Lonnie Earnest

ALTAMONTE CENTER
for PSYCHOLOGICAL SERVICES
498 PALM SPRINGS DR. STE 270
ALTAMONTE SPRINGS, FL

D0602394

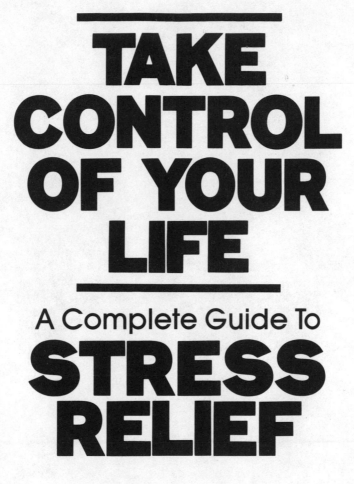

TAKE CONTROL OF YOUR LIFE

A Complete Guide To STRESS RELIEF

TAKE CONTROL OF YOUR LIFE

A Complete Guide To

STRESS RELIEF

by Sharon Faelten, David Diamond
& the Editors of *Prevention*® Magazine

Rodale Press, Emmaus, Pennsylvania

Printed in the United States of America on recycled
paper containing a high percentage of de-inked fiber.

Book design by Linda Jacopetti

Library of Congress Cataloging-in-Publication Data

Faelten, Sharon.
    Take control of your life.

    Includes index.
    1. Stress (Psychology)   I. Diamond, David,
1952–   . II. Prevention (Emmaus, Pa.)
III. Title.
BF575.S75F34   1988   155.9   87–37667

ISBN 0-87857-757-2   hardcover

2 4 6 8 10 9 7 5 3   **hardcover**

Contributors to this book include:
Editor
Carol Keough

Executive Editor, *Prevention*® Magazine
Health Books
William Gottlieb

Writers
Martha Capwell
Gale Maleskey
Thomas Shealey
Lewis Vaughn
Jennifer Whitlock

Research Associates
Christine Dreisbach
Karen Feridun
Ann Gossy
Staci Hadeed
Alice Harris
Karen Lombardi
Bernadette Sukley

Assistant Research Chief
Holly Clemson

Associate Research Chief
Susan A. Nastasee

Office Personnel
Roberta Mulliner
Kim Mohr
Kelly Trumbauer

Group Vice President, Health
Mark Bricklin

CONTENTS

TAKING CONTROL

The account exec is sick of dealing with a difficult client. The new concept he presented as a sure winner just became a big loser, and the project was terminated—with extreme ridicule. What's more, the advertising budget has just been cut and the sales quota upped. It's been a bad day. Squinting at the little bit of blue sky visible between New York's towers, our executive wishes for a simpler life. "Maybe I should move out to Iowa or Kansas and be a farmer. Fresh air, lots of sunshine, communion with nature—that's the way to go," he muses.

But in the scorched cornfields of Kansas, a farmer is squinting at the same blue sky. And cursing it. No rain, no grain in the farming biz. "Maybe I should get a city job—something not so dependent on the weather," he thinks.

Working the land, working the system, not working at all—it seems as though any and every lifestyle is filled with stress. The career woman envies her sister who stays at home with the baby, while the young mother wishes she could get out of the house and talk to grownups now and then. Every one of us experiences a good amount of stress almost every day. Some people seem to take it in stride, while others are overwhelmed.

What accounts for the difference? What enables some individuals to not only cope but *thrive* in the face of trouble, and others to crumble?

The answer seems to lie in the way we *perceive* a situation. Given the same set of circumstances, one person may see a crisis where another finds an invigorating challenge. The difference in perception may explain why an astronaut can step into outer space, while others are too afraid to step out on a stage. The key to controlling stress, the experts say, is learning to see things in a certain way.

Suppose your job requires you to move to another city. It means you'll have to sell your home and buy a new one, leave your old friends and live among strangers, ease your children into a new environment, learn to do a new job while working for a new manager. Stressful? You bet! But this stress can be handled. Let's view these circumstances as an exercise in perception.

How would you feel if you had to sell the house and buy a new one? You may see it as a hassle—which it is—but you also may recognize it as an opportunity to make a profit on your old home, allowing you to buy a better one. And yes, you will leave your old friends—but you know you'll make new ones. The children will become more mature and experienced, the new job will be a stimulating challenge. You get the idea: Stress is an opportunity for growth and excitement if viewed in the proper perspective.

Here's another factor: People who successfully cope with stress are usually very committed to what they do. Some overriding goal or belief gives them purpose, purpose that gets them through life's inevitable crises. What's more, stress-resistant people exert some control in their lives. They seem to have a knack for handling external stresses like deadlines or delays. They cope, not crumble, when a crisis like illness or job loss hits. And they manage to keep internal stresses like guilt and worry in perspective. You might call these factors the Three C's of stress management—challenge, commitment and control.

How, exactly, does a mere mortal learn to trade the fight-or-flight responses to stress that helped our ancestors survive for these Three C's? How can we change the way we react to stressful events? This book shows the way. Experts in stress-management techniques have offered the latest advice for handling everything from the most mundane but truly stressful trials to dealing with life's more traumatic events. This book opens the door to a happier, healthier, more satisfying life.

Part 1

HANDLING EVERYDAY HASSLES

Chapter 1

BAD NEWS

Good evening. This is Peter Jennings with the 6 o'clock news. Today, no jumbo jets crashed, no children lost their lives in tenement fires, and terrorists took a day off from bombing airports. Thank you, and have a good night.

That's a fictitious news account, of course. Actual news broadcasts are 23-minute dramas of murder, mayhem, tragedy and misfortune (with time out for advertising) calculated to *induce* stress in you, the viewer. TV insiders call it "anxiety journalism." Producers—and advertisers—know that when you're scared, you pay attention, and you won't change the channel.

"A purpose of broadcasters is to assemble people for the advertisers so that buyers are receptive to their products and services," says George Gerbner, Ph.D., dean of the Annenberg School of Communications, University of Pennsylvania, Philadelphia. "Although the industry doesn't use the terms 'anxious' and 'insecure,' that is the state they cultivate."

Bad News: Just Another Prime-Time Drama?

We don't advise a head-in-the-sand attitude toward news—keeping informed is essential. If a major hurricane is crawling up the coastline, headed for your hometown, you should know about it. And you should know about the African famine and the desperation of the homeless, as well as the stalled commuter train. Even the news media's strongest critics are the last to advocate bland, air-brushed, good-news-only journalism that soft-pedals bona fide threats to our safety and well-being. Bad news is a fact of life. But there's something about electronically transmitted news that compounds the resulting stress, sometimes unnecessarily.

"A printed word description is easier to take than a pictorial presentation of the same news, and a filmed 'dramatization' is probably the hardest to take and assimilate in any useful way, because you see only what the camera wants you to see," explains Robert M. Leibert, Ph.D., who served as principal investigator for the National Institute of Mental Health's program on television and social behavior some years ago. "Information is left out and questions are left unanswered. The editing process exerts more control than with print media. Even if you read a biased commentary, you will be more aware of the bias—and less manipulated—than if you hear it."

"What we see on television is not representative of real life, but an exaggerated and unrealistic picture that generates anxiety," says Dr. Gerbner.

"We know that 'people dislike surprises,' " say John Urquhart, M.D., and Klaus Heilmann, M.D., in their book *Riskwatch*. "But sudden bad news certainly sells newspapers and draws people to their TV screens or radios. The fact that 'bad news sells' is nothing new, but what is new in the historical sense is the instantaneous dissemination of news, one of the gifts of modern electronic technology.

"The quantity and timing of information in today's world can scarcely be faulted," continue the authors, "but who can say that it does not play much more to our fears than to our understanding?"

"Television is superb for conveying emotions but practically opaque for the transmission of sustained thought," remarks Edwin Diamond, former head of the News Study Group at New York University and author of *Good News, Bad News* and other books concerning television and social attitudes. As a result, the media may report the news quite responsibly, yet still leave you more stressed than the facts warrant.

That residual stress is especially ironic when you consider that part of the reason we watch or listen to or read the news is for reassurance, according to one former network news producer. "The 'average' home viewer wants to know right away, in headline form, mainly two things: First, is my home safe? and second, is the world safe for the next 24 hours?"

"Many people depend on TV for most of their information," says Dr. Gerbner. "But studies show that the more people watch TV, the more insecure they tend to be."

Spare Yourself Some Grief— Control What You View

The antidote to anxiety and insecurity generated by bad news, says Dr. Gerbner, is a better understanding of how the news is put together. "What people need to do is take a fresh look at a familiar medium," he says. Here's how.

Read background stories behind the two- or three-minute doom-and-gloom bulletins. "We can't tell the whole story," John Chancellor once said. "A television news program is a . . . sort of front page." By the same token, read analysis and commentary in addition to headlines and news stories. Deeper understanding can dispel unwarranted fears generated by bad news.

Read first, watch "pictures" later. "To really enhance understanding and manage your reactions to the news, the best approach is to read the printed version first and then listen to the broadcast, rather than the reverse," says Dr. Leibert, "much as you would read about countries you plan to visit before leaving on a trip, not after you return home and have seen the sights."

Don't watch the news during dinner or before you go to bed. "Live remotes" of fires, freeway crashes and twisted masses of unrecognizable metal may upset sensitive viewers. And the last thing your nervous system needs before you toddle off to dreamland is to learn that the crime rate is up, employment is down and your favorite ballpark snack causes cancer in rodents who should know better by now.

Be your own program director. If you have a VCR, tape the broadcast and watch it at your convenience. (And if human tragedy unduly upsets you at *any* hour of the day, you have the option of fast-forwarding past graphic shots of body bags and other gratuitously grim "news.")

"Yes, bad news is inescapable," says Dr. Gerbner. "But you don't have to let it manipulate you. Be selective. Read more. Use the VCR. That way, you program the news, it doesn't program you."

Chapter 2

BOREDOM

Do you find yourself eating everything in sight or perhaps not eating much at all?

Are you waking up earlier and staying up later or can't you drag your head off the pillow?

Is your mind a blank or swirling with random thoughts?

Are you peevish with your loved ones, taking dumb risks or having a lot of little accidents?

If you answered yes to any of the above, your problem might simply be a case of boredom. Stress experts are waking up to the broad range of physical and psychological symptoms that result from being understimulated by the challenges of our daily lives.

Boredom can make it virtually impossible to perform simple work tasks, tasks that are ordinarily part of our regular jobs. That's why boredom is among the major stress-related reasons we fail at our jobs, according to Arthur Witkin, Ph.D., an industrial psychologist at the New York career counseling firm of Personnel Sciences Center and professor at Queens College of the City University of New York.

"Most articles on stress deal with the overload side of stress, people being overwhelmed," says Augustin de la Pena, Ph.D., associate professor of psychiatry at the University of Texas Health Science Center, Dallas. "But the *underload* side of stress in adults is the predominant side of stress." What Dr. de la Pena calls underload, most people call boredom. *Why* are so many of us so bored?

As we grow, our brains gain the capacity to process ever-increasing amounts of information. It's kind of like computer software that helps us deal with or predict our environment. But when we're bored, the understimulated brain structure signals itself to increase the input of or sensitivity to information.

This continued growth and its resulting demand for ever more stimulation explains why what excited us as kids bores us as adults. "Most people try to get back to that intermediate range of information flow, to regain the fun and interest, and wind up on the overload side," says Dr. de la Pena.

Without conscious restraint, our brains will go to any length to combat boredom and seek new challenges. Boredom, for example, can increase the possibility of illness and/or the complaint of illness. Back pain, some eating disorders, high blood pressure, some kinds of cancer and other problems can be created by the brain to make its work more interesting, says Dr. de la Pena. Some people respond to boredom by becoming sleepy, but for others, insomnia is a by-product. According to Dr. de la Pena's research, the chronically bored brain pursues the stimulation of an increased level of REM (rapid eye movement), or dreaming, sleep. "The more boredom, the quicker one gets into REM sleep," he says. But since REM sleep signals the brain to wake up, those who fall rapidly into REM sleep also find themselves waking up earlier than they want.

Keeping control of the physical results of boredom may be a simple matter of systematically increasing our daily challenges (and thus also increasing our brain-satisfying information flow) without overdoing it. If you've been playing dominoes for years, it might be time to take up chess. Forsake the television set to play the piano, study a foreign language or go out on the town. In other words, make a conscious effort to feed those hungry brain structures something fresh and meaty. Meditation (see chapter 76) can teach you to increase your sensory awareness if you are understimulated.

Put Some Fun in Your Life

When patients of Arthur Freeman, Ph.D., a psychologist at the University of Pennsylvania's Center for Cognitive Therapy in Philadelphia, complain of being bored, he instructs them to do two things. First, they are asked to determine their level of boredom on a scale of one to ten. Then he tells them to make a list of things that are mildly stimulating, moderately stimulating and very stimulating. "They have to determine for themselves what their needs are and what they find stimulating. Then they can be helped to go after it," he says. "For one person it might mean inviting someone over to dinner and creating an elaborate meal; for another person it might mean working out at a gym. Someone else might find it stimulating to rent a movie. They have to very consciously set goals for themselves that will alleviate the so-called boredom. I find doing selected activities helps almost immediately."

Be sensible, however, when selecting your antiboredom activity. "A person who is bored may decide to drink, a person who is bored may decide to use drugs," says Dr. Freeman. "Eating, too, is something people do to arouse themselves when they are bored."

Boredom with work is the result of the same understimulation that causes physical ailments or sends people into eating binges, and with 40 hours or more of it a week, it is something that should not be underplayed.

The number one complaint among 9,000 workers surveyed for the book *Stress in Organizations* was "feeling isolated and bored" at work.

Testing for Tedium

The first thing is to identify boredom—as opposed to a temporary "situational" emotional problem—as the culprit. At a very minimum, some of the symptoms of occupational boredom include a fluctuation of attention, absenteeism and irritability, which industrial psychologist Dr. Witkin describes as "the neurotic conflict that comes with being forced to do what you don't want to do." At its maximum impact, bored workers find themselves—without reason—to be helplessly incompetent. (In Dr. Witkin's words, "The inability to do what you're supposed to be doing.")

Those of us who are employed in large organizations, where the work can be dreadfully routine, are often in the best position to tackle occupational boredom. Over the past several decades business management has developed some sound psychological procedures such as aptitude testing to determine growth potential for employees who are in jobs or occupations that bore them. Most major corporations employ a human resources department whose function is to ensure that round pegs are in round holes, that employees' skills are best utilized in jobs that interest and challenge them.

For those working in such organizations, the advice is simple: Ask your employer to test your aptitude and, if the results warrant, find you another job within the company. If it turns out that you are well suited for your current job and no other, ask about the possibility of being given additional responsibilities.

Employees in smaller organizations will probably have to take matters into their own hands. The first step is to contact a career counselor. The International Association of Counseling Services (5999 Stevenson Avenue, Alexandria, VA 22304) is the accrediting organization for counseling centers, and it will provide a list of accredited counseling centers state by state (send a stamped, self-addressed envelope). Career counselors are listed, but only as part of a larger group. B'nai B'rith, YMCA and a few other nonprofit organizations offer career counseling on an ability-to-pay basis.

"A professional counselor may help you discover new options," says Dr. Witkin. "Those options might include adding new responsibilities, getting a second job that is more challenging than your boring one, or taking on a hobby." At the absolute worst, a psychologist can teach a bored-to-tears employee how to adjust to the situation. A little scheduling, for instance, can go a long way toward alleviating boredom. Tedious tasks can be grouped together and accomplished in the morning, leaving the afternoon free for more interesting projects. Whatever the specific strategy, the advice of professionals is the same as that offered to those suffering from off-the-job boredom: Set realistic goals for yourself and go after them.

Dr. Witkin asserts that "there is no such thing as a boring job." He would probably be scoffed at by anyone who has spent time on an assembly line. But many individuals are attracted by the challenge of successfully completing an assembly task and by the camaraderie of participating with a group of friendly co-workers. In jobs, what's boring to one might be engaging to another. The same rings true for people.

The People Who Bore You

Mark Leary, Ph.D., an assistant professor of psychology at Wake Forest University in Winston-Salem, North Carolina, is coauthor of a report that lists the qualities that make a person boring. (It even established a "boringness index.") It has made Dr. Leary one of the nation's few experts on dealing with uninteresting people.

The Wake Forest study suggests that the people who are most boring are those who complain about themselves and their lives, as well as those who mutter trivialities. These bores are even more annoying than people who overuse slang or try too hard to be nice, according to the research.

"They interfere with communication and deprive us of rewarding social interaction." says Dr. Leary. "The frustration comes from not being able to interact as easily as we would like. We'd like to have rewards from our relationships just the way we'd like to have rewards from our jobs." In Dr. Leary's opinion, boring jobs are easier to change than boring people. "There are certain things you can do to change a boring job; you can often make it more interesting if you can get your employer's cooperation. But when it comes to changing a person, you need to change the way they interact." You need to teach them interpersonal skills.

To help convert boring acquaintances into tolerable ones, you could focus discussions on interesting things. If you both root for the home team, by all means discuss the repercussions of that error in the seventh inning. For friends and lovers, the advice is not as simple. "If you're really trying to bring out a spouse or a loved one, one of the best techniques is also one of the hardest—letting them know when they're being boring," says Dr. Leary.

He suggests you establish a manner of communication in which they encourage you to point out to them when their discussion treads mercilessly into areas that most people don't find interesting. Can you imagine yourself saying, "Dear, I'm so happy you could repair the brakes yourself, but I'm just not interested in the details"? Can you imagine your loved one's reply? Be aware that it's touchy telling someone he's a bore. "Unfortunately, it's much easier to tell a loved one or friend that they're untidy," says Dr. Leary.

The crusade against boredom has become a cottage industry for Alan Caruba, a writer and public relations consultant in Maplewood, New Jersey, who has given birth to The Boring Institute. A self-professed expert on boredom, Caruba sells a $2 poster that lists "25 Ways to Avoid Boredom" (they range from number 1, "Read a Book," to number 25, "Turn Off the TV"). And he is endlessly pursuing publicity for National Anti-Boredom Month, his designation for July. "It's July because if the first six months of your year have been boring, July is an opportunity to examine what aspects of your life have been boring—job, school, housework, whatever—and spend the other months changing it, to get yourself out of the rut of boredom," he says. For Caruba, at least, the crusade itself is one antidote for boredom.

Chapter 3

CAR TROUBLE

Sometimes it seems as if car ownership must have been written into the Bill of Rights. With more than 130 million of the vehicles on U.S. roads, Americans drive more than one-third of the world's cars. But our transportation of choice is also one of our biggest headaches: It's an engine that fails to start as you try to head to work on a blustery Minnesota morning, a tire that blows out as you enter the Lincoln Tunnel, the overheated engine during the freeway backup.

In the scope of the universe, these troubles are trivial, but as far as everyday setbacks go, they are among the most costly and, because they are seldom anticipated, among the most frustrating.

So the strategy for reducing the stress of unforeseen car trouble is to take charge of your vehicle. As much as possible, it should be you who controls the car, not vice-versa.

Start out by avoiding the trap of driving beyond your means. "Amazing as it seems, it's possible to be happy driving a $6,000 car," says Andrew Tobias, a financial writer and author of *The Only OTHER Investment Guide You'll Ever Need.* He says, "Rather than buy a $16,000 car that you have to finance, buy a $6,000 car that you can afford. You'll get ahead of the game and get off the stressful treadmill."

Trading down helps you avoid the stress of car trouble in two ways. First, the most expensive models are generally costliest to maintain and insure. And second, if you are not forced to meet monthly payments for the car itself, you might be in better financial shape to properly maintain your car and even weather the unexpected. "If it's embarrassing to drive up in a $6,000 car," says Tobias, "just tell people your Jaguar's being repaired."

Triple-A Troubleshooting

One of the simplest, smartest and least expensive ways to reduce the stress of car ownership is to join the 27 million car owners who belong to the

American Automobile Association (AAA). Annual membership ranges from $14 to $70 (average is $35), depending on which of the 161 affiliates you join and which services you select. At the very least, you will get emergency road service and towing, as well as such travel services as route advice and free maps. The membership fees include discounts on lodging and rental cars, insurance and financial services. (Contact your nearest AAA affiliate or call the AAA toll free at 1–800–336–4357.)

And even if you don't intend to ever raise your car's hood, it makes sense to shell out $12.95 for the *Chilton Repair and Tune-Up Guide* for your model. Their basic repair guides cover every aspect of 125 car models. For non-do-it-yourselfers, these books unravel the mysteries of your automobile's innards and can make you more conversant with—and less intimidated by—your auto mechanic.

The people who feel least in control when car trouble occurs are those of us who don't budget for it. "A prudent car buyer will factor such expenses as insurance, taxes and standard maintenance into the price," says Daniel Kegan, Ph.D., a Chicago organizational psychologist who has researched the topic of the psychological meaning of money. He suggests car buyers check published reports on their model, particularly the data that indicates which parts are likely to wear out. That way a car's owners can save toward anticipated repairs. "Figure out how many miles you drive a year and estimate when you'll need new tires. Or look at other people's experience and see what's coming up," Dr. Kegan advises.

To get in the habit of planning realistically for car surprises, Dr. Kegan recommends that car owners make an estimate of what they think they will spend on their cars for a six-month period and then see how close they come to the projection. Those who budget 10 percent of their general expenditures for unexpected expenses will find themselves better prepared for car trouble.

From a psychological perspective, Dr. Kegan tells us to pay attention to our feelings. "The more someone is attuned to their feelings and the more they know why they behave the way they do, the more they can be in control of themselves and their spending," he says.

"If you know you're the kind of person who takes that 'stitch in time,' who changes the oil regularly, you'll have fewer surprises. If you're not that kind, expect surprises and expect to spend more of your time and money on repairs," he says. "The more you can think ahead, or force yourself to, the better off you'll be."

A single example: Those of us who live in the North should designate a car winterization day sometime in mid-November and arrange to take the car in. Does mid-November seem too early? It's not, according to Dr. Kegan. His reasons are more "motive" than "automotive," however. "By planning ahead," he says, "you're more likely to be prepared when bad weather hits."

Chapter 4

COMMUTING

Freeway crawlers in Southern California's San Fernando Valley can tune their car radio to KWNK-AM for instant temporary relief from the morning rush. Sometime around 7:45, radio personality "Sweet" Dick Whittington spins exercise music and leads commuters in "aerobics" for the rush-hour bound. "Lift your left bun. [Pause] Lower your left bun. Lift your right bun. . . ." For more than a decade, Whittington's "The Aching Buns Boogey" feature has created a rare, pleasant diversion from the tense monotony of commuting to work by car. But it's not much.

Whatever the mode of travel, there's no question that commuting is stressful. It's particularly vexing when travelers find the situation out of their control. The traffic jam, the stalled subway train are likely to bring out the worst in even the least aggressive folks. In fact, it is "laid back" Type B personalities, not the traditionally competitive Type A's, who are more sensitive to traffic stress, according to Daniel Stokols, Ph.D., a University of California, Irvine, social ecology professor. He studied 100 traffic-congestion-plagued commuters and determined that the Type B personalities among them performed worse and had higher blood pressure readings when they arrived at work than did the Type A commuters.

In 1984, anxiety over arriving at work late caused 27,619 subway riders to phone New York City's Transit Authority for official "late slips" to take to the office. To reduce the number of individual telephone requests for subway delay verifications it received, the Transit Authority in 1986 began signing up major New York employers, who are now informed when subway trains are late.

Take Control

Such programs help a little, but there are stress-reducing steps commuters can take even when the train runs on time or the traffic is a breeze. *The key*

12

is in seizing as much control of the commute as is possible. Jerome E. Singer, Ph.D., a professor of medical psychology at the Uniformed Services University of the Health Sciences in Bethesda, Maryland, studied train commuters in Sweden and car commuters in the United States and determined that "the extent to which people feel they can control the situation is more important than the physical characteristics of the route."

In his study of rail commuters, for instance, he determined that those whose trips lasted 1½ hours experienced less stress than those who rode for 45 minutes. The reason: The longer riders boarded earlier and had the opportunity to choose well-located seats; those who boarded later saw that the territory had already been carved up and felt they had little control.

How to take control of your commuter stress?

Drive your car alone. If you like to exercise control over the route you take, your traffic behavior or the atmosphere in the car, it makes sense to go alone. But if the social atmosphere is more important than controlling the ride, travel in a van or car pool.

Make some conscious stress-reducing driving decisions. "Don't contest everybody trying to change lanes. If you let someone in, you are exercising some control. By doing so, you make it less stressful for yourself," says Dr. Singer.

Get a mobile phone. That way you can phone ahead if you're running late.

Sign up for a flexible work schedule. If your company offers it, a flexible work schedule will enable you to commute during non-rush hours.

Ride trains in a group. While you may not enjoy having others in your *auto*, riding on a train with your friends will establish the internal atmosphere of the car, suggests Dr. Singer.

Sleep on the train. New York's Metro-North commuter rail ferries 180,000 riders each day and figures a lot of them use the time to catch up on sleep. The color-coordinated interiors of its cars combine shades that are calming to the senses.

Read on the train. In one busy commuter train station, the DeKalb Public Library and the Metropolitan Atlanta Rapid Transit Authority installed a prefabricated, modular, 160-square-foot kiosk—a special library for commuters. The "read and ride" library branch is open during the commuter rush (6:30–10:00 A.M. and 3:30–7:00 P.M.). "Many of our users are commuters who would like to read but don't have time to get to the library," says Barbara Loar, the library director responsible for the project. "People are hungry for information. Whenever they have a spare moment, when they ride a train or ride a bus, it's an ideal time to add to their knowledge."

Chapter 5

COMPETITION

"The world is not a football game," says Elliot Aronson, Ph.D. That simple sentence sounds like the practical advice of a caring grandparent who knows better, who knows that for many people the world *is* a football game but knows also that life would be less stressful if it weren't viewed as such.

The University of California, Santa Cruz, psychology professor once conducted several experiments on elementary school classes. In the experiment, students were taught to cooperate, not compete, on projects. The clear results were superior performances, as detailed in his book, *The Jigsaw Classroom*. "They achieved better grades on exams, their self-esteem improved, they liked each other better, ethnic stereotypes diminished and absenteeism decreased," says Dr. Aronson.

The evidence against competition is growing rapidly. In 1985, Robert Helmreich, Ph.D., of the University of Texas, Austin, and his associates studied seven different groups of people, groups as diverse as scientists, undergraduates and airline reservations agents. Dr. Helmreich, a psychology professor, determined that on a consistent basis, in work and in school, the participants who exhibited the most competitive personality traits were those who performed worst.

Interesting news. But how does this information help those of us who try to seek out a living in workplaces that are only slightly less competitive than the Army-Navy game? How does it help those of us who find our friendships soured by an undeclared contest? How can we keep competition in proper perspective?

"It's hard to," answers Dr. Aronson, "because the whole society, from kindergarten on up, is geared toward competition." Dr. Aronson's the-world-is-not-a-football-game advice is a start in the long task of putting stressful competition in its place. Robert L. James, M.D., an assistant clinical professor of psychology at UCLA, adds, "A person needs to ask 'What's really at stake? What's the worst thing that could happen if I lose?' "

He echoes the sentiments of many health professionals who believe

Keeping Up Is Hard to Do

Among the most irksome forms of competition is the unspoken rivalry with friends and neighbors over status. The sports car, the backyard pool, the new dinette set—these possessions often aren't bought because we *need* them. They're bought to use like flashing neon signs signaling to the Joneses, "RICH, RICH, RICH." Then we can only hope they don't buy a "sign" that says, "RICHER, RICHER, RICHER."

Once trapped in such a game, it can be stressful, frustrating and *expensive* to keep up. "If people are in such a competition, it's important for them to recognize it and to know what's motivating them," says Lillian Rubin, Ph.D., psychologist and senior research associate at the Institute for the Study of Social Change, University of California, Berkeley. "Such behavior can be controlled and devalued," she says.

Paul Wright, Ph.D., a psychology professor at the University of North Dakota who has studied male friendships for nearly two decades, says, "Try to adapt a more balanced perspective on what is important in life. Recognize that there are rewards in life other than material successes—like having friends and keeping friends. I know, it's easy to say and hard to do."

So count your rewards and seek your own rewards. But don't worry about measuring up to the folks next door. "In most situations, another person's gain does not have to be our loss," says Elliot Aronson, Ph.D., a professor of psychology at the University of California, Santa Cruz. "That's something that has to be taught in elementary school."

competition is not uniformly unhealthy. "It depends on each individual's reaction to competition," says Dr. James.

"Acknowledge that there's nothing wrong with competition unless you're out to annihilate the other person," says Lillian Rubin, Ph.D., psychologist and senior research associate at the Institute for the Study of Social Change, University of California, Berkeley, and author of *Just Friends: The Role of Friendship in Our Lives.*

Initially, those of us who are concerned that competition is too pervasive could take a survey of our own competitive impulses. That involves understanding what kind of competitors we are, why we compete and what's at stake when we do.

Sam Osherson, Ph.D., author of *Finding Our Fathers*, explains that our competitive behaviors are rooted in childhood experience. The patterns of competition we learned as children competing with parents and siblings are revived in the workplace family. So we have our backgrounds to blame for the manner in which we compete—or how well we compete. Then we have employers who often deliberately pit workers against each other in the belief that everybody's performance will be improved.

Calling for Time Out

At its harshest, competition stirs up basic fears of survival, fears that are not realistic in some work environments. For those who don't want to compete or who don't feel comfortable in such an atmosphere, the wisest move often is to get out before too much damage is done. Even if you survive the job, you might lose your health. "If survival in the workplace is on the line, then competition will lead to chronic elevated levels of stress that certainly can be related to causing illness," explains Dr. James.

"The art of living involves finding what kind of lifestyle is most suited to a person. There are people who are not well suited to highly competitive environments. Bow out of a competitive line of work if it doesn't fit your personality," he says.

But that doesn't necessarily mean you have to find a new job because, in your current one, you're routinely "tackled" by fellow employees. Instead, you might try learning how to deal with and control the competition rather than be shocked when it occurs. "Accept it as something that's normal and learn the skills for managing it," suggests Robert E. Lefton, Ph.D., an organizational psychologist and president of Psychological Associates, Inc., in St. Louis.

"In the workplace, a lot of stress is produced by competitive interpersonal relationships. So you can teach people how to have better people skills," Dr. Lefton says. Consider how you handle disagreements with co-workers.

"When it comes to routine disagreements, you've got a choice," he continues. "You could squelch it, going along as though a disagreement doesn't exist. Or you could treat it lightly. Or you could acknowledge it, which involves probing and problem-solving.

"Suppressing, smoothing over or avoiding can spin up to a very high degree of stress. Problem-solving is the most effective means of dealing with a disagreement. It can be stressful up-front, but the long-term results are good," he says.

Here are Dr. Lefton's solutions to a touchy, competitive workplace problem.

Suppose you frequently find yourself arguing with someone at work. You could confront that person in a negative "win/lose" manner, warning that "If you try to get me, I'll get you." Or you could smooth it over, saying, "Well, we argue, but it's really not *that* significant." Neither of these responses will lessen stress. The first is a declaration of war, and the second just submerges the tension and feelings of distress. Instead, you might try a third option. You could openly state your concern, saying, "I'm very upset and concerned about our constant arguing. As a result of our bickering, our discussions deteriorate and our work suffers. What can we do to solve this problem?"

According to Dr. Lefton, "Anything that requires confrontation requires courage and assertiveness. For some people that's stressful. But when you weigh it against possible long-term gains, you can save a great deal of stress. There's no magic. All you can do is increase the probability that you'll relate better."

A "Buddy System"

Business consultants tell employees to try to have good relations with workplace competitors. But if that notion sounds contradictory, consider the awkward—and often destructive—role that competition plays in friendships.

In her book on friendships, Dr. Rubin explains that in male friendships, "The competitive thrust is overt and direct; with women, it's hidden from view, too often covered with a smile, a veneer of warmth and friendliness that bodes ill for the kind of trust a friendship requires."

The bottom line is that most men, because they are openly competitive, have difficulty forming intimate friendships. Most women, because they are unwilling to acknowledge competition with friends, may destroy the intimate friendships they have. "Women's inability to deal directly with competitive feelings is a source of difficulty in their relations with each other. For whether the motive is to compete or to avoid competition, it creates a similar distance between friends."

There's another problem. Dr. Rubin points out that it's particularly stressful to compete against someone with whom you have an emotional involvement. "You want to win," she says, "and don't want to win."

One step toward keeping competition between friends from getting out of hand: Acknowledge the competition, acknowledge the feelings of jealousy and guilt. And acknowledge the affection. Dr. Osherson says that between men, at least there's a strong undercurrent of affection beneath the competitive surface.

"Healthy, mature relationships include mixed feelings toward those whom we love," says Dr. James. "Real maturity, real intimacy requires working through these feelings, embracing these feelings and coming to terms with them as a normal, healthy part of the human experience, rather than denying them, throwing them out the window." As with the competitive co-worker, tell your friend how you feel.

The outlook for competitive friendships does not have to be bleak. Paul Wright, Ph.D., a University of North Dakota psychology professor who has collected data on 5,000 male friendships since 1968, says, "When men become really good friends, the competitive element disappears. It's a matter of just gradually lowering guards and becoming more secure with one another."

But developing such friendships with "strong security value" takes time, he says. And they are not limited by gender.

Dr. Helmreich warns that it's "darn hard" to view the world in noncompetitive terms if the people we encounter are relentless competitors. Still, you can set a cooperative tone by relaxing.

"Look at one another as being on the same team rather than needing to beat each other," says Dr. Aronson. "In most situations, doing well does not have to be consistent with beating someone. Relax," he says. "Do the best you can and cheer for the others to do as well."

Chapter 6

DEADLINES

Tia O'Brien, a political reporter for Philadelphia's KYW-TV, arrived at work at 10:00 A.M. and immediately traveled cross-town to cover a relatively routine and predictable assignment. She would have enough time, she figured, to gather tape, do her interview, travel with her cameraman to different parts of the city to get on-camera reactions and then return to the television station to write her story, shoot a "stand-up close," edit the story and fight for time on the 5:30 or 6:00 P.M. newscast. It was to be an easy, well-paced day.

But shortly after noon the day was thrown into a frenzy. The state treasurer—recently convicted of bribery—killed himself during a news conference.

O'Brien instinctively knew that her original story was now nothing more than a ten-second announcement for the news show. She had to quickly shift gears and rearrange her day in order to meet the same 5:30 deadline, but with a vastly different and exceedingly more difficult story.

First she mentally calculated how much time it would take to gather and produce the breaking suicide story. By 1:00 P.M. she knew that her new assignment was to produce the "reaction" story and that she would have to begin the final editing stage by 5:00.

She had to factor in the snow-covered roads, unavailable sources, the difficulty in tracking down "background" film of the late state treasurer and the reluctance of other politicians to offer taped reaction to the suicide. And as happens every day, she had to be realistic in accounting for other possible setbacks: tape editing machines that are being used by other reporters or faulty camera equipment—a bad battery, for instance—that could send her mercilessly behind schedule.

"I always keep a mental timetable as the day goes on. I have to calculate backward how much time each process could take. In other words, by 1:00 P.M., when I started out on my new assignment, I knew I only had four hours left before I had to start editing," she says.

Given the city's snow-paralyzed streets, O'Brien opted to do telephone interviews. "When the blizzard intensified, I knew that I would jeopardize my whole piece if I left the building," she says.

In the end, it all worked out because O'Brien, like most successful people, has mastered the difficult art of meeting deadlines. As the example suggests, meeting deadlines—and reducing the stress of deadlines—is often a matter of setting up priorities, scheduling your time accordingly and making an effort to stick to both priorities and schedule. The strategy is the same for a television reporter's minutes-away deadline as it is for a bookkeeper's quarterly deadline or an academician's years-long deadline. By prioritizing and scheduling, you gain control.

Being Realistic about Your Time

"Many people are unrealistic about time. They either overestimate how long something will take or they underestimate," says Jane Burka, Ph.D., a Berkeley, California, psychologist. "The first thing to do is anticipate realistically how long a task will take and how much time you can spend on it. For instance, if a project is due in a week and you're feeling optimistic about that deadline, check your calendar. Are your in-laws coming to visit on one of those days? Do you have an all-day meeting another day?"

"You have to take steps now to ensure that you'll complete what you have to do. For instance, tell your secretary *today* that you have to be uninterrupted tomorrow while you work on your project. Working without interruption would be difficult to do when it's already tomorrow and your phone's ringing all day," adds Ronald Drabman, Ph.D., professor and director of clinical psychology at the University of Mississippi Medical Center.

If you've set aside the time to work, you should also have a clear sense of your priorities, suggests Dr. Drabman. You have to consider all the tasks you have to do, then put them in order of importance. And chances are, if you don't get to some of the lower priorities on your list, they weren't very important—or they were things you couldn't possibly have done, given your timetable.

In addition to putting tasks in order, you also should prioritize your deadlines. "One thing that is helpful in reducing the stress of deadlines is to make up in your mind which deadlines are really important and which ones are flexible," says Dr. Burka. "On one hand, you might say you want to finish reading a book by Friday, or you want to get a new job by Christmas. Those are self-imposed deadlines, which can be flexible. Then there are deadlines of real consequence—such as the date by which you must pay your traffic tickets or register your car. These deadlines are inflexible. Meet them first."

Gaining Control

To gain control, think of doing the project in very specific steps. "Rather than saying you have to have the quarterly report completed by Thursday and proceeding blindly, break down the project into very small and manageable tasks. For a six-page quarterly report, you might have to gather the financial data, talk to three people in your department, look at the last two years' worth of reports. Realistically assess the time required for each," says Dr. Burka, coauthor of the book *Procrastination: Why You Do It, What to Do about It.*

To minimize the stress of a deadline, Dr. Burka suggests you pick out the first step you can accomplish within 15 minutes and do it. "A person can stand almost anything for 15 minutes," she says, "and you may feel better that you're on your way to meeting your deadline. Then make a note to yourself about what you have to do next."

Breaking up a project, making a deal with yourself to work only 15 minutes and rewarding yourself for completing a task are methods of seducing yourself into working toward your deadline. There are others. "I simply turn on my computer," says T. Thorne Wiggers, Ed.D., a counseling psychologist at George Washington University, Washington, D.C. "That way, I figure that I might as well write just the beginning of whatever it is I have to write, since the computer is already on. Or if I'm preparing my taxes, I'll collect all my receipts. Then I say to myself, 'Now that I've got all the receipts together, I might as well sort them into categories.'"

The Procrastinator's Profile

Such tips are fine, but a person plagued with a tendency to procrastinate should also look below the surface to understand why he or she has trouble meeting deadlines.

Some procrastinators take *every* deadline so seriously that they can't distinguish between those that are rigid and those that are flexible. Such people "have to question their assumption that they are being judged by every challenge that they face. They need to realize that doing everything is impossible and that the stress of perfectionism is very costly," says Dr. Burka.

Other people procrastinate out of rebellion. For instance, they may delay paying taxes because they are angry about having to do it. Still other procrastinators operate out of a fear of failure. They figure that if they procrastinate and then don't do well, they can blame the procrastination rather than their ability. "What they're doing is protecting themselves from finding out if they would or wouldn't fail if they didn't procrastinate," says Dr. Wiggers.

Then there are people who use deadlines as motivators. They might do well at meeting deadlines, but the process takes its toll. These are people who cling to the motto, "I can only work under pressure."

Dr. Wiggers is skeptical of such a statement. "I ask those people how it feels working under pressure and to describe to me how it would feel if they did the work over a long period of time relative to a short period of time. I ask them what the quality of their work would be like if they took the time instead of jamming it up against a deadline. For some people it might be fine. But for others, there are signs that it isn't. They complain of ulcers, headaches and of drinking too much to deal with the stress."

For some, however, cramming really is best. Dr. Drabman divides most people into two groups in terms of how they accomplish tasks: plotters and crammers. Plotters chop off sections of work and proceed accordingly. Crammers wait until the last minute and work in a panic.

"Parents often tell children they have to be plotters. That makes sense except that lots of successful people function fine doing things at the last minute," he says. "So sometimes we try to be a way we are not, to be plotters instead of crammers, and that causes stress. Our natural inclinations could be successful. So the first thing you should do is whatever comes naturally to you. If what comes naturally doesn't work, if it provides stress, then you'll have to change.

"If you're a natural crammer, for instance, and you need the tension cramming induces but you find your cramming is causing too much stress, you could at least set some subgoals. That is, cram for parts of a project at a time."

Chapter 7

DIETING

We all know that stress can trigger the "nervous munchies." But can dieting itself leave you tense, irritable, angry and frustrated?

"No question about it," says Michael R. Lowe, Ph.D., director of the weight management program at Temple University Medical Practices in Philadelphia. "Trying to lose weight is both physically and mentally stressful.

"To begin with, the very fact that you are trying to lose weight implies dissatisfaction with your present shape. Pressures to lose weight are greater among women," says Dr. Lowe. "Being bombarded with image after image of ultra-thin, high-fashion role models can reinforce the feeling that no matter how much you diet, you're not going to be thin enough or attractive enough.

"The physical effects of dieting are stressful, too, because evidence indicates that the body resists attempts to lose weight," says Dr. Lowe. "Feelings of hunger and lethargy triggered by food restriction are stressful, especially coupled with visual food cues, like food stands, restaurants and magazine ads, all around us. Altogether, constantly saying no to desired foods leaves you feeling frustrated, deprived and stressed."

Taking the Torture Out of Eating Less

Short of abandoning all efforts to control your eating habits, what can calorie counters do to avoid dieting themselves down to a bundle of nerves?

Plenty. The following tips can counteract many of the feelings of resentment and deprivation that make weight control torture to body and soul.

Ask yourself if you *really* need to lose weight. "Many people who are dissatisfied with their size aren't really overweight, but they're either on a diet or feel they should be," says Dr. Lowe. If you have good reason to feel fat, though—if you weigh 20 percent or more above the recommended weight for your height—then you need to face some facts.

Accept the fact that you will never be able to eat whatever you like,

whenever you like, in any amount, without gaining weight. "If people want to lose weight and keep it off, they first have to accept the fact that they will never be able to return to their eating habits of the past," says Dr. Lowe. "In our program, we find it useful to describe an overweight tendency as a kind of handicap. And as with other physical handicaps, the people who ultimately adapt best are those who can get past the feelings of anger and injustice, strive toward new goals and develop new feelings of pride at having overcome their 'handicap.' "

Don't cut back drastically. "Drastic efforts—a few weeks of strict discipline and extreme self-sacrifice—are usually followed by a return to old eating habits, leaving people feeling guilty and disgusted with themselves," says Dr. Lowe. "Instead, cut back gradually."

Don't adopt very odd or specialized diets. "Highly idiosyncratic diets that force you to eat only a few foods will also leave you feeling very deprived," says Dr. Lowe. You're apt to feel edgy and irritable. Odd diets are also hard to follow if you work outside the home, attend social functions and otherwise lead a normal, active life.

Build indulgences into your program. "If you say, 'I'm never going to eat ice cream again for the rest of my life,' you are aiming for the impossible and setting yourself up for failure," says Dr. Lowe. "Black-or-white, all-or-nothing thinking can undermine the very thing you're trying to achieve. So allow yourself an occasional stop for an ice cream cone (but don't keep a half-gallon carton in the freezer)."

Congratulate yourself on the victories and a healthier way of life. "If you lock yourself in a mind-set of, 'How much longer can I endure this?' you will feel upset, frustrated and angry," says Dr. Lowe. "But if you focus on the healthful benefits of weight control, feelings of inferiority and deprivation give way to pride, and your new diet becomes a morale booster."

Plan ahead. It's one thing to be obsessed with food (which many dieters are) and quite another to plan ahead in order to stick to your diet.

"Weight-conscious people need to be more mindful of what they're going to eat, and not make on-the-spot decisions at mealtime," says Dr. Lowe. Otherwise, you may end up eating high-calorie foods by default.

"Plan menus, shop for food, prepare for food-centered situations," says Dr. Lowe. "If you're going to a party, prepare to decline food when it's offered. Or set limits to how much you will eat. Or eat sparingly earlier that day."

Don't let others coax or bully you off your diet. "No one, hosts and hostesses included, has the right to pressure you into eating or drinking something you shouldn't," says Dr. Lowe.

Losing weight is no piece of cake. But it doesn't have to be torture, either.

Chapter 8

DISAPPOINTMENTS

Consider the view from above. You are on the moon looking down at the earth. Somewhere below, a person's blood pressure is rising, his nights are sleepless. He yells at his kids, berates his wife, cannot concentrate at work and finds no joy in recreation. The reason for all this stress? He is disappointed that the new car he purchased is a lemon.

Sure, owning a car with flaws is frustrating. But consider the view from above: One car isn't going to mean much in the scheme of things. Ten years from now, it won't matter at all. So why should you let such a disappointment interfere with your health and emotional well-being?

Whether they are minor letdowns, like buying an unsatisfactory product, or major defeats, like discovering you are infertile, disappointments are always stressful. But the difference between letting them destroy you and letting them challenge you is a simple matter of attitude, and of understanding what disappointments show us about how we view ourselves.

Let's start off with a disappointment almost every working person has experienced at least once: the trauma of not getting an anticipated promotion.

What happens when you are denied a promotion, is that someone is pointing out to you that you're not worth very much. And if that catastrophe has you feeling brutal about yourself, the big thing to recognize, according to organizational psychologist Maury Elvekrog, Ph.D., is how much your self-image, your self-interpretation and your values are totally tied to a promotion and to job prestige. He says, "Ask yourself, 'Do I have no value, no reason to feel good about myself except for the job?' "

In this case, as in most disappointments, the stress is basically a function of your own mind. It's not being passed over for the job, it's the meaning you attach to it that causes the stress. "It is almost never really the practicality of such a situation that causes problems, that the lack of finances will throw the person and his family into debtors' prison," he says. "The big problem is the blow to the ego."

So if you're feeling totally put down by such a disappointment, it's time

25

for a little self-examination. People acquire values from our culture, from their parents and from peers, and they rarely look at them objectively. Start now. Sit back and ask yourself about your life values. Is there an overemphasis on job prestige? "One's values don't have to depend just on that. In fact, for people whose values depend totally on such external things as advancing at work, the stress never ends because you might never advance enough for your own liking," says Dr. Elvekrog.

Making It Hard to Rebound

The real key is the kind of message the person sends himself about the disappointment. If the person says to himself, "I must be a lousy person because they didn't hire me for the job," it's needless personalization. In fact, work by several researchers has shown that people who tend to blame themselves for misfortune are more susceptible to disease. And there is evidence that self-blaming and other defeatist types create a self-fulfilling prophecy. It pays for them not to be optimistic.

And people often make a catastrophe out of something that doesn't have to be a catastrophe. Those who experience any disappointment, even one as traumatic as losing a child through a miscarriage, should remind themselves that the sad event doesn't mean they can never be happy again.

"People say their life will never be satisfying again. And in communicating that feeling to themselves, they feel worse than just the experience of the loss. They've made the loss that much stronger," says T. Thorne Wiggers, Ed.D., a counseling psychologist at George Washington University, Washington, D.C. "It's sad when any disappointment happens, but it's not the end of the world." A doom-and-gloom attitude also makes it hard for the person to rebound in a positive way.

How you respond to major disappointments can have a profound impact on your life. John Snarey, Ph.D., conducted a study that examined how 52 men who experienced infertility coped with the problem over several decades. The results can teach people a great deal about the preferable methods for dealing with disappointments.

The men were divided into three groups, according to what kind of "replacement" they sought to cope with the stress of involuntary infertility. Members of one group treated themselves as their own babies, becoming preoccupied with activities such as body building, activities that Dr. Snarey describes as narcissistic. Another group's members found their replacement in objects, devoting themselves to a house, car, boat or the like. The third group's members became involved in vicarious childrearing by substituting the child of a relative, friend or neighbor for the one they couldn't produce.

By tracking the groups to midlife, Dr. Snarey found among the narcissistic group that 80 percent were divorced and 20 percent reported being unhappily married. In the group that found a substitute in objects, 50 percent were happily married, 25 percent were unhappily married and 25 percent were divorced. In the group that substituted vicarious child rearing, 90 percent reported being happily married.

For those who must bear the burden of involuntary childlessness, Dr. Snarey says, "Find important substitutes, other living human beings. I would caution people not to focus on themselves."

From Lemons, Make Lemonade

Solutions to disappointments aren't always easy. But Ronald Nathan, Ph.D., associate professor of psychiatry and family medicine at Louisiana State University School of Medicine in Shreveport, says to look for the opportunities that exist behind the disappointment.

Dr. Nathan is coauthor of the book *The Doctors' Guide to Instant Stress Relief.* And he's got a strategy for the age-old disappointment that accompanies lemon car models.

"The first step is to relax. Change your expectations and thoughts that the car will be perfect. Anticipate the inevitable problems, but not to the extent that you dwell on them," he says.

"A big part of stress comes from feeling out of control. So bring things under control as much as possible. Take out a pad and pencil and write down the things that are wrong with your car, when you want to bring it in for repair," he says, then adds, "Use this as an opportunity to employ your assertive skills."

Take the stress out of what you're telling yourself. Don't blame yourself. And see how this disappointment fits into the big picture from above.

Chapter 9

DUAL-CAREER HOUSEHOLDS

How's this for a morning routine?

Johnny, the ten-month-old human alarm clock, shrieks his morning call at 6:10 A.M. on this rainy Monday instead of his usual, dependable 5:40. While Mom tends to Johnny's diaper, furiously working to recapture the forever-lost half hour and mentally outlining the assignment she will give her earliest seventh-grade class, eight-year-old Mary is telling Dad that she thinks, just thinks, she has a sore throat, but she wants to stay in bed five more minutes to decide. And can she have a glass of water? From inside the bathroom, Dad yells something unpleasant about getting the wrong brand of razor blades. In the kitchen, Mom uses one hand to feed Johnny, the other to put up coffee. From her bed, Mary is shouting out her breakfast order and shouting out her lunchbox order, but she'll repeat them both as she emerges from her room and races for the closed bathroom door.

Dressing, Dad discovers the dry cleaning, containing all his suitable shirts, was never picked up the previous afternoon, then finds the crucial notes for an 8:30 budget meeting have vanished.

Mary is dissatisfied with her cereal, hesitant to brush her teeth, unable to recall where she left her galoshes. Mom escapes Johnny for a two-minute shower, drips water on the kitchen floor as she slaps together peanut butter and jelly against Mary's squeals of protest. Eventually, the right papers are located and the wrong shirt will have to do. With the school bus making its way down the block, neither Mary nor Mom is dressed. Dad has missed his usual commuter train, and the one after it, and he will miss the one after that—God knows, maybe lose his job—if he can't maneuver Johnny into the car seat and deposit him in the day care center within the next 15 minutes.

With only slight variations, such mornings are standard operating procedure in families where both spouses work. "People are more pressured in the morning," says Clifford Sager, M.D., director of family psychiatry at the Jewish Board of Family and Children's Services in New York. "And it is very important to be organized, very important to be considerate. When people are rushed in the morning, they might not be thoughtful and, if they're annoyed at their mate, they can be spiteful. It's all very stressful."

How Many Remedies Can You Find?

There is a host of relatively simple remedies for the above madness. Here are some recommended by Dr. Sager.

First, no one in their right mind would depend on an infant's schedule to wake them up, regardless of how regular the baby is. It's an adult responsibility. Set your alarm clock or clock radio, or attach a timer to your television.

If you've got one bathroom, stagger the times you wake up so one person can use the facilities before the other.

Pack lunch for your children the night before. That way you can simply reach into the refrigerator and retrieve it in the morning. Also, if the lunch is prepared in advance, there is less of an opportunity to place a lunch order the next morning ("This is what you said you wanted last night. . . . ").

Organize your clothes and your kids' clothes before going to bed. An eight-year-old should be able to lay out her clothes the night before, with only minor parental consultation. And if you suddenly remember the forgotten dry cleaning at night before going to bed, you're in a better position to figure out an alternative wardrobe selection for yourself.

And while you're doing so much advance preparation, set the breakfast table before retiring for the night. And get yourself one of those coffeemakers that operates by timer.

"The two most important things are advance planning and getting your kids to be as independent and do as much as their ages and capabilities allow," says Dr. Sager.

And what about the sore throat? "You have to make a list of at least three backup people who can come over quickly to stay with a sick youngster. They should be people with whom the children are familiar," recommends Dr. Sager.

More Working Mothers, More Hassles

These hassles are a part of everyday life in an increasing number of households. According to the latest U.S. Department of Labor statistics, 55 percent of all married women work—that's 28.2 million women—and 61 percent of the nation's married mothers work.

Those figures are climbing rapidly. Women now comprise 44 percent of the United States workforce, and the Labor Department predicts that by 1995 they will represent 60 percent. Not only are more married women working than ever before, but they are proving to be competitive with men on the earnings front.

Whether both partners work because of financial pressures or in pursuit of personal satisfaction, dual-career couples, for the most part, must blaze their own trail, arrive at their own solutions to the special needs of the arrangement. Two-career couples have become solidly entrenched in our culture, but our society still offers little in the way of institutionalized solutions. Few corporations provide child day care. Flexible work hours and job-sharing arrangements, two once highly touted solutions for dual-worker households, have been shunned by all but a handful of employers.

The Childcare Dilemma

There's a wonderful Doonesbury comic strip in which cartoonist Garry Trudeau captures the unsettling spirit of day care. A child being picked up from a home-based day care center tells his mother: "I was crying because all the other children went home and you were late again, but Mrs. Wicker gave me Oreos and let me watch cartoons and I called her 'Mommy' by mistake." Mother looks at the child and says, "You play hardball, kid."

Whether it's employer-run or university-affiliated, whether a nanny comes to your house or you drop off your kid with a neighbor who owns every toy ever made, whether there are provisions for children with the flu or child development specialists on hand, the bottom line is likely to be the same: You have nagging doubts about what's going on with your kids.

Those nagging doubts can impact on your productivity at work and on your relationship with your child. Even parents who can afford the best care worry that they may be shortchanging their youngsters.

For most people, childcare can be a troublesome arrangement indeed. But there are steps you can take to eliminate some of your worries. Here's a day care center checklist, provided by Ellen Galinsky, director of Work and Family Life Studies at Bank Street College in New York and coauthor of the forthcoming *Family Matters in the Pre-School Years*.

1. What's the relationship between the childcare provider and the child? Do they care about the child? Do they pay attention to the child?
2. What's the discipline that the childcare provider uses? Do they see so-called bad behavior as something to be stopped and punished or as a chance to teach children how to solve problems, how to learn self-guidance and how to handle stressful situations? For instance, if two kids are hitting each other, is the childcare provider likely to say something on the order of,

"You're bad, that hurts," or "You both want that fire truck, but can you think of a better way to solve that problem?"

3. Does the childcare provider encourage the child to talk, to think, to describe things, to express himself or herself?
4. Is it a stable childcare facility? Is there a high turnover rate among employees, or is there some consistency?
5. Are there enough adults to take care of the kids? And are groups small enough to keep your child from being overwhelmed? For kids under age two, it's best to have one adult for every three children, according to the National Association for Education of Young Children, an accrediting agency for center-based (as opposed to home-based) early childhood programs. Two-year-olds should be in groups no larger than 12, three- and four-year-olds in groups no larger than 18. And there should be two adults on hand at all times.
6. What's the training of the caregivers? Have they attended courses on childcare? Do they read about it?
7. Is there enough space? Are there interesting materials for the children? Do they have things to do based on their ages?
8. What's your relationship with the caregiver? Is it supportive? Does it make you feel guilty? Does the individual subtly make you feel terrible? (Example: "Your child always behaves with me. I don't know why he cries with you.") Such comments can create conflict between the child and the important adults in his or her life.

For a copy of the brochure "How to Choose a Good Early-Childhood Program," send 50 cents and a self-addressed, stamped, business-size envelope to the National Association for Education of Young Children, 1834 Connecticut Avenue NW, Washington, DC 20009.

Setting Priorities

Managing the stress of being part of a dual-career family is often a matter of using time efficiently, being organized, sharing responsibilities as a family, taking an interest in your child's well-being (feeling comfortable about their childcare, for instance) and understanding your limitations.

"Understand the power that your expectations have in your judgment of yourself," says childcare expert Galinsky. If you believe all your time with your child should be quality time, you may be setting yourself up for unrealistic expectations. Many psychologists believe "down time" is equally important. And besides, "No human relationship can be perfect all of the time," says Galinsky.

"Don't expect things in your household to be done as well as if that were your top priority," says Ross Webber, Ph.D., a management professor at the Wharton School of the University of Pennsylvania. Dr. Webber, who has written several books on time management, including *A Guide to Getting Things Done*, recommends you "prepare yourself psychologically" to lower your expectations, whether for the quality of your meals or the neatness of your kid's room.

Dr. Webber suggests you segment your time. Pick two days a week for your special meals, days when you know you'll be able to get home early or be able to shop for food. "The fact that you know you will have those two special meals will make you feel in control of at least part of the week and make you better able to deal with the fact that on the other days you won't be having dinners like mother used to make," he says.

There's a similar approach to cleaning your kid's room. Pick one day that you'll share with your child the experience of cleaning up his or her room. You'll know that it will be clean at least one day (or one hour) a week, and that may help you through the time when you know it'll be a mess. There's a psychological fringe benefit to doing the straightening up together. The child will associate the cleaning process as a positive experience, and may not shun the task when he or she is old enough to do it alone.

If you think your house should look perfect all of the time, maybe you should think again. "In the scheme of the universe, doing things with your kids is going to be more important to you than having no dust," says Galinsky. In general, "Figure out which of the 'shoulds' matter to you and which are cultural hangovers," she says.

Every dual-career household fits into one of four strategic frameworks, according to Dr. Webber.

• Couples who put their career second in importance to their relationship or family. Couples who operate this way tend to find it relatively easy to make time-sharing deals. The downside is that there could be adverse consequences to both careers and that, as years march on, one member may end up resenting the bargain.

• Couples who agree that the husband's career comes first and the wife's is secondary. The wife bears the burden of keeping the household moving. This arrangement tends to work the best, as unfair as it might be.

• Couples who put the wife's career first and the husband's second. This is the most difficult arrangement to sustain because most men are conditioned to be the successful partner. They may become unhappy as they begin to see themselves falling behind their peers. Such arrangements work best if the husband is in a nonorganizational work situation—such as an artist who works at home.

• Couples who both put their careers ahead of the relationship or family. Chances for success of both the relationship and careers are slimmest in such households.

Dr. Webber says that devising a strategy for sharing responsibilities and managing time may depend on which framework your marriage falls under. It also depends on the demands of your jobs. The simplest means of sharing chores is to arbitrarily alternate on a daily or a weekly basis. But that arrangement doesn't allow for much flexibility in case one partner's workload increases. On the other hand, if you alternate your chores based on how busy you are at work, you may be headed for conflict. One spouse may feel that the household work is unevenly distributed. Most successful couples work out a plan for sharing the household duties that matches their needs and dispositions.

Dividing Responsibilities: How Successful Couples Do It

Max and Jane Carter of Upper Darby, Pennsylvania, would make a perfect study for time-management researchers. Until a few months ago, they both worked full-time as teachers and they both were full-time graduate students. And they have three kids. The coursework has ended for Max and Jane—both of whom are in their thirties—but the organizing strategies remain well entrenched in the household.

"We divide up tasks and responsibilities so there's a clear sense of who does what and when," says Max. "You have to establish clear expectations so you don't assume the other person knows what's going on. Things need to be expressed."

Here's how the Carters divide up the chores. Jane cooks the meals. Max cleans up after the meals. Max prepares breakfast with the help of their 11-year-old daughter while Jane gets the 4-year-old ready for day care. Max cleans up after breakfast and cleans the house on Saturday mornings. Jane does the laundry.

During the course of their four-year marriage, Robert and Gayle Stewart of suburban Washington, D.C., have developed a simple method of divvying up the work: She takes care of everything inside the house; he handles chores outside. "I take care of all the money, all the bills, and if something needs to get done inside the house, I either do it or get it done," she says. "If it's outside the house—mowing the grass, digging out the snowbound cars—he does it."

It is an arrangement that suits each partner and may be crucial to their own particular situation. Both Robert, 39, and Gayle, 35, are captains in the Washington Police Department. She works the midnight-to-7:00 A.M. shift; he works from about 7:00 A.M. to 3:00 P.M. "Some mornings I come home and, if he hasn't left yet, I literally push him out of bed," says Gayle. "When he comes home, I'm getting ready for bed."

"I like to cook," says Yona Dansky, 38, a Philadelphia teacher, "so I do the meals. I have them all planned a week in advance." Her husband, Howard, 39, likes to flee the confines of a small house, so he shops for food and takes care of the cars. They split the cleaning: She does the laundry, he vacuums. Another dual-career couple alternate chores on a weekly basis. One week he shops and cooks while she does the laundry. The next week they swap. If a partner's shop-and-cook week coincides with a particularly rough work week, there's little room to wiggle out of the commitment. The partner winds up spending Sunday cooking food for the week.

Judy Green and Michael Scheible prefer to take turns with the chores, but they do it on an ad hoc, daily basis. Because their work schedules are fairly flexible, they are able to alternate the daily workload: Some days he babysits the two children while she cooks; other days she babysits while he cooks. It depends, for the most part, on their jobs.

She works on the copy desk of the *Sacramento Bee*. He is chief of program planning for the California Air Resources Board. Michael often is able to take work home; Judy was able to arrange a 24-hour work week that involves working either all mornings or all afternoons. Her employer pays her at the hourly rate she earned as a full-time employee, before having kids and dropping back to part-time work. With the two incomes, the family can afford the $800-a-month bill for outside day care.

When the Family Takes Priority

Judy Green and Michael Scheible are among the folks who have very clearly established from the start that the family comes first and career advancement concerns come second. It's a commitment that required Judy—the spouse with the most flexible job—to reduce her work week from 40 hours to 24 hours for the years that her children are young. She even forfeited a coveted promotion in the process.

The couple recommends that by setting your priorities—and by sticking to them—you are managing some of the strain. "Your values have to be clearly set," says Michael. "If you make our kind of choice, putting careers behind family, life is a lot easier. But you have to make that priority very clear to yourself. Between two jobs and keeping a household going, there's never enough time. You have to give something up. If you give up your family, you feel guilty; if you give up your job, you feel as if you let your co-workers down and are not progressing as far as you can as fast as you can. If you do everything, you're pooped all the time."

Plans That Work

Busy couples develop tricks for getting things done. If Yona and Howard Dansky have household business matters to discuss with each other, they do it over the phone. If they can't get it settled during the workday, they will call each other up from different rooms at home. They've discovered that their two children are less apt to interrupt them when they're talking on the phone.

Other couples who must commute distances to work have struck upon the wonders of a car phone for accomplishing such personal tasks as ordering birthday gifts.

Both partners must be flexible and willing to experiment and innovate. In fact, an extensive study conducted by psychologist Joseph H. Pleck, author of *Working Wives, Working Husbands,* indicated that the more housework and childcare a husband in a dual-career marriage performed, the happier he was. Indeed, the couples who appear to succeed at the dual-career lifestyle are those who are the most cooperative.

Helping around the House

What about the spouse who feels overburdened with an unequal share of household chores and responsibilities? How to get a partner to lend support?

In his role as president of the Institute for the Development of Emotional and Life Skills, Bernard G. Guerney, Ph.D., teaches people constructive strategies for dealing with such conflicts. "These require skills most people don't have," he says.

"They have to learn to take the other person's perspective and let the other person know they respect their point of view and feelings. Most people only want to get their own point of view across and feel that to respect the other person's point of view would go against them. But the opposite is true," says Dr. Guerney. He gives two examples—one wrong, one right—of trying to get a spouse to pitch in with some help around the house.

Wrong: "I think you're a very inconsiderate person to have me be doing all of the cooking all of the time."

"You should be telling your partner what it is you want and how you feel in a way that's least likely to be threatening to the other person and most likely to make them want to cooperate," he says. "We teach people not to talk about the character or motives of the other person ('you're very inconsiderate'), which leads the partner to respond defensively, nor to indulge in overgeneralization ('all of the cooking all of the time'), which invites counterattack that the overgeneralization is not true. And it usually causes the discussion to deteriorate." Also, by not telling the other person how you feel, you make it hard for them to empathize.

Right: "I'm feeling overwhelmed, very frustrated by the amount of work that I feel obliged to do around the house, and I feel discouraged about the amount of help I get from you. You could be a big help to me if you were willing to do some of these things."

After making such a statement, the next move is to stop talking and start listening to your spouse's reaction. Listen to your partner express his or her feelings.

"You want a constructive approach to problem-solving. So share your ideas, discover the basic issues and how you feel about them and what it is you want. Then you have to reach the solution where you get the most of what you want," says Dr. Guerney.

Dr. Guerney says that most people wait until the wrong moment to launch into their attack—when they can't take it any longer. They will be expressing negative emotions, crying or doing things that will frighten or put off the other person. "Instead, frustrated partners should discuss a problem before it becomes a hostile issue," he recommends.

Caring for the Sick Child

So who stays home with the sick youngster? Dr. Webber says there's no question that the illness of a child is the most conflict-invoking situation that faces a dual-career family. And it's usually the wife, he says, who makes the sacrifice and stays home. A recent survey of 400 working men and women with children under age 12 indicated that 38 percent of the men and 59 percent of the women missed a workday in the past three months due to family obligations. "When push comes to shove, her success or the risk of offending her organization is less than the man's."

There's a double bind, says Dr. Webber. A woman who asks for time off is usually treated more graciously by her organization than a man would be. So for her, it's less stressful. But in a way, the organization expects a woman to be less committed to a career. When she asks for time off to stay home with a sick youngster, it verifies the organization's stereotype and expectations that the woman isn't serious about work.

If a man makes the request, the employer may be surprised—and angry. When promotion time rolls around, a boss may reason that if the man can't manage his family (and arrange for someone else to care for the ill youngster), he won't be able to manage the budget committee.

What's the solution? "It's a consideration that has to be worked out in advance, if possible," says Dr. Sager. "They have to sit down and talk it over. If one of them has a boss who's impossible, that has to be considered. But a backup plan is good to have, perhaps a list of people who will look after the kids in a tight situation, people the kids like being with. A plan is necessary because with kids you're always going to have these problems. But the decisions should not be made unilaterally."

He adds, "Even in couples where one partner stays home and takes care of the house, decisions should not be made unilaterally."

Keeping Spirits Up

It's not always easy to leave the job behind and plunge into family life at 5:00 P.M. (or 6:00 or 7:00 P.M., as the case is likely to be). Making a direct move from harried employee to harried parent may not be fair to yourself, and it certainly isn't fair to your kids.

When you get home, stop for a moment to relax before rushing into your next bout of activity. It may take some practice, but you will find yourself better able to manage the stress of your busy lifestyle.

T. Berry Brazelton, M.D., professor of pediatrics at Harvard Medical School and chief of the child development unit at Boston's Children's Hospital, says it's important to save up some energy so that when you get home you'll have enough for the children. Pacing yourself might mean not going the unnecessary extra mile for your employer, but the long-term benefits may be well worth it. And Dr. Brazelton offers some other advice.

Compartmentalize. When you're at work, try to think about what you're doing at work. When you're at home, think about what's happening at home. Try not to bring work home from the office; try not to take your family worries into work.

When you get home, gather the kids up and be with them as a family before you do anything else. If you have an infant, just spend some time cuddling. If you have older children, just sit there and talk to them. The point is to get back together as a family. Then you can do the housework or prepare dinner. "It gives them the feeling that you've got time for them, that you're not just still at work—but now doing it at home."

In her book *The Working Parents Survival Guide*, Sally Wendkos Olds offers additional tips for easing the transition between work and home. Among them she recommends finding 15 or 30 minutes of peace in exercise, meditation, a shower or bath, watching the evening news, reading the mail to your favorite music, eating an appetizer. Or, "Get off the bus two stops earlier than you have to and walk the rest of the way home. The exercise is good for you, and the fresh air acts as a decompression chamber." Driving? "Detour by the park for a ten-minute stroll to accomplish the same effect," she writes.

Keeping the Marriage in Tune

Keeping the household humming is just one major objective facing the dual-career couple. The other is to keep the marriage itself in tune. And the two-paycheck household may harbor a host of special stresses—even if both partners have no problem sharing the chores, organizing their time, finding the perfect childcare strategy or keeping the family matters in order. There's still the marriage to de-stress.

When a housewife decides to work outside of the home, unanticipated conflicts often accompany the second paycheck. First off, the husband may begin to feel insecure. "The work is something like a baby coming into the household. The man finds himself competing for attention," says Judith Kuriansky, Ph.D., a clinical psychologist with the Center for Marital and Family Therapy in New York. The result, for many couples, is that a subtle battle over control of the relationship might rage beneath the surface of the marriage. It could undermine both the marriage and careers.

To eliminate the stress brought on by such changes and worries, Dr. Kuriansky recommends a frank discussion. "They really have to discuss the questions. What are their fears and fantasies? Is he worried that his wife will have an affair with a co-worker? What are his concerns about giving up control? Only by bringing it out in the open can you dissipate such problems," she says.

Today, one in five married women brings home more money than does her husband. And the group's ranks expand each year, as women gain status and advancement in new careers. Partners may begin to think of their value in the relationship in terms of how much money they are able to contribute. Such competitiveness can work to subvert a partner's career. Explains Dr. Kuriansky, "Obviously, if a couple has a good relationship, they want each other to go ahead. But they can be carrying over sibling rivalries." Sibling rivalry seeps into a marriage in the form of criticizing a partner's work. Dr. Kuriansky instructs her clients to write down statements they make about their spouse's work. She then asks them to determine whether the statements are positive or negative, critical or supportive. "Step back and distance yourself to gain a different perspective," she says. You may be surprised to discover that you aren't talking to your spouse but to a sister or brother."

Sibling rivalry is not the only behavior from an original family that creeps into a marriage. There are expectations of how one's spouse should act. On the one hand, a man might be attracted to powerful women and want a wife who is more independent and has more status and more earning power than his mother. On the other hand, he still wants to be mothered by someone who is relatively docile because that's the way he was raised. Says Dr. Kuriansky, "Half the battle is realizing what your real attitudes are and whether or not you may be following your parents' patterns."

Chapter 10

EXECUTIVE STRESS

Question: What's the difference between an executive and a tightrope walker on a greased wire above the Grand Canyon with no net?

Answer: The executive's under more stress.

If you're nodding your head at this lame joke, you must be an executive.

Executives know that they have their own tightropes to walk, balancing between success and failure, vigor and exhaustion, recognition and blame, and that stress accompanies every step. Indeed, enormous stress is part of the image of the American executive. We picture this: A harried man or woman burning the midnight oil at a massive desk piled high with papers, perspiration on the brow, sipping the tenth cup of coffee, then, in another moment of frustration, snapping a pencil in two.

The image, of course, doesn't quite fit all executives. But there's no denying that stress is a big part of executive life and that it can have serious consequences, both physically and mentally. Ulcers, migraines, heart disease, fatigue, sleeplessness, depression, anxiety, anger, low self-esteem—these and other symptoms, research says, may be the executive's lot if stress isn't managed.

And managed it can be.

The heartening news from stress experts to executives is this: Even though stress is an inescapable part of your job, you can—with proper techniques—handle it effectively, and even turn it to your advantage.

Pushing the Stress Buttons

What are the sources of stress for the executive? If you can answer that one, you're well on your way to bringing executive stress under control.

In a study of 300 managers from 12 major companies, John H. Howard, Ph.D., of the University of Western Ontario, pinpointed four factors in executive jobs that seem to produce the most stress.

A feeling of helplessness. When executives are prevented from acting out their proper roles, they feel helpless, impotent—and this feeling engenders tremendous stress. For example, you may work hard to develop reasonable solutions to some tough problems, but can't apply what you know because of constraints within the organization. The wielding of power, therefore, is a remedy for stress.

Uncertainty. When you're not sure of the facts (about company policy, the vagaries of proposed budget or anything else), decision making is hard—and stress increases.

Urgency. The executive's day is filled with tasks that demand great attention and effort—right now. "On average," Dr. Howard says, "managers do something different every seven minutes. Their jobs are characterized by brevity and fragmentation and stress."

Overwork. Like the executive in the popular mind, the real executive typically strains under a huge workload. Executive jobs, says Dr. Howard, are often "much work at an unrelenting pace."

As Dr. Howard's study reveals, these four stress-producers crop up in all kinds of on-the-job situations. He groups these situations into categories that probably will sound disconcertingly familiar to most executives. Here are a few of the categories.

Poor management or boss. For the 300 executives in the study, having to deal with bad management was the single biggest stress-producing situation to be in. They said that what causes the most strain and tension is poor planning, bad direction and chronic indecisiveness.

Lack of authority or blurred organizational structure. As far as the executives in the study were concerned, the second biggest stressful situation is having a job to do with no authority to do it. Almost as bad is having to work where organizational boundaries are fuzzy—where job descriptions are too vague and bosses are too plentiful.

Promotion and recognition. When you're uncertain about future promotion or you never get any praise or recognition from top management, you're going to be stressed. Perhaps *very* stressed. Many of the executives in the study found these situations to be particularly painful—and complained that they didn't know what criteria they were being judged by or what they needed to do to get promoted.

Company politics. When work becomes political, it becomes stressful—especially when office politics influence promotions, the use of power, transfers and allocation of supplies and equipment.

Personnel problems. Executives must manage people. And when those people aren't doing their jobs or they have personal problems, the executive gets hit with a wave of stress.

Stress Inoculations

One obvious strategy against stress is to eliminate or change the situations that cause it.

But wait a minute. You can't always avoid stressful situations. Often you can't even *change* the situations, not even one little bit. So what's a stressed-out executive to do?

You build up your stress resistance. That, in effect, is what some stress experts are recommending. They say that by changing your approach to stressful situations, your perceptions of them, you can actually make yourself resistant to stress and its awful consequences.

"We think of stress as something that's 'out there,' " says Paul J. Rosch, M.D., president of the American Institute of Stress. "Well, it's not 'out there.' It's all in how you perceive it. Look at how two people might experience a roller coaster ride. One has his back stiffened, his knuckles are white, his eyes are shut, his jaws are clenched, just waiting for it to be over. The wide-eyed thrill-seeker relishes every plunge and can't wait to do it again."

Researchers Suzanne Kobasa, Ph.D., and Salvatore Maddi, Ph.D., have taken a first-hand look at the link between executives' attitudes and stress resistance. They studied executives involved in the 1983 Bell System breakup and found big differences between executives who withstood the stresses of organizational change and those who knuckled under.

First, they found that executives bothered the least by stressful circumstances had fewer illnesses than executives who had trouble coping with the same circumstances. No surprise. But what was significant was that Dr. Kobasa and Dr. Maddi were able to pinpoint what seemed to "inoculate" many of the executives against stress.

The key stress-resistance factor, say the researchers, was "personality hardiness." "Hardiness is not the mental counterpart of a strong physical constitution," says Dr. Maddi, coauthor with Dr. Kobasa of *The Hardy Executive: Health under Stress*. "Rather, hardiness is a set of beliefs people have about the world and themselves and the interaction between the two."

According to these experts, these beliefs or attitudes enable the executive to defuse stress by looking at stressful situations in a unique way. The hardy (stress-resistant) executive thinks, "The situation is not completely unmanageable; it's something I can control, at least to a degree. And it isn't a trivial or thoroughly terrible problem—it's actually interesting and important. And I don't really think of it as threatening to me—it's a challenge."

Such a stress-defusing outlook enabled some executives in the Bell System breakup to actually enjoy stresses that were making other executives' lives a nightmare.

Fortunately, say Dr. Maddi and Dr. Kobasa, this outlook isn't something that you either have or you don't—it can be *learned*. They've already successfully taught executives the psychological techniques that embody the stress-busting outlook.

Here are some of the key techniques.

Focusing. This involves discovering what's truly stressful to you about a situation and why—the idea being that understanding your stress lessens it and gives you some control over it. The technique may sound simplistic, but often people may think they know why something is stressful to them but are way off-base.

For example: John has a report to prepare on improving his department's efficiency, and he's getting nowhere. The deadline's closing in—and so is stress. John thinks he knows the source of the stress: "They never give you enough time to do anything in this place," he says.

But then he tries focusing. He takes a closer look at his emotions regarding his predicament and realizes to his surprise that he feels fear. He traces the fear back to grammar school, where he was afraid of failure—and often simply didn't do assigned work to avoid failing at it. He realizes that he's doing the same thing now. And this insight seems to cut his problem down to size, to at least make it capable of manipulation.

Situational reconstruction. This method disarms stress by putting a stressful situation in perspective. It's most useful when you run smack into a really big stressful event in your life, especially one that you become obsessed with.

After a stress-producing event, you try to imagine specific ways that the

Stress First-Aid for the Executive

It's only 9:22 and already the boss is steamed, your big project is snafued and you just got enough stress in ten minutes to last you all day. You'll eventually get the mess straightened out, but what can you do right now for on-the-spot stress relief?

A lot, say stress experts. Here are some of their best suggestions for rapid easing of the effects of stress—so you can get on with the job of being a top-notch executive.

• Stretch yourself. Dissipate the tension in your muscles by giving them a nice long stretch. Select a muscle group (legs, arms, neck, back, whatever), gently and slowly stretch them until you feel a tug, hold for 10 to 30 seconds, then release. You can do this throughout your whole body or just in the muscles that are tensed up.

• Walk it off. When tension is high, don't sit. Get up and take your stress for a stroll. A brisk 10- or 15-minute walk can reduce muscular and nervous tension.

• Take a trip—in your mind. By visualizing a stress-free scene that appeals to you, you can actually unwind the tension you feel. Lock the door to your office, sit back and "see," as vividly as you can, the sandy shores of your next vacation, or a single magnificent rose. Use as many senses as possible to experience your stress-reducing vision.

• Take a breather. When you're uptight, your breathing becomes rapid and shallow. Decrease stress by deliberately breathing more slowly and deeply. Take seven seconds to inhale, then eight seconds to exhale. Then repeat this for five minutes—or longer if necessary.

• Practice executive P.R. The technique known as Progressive Re-event could have been worse and better. Then you visualize what you could have done to make the better outcome a reality.

Often the result of this exercise is that you realize that you do have options, that you can exert some control, that you can use your imagination to head off future stresses. And, as Dr. Kobasa explains, "when you realize how much worse it could have been, you know you didn't mess up as much as you might have."

Compensatory self-improvement. This is the technique you use when you run up against the "executive stone wall"—the stressful situation that can't be changed.

Step one is to be realistic. "If no amount of situational reconstruction provokes a sense that a stressful event can be transformed," say Dr. Maddi and Dr. Kobasa, "then that event is a given, and is best accepted as such."

Step two is to realize that you can still have control and success in other areas of your life, then set out to prove this to yourself. Pick out an important

laxation is a perfect stress-releaser for the office. The first time you try it you may need some privacy (in your office or the washroom, say) so you can concentrate. But as you get better at it, you can use it to de-stress yourself anywhere.

First, sit down, lean back and close your eyes. Then clench your right hand, tensing the muscles in your wrist and forearm. Hold for five seconds, concentrating on the tension building in your hand. Then release, letting the tension drain away and paying close attention to the feeling of relaxation. Repeat this sequence of tension and release in your left hand, then your upper arms, shoulders, neck, back, face, legs, feet and toes.

• Open the pressure valve. If you're steamed up or stressed out about something, open your mouth and let out the pressure. No kidding. Talking is one way to do this. Sometimes the quickest way to ease tension is to discuss it calmly with the people involved in the tension-producing situation. If you can talk out the conflicts you're having with someone in a detached manner—without adding fuel to the fire—you'll be able to depressurize yourself and the whole situation. Even talking things over with friends outside the stressful situation can help.

Another way to open up the stress-release valve is to have a good laugh—or a good cry. Laughing at your predicament can restore calm and give you a more productive perspective. Crying—which every good executive wants to do occasionally but usually won't—may do its stress-easing by carrying away some of the body's potentially harmful chemicals in tears.

personal deficiency that can be changed—and work to change it. If you're hitting the stone wall at the office, work to overcome your fear of skiing or your lack of poise when giving speeches or some failing in parenthood.

The technique takes the bite out of stress by giving you an added sense of power, by widening your scope of possible actions, by undercutting obsession with a hopeless situation.

The Power of Expert Coping

Like Dr. Maddi and Dr. Kobasa, other stress experts have investigated what distinguishes executives who cope well with stress from those who can't—and they've come up with some surprising data. Many researchers found that the "competent copers" use simple antistress strategies that other executives ignore. Unlike those ravaged by stress, the coping executives:

- Postpone thinking about problems until an appropriate time.
- Easily detect fatigue in themselves and respond to it by cutting the workday short or taking time off during the week.
- Size up stressful situations and decide which aspects are worth worrying about and which can be ignored.
- Delegate tasks to others, especially when stress starts to increase.
- Know when perfection is possible and when it isn't.
- Get regular exercise.
- Take vacations.
- Aren't afraid to laugh at themselves.
- Talk to others—colleagues, friends, spouses—about job pressures.
- Expect the unexpected. They therefore try to allow time and energy to deal with the inevitable stressful events that come out of left field.

Chapter 11

FAMILY FEUDS

Most of us want a warm, loving family. We wish we'd get along the way the Cosbys do. So why do parents and children or brothers and sisters choose up sides and feud like the Hatfields and the McCoys?

It could be because we *expect* so much. "We want things from family," says Jacob Tebes, Ph.D., assistant professor of psychiatry and psychology at Yale University School of Medicine, New Haven, Connecticut. "We want things like intimacy, security and predictability." One big thing many of us still seek—even in our middle years—is approval. "The 'approval trap' is the major cause of nearly every dispute with your parents," says Leonard Felder, Ph.D., a psychologist in Santa Monica and author of *A Fresh Start: How to Let Go of Your Emotional Baggage and Enjoy Your Life Again* and coauthor of *Making Peace with Your Parents*. "That's when you each want each other to conform to your expectations and needs. It can block your feelings of love because you either wish your parents were different, resent that they're not, feel driven to defy or conform to their values, or feel defensive and unloving when you are with them."

With brothers and sisters, the basis for a feud is often jealousy. In comparing ourselves with our siblings, we can help or hurt each other's sense of personal worth in achievement and success, sexuality and beauty, and social relations with others.

And with any relation, we can get locked into roles. "Children often give a lot of power to their parents and older siblings," says Dr. Tebes. "As they get older, they must learn to see their relatives through the eyes of an adult. They must recognize their own power and accept the limitations of their relatives. If they don't, they may be constantly disappointed."

The Nature of Grudges

Persistent grudges can leave you fuming after each phone call, dreading family get-togethers, and yet feeling guilty if that relative becomes ill or dies.

45

Family feuds can even interfere with relationships that have nothing to do with family. "You may find yourself overreacting to anyone who reminds you of your brother, your cousin or any other family member you detest," says Dr. Felder. "When your spouse, friend or co-worker does anything that resembles the relative who gets on your nerves, you may unknowingly dump a load of resentments on that undeserving person."

And feuds can be self-perpetuating. "When a relative raises intense feelings such as anger, sadness and hurt, you may react in a negative way, such as yelling or accusing," says Dr. Tebes. "And that prompts the relative to act the same. So you get into a negative communication loop."

Backing Out of a Feud

You may never be best friends with the aunt who bugs you, but you can let go of the hurt and anger. You can get out of the rut you're in and start enjoying this person more.

First, understand the other side. In most feuds, each of you is firmly convinced that the other guy is wrong. "Often, we assume that we should convert or reform our relatives to our way of thinking," says Dr. Felder. "We want to prove that we're right."

But in many cases, there's no right and wrong person. There are just differences in opinion—different religious beliefs, political parties, lifestyles, hairstyles, careers, moral values and personalities. And we each fight to prove our ways are right.

And the more we keep fighting, the worse it gets. "What you resist persists," says Dr. Felder. "Let's say your mother doesn't like your new girlfriend, and tells you so. The more you try to resist her point of view and try to convince her that she's wrong, the more she will persist in trying to convince you that she's right."

Instead, next time your relative says something you disagree with, try to understand his feelings, experiences and attitudes instead of attacking him. If necessary, do a little research on that person's behavior.

"I had a patient, Vicki, who married a man who came from a different religious and ethnic background," says Dr. Felder. "Her parents reacted so strongly, she eloped, and they remained distant for years. So I told Vicki to research their point of view. She talked to aunts, uncles, and cousins and read several books on the subjects of intermarriage and religious identity. The more she understood about the personal and cultural reasons why her family had been so intolerant, the easier it was for her to work through her resentments."

Next, be assertive, not aggressive. Understanding the problem relative does not mean you must bow to his or her wishes. On the contrary, you should stand up for yourself. In fact, if you don't assert your own rights, you may perpetuate the conflict.

Let's say you have a mother who plays the martyr. "The martyr parent maintains control by making you feel inappropriately responsible for her suffering," says Dr. Felder.

With a parent like that, you may feel as though you can never win. You either comply with her wishes and feel resentful, or disobey and feel guilty. Either way you lose.

You probably can't change your parent's feelings, but you can give up your role in the melodrama. "Next time your dad says, 'If you love me, you'll do as I say,' don't yell." says Dr. Felder. "Instead, say, 'You've done your job as a parent by sharing your concerns, so now you can relax. Even though I don't always do what you like, I still love you.' "

And the next time your siblings make some snide remark that makes you feel inferior, don't burn up. Don't attack or hold your anger inside. "Stand up for yourself by saying, in essence, 'That hurt, here's why, and here's what I need so I won't be hurt again,' " says Dr. Felder.

Third, try to stay calm when you're under attack. Of course, it's not always easy to remain calm when your uncle tells you (again) that you'll never amount to anything. Here's a suggestion for keeping your cool.

"Try a 'guilt desensitization' exercise," says Dr. Felder. "Think of the five most common zingers your relative hits you with. It could be 'You're getting fat,' 'Why don't you call me more often?' 'When are you getting married?' 'Are you still wasting your life in that lousy job?' and so on. Record these phrases on a tape recorder and listen to them again and again. The next time you hear them, think to yourself, 'There it is, number three again.' "

Finally, discharge your rage. Despite all your efforts to be reasonable, you may still need to let off steam. "When you want to scream, and you don't do anything, your body suffers," says Dr. Felder. "Half your muscles tense as if to strike back in anger while the other half work doubly hard to suppress your reaction. It's like trying to drive with one foot on the gas and the other on the brake. I know people with family problems who get all sorts of physical symptoms—headaches, backaches and tension—when they visit their family for the holidays."

Suppressed anger can hold back your spontaneity and warmth and your ability to enjoy your relatives. But dumping it back on your relatives will just make the feuding worse. So dispel your anger by yourself. Write a scathing letter to your rival relative, listing every resentment, but don't send it. Yell at the top of your lungs into a pillow or in the car with the windows rolled up.

"Jump up and down and yell 'Get off my back!' But do it in private," suggests Dr. Felder. "That can be the quickest and easiest way to transform an oncoming 'downer' mood into laughter and emotional release."

Plan Smoother Get-Togethers

"Most family members see each other only at large group events," says Dr. Felder. "But when too many egos are gathered together, it's next to impossible to have a relaxed and satisfying conversation with any family member, especially the one with whom you've been having trouble. Too often, a few overbearing relatives dominate the conversation while the rest sit back and pray it'll be over soon."

Next time, try to do something both you and your problem relative enjoy. Take Dad to the ball game, go shopping with your sister. Ask your overly critical aunt and uncle to stroll in the park with you.

And try to notice the good points in this person. "If you're distant from a relative, try this exercise: Each of you tell the other 3 things you like about them," says Dr. Felder. "Then, instead of concentrating on the 50 things you hate about each other, try remembering those 3 good things."

Set new rules for length and frequency of phone calls and visits. "If your brother comes to visit for a month, and you drive each other crazy after five days, try a five-day visit next time," suggests Dr. Felder.

And make touchy subjects off-limits, if necessary. "If you just got a divorce and you don't want to be questioned about it, you can tell your relatives you don't want to discuss it," says Dr. Felder. "Tell them you need lots of love and support and you need the subject to be off-limits because you're so sensitive about it."

And keep working at the relationship, because it's worth the effort. Many people come and go in our lives, but our families are with us forever.

Chapter 12

HOLIDAYS

It's Thanksgiving Day. It's 5:00 in the afternoon. You have a houseful of very hungry guests eyeing the barren dining room table. As you check the turkey for what seems like the zillionth time, it finally dawns on you. The bird is not going to be cooked in time for dinner. In fact, it's *never* going to be cooked. The oven is broken.

Is your day spoiled? Are you going to fume and sputter and apologize until your last guest leaves? Or are you going to put out some lunchmeat and hope for the best?

If you're like Jerry Burnam and his wife, Pat, you'll head straight for the bologna.

"That's the kind of situation, where, if you're inflexible, or if you decide you're going to have a miserable time, you can be sure you will," says Burnam, a University of Illinois professor of leisure studies. He and his wife have learned to be just the opposite, to go with the flow. "We ate our bologna sandwiches, looked at slides, talked, laughed and ended the evening in a good mood." In fact, their dinner that day became a standing joke. Years later, their now-grown son still asks if the turkey will be cooked.

The holiday season offers its own special stresses. Most of us enjoy buying or making gifts, going to parties, baking cookies and seeing friends and relatives. Some of us even enjoy Alvin and the Chipmunks and mimeographed Christmas greetings. But too much, even of these good things, can generate a lot of stress.

And not everything about the holidays is pleasant. These particular days seem to magnify certain aspects of our everyday life. If we sometimes feel lonely, for example, we feel especially lonely during the holidays. If we miss a family member, we miss them most of all at Christmas time. And the marking of a new year brings into focus all the issues that have been bothering us year-long.

"This time of year is a milestone for people," says Lynn Rehm, Ph.D., a

University of Houston psychology professor. "It's a time when we evaluate where we are since last year or earlier Christmases, and how we stack up to idealized images of family life. It can be a stressful and unhappy time for us when we feel our lives don't measure up in some way."

It's possible to plan ahead to eliminate at least some holiday stress. This is *not* the time to air long-term grievances or regrets, but it's important to make note of the issues that do arise, particularly in family relationships, so that you can deal with them later, hopefully *before* next Christmas!

Tradition versus Time

Remember the poppyseed cakes Mom used to bake for the holidays? Your mouth may water just thinking about them, but it's not easy rolling dough at night when you've been busy earning it all day. Women, especially, can feel guilty when they realize they just can't do everything they think they "should" to prepare for the holidays.

"Women need to realize they can't be the perfect wife, mother and worker all at the same time," says Herbert Freudenberger, M.D., a New York City psychiatrist and author of *Women's Burn-Out*. "People need to prethink the holidays, to anticipate as many problems beforehand as possible, and to make plans to avoid them."

Rather than trying to do everything themselves, for instance, or abandoning tradition altogether, women need to delegate holiday tasks to their husbands, children, friends and relatives. "*Do* have dinner at your house, if that's what you want," Dr. Freudenberger says. "But ask your guests to bring a dish. Most people actually like to contribute, and then you don't have the pressure of having to do it all."

And help the hostess if you're visiting for several days with friends or relatives, Dr. Freudenberger says. "Offer to take everyone out for one meal a day. That way, mother, sister or whoever doesn't feel tied to the kitchen throughout the holidays."

You can take some stress out of gift-giving by shopping at off hours and ordering through the mail. Or don't buy gifts at all. Teenagers, especially, prefer money to a hastily bought gift.

Also allow extra time to deal with holiday hassles—getting stuck in traffic, driving to the airport, dressing for parties and wrapping gifts. And be sure to schedule some daily "down time" to take a bath, exercise or simply rest.

Plan time to do the things you really need or want to do, then write them on a big calendar. If you really want to make those poppyseed cakes, prepare the dough one night, the filling another, and bake them on a third.

And decide to enjoy yourself, even if everything doesn't get done. Things don't have to be perfect, as the Burnams will tell you.

Gifts versus Money

Are you still paying for Christmas in July? "Money is something people absolutely need to look at ahead of time and set limits on," Dr. Freudenberger says. "I regularly see people after Christmas who have run up $5,000 credit card bills and who are very distressed about it."

Spending so much money can represent something else. For one busy worker, who spent at least $1,000 on each of his children at Christmas, it meant making up for the time he hadn't given them during the rest of the year. "For others," Dr. Freudenberger says, "being extravagant at Christmas time is a way of denying to themselves the economic bag they are in," especially if they're in debt or have lost income.

If you're financially strapped, first admit it to yourself. Then talk with your kids about what gifts you can afford this year. "Unless they're totally spoiled, you'll be surprised how accepting they'll be," Dr. Freudenberger says. "Say, 'Daddy's been sick (or laid off, or whatever), and we don't have the money to give the same kind of gifts this year, so let's talk about what we *can* buy.'"

Being broke can be a good reason to start moving away from the notion that material gifts are the only way to express affection. Instead, give children some things that cost nothing but that they'll like—breakfast in bed, making their beds for them, teaching them to play poker. And suggest they do the same for other family members.

"We really learned what Christmas was all about the winter I lost my job," says Bob, a former steelworker. "You know that saying, 'We ain't got much, but at least we got each other?' Well, that's what it was like. We were real worried and all, but somehow that made us closer. We had to let one another know how much we cared, *without* presents."

Expectations versus Reality

Even in Hawaii, come December 25, people tend to dream about a white Christmas and riding to each other's houses in horse-drawn sleighs, Dr. Rehm says. "That image sure is hard to shake." So, too, is the childhood belief that everything is supposed to be just wonderful. We are primed to be full of great expectations, and so we're set up to be disappointed.

The antidote to disappointment is to make a good, hard reality check. "Your family relationships are going to be the same at the holidays as they are any other time of year," Dr. Rehm says. "Don't just magically hope that you'll get along better because you will see this person at Christmas. If you want to improve a relationship, make long-range plans. Make plans to get together during the year, or to write or phone more often. Do whatever it takes."

If you need to patch things up with someone, don't wait until they walk through the door on Christmas Day. Talk with them at least a month before the holidays, Dr. Freudenberger says. "Clear the air a little bit before you visit. Apologize for whatever it is, not calling or writing, and let them express their anger. Let them know you're happy to be talking it out, and that you'll be glad to see them in a few weeks."

Is this the first Christmas since you were divorced? If so, it's very important to plan ahead for your children. Who gets them, and when? And will the children have a say in where they spend the time? If it's the first Christmas for you without your children, it may make sense to go on a winter vacation. Being with strangers who are in the same boat will help you take your mind off missing the kids.

If you're introducing your children to a new mother or father, or boyfriend or girlfriend, preparation beforehand is a must if the children are to feel comfortable in a new family, Dr. Freudenberger says. "Have photographs with the names written on them of the people the kids are going to meet. Sit down and talk about the people with your children." It's also important that the children have some routine during the visit. Give them quiet time to rest and talk, or just play by themselves.

Is this the first holiday since Mom or Dad or Grandma died? Don't wait until the holiday arrives to come to terms with it. "Some of the young people I see feel like they don't have much of a family anymore," Dr. Freudenberger says. "But sometimes they can put together a real family Christmas. They'll invite everyone to their place (or take turns). They're impressed to see how many people are just looking for someone to take charge. That tradition, that ritual, can continue if someone in the next generation is willing to pick it up."

Christmas is a spiritual time of year, whether we're Christian, Jewish or Moslem. And it's a good time to take a look at who we are and how we're living our lives. Try to get away from what you think Christmas "ought to be" and make it what you *want* it. What really gives you pleasure this time of year? How can you just relax and enjoy the company of friends and family? "That," Jerry Burnam says, "is what you should do with Christmas, *and* with your life."

Chapter 13

HOUSEWORK

Most people hate housework. A survey of 3,600 people, conducted by researchers at the University of Michigan in Ann Arbor, found that, for most, housework ranked *last* on a list of 25 activities rated in order of preference.

When quizzed further, the few who didn't mind housework said they "felt good about having a clean house." It seems the best anyone can manage to say in defense of housework is that it's like beating your head against a wall—it feels so good when you stop.

How to Prevent Housework

"Fast, easy, orderly and *less* daily upkeep for the entire house, inside and out, will take pressure off the entire family and give you time to enjoy life again!" says Don Aslett, coauthor of *Make Your House Do the Housework* and several other best-selling books on housework. "The key to cutting housework is to look at each chore and ask, 'How can this be prevented?'"

The following tips are examples of how a little ingenuity can cut housework down to manageable levels.

Stop dirt in its tracks. Most dirt marches into your house on people's shoes. Once inside, it takes a fleet of mops, vacuum cleaners and carpet sweepers to get it back out. So install industrial entranceway mats at every door. Sturdy nylon fiber mats, often used in offices, supermarkets and other commercial buildings, are best, says Aslett. "Nylon creates a static charge that actually helps pull particles from your shoes and clothes."

Keep your decor simple. "If pictures are hanging on a wall instead of sitting on a table, they won't have to be straightened, dusted around, worried about or picked up after they topple," says the author. By the same reasoning, one lovely vase is pleasing to look at; a table full of knickknacks needs a museum curator.

Clutterproof your house. One homeowner, tired of a messy tabletop in the entryway, removed the table. "There was no longer a handy place to set junk," says Aslett in his book. "At least half of housework is caused by clutter," he says. So removing "clutter magnets" can cut your housework by 50 percent.

Create a control center in each room. Keep keys, mail, grocery lists and phone messages in one area—a bookshelf in the kitchen, for instance. Then, instead of having the entire room to clean, it can be dealt with in one stop. "Plus, everyone will know where these things are," adds Aslett.

Stacked plastic bins make excellent clutter-control centers in the kids' rooms. Clearing up the obstacle course of toys, games and books won't be nearly as much of a project.

Rethink your kitchen work area for maximum convenience, floor to ceiling. Start by storing your cookware within easy reach of the main work area—the spot between the sink and the range—so you don't have to dart back and forth like a squirrel on amphetamines to prepare meals.

Demilitarize the toilet zone. Even if the tub has a bigger ring than Liz Taylor's, the bathroom will automatically look presentable in minutes if you can quickly clean the mirror and sink, says Aslett in his book. So clear the decks of hairbrushes, combs, shavers, toothpaste, makeup and hair dryers. Stash grooming paraphernalia in drawers, on shelves, on hooks or in one big crock on the corner of the vanity.

To eliminate soap scum "soup," use liquid soap from a pump bottle in the sink and the shower. And hang an extra towel rack to keep soggy towels and washcloths off the floor.

Democracy at Work

Short of hiring a live-in janitor, though, some housework will remain. To de-stress essential chores:

Ask for help. "Many people never get help with the housework because they don't ask for it," says Aslett. "And the truth is, 90 percent of housework is created by people—namely husbands and children—who are accustomed to having someone else pick up after them. So making each household member reponsible for his or her own mess is a big help." Perhaps you could also persuade one of the neighborhood kids to vacuum or do windows in exchange for a ride to the movies or shopping mall.

Divvy up chores based on individual likes and dislikes. Everyone has some chores they hate less than others.

Decide what you can be flexible about and where you won't compromise. So says one busy lawyer and college professor whose husband, despite a combined household income in six figures, refuses to hire house-hold help. Is it absolutely imperative that you can see a perfect reflection of yourself in the toaster? Probably not.

Easy Maintenance, by Design

"When furniture and fixtures wear out, or walls, floors and ceilings need repainting or re-covering, use low-maintenance materials," says Aslett. When choosing materials, ask yourself, 'Is it easy to clean?'" The last thing you want in the kitchen, for example, is flocked wallcovering, ornate hardware or other high-maintenance frills.

"Every room in your home can be changed to cut some need for cleaning," says Aslett. And every step that frees you from housework is a step closer toward a Home Sweet Home.

Chapter 14

LONELINESS

When Robert Weiss, Ph.D., a sociologist from the University of Massachusetts, Boston, who has conducted research on loneliness, delivers his classic line on the pervasiveness of that affliction, he conjures up a strong image. "Loneliness," he says, "has about the frequency of colds in the wintertime."

Why should loneliness occur so often? And who are the people who suffer this black emotion? Are they the elderly? The solitary widows wrapped in blankets, sipping tea? No. Not the old but the young, Dr. Weiss reports, complain most of feeling lonely.

"People have an image of the aged living alone, deserted by their family. That's not the case. The group most likely to experience loneliness are those in late adolescence, and it continues up to young adulthood. Just think of the music these people listen to, and how often loneliness is a theme," says Dr. Weiss. That loneliness tapers off during the years when people pair off in permanent or semipermanent relationships, or when they gain an increase in self-confidence, an acquisition that makes the world less threatening and thus makes them less vulnerable to loneliness, Dr. Weiss explains.

In the intervening years, until that self-confidence develops, many people blame themselves for feeling lonely. "People who are lonely, like people who are depressed, often attribute it to something being wrong with them. They say something like 'I don't have social skills' or 'I look bad,'" says Cecilia Solano, Ph.D., a professor of psychology at Wake Forest University, Winston-Salem, North Carolina.

Loneliness sometimes just develops because of a person's surroundings. Young people, for example, might easily suffer from "situational" loneliness. This feeling occurs when a person is separated from parents or from the high school gang. It's the same loneliness people of any age feel when they have recently moved, or when they are separating or getting divorced.

It's important for anyone who is plagued by loneliness to understand the cause of their loneliness, to connect it to their situation as a newcomer, widow, or any other changed status. "It's an extremely common phenomenon, so people shouldn't feel that it's something odd about them," says Dr. Solano.

Once you fully realize that there's a good reason for your loneliness—that it's natural, in fact—you should find ways to improve the situation. What you shouldn't do is fall into the trap of blaming yourself and feeling helpless.

Making Changes

If you've diagnosed your loneliness as a temporary thing, the process of making changes can begin. Start to focus your energy on activities that will put you in touch with both yourself and others.

First, push the loneliness to the back of your mind and devote some time, no matter how little, to a hobby, sport, spiritual pursuit or talent that you can pursue alone. That's right. Do something that will help you feel comfortable being by yourself. An absorbing and enjoyable activity will make you feel less desperate to meet people and will help you build confidence and self-reliance—traits others find attractive.

Next, find activities that will focus your attention on other people and relieve you of your temporary loneliness. Do some volunteer work at an organization where you are bound to meet like-minded people. Take a night school class in anything that interests you, whether it's Renaissance painting or assertiveness training. If you play tennis, check local tennis clubs for notices of tennis socials and attend one. "Try to pick an activity that you'll be reasonably comfortable with. It might be less anxiety producing than going to a bar," says Peter Stein, Ph.D., author of the book *Single Life*. His studies indicate that single people are relatively free from feelings of loneliness if they are hooked into friendship networks or are involved in professional counseling.

Suggestions for Older People

Widows, widowers, or even retired couples living miles away from family can consciously try to replace their departed or distant loved ones with friends. Among the solid suggestions in her book *The Survival Guide for Widows*, Canadian author and playwright Betty Jane Wylie offers a particularly imaginative one: "Make fudge with a child. If you don't have one the right age, borrow one."

Here are two more of her many suggestions.

"Crawl into a hole and pull the hole in after you. Sometimes it's so bad that's all you can do. While it's no permanent solution, it's okay to occasionally go ahead and brood. Wallow in it. Cry. Feel sorry for yourself. But don't try to share this with anyone. When you're fit for human companionship again, emerge, like a butterfly from a grubby cocoon."

And, "Forgive someone. There's a lot of residual anger flying around in you. When you're in one of these moods, pick out someone you really feel resentful of and forgive him or her. Do something for her: Bake her a loaf of bread or invite her for lunch or write her a note. Free of even a fraction of your burden of anger, you will feel much better."

This advice holds true for people of all ages. And when it comes to older people, research indicates that friends might actually do a better job than family at relieving the stress of loneliness. Ann Gerson, Ph.D., coauthored a study of 158 older people in Winnipeg and discovered that fact. "The older people who had a network of friends and no family felt less lonely than people who had family around and no friends," says the Salt Lake City psychologist.

So for older people, the message is clear: If possible, create a retirement situation where there is a built-in network of retired people that might be easy to fit into. For the families of older people, the study provides something new to consider. If you're thinking of moving an older relative in with you to take care of them, maybe you should think again. Should the move deprive them of their friends, that consideration would be greater, perhaps, than the physical care you would provide, says Dr. Gerson.

Chronic Loneliness

Sometimes loneliness has nothing to do with moving to a new town, divorcing or aging. Sometimes loneliness is a chronic condition that lasts for years. It's a serious condition because the physical consequences can be deadly. In his book *The Language of the Heart*, University of Maryland psychologist James J. Lynch, Ph.D., writes: "All the available data pointed to the lack of human companionship, chronic loneliness, social isolation, and the sudden loss of a loved one as being among the leading causes of premature death in the United States. And while we found that the effects of human loneliness were related to virtually every major disease—whether cancer, pneumonia or mental disease—they were particularly apparent in heart disease, the leading cause of death in the United States. Evidently millions of people were dying, quite literally, of broken or lonely hearts."

Seeking a Solution

The only way to end chronic loneliness is to make friends—an act requiring self-confidence and social skills many lonely people don't have. Both, fortunately, can be learned.

Among the more innovative forms of learning to make friends is something tailor-made for chronically lonely or shy people: social skills groups. (Many of them exist in the United States, some of them even at the elementary and high school levels.)

In such a group, people can learn how to initiate a conversation with a stranger, how to conduct a telephone conversation, how to give and receive a compliment and even how to ask for a date, says Karen Rook, Ph.D., of the University of California, Irvine. People "role play" how they would interact with others and try new ways of interacting. They get feedback on the order of "Gee, Bob, are you aware you looked at your feet during the entire discussion? Let's try it again with eye contact."

Sometimes videotapes are used. Sometimes group members are given homework to initiate a conversation on a bus, for example, and report on it. The lessons get increasingly difficult over the 10- or 12-week course, but the results are certainly worth the effort. For information on social skills groups, contact a community mental health center. If you live near a major university with a psychology department or clinical psychology clinic, inquire there.

If you want to change the way you relate to people but prefer doing it on your own, you can start by thinking about how to make friends in strategic terms. For instance, instead of going to a social function and standing in the corner, think about what you can do to take control of things you say and do. Remind yourself to ask questions and to listen to the responses, to be friendly and to be interested in people. And if possible, to try to make a friend.

The Intimacy Cure

Feeling really close to someone is tough for men in general and for college-age men in particular, according to Harry Reis, Ph.D., a professor of psychology at the University of Rochester, New York. "Men socialize as much as women, but women socialize more intimately. While men might be playing sports, they're not talking about their feelings and making intimate contact. It's intimate contact that helps avoid loneliness."

It's obvious, then, that Dr. Reis advises the lonely—regardless of gender—to try to become close to others. "Have interactions in which you open yourself up to other people and get close. Talk about how you really feel about the kinds of things most people don't usually talk about, fears and anxieties. And get into those discussions in some depth," he says.

How to determine with whom you should try to get so close? Carolyn Cutrona, associate professor of psychology at the University of Iowa, suggests you make a list of the people that are around and determine who among them are likely to develop as meaningful, rewarding friends.

If you figure you'd rather spend your time searching for the ideal lover instead of developing friends, figure again. Regardless of the fact that many chronically lonely people feel they must find a romantic relationship to overcome their loneliness, a perfect love will not necessarily make loneliness disappear. And Cutrona warns that by searching for the perfect lover, you might overlook the potential loneliness cure that exists in good friends.

Chapter 15

ON-THE-JOB STRESS

The 40 hours or more you spend each week at work represents a large chunk of your life. And if you think a bad work scene doesn't take a serious toll on your body and mind, pay attention.

Robert Collier Page, M.D., studied 100 employees who were placed in jobs that did not meet their level of intelligence or match their aptitudes, personality, behavioral characteristics and aspiration. After carefully examining the employees, this early student of workplace stress and one-time medical director of Standard Oil Company of New Jersey (now Exxon), learned that they suffered from sleeplessness, headaches, despondency, stiffness, backaches, fatigue and gastrointestinal symptoms. None of them were found to have a disease as such. Rather, their symptoms seemed to stem from their jobs. In his landmark 1963 book, *Occupational Health and Mantalent Development*, Dr. Page writes: "If no one else happens to observe what is happening, the individual will continue to push himself blithely into the performance of tasks against which his entire inner being rebels. Eventually this inner being or subconscious will strike back in the only way it knows how, by producing a symptom of illness to warn the misassigned that it is time to stop, look and listen."

It gets worse, he writes. "The same habits of self-deception which he has acquired in order to stick to his job will enable him to shrug off the first minor symptoms of potential functional illness. . . . If by this time he is fairly well advanced into his middle years, this creeping loss of health will be progressive and, when he is finally forced to recognize his true predicament, irreversible."

An Abundance of Research

In the decades since that study, an abundance of research has linked job stress to illness. The link is so great that Paul J. Rosch, M.D., president of the

60

American Institute of Stress, says, "Stress in the workplace may well be the number one health problem for the working adult population in the United States." Here's a sampling of stress-related illnesses.

- Working excessive hours and holding down more than one job has been associated with coronary heart disease.
- Monotonous work has been associated with job dissatisfaction, poor mental health, coronary heart disease, peptic ulcers and gastritis.
- The stress of conflicting job demands has been linked to depression and such physiological strains as increased heart rate and increased blood pressure.

What, exactly, makes working so stressful? For one thing, a lack of control. A study of nearly 1,500 workers found that nonparticipation in the decision-making process at work was related to low self-esteem, escapist drinking and overall poor health. Those were the same symptoms of workers who faced an uncertain employment future.

For another thing, feeling angry. A team from the University of Pittsburgh's Department of Epidemiology compared those who frequently experience anger-producing job stress *and* suppress their anger, with others. What researchers found is that people who experience job stress and suppress their anger have a greater risk of high blood pressure than those who either experience similar levels of job stress or suppress their anger. The trouble comes from experiencing both stress *and* suppressed anger, according to Eric M. Cottington, Ph.D., an epidemiologist from Pittsburgh's Allegheny-Singer Research Institute, who headed the research team.

What is a worker to do about lack of control or on-the-job anger? One approach is to change the job so that it becomes less stressful. The other approach is to change the person's reaction to the job.

Changing the Job

"One option is to develop a strategy for changing the work environment. Calmly, rationally and with a well-devised plan, ask your boss for more guidance, more freedom, more money—whatever it is you need," suggests Dr. Cottington.

You can work to change the job with the help of a boss, co-workers, a labor union or other organization. That can mean changing the responsibilities or the hours. It also can mean organizing a lunch-hour volleyball game.

If you can't improve your workplace, maybe you can improve the way you view it. "An employee who feels he has control over what he is doing is a much happier and healthier employee," says Stewart G. Wolf, Jr., M.D., professor of medicine at Temple University, Philadelphia, and director of the Totts Gap

Medical Research Laboratory in Bangor, Pennsylvania. You can reduce the stress of any job by seizing as much control over the situation as possible.

Let's go to work with Bobbi White, the office manager for a busy Pennsylvania car mechanic shop, to see how she manages to achieve a level of control over a tough situation. White often finds herself in an awkward place: between customers who are griping about getting their cars repaired and mechanics who sometimes cannot accommodate the onslaught of ill vehicles. "The favorite thing that customers do is to make their problems your problems. They call up and say, 'What do you mean you can't take me today? My inspection runs out,' " says White.

Her response? "I just put it back squarely on their shoulders. I just make them aware of the fact that they had three months in which to get their car inspected. I don't say it abruptly. But I tell them that they had the time to do it earlier and that I'd be happy to make an appointment for the first available time. They have to settle for it. I can't tell a mechanic to hurry up. You'd be rushing something that involves safety," she says. "I tend to get extremely bothered by people who yell at me. But I can't yell back. The worst I'll do is get abrupt."

"She's doing the right thing," says Albert Finestone, M.D., associate dean of continuing medical education at Temple. "If they delay until the last day for car inspection, she can dump the stress right back on them." White's real problem, however, is more complicated than handling disgruntled customers. She has to fit clients' car repairs into the mechanics' schedules—and she has no control over the number of cars needing to be fixed or the schedules.

"When you're placed in a situation where things are beyond your control, this creates an enormous amount of stress," says Dr. Finestone. "It's the same problem facing a waiter whose food is backed up in the kitchen trying to satisfy an impatient diner. I would suggest he recognize it's not his fault, go back to the customer and say: 'Look, the kitchen's backed up, I guarantee I'll be in there trying to rush the cook, but that's the situation.' Meanwhile, if you can't stand the heat, get out of the kitchen."

The Value of Peer Counseling

Sometimes it's helpful—or downright crucial—to talk about your job stress with co-workers. That's the lifesaving lesson learned by Ed Donovan of the Boston police.

Donovan had been a police officer in Boston for only five years when he reached his limit. He no longer could handle the day-to-day dealing with danger or take the responsibility of having to make major decisions in a split second that would affect him for the rest of his life. He couldn't live with the image that he was supposed to be Superman, that he was not supposed to have problems but was instead expected to solve others' problems. He couldn't face the daily descent into society's low depths. Few professionals are subject to as much stress as policemen are, and Donovan simply could not take it. So he overdrank; he became addicted to drugs. One day he stuck a gun in his mouth and tried to pull the trigger.

He found he couldn't take his own life.

Donovan didn't trust psychologists. He realized the only people he could turn to were peers, the two cops who ran an alcoholism program for the Boston police. Eventually, their peer support helped Donovan learn to deal with the stress of his job. And as chronicled in his book, *The Shattered Badge*, it led him to launch the Boston Police Department Stress Program, perhaps the most extensive stress-reduction operation serving law enforcement. Donovan is still its director.

Boston's 13-year-old stress program has helped thousands of area policemen deal with the particular stresses of being a cop, a profession whose members, Donovan says, are among those least likely to seek advice from mental health professionals. "How much more macho can you get than swaggering around with a gun?" he says. And because of Donovan's experience, the Boston program relies primarily on peer counseling; professionals are used only for backup.

"We can get a cop to open up better in front of three or four other cops than in a one-on-one situation with a psychologist," he says. The program includes training, education, counseling, group therapy and crisis intervention. And among some 200 police department stress programs in the United States, Boston's is the only one that operates autonomously from the police department's administration. That way, cops under pressure feel secure that their group therapy discussions—which often focus on problems emanating from above—won't reach the ears of their superiors.

The experience in Boston underscores three crucial points. First, there's nothing wrong with admitting you have difficulty coping with the stress of your job. This holds for all jobs, even those that are substantially less demanding than police work. Second, there's an abundance of relief to be gained by talking over your workplace woes with co-workers you can trust. And third, there are professional career counselors waiting in the wings if you feel your peers lack the skills to help or if you begin to threaten a relationship by overindulging in your miseries.

If you are not comfortable discussing your job-related stress with company personnel, try an outside professional. (For a list of certified career counselors in your community, write to the International Association of Counseling Services, 5999 Stevenson Avenue, Alexandria, VA 22304.)

The sad news is that even where good in-house help is available, some folks refuse to seek it. Last year five Boston police officers committed suicide. Ed Donovan says, "Four of those could have been prevented if they were referred to us."

The Dreaded Raise Discussion

"An enormous change can take place in one morning when a demanding boss comes by to say, 'You've done a great job. We couldn't get along without you,' " says Dr. Wolf. "That kind of comment from a supervisor can make you feel that you're important, that you're somebody with a well-defined place who does things that are appreciated."

Unfortunately, few bosses are that thoughtful and appreciative. Many are downright hostile. And so, if you want to better your relations with your boss, *you'll* have to do the work. A better relationship can improve your work environment and even increase your odds of getting what you want. Take the dreaded raise discussion as an example.

"One of the biggest mistakes employees make when they finally decide to ask for a raise is that they don't relatively assess a few things," says Peter Wylie, Ph.D. "They don't consider their perceived value on the part of the boss—how dispensable they are. And they're also not good at putting themselves in the shoes of their boss."

Dr. Wylie is coauthor of *Problem Bosses: Who They Are and How to Deal with Them,* and he suggests that before you march in and make your little plea for a raise, you should do some homework.

Develop a well-worked-out rationale for why you deserve a raise. Be realistic. The fact that your production increased over the past six months may reflect added support personnel more than your own performance. Therefore, objectively construct a case for a raise. Outline your argument on paper and back it up with a strong verbal presentation that you rehearse to persuasive perfection, suggests Dr. Wylie.

And even if you're a prime candidate for a raise, keep in mind that your boss may have a host of reasons why he must turn you down. There are good times and bad times to ask for raises. Obviously, when profits are down, budgets are tight. If that's the case, you probably won't get a good hearing from your boss, regardless of how worthy you are. And often your boss can't make the decision on his own. So you need to understand how the chain of command works, who your boss has to go to for approval and the degree to which your boss is weak in fighting for your case, says Dr. Wylie.

If your request is turned down, make certain you understand why. If the company has imposed a freeze on salary increases, find out when the freeze will be lifted and what your chances are for a raise at that time. Should your boss inform you that your performance does not merit a salary raise, ask him what you need to do to get back on track. Tell him you appreciate getting feedback on your performance. Make it clear that you're serious about improving. If possible, offer to establish work goals that will lead to an eventual raise, then achieve them.

"The important function of an employee is not simply to be a passive recipient of what's handed down from above," says Dr. Wolf. "You've got to learn to react to the machinery. You have to learn diplomacy. You have to have a reasonable case. And you can't exaggerate. If you've got three things to say and one's shaky, your boss is going to focus on the shaky one and ignore the others," he says. "Don't say too much, and stick to the strong points."

A Job You Can't Handle

Say your employer promoted you into a coveted management job but you find yourself overwhelmed by the new responsibilities and are constantly unhappy. The advice from Beth Ann Wilson, a Philadelphia career counselor, is basic: "Be clear why the situation is not working."

Ask yourself whether the problem is that you don't like the job or that you just don't have the skills to do the job properly.

By taking a strong look at the situation, many people discover they simply lack appropriate job skills. If that's the case, go to your boss or personnel administrator and ask for training in how to manage or how to delegate. That's a strategy that gets you needed training while also demonstrating your maturity and desire to do a good job.

De-stressing an Unrewarding Job

Many of us suffer in jobs that are unrewarding, and for one reason or another we cannot quit or shift jobs right now. How do you remove yourself from the stress of such a bad work scene? Career counselor Wilson provides a practical list of suggestions.

• Build up other things in your life. Volunteer to do something in the community that's rewarding to you and gives you satisfaction.

• Take a course in a hobby or to develop a new skill that can help you eventually land another job.

• Talk to people who work in similar jobs—a teller at another bank or a teacher at another school.

• Identify what you want to do next, career-wise or job-wise. Then focus a fixed amount of time each day on helping you get there. That time could be spent working, for example, on the United Way campaign to make yourself more visible to potential new employers in the community.

• Get out of the building, if only for ten minutes at lunchtime. A walk will help relieve stress.

• Figure out the source of your stress. Focus on whether or not it is your fault and, if so, whether there's anything you can do about it. If you've determined you're not at fault, be very clear that it's not you that's contributing to the stress.

• Talk to someone about your situation who will help you develop an objective perspective. It doesn't have to be a professional; it could be someone at work whom you trust.

Maybe You'd Better Start Looking

The fear of job-hunting, the fear of being unemployed and the fear of winding up in an even worse situation keeps people trapped in miserable, stressful jobs. "People come in and tell me that at least they wake up in the morning and know exactly how miserable they'll be. There's some comfort in that familiarity," says Wilson.

Even people who quit a job to look for a new one have more control than those who stay, lose interest to the point that they cannot function well, and are eventually laid off or fired. There's little to be gained by staying in an unhappy job if you can devise a careful strategy for a job search. Be honest with yourself: Do you really need to stay?

Each Monday evening Beth Wilson runs a support group for people who are employed but are looking for new jobs. The point of the discreet group is to motivate its members, to provide group support and to make participants accountable for their week-to-week job-seeking activities. If you don't think you can develop and stick to a job search on your own, check with a local career counselor about a job-seekers' support group in your community.

When There's Not Enough Stress

Finally, some people find it difficult to perform in laid-back workplaces. They flourish in antagonistic environments and thrive on anxiety. "These are people who get into organizations that are so supportive they can't stand it. So they might find themselves instigating things at work," says Wilson.

The problem is particularly relevant in companies that are following the current trend of giving an employee vast amounts of freedom to accomplish projects at the worker's own pace. The presumption is that employees will work harder and be happier if they are doing their own thing and are out from under constant supervision. But by merely giving an employee a project and saying "work on this for six months," an employer might be doing the worker a disservice.

"You're coming from an educational system that's structured and a background that's structured. So when you go into an unstructured job where you're told to use your creativity, you're subject to a lot of stress," says Wilson. It may be great for some people, but it's torture for others.

In such a situation, Wilson suggests you try to structure your own workload so that you will impose some pressure on yourself. Set personal deadlines. If you're on a long-term project and don't feel comfortable about the lack of guidance or supervision, tell your boss you'd like to meet every two weeks for 15 minutes to discuss what you're doing.

If your workplace is too stress-free for your liking, you can compensate by structuring high-pressure after-work activities. Play a highly competitive sport. Volunteer to work on a rescue squad. Or you can seek out a job in a high-pressure industry or in a company whose corporate culture runs on stress. But it's important to look at what you need and what has worked for you in the past.

Chapter 16

PERFORMANCE JITTERS

Here's an incredible fact: Among our top ten fears, the fear of death ranks number six. So what's number one? It might surprise you, but holding first place among our fears is the fear of speaking before a group. This, according to a market research study of 3,000 Americans.

Those who aren't petrified to speak or perform before an audience may go on to flourishing careers in politics, theater or television. The rest of us just suffer, avoiding and dreading that semiannual presentation before the budget committee or the toast we agreed to deliver at our friend's wedding. We may even go into a fit of madness if we host a party.

Doctors classify such performance anxiety as a form of social phobia, the fear of doing anything under scrutiny that can result in humiliation. Most of us are all too familiar with the symptoms: sweaty palms, shaking, voice tremors, rubbery legs. That's the "fight-or-flight" reaction, our body's natural response to fear. Inside our bodies, the adrenal glands shoot the hormone adrenaline (also called epinephrine) into the bloodstream. Blood pressure climbs, heartbeat increases, and blood vessels to the digestive tract narrow, while blood vessels to the trunk's muscles expand, according to Patricia Normand, M.D., instructor in psychiatry at Harvard and associate director of psychopharmacology at the Cambridge Hospital in Boston.

The Adrenaline Rush

For some folks, the shot of adrenaline produces a high. But for many, it's a tormenting discomfort. Yet whether your performance anxiety happens once a year or once a day, there are ways of overcoming it.

Say you get particularly nervous when you are about to deliver a toast before a wedding party. Obviously the best thing to do is be well rehearsed. So practice the toast, simulating it before a group if possible, advises Valerie

Adami, an actress and instructor at Weist-Barron in New York City, a school that teaches acting for television commercials.

The same simple advice holds true if you are delivering a speech. The more nervous you ordinarily get, the more prepared you should be. "It's less stressful if you know what you're talking about," Adami says.

In either case, you should avoid things that make you nervous, such as caffeine or nicotine. Alcohol, too, can be detrimental. Initially it may calm you down, but often it later produces anxiety. And tranquilizers tend to slow down your motor skills.

Relaxation Techniques to the Rescue

The advice gets a great deal more complex if your performance anxiety is a constant affair. In that case, there are relaxation techniques to help you cope.

Systematic desensitization. This is a process in which you relax your muscles and then imagine yourself performing a series of situations, progressing from something simple like speaking to a few friends and leading up to a speech before a huge auditorium.

Flooding. This technique requires you to confront your fear directly and work through it. If you fear public speaking, you could deliver the dreaded speech before a therapy group. You learn that you can survive such a trial.

Modeling. This method requires you to watch other people, even if only on videotape, satisfactorily perform a public speech. By observing, you lose some of the fear of doing it yourself, says Dr. Normand.

If your stage fright is so bad that you structure your life to avoid even rare performances—you turn down a job promotion because the new position requires you to deliver an occasional speech—you may be a candidate for medical intervention. A medication such as propranolol may be prescribed, to be taken a few hours before your performance. It works by blocking the effects of the adrenaline your body produces. You won't sweat, you'll stop shaking and your heart palpitations will cease.

Telling Yourself You Can

Then there's the powerful force of positive thinking to get you to overcome your jitters. Positive thinking is a keystone in the decades-old advice preached by Dale Carnegie to salesmen and others who flocked to his lectures and purchased his popular books *How to Win Friends and Influence People, How to Stop Worrying and Start Living* and *The Quick and Easy Way to Effective Speaking.* Carnegie's philosophy contends that almost anyone can speak in public if they have self-confidence and an idea that is boiling and stewing within them. What he taught those who crowded his classrooms, and what his instructors continue to teach, is that to develop self-confidence, you must do whatever it is you fear doing and get a record of successful experiences under your belt.

If you feel you would benefit from the instruction, the group support and the intensified practice of a Dale Carnegie course, why not sign up? The basic public speaking course runs 14 sessions and costs approximately $800. For information on courses in your area, check the yellow pages in your local telephone directory.

The Nervous Host

You can have performance anxiety about almost anything, but some people experience their worst anxiety when it comes to hosting a party. "The thing to do," says Dr. Normand, "is question why you are being so nervous about having a party. You might separate the worry about what people will think of *you* from what you are actually doing. That separation will help make you less nervous. Then you can realize that it's not the end of the world if not everyone thinks it's the best party ever given. Ask yourself why you're being such a perfectionist."

Facing, then getting over, such unrealistic expectations of yourself may free you from the grip of performance anxiety.

Chapter 17

TRAVEL

Travel has always been fraught with uncertainty and stress. Consider the inconvenience and hassles travelers like Marco Polo had to deal with back in the 13th century. A typical journey to the Far East began with a sea voyage to Constantinople. Ships were manned with armed soldiers and traveled in convoys in defense against pirates who beleaguered the Mediterranean. In the event of attack, passengers were expected to lend a hand with a crossbow.

Pirate attacks or no, conditions were still taxing. Passengers below decks slept amidst bilge water, damp sand and vermin. The privy was a small bucket hung over the side. In rough weather, it was "out of order" altogether.

By comparison, even today's grungiest gas station restroom looks like a tour stop on "Lifestyles of the Rich and Famous," and budget cruises seem quite luxurious.

Yes, 700 years later, travel is much easier—but still stressful. Bad weather can still spoil a vacation. Traffic, detours and delays, lost reservations, missed connections and other glitches can—and do—create tension. Yet there are plenty of ways to head off travel-related stress right from the outset, before you even leave home.

The Secret to Stress-Free Travel: Plan Ahead

Cecil and Celeste always plan their vacations months ahead of time, and they begin to pack a week or two in advance, to avoid a last-minute frenzy of searching for out-of-season clothes, tennis rackets or luggage keys. The night before an early departure, they set three alarm clocks—one windup in case the power fails—to be sure they don't oversleep. And they allow themselves time to check that all the doors are locked and the appliances are turned off before they leave the house. They usually arrive at the airport with time to spare, having allowed for a flat tire or other unexpected delay. They check their baggage and sit down to enjoy a relaxing cup of coffee while they wait for their flight.

Darby and Joan, by contrast, tend to wing it. On a recent trip, for example, they set their alarm for 5:00 A.M.—"leaving us a whole hour to pack before we leave for the airport," says Joan. But they overslept, so they packed in ten minutes flat. The drive to the airport took longer than they expected and they boarded their plane during last call. When they arrived at their destination, Darby and Joan discovered they'd forgotten a few key items—and all week they wondered if they'd remembered to turn off the coffee pot. Their trip began in a frenzy that set the rhythm for the rest of the trip.

"Planning ahead is the best way to reduce the stress of travel," says Stephen A. Shapiro, Ph.D., psychotherapist and coauthor of *Time Off: A Psychological Guide to Vacations.* "Although it cannot assure a successful holiday, it is perhaps the best defense of all against a disappointing one."

Planning ahead also helps to prevent the pretravel jitters—nagging doubts and worries that can gnaw at travelers the last few days before departure: Will the kids/house/my parents be all right while I'm away? What if things go haywire at the office? What if I run out of money? What if I get bumped from the flight? What if the weather is terrible?

Granted, it's impossible to foresee—and prevent—every possible glitch. But neither should you assume that somehow everything will turn out all right, with little or no effort on your part, says Dr. Shapiro. Planning is vital whether you're spending the weekend at your cabin in the mountains or touring Europe for three weeks.

Learn about your destination. Whether you're headed for Myrtle Beach or China, the more you learn about your destination—geography, climate, customs and accommodations—before you get there, the less likely you are to have your trip spoiled by unpleasant surprises.

"I was once in Siberia," muses travel writer and novelist Paul Theroux, "and I recall an Australian saying to me in a complaining way, 'It's *cold* here!' In Peru, an American woman said to me, 'I hate these hills—they're too steep.' We were in the Andes."

Useful resources include:

• *Triptiks,* which give routes and mileage to destinations throughout the United States, are available to members free of charge from your local chapter of the American Automobile Association (AAA).

• *Background Notes,* inexpensive, factual pamphlets containing current information on the people, culture, geography, history, government, economy and political conditions of about 170 countries, are available from the Superintendent of Documents, U.S. Government Printing Office, Washington, DC 20402. Prices vary.

• *Consumer Reports Travel Letter,* Box 5248, Boulder, CO 80322.

• *Baedeker Guides, Fielding Travel Books, Fodor's Modern Guides, Frommer's Dollarwise Guides* and *Rand McNally National Park Guide,* among others, are available in paperback in the travel section of most bookstores.

• Brochures ("Cruise Safety," "Hotels: An Insider's Guide," "Overseas Travel," "Packing Tips," "Traveling Safely" and "Travel Tips"), are available from travel agents who are members of the American Society of Travel Agents.

Also, publications devoted to your particular sport or interest—hiking, skiing, fine dining and so forth—regularly report on travel destinations.

Learn as much about yourself as possible. "Ask yourself, 'What do I really like or dislike?' " says Dr. Shapiro. If you hate the cold or steep hills, for example, don't go to Siberia or the Andes. If you hate sitting around doing nothing, don't plan to spend all week on the beach.

"That might sound like common sense, but you'd be surprised at the number of people who show up at travel agencies without the slightest idea of where they'd like to go or what they'd like to do when they get there," says Dr. Shapiro. "So they end up on trips totally unsuited to their needs—and blame their spouse or their travel agent."

Enlist a travel agent. Look for an agent who has experience booking the type of trip *you* are planning—package tours, cruises or strike-out-on-your-own jaunts. He can save you time and aggravation by making phone calls, comparing hotel rates and airfares, determining the best routes and taking care of other laborious tasks, at no cost to you. A travel agent should also be able to tell you if a cruise is geared for families or singles, what hotels are close to your meeting or airport and provide other information that can make the difference between a good trip and a great trip. (Keep in mind that every travel agent can't be expected to have visited every destination. The more research you do, the better a travel agent can serve you.)

"Bump-proof" your reservations. Make reservations as far in advance as possible, then guarantee your reservations against late arrival by making partial or complete payment or giving a credit card number. When traveling by plane, confirm your reservations 72 hours before departure and at each stopover, even if you hold the tickets in your hands. Arrive well ahead of departure time—one hour for domestic flights and two hours for international flights.

Carry a phone credit card. Charging calls to your home phone is enormously helpful should you need to untangle snafus—like a change in itinerary or a medical or financial emergency—while you're away.

Guard your passport carefully. Without your passport, you can't leave a foreign country or reenter the United States. Replacing it causes major delay and inconvenience.

Pack your travel wardrobe in two bags instead of one. If one bag is lost, you will still have some clothes to wear.

Remove old claim checks from your luggage. Otherwise, baggage handlers may mistakenly send your luggage to the wrong destination.

Wear or pack comfortable walking shoes. Nothing can ruin a trip like sore feet.

Take along a paperback book or two. Mysteries, crossword puzzles, the travel-size version of Trivial Pursuit or other amusements take the stress out of delays for passengers stuck in airports, traffic jams or other trying circumstances. "Having something to do is especially important for people who get real fidgety whenever they have to wait," says Dr. Shapiro.

Let someone know where you're going. Leave a detailed itinerary (including names, addresses and phone numbers of persons and places to be visited) with friends or relatives so you can be reached in an emergency or get money in hurry. For added peace of mind, ask a trusted neighbor to periodically check your premises while you're away.

Delegate someone at work to handle problems that can't wait until you get back. Tell your backup, in advance, what to do in the event of various possible emergencies.

How to Handle a Glitch

Sometimes, no matter how well-informed and thoroughly prepared you are for a trip, things go wrong. Bad weather, for example, is totally beyond control and can sabotage the best-laid plans.

"If your trip isn't working out, do something to make it right," says Alan J. Tuckman, M.D., coauthor of *Time Off*. "I remember one time we all flew out to Taos to ski, but heavy rains triggered mudslides and ruined the slopes. We hung around for a day and a half, then repacked, flew back to New York and drove up to Mt. Snow, where the powder was fabulous, to ski."

Getting angry or disgusted does nothing to solve a problem. Rather, it may escalate tension and will certainly distress your companions.

"Flying into a rage when things go wrong is the *worst* way to handle the situation," says Dr. Shapiro. "You have to deal with what you've got. Look at your options. Make a new plan. Because if you feel competent and view a problem as a challenge, that will lower your stress level."

So here are some suggestions for handling problems that may occur.

Be flexible. The ability and willingness to improvise can salvage what's left of your trip, say Dr. Tuckman and Dr. Shapiro. If you find that your favorite beach on Cape Cod is infested with black flies, for example, go whale watching instead. If the hotel you planned to stay in has your room reservations but no rooms, have them book you elsewhere (the alternate hotel could be *better*). Construction delays on the interstate? Take the scenic route—and your camera.

If you can't change the situation, change your attitude. Learn to accept a certain amount of poor service or incompetence (the root causes of so many travel glitches).

"People often have images of the perfect trip, where everything goes like clockwork," says Dr. Shapiro. "And that illusion is their worst enemy. Some things *will* probably go wrong, but that doesn't automatically ruin the entire trip."

Suppose the worst happens and your trip is a total disappointment? "Conduct a post-mortem on your trip," suggests Dr. Tuckman. "Ask yourself, 'What went right or wrong?' and 'What can we do about it next time?' "

After all, experience, good or bad, is what divides the "tourists" from the "travelers."

Chapter 18

WORKAHOLISM

Let's start with the basics: There's nothing inherently wrong with workaholics. That's the conclusion of an in-depth, landmark study on the subject by Marilyn Machlowitz, Ph.D., a New York industrial psychologist and author who professes to be a workaholic herself.

Dr. Machlowitz's book, *Workaholics, Living with Them, Working with Them,* blasted workaholism's bad reputation. People who are addicted to work, she suggested, often are surprisingly happy. True, a workaholic may be working all the time. But he or she also may get an abundance of pleasure from the job—more pleasure than from tennis or opera or family life.

"People whose life is their work are doing that because they like what they're doing," says Richard G. Lonsdorf, M.D., a psychiatrist and professor of law at the University of Pennsylvania in Philadelphia. Dr. Lonsdorf sees many patients who are in the legal profession—a vocation noted for its long hours. "Although there are some compulsive people who are compulsive about anything, it's true that workaholics often are very healthy people," he says. "And you usually don't find workaholics in jobs that don't interest them."

"It's the *inflexible* addiction to work that's unhealthy," says Robert Rosen, Ph.D., director of the Institute on Organizational Health at the Washington Business Group on Health. "If you're avoiding something or if the need for manipulation and power becomes the overriding fuel for the commitment to work, you're placing yourself at risk of affecting your health."

But that's not always the standard profile. "Some workaholics are just enthusiastic about their work and could do it 24 hours a day, seven days a week, without resentment or bitterness," says Maurice Prout, Ph.D., director of cognitive behavior therapy at Hahnemann University, Philadelphia.

The problems arise when you mix these curious animals with non-workaholics. It's easy to understand how people who don't get such a tremendous satisfaction out of long hours on the job can resent those who do. And there are other problems. Working for someone who lives to work can make your life miserable if you aren't so inclined. It's also easy to be angered

76

at a loved one who is married to work and treats you with somewhat less regard. The spouse, lover, parent or child who is bent on reforming a workaholic is bound to meet with frustration. And then there's the overstressed existence of 40-hour-week types whose co-workers (read: competitors) are workaholics.

To Reform or Not to Reform

Fears that workaholics shorten their lives through stress may be unfounded, according to Dr. Machlowitz. It depends on the individual's response to stress. Some people flourish in stressful jobs, particularly if they feel they can exert some control over events, if they feel deeply involved in the activities of their lives and if they anticipate changes as exciting challenges. Others may be virtually incapacitated by the same level of stress, regardless of the potential psychic rewards. It's important to understand which type you are, and, as much as possible, to live within the structure dictated by your own personal needs.

But that doesn't mean workaholics are destined to live out their years alienating family, friends and co-workers, missing out on the marvelous non-work-related joys of life. If you are a workaholic and want to end the resentment that may be building up around you, or if you want to gain value from things other than work, there are steps you can take.

First, pay attention to the words of Dr. Lonsdorf when he says, "It's an enormously egotistical thing to be a workaholic. It says to people around you that what you're doing is more important than they are." He adds that when workaholics understand the impact of those words, they often work to modify their values.

Get to know what's at the root of your workaholism, even if it takes a therapist to help you do it. It could be a compulsion. "Often workaholism is an escape from something else—difficulties in interpersonal relationships, an inability to achieve intimacy," says David Sirota, Ph.D., a New York industrial psychologist. "Or it could be their own particular compulsion to see themselves as working all the time," he says. That may be understandable, adds Dr. Prout, because "culturally, we're rewarded for the concept of working hard early on. If you didn't get a good grade, a teacher may have boosted it for effort." Or it could be that your entire self-esteem is connected to making more money than others.

Then there's the matter of corporate culture. At many companies, long hours are a fact of life. Many psychologists suggest you take some responsibility for your own long hours. Ask yourself, are they really necessary?

Often workaholics have convinced themselves that their long hours are required, but that's not always the case. Unless you work for an organization that is understaffed, you should not have to put in the 60-hour work week that is standard among workaholics. Chances are that you are squandering at least 10 of those hours on trivialities or on make-work projects. Often, work-aholics who are pressed to examine their activities will determine that they waste time for one reason or another.

But if you're dismayed at the prospect of spending those ten extra hours at play, don't fret. "You don't have to do what other people define as play. If you do that, you'll just wind up with the desire to go back to work. Instead, you have to define what form your play is going to take," says Dr. Prout.

So your "play" time could mean volunteering to "work" with a nonprofit organization or charity. Or your "play" time could mean "working" on your house. It's your time, your decision. Channel your work addiction into some-thing constructive.

When the Family Loses

But if your workaholism is frustrating your family—and if you want that to change—it won't make sense to exchange your hours at work for hours at the Red Cross or hours spent papering the den. Your family needs you, and giving them the time they deserve may require a systematic approach.

Start by scheduling regular time to be with your spouse. "Do something every Thursday night. Hire a babysitter and go someplace, even if it's just a ride around the block," says Dr. Lonsdorf. He suggests you force yourself not to work. Buy tickets for 13 baseball games and attend them all with your kids. Get involved in activities that used to give you pleasure—or try new activities. One caution, however: Attempt to maintain a relaxed attitude. Should you develop an interest in hiking through the woods with your spouse, try not to become obsessed with the identification of every item of flora and fauna if it makes your partner feel as though you're still at work.

If overtime forces you to miss your kid's performance in the fourth-grade pageant, you should explain to the youngster that you cannot make it to the event and ask what he or she would enjoy doing together in its place. "The only way you can diffuse a child's resentment is to give him or her more time, not only so-called quality time, but 'down time' as well—time when you do nothing but talk," says Dr. Prout. And remember that there's nothing wrong with writing into your calendar: "Saturday afternoon: Play in sandbox with Johnny."

That brings us to the old joke about married couples who are so busy that they have to "pencil" an episode of sex into their crowded calendars. Dr. Lonsdorf thinks that's not such a silly scheme if it ensures the couple will take time away from work to enjoy time together. "The notion that sex has to be spontaneous to be good is baloney," he says.

And keep things in perspective. "Decide whether you want your family to feel they're last on your list," writes Dr. Machlowitz. "You really are more indispensable to those at home than you are to those at work. Your parents will appreciate your presence at their golden anniversary party more than your colleagues will miss you at a company dinner." And it's not just the big events that count. She continues, "Showing up to watch your child's basket-ball team practice counts more than merely making it to the championship game." Above all, adds Dr. Rosen, open a dialogue with family members so that they feel comfortable telling you if their needs are not being met.

Living with a Workaholic

If you're on the other side of the equation, a workaholic's resentful loved one, you've got a decision to make. Do you want to remain in a relationship with a person who may or may not want to reform?

There *is* some point to trying to change a loved one, says Dr. Lonsdorf. "It's legitimate for a wife or husband to say 'I married you because I wanted to share your time and interests and you're not doing it.' " But even when workaholics express an interest in changing, they may not. Don't believe a workaholic spouse who says he or she will cut down on hours after reaching some goal such as an anticipated promotion or the attainment of a particular salary level. The new position may bring more responsibilities—even more overtime. The new salary level may only set the stage for a subsequent salary goal. And how do you know your loved one really wants to end his or her devotion to work?

Let's first assume you opt to live with your workaholic. Keep in mind that your life together will demand an abundance of compromises. You can try to interest your spouse in old activities that gave you both pleasure at a time before work became so important—if any such activities existed. Or you can try to engage your spouse in new activities with scheduled-in "play" time. But if your workaholic isn't interested in changing, you don't have to let your spouse's enthusiasm about work rob you of the opportunity to enjoy life on your own. "You may have to develop activities on your own so you can grow and mature," says Dr. Prout.

In any event, try to make the time you do spend together as enjoyable as possible. Work to minimize the stress of everyday household hassles. Don't get into the habit of resenting a workaholic who won't help around the house. Instead, if you can afford it, pay someone to help with the household chores. Don't spend your precious time together doing things you don't enjoy doing.

Anticipate some readjustment problems if you get your workaholic to reform. You and your family may have adapted to your status as second fiddle, and you may be angry or alienated. Now you must deal with a change in your relationship to the workaholic. Expect your workaholic to be irritable. After all, you're taking him or her away from something that's rewarding and important. Your workaholic may even become depressed. "There's a chance that the workaholic may resent the changes. There's the possibility that they'll be sad because their needs aren't being met," says Dr. Rosen. Often, professional help in the form of individual or family therapy is the best answer.

When You Work for a Workaholic

In the annals of business, there are legends about the heads of major corporations who relinquish corner offices with sweeping views in favor of an office with a window from which they can see the company parking lot—and keep track of the comings and goings of employees.

That's a great environment for workaholics. But if you're not one, and your organization worships overtime hounds, you're probably in for some trouble. "If your boss is a workaholic, he or she may say, 'I'm the boss and everybody's working for me,'" says Dr. Prout. "It could be the kiss of death for someone who's not in there seven days a week."

"You probably can't change a workaholic boss," says Dr. Machlowitz. But you probably can put up with one if you know it is only for a specified period of time. Some people accept a job with a workaholic boss only long enough to gain experience to move on. This strategy is wise only if you have some assurance that the job (and its long hours) will make way for something that better suits your personality. In general, you probably won't survive over the long run. Square pegs don't fit into round holes. "I would never advise people to conform to a pattern of a boss if in fact they're not that way and the job doesn't require it," says Dr. Sirota.

One obvious strategy is to try to discuss the problem with your boss. "If working long hours of overtime is not the way you choose to lead your life, tell your boss. Put it on the table. In my experience, often it works—say, 90 percent of the time. The difficulties occur when it's not discussed," says Dr. Sirota. But he adds one caveat: The individual must be producing top-notch work to achieve a positive response.

There are ways of protecting yourself from getting in the employ of a workaholic in the first place. "Past work experience is the best indicator of future work experience," says Dr. Machlowitz. "So in the interview, ask your potential boss about part-time jobs he had in college. Try to determine if he is a person who just does the minimum or who may be a workaholic." Ask others at the organization whether long hours are required.

If You're the Workaholic

Just as it can be catastrophic if you're a 9-to-5'er in the employ of someone who is wedded to work, it can be a terrible mismatch if you're a workaholic and your boss isn't. You'd think that any employer would be thrilled to have someone so dedicated to a job. But that's not always the case. Many bosses, particularly those in large, competitive organizations, feel threatened by a workaholic subordinate. They may convince themselves that the workaholic is after their job. "If you're a workaholic and your boss isn't, it can be very threatening to your boss. You've got to be sensitive about that," says Dr. Rosen.

Dr. Prout advises against telling your boss that you merely enjoy working endless overtime and that you're not after his or her job. "The boss won't necessarily believe you," he says. Instead, he suggests you find another place to spend your extra energy. Volunteer at a nonprofit organization. Work with your family at home. Or find a job in an organization that appreciates your drive and capacity for work. But if you need to stay in the mismatched job, Dr. Rosen suggests you stay late only if you're very conscious not to threaten the boss.

The Co-worker Trap

Pressure from peers, as well as from bosses, lengthens the workday. Dr. Sirota tells of one transportation company in which employees feel compelled to come in on Saturdays, even though there is nothing to do. So they chat and go to lunch. It's all part of a game of one-upmanship that people play. The winners are those who stay at work the latest.

Actually, the winners are those who don't succumb to such pressure. To exit yourself from the game, be comfortable with the fact that you are not a workaholic and don't have your self-esteem based on the number of hours you put in—regardless of what others do. "You have to be comfortable with who you are, with your values, your interests and your goals in life," says Dr. Rosen. "It's very easy to be swayed by what other people do and think." He says you should ask yourself, "Am I going to let other people's workaholism affect my sense of self?"

And it works the other way, too. Your slavish devotion to the job may be building up resentment on the part of co-workers who get value from other things in their lives besides work. Be sensitive to their feelings. "Co-workers are going to be very jealous because when it comes time for a promotion, everybody knows who's going to get it," says Dr. Prout.

That's right, the workaholic probably will succeed faster than colleagues who aren't so inclined. Unless, of course, the workaholic isn't producing more than his or her co-workers, despite the lengthy hours. Or unless the workaholic's work habits have antagonized other members of the organization. Or if the workaholic's boundless energy and capacity for work simply aren't valued by the employer.

Part 2

CONTROLLING SELF-MADE STRESS

Chapter 19

ANGER

In Japan, an individual who feels angry is not likely to lash out at the object of his anger with a torrent of furious words. Instead, he will show it by excessive politeness and a neutral expression.

Among the Mbuti hunter-gatherers of northeast Zaire, humor is routinely used to dissipate quarrels. Individual disputes turn into full-scale tribal laugh fests.

The Utku Eskimos are likely to ostracize anyone among them who loses his or her temper, regardless of the reason.

Welcome to the fascinating world of anger. Virtually every culture has its own rules that spell out the socially acceptable causes and the permissible methods of expressing the emotion. In our culture, the way we think about anger—and how best to handle it—is changing.

For years the popular wisdom was to vent all anger. Those who suppressed anger, it was argued, risked everything from ulcers to heart attacks to overeating binges, not to mention disastrous relationships. Now experts suspect that such a universal link between anger and physical ills may be overstated, and that people who express their anger without hesitation or reflection may want to consider the potentially devastating social consequences of their actions. Sometimes the "let-it-out" philosophy is counterproductive.

Let's start with the link between suppressed anger and illness. In the controversial book, *Anger, the Misunderstood Emotion*, social psychologist Carol Tavris, Ph.D., drew on a great number of research references to write that "the popular belief that suppressed anger can wreak havoc on the body and bloodstream had been inflated out of realistic proportions. It does not, in any predictable or consistent way, make us depressed, produce ulcers or hypertension, set us off on food binges, or give us heart attacks."

She wrote that ulcers, traditionally considered the ultimate symptom of suppressed emotion, "turn up among people who express anger readily and among those who don't." It may partly have something to do with your genes. "If you have a particular kind of genetic capacity and are socialized in a

84

certain way, chances are you might [get an ulcer]. We still don't know," says Ernest Harburg, Ph.D., a University of Michigan senior research scientist.

Just as some individuals may be genetically predisposed to heart disease, some seem to be genetically predisposed to having a greater capacity for anger. However, the way people *express* their anger will vary with the social and psychological environment.

Dr. Harburg studied how the anger responses of 2,300 individuals in Detroit impacted on their blood pressure. Whose was lower, those who kept anger in (Anger-In) or those who freely expressed anger (Anger-Out)? Neither. Significant numbers of both groups experienced high levels of blood pressure arousal. And other research by Dr. Harburg linked unexpressed anger with early mortality. But while he cautions that it's only a hypothesis that suppressed anger is a risk factor that can lead you to an early grave, he adds: "If you play the percentages, you'd find a better way to deal with anger." Fortunately, there's a third method of handling anger: reflective coping.

Reflective Coping

Both Anger-In and Anger-Out are reflexive responses. They just *happen*, like when the doctor tests your reflexes by hitting your knee. When you're angry, you don't necessarily *think* about what you're doing. And you certainly don't think constructively—for example, considering ways of getting to the root of it. That's why many psychologists now recommend reflective coping as a way of dealing with anger. You don't lash out at someone. You don't sit and stew. Instead, you think about the source of your anger, about the consequences of your response. "People who respond with reflective handling of anger seen to have lower blood pressure, on average," says Dr. Harburg.

Keep two things in mind. First, as we understand from the Eskimos and others, the way we express our anger is something we learned how to do. It doesn't come naturally. So you can learn to cope in new ways—whether it's a matter of keeping a diary of your anger so you can track its ebbs and flows and your responses, or whether it's a matter of learning relaxation techniques as a way of responding to what in the past would have sent you flying off the handle.

The second thing to keep in mind is that reflective coping techniques don't mean that you can never tell a boss or a loved one precisely how you feel. You can. The difference is that you do it in a constructive manner.

Dr. Harburg gives this simple example. The boss flings open his door, emerges and yells at the near-top of his voice: "Where's that report you owe me? Haven't you finished it yet?" If this is, in fact, a wrong accusation—if you already put the report on the boss's desk but he hasn't discovered it—you can simply stand up, look him in the eye and say, "I already put it on your desk. And I don't like it when you yell at me like that."

Finding What's Good for You

There are two reasons for expressing anger, according to Dr. Tavris—to make the other guy feel as bad as you do, and to draw the other person's attention to the fact that something is wrong that you want fixed. Sometimes losing your temper is the only way to let a person know how serious the issue is, which is why our culture permits it. Dr. Tavris believes anger should be expressed only in circumstances that satisfy three conditions: when it represents a legitimate plea for justice; when it is directed at someone who is the cause of the anger; and when it would correct the situation or not cause retaliation.

But suppose you find yourself constantly yelling at your kids and getting temporary relief, yet later feeling remorse over your own behavior. It could be time to look for a strategy that works better for you—a strategy in which the object of your anger is open to your message and a strategy that you feel comfortable with over the long run.

Many psychologists agree that a rational method for handling your anger is often the best approach. But some people just seem to blow their top, despite lots of promises that they'll never do it again. If you think you have no choices and control over how you respond, you might try this "thought system." In his book *Anger: How to Live with and without It*, Albert Ellis, Ph.D., offers a step-by-step method to change and undercut irrational responses to anger. You may never throw another tantrum.

Foremost, he says, "Acknowledge that it's *you* who creates the anger." Someone may displease or frustrate you, but they don't create the anger. Second, he suggests you rate people's behavior instead of evaluating them as a whole. "Acknowledge that there are people who do badly, not rotten, bad people," he says.

"That diminishes the anger, but you still have the displeasure of the act, and you have to decide whether to assert yourself or not. If it's a friend or family member you're angry with, you can feel free to tell them. Your diminished anger will enable you to be assertive, but without the aggression that is likely to either intensify your anger or alienate your friend. If it's your boss you're angry with, you may not be as free to assert yourself without consequences," he says. What many therapists suggest is that you tell friends about the anger if you can't tell the boss.

"Try to understand the circumstances that are provoking the anger in the first place, whether they are stored memories from the past or from the current predicament," says Charles D. Spielberger, Ph.D., director of the Center for Research in Behavioral Medicine and Health Psychology at the University of South Florida. "If you know what provokes the anger, you have lots of choices. You may be able to avoid people who make you angry. And if you can't avoid them, you may be able to anticipate that they're likely to make you angry. So you can develop alternative ways of coping." Try taking a deep breath, for example, and slowly counting to ten.

Chapter 20

FRUSTRATION

Non possunt primi esse omnes in omni tempore.

—Laberius

Frustrations seem to come in three sizes.

Little frustrations: A busy signal on the phone; a red light; a quotation in a dead language, untranslated. Little frustrations come every day; they bug us but are quickly forgotten.

Middling frustrations: Driving 20 miles to your favorite restaurant to find it closed; driving 19 miles to your favorite restaurant and running out of gas; discovering your favorite restaurant is now a muffler shop. These midsize troubles really bug us, and can linger.

Big frustrations: Training rigorously for ten years in anticipation of the 1980 Olympics, only to see it cancelled. Kurt Thomas, 26, was then rated the best male gymnast in the country, a good bet for several gold medals.

"At first I didn't believe it," says Thomas. "My whole mind went blank. My body just gave up. I quit training."

Frustration is stress that comes when things turn out not quite the way we wanted them to, when we can't accomplish something we set out to do or when we feel cheated, foiled, thwarted or baffled.

Find your patterns. Although Kurt Thomas never went back to competitive gymnastics, he did eventually get over his enormous frustration. According to Richard Lane, M.D., assistant professor of psychiatry and psychology at the University of Health Sciences/The Chicago Medical School, the way each of us handles frustration is partly genetic (we are not all born with the same temperament) and partly environmental (how well we have learned to deal with life's upsets).

Frustration isn't always cause for self-analysis. (In Thomas's case, it's hard to see how anyone would not have felt frustrated.) But, says Dr. Lane, "intense reactions to something seemingly benign often resonate with important issues earlier in a person's life." He suggests the next time you feel overly frustrated you look within, and look back.

For example, if dealing with your boss constantly drives you up a wall, if your last parking ticket made you curse all cops, if nothing your elected officials do ever seems right—you just might have a problem dealing with authority figures. Could it all have begun with dear old dad?

Recognizing a pattern such as this one, says Dr. Lane, could be an important step toward overcoming your frustrations. If this pattern is yours, next time the boss rejects your work, ask yourself how this may mirror your dad's harping on you about schoolwork. Recognize the similarities in the situation and you can more easily recognize the differences—and this, says Dr. Lane, is the important thing. You are *not* still in the third grade, and your boss is *not* your father.

Take action. Allan Markle, Ph.D., a behavioral psychologist at the Veterans Administration Medical Center in North Chicago, believes there's a lot we can do about handling frustrations, regardless of their psychological roots.

He suggests the following:

• Decide whether there's anything you can do about the situation, and if there is—do it. The light at 23rd and Vine drives you crazy? . . . Take 22nd Street.

• Don't "awfulize." If you must, consider the possibility of nuclear holocaust to understand that your puppy missing the paper isn't really the end of the world. Check your words: If you say "Oh God, this is a catastrophe," on a weekly basis, you're awfulizing.

• Don't ruminate. If your life's failures keep popping up in your mind—don't let them! A good exercise is to slap your thigh or snap a rubber band against your wrist every time you catch yourself dwelling on past frustrations.

• If all sorts of things get to you, consider learning various relaxation techniques.

Accept life's fizzles. According to William Knaus, Ed.D., author of *How to Conquer Your Frustrations*, frustration is not something that can be blotted out of our lives. Rather, it is something we must learn to tolerate.

"One must accept frustration as part of the price for getting things done," says Dr. Knaus. "There's no getting around it: You simply have to accept that things aren't going to be the way you want them to be all of the time. You can't always win."

Funny, that's just about what Roman playwright Laberius said 2,000 years ago. *Non possunt primi esse omnes in omni tempore*—"All cannot be first all the time."

Chapter 21

GUILT

In the world of emotions, guilt has been given a bad rap. For a while it was in vogue among pop psychologists to dub it the "useless" emotion and to attempt to banish guilt and its many stressful side effects from the psyche. But recently, therapists have been working to restore guilt to its rightful place among our emotions. Without guilt, they ask, how many of us would cheat on our taxes? Without guilt, they ask, how many of us would never be kind to our parents or children or co-workers? "The sense of guilt you feel is what makes you human," says psychiatrist Willard Gaylin, M.D., author of *Feelings: Our Vital Signs*. "Be grateful you have it."

Guilt is a form of self-punishment. It is a reaction to an event or situation, and when it motivates us for constructive activity, it is both healthy and useful, says Salvatore V. Didato, Ph.D., a Scarsdale, New York, psychologist, syndicated columnist and author of *Psychotechniques: Act Right, Feel Right*.

Healthy Guilt, Unhealthy Guilt

Here's a simple example of the constructive nature of guilt. Say you were abrupt or abrasive to a co-worker. As a result of your words or actions you somehow bruised their self-esteem. You feel guilty, and to neutralize the guilt you apologize to the person, or you do a good deed to help the person, or you give them more of you and your time.

Here, on the other hand, is a typical example of unhealthy or unrealistic guilt. Say your mother dies. You search the past for situations where you may have offended her. You come up with a cluster of circumstances where you may have disappointed her—forgetting her birthday, not going home for Christmas and the like. So you lapse into a guilt pattern that causes you to behave differently. You mistreat people. You engage in self-critical thoughts.

You find yourself becoming too passive or unassertive in situations where you feel you don't deserve to win.

"Guilt is the agonizing sense that you have betrayed an internal value of your own, and its relief often requires—and invites—punishment," says Dr. Gaylin. And because it's akin to anxiety, it can cause stress. So if you're feeling guilty, the obvious issue to explore is whether your guilt is of the healthy or unhealthy variety.

The situations that make us feel guilty have their roots in our culture and in our families. Harry E. Gunn, Ph.D., author of *Manipulation by Guilt: How to Avoid It*, believes that all guilt originates from the fear that a parent will harm us for what we do—or even think. So the dynamics for guilt have been firmly established in childhood.

But many of the principles we learned in childhood—and by which we are dominated—are not appropriate for our lives today. And they can be a source of unhealthy guilt. Despite the widespread changes that have resulted from the women's liberation movement, for example, many women still feel guilt-ridden because they have careers, something that was taboo in their mothers' generation.

"The thing you would have to do in that case is to go back and track down the roots of your thinking," says Dr. Gunn. "Where did you get the idea that it's bad to have a career? Was it something your kid said? Was it an article you read? Very often in this search, people can trace their guilt to their parents. Then they have to ask themselves, 'Do *I* think it's wrong to have a career?' " he says.

Unadmitted Guilt

What made us feel guilty as youngsters often still can. As a result, many people are carrying around guilt that is no longer appropriate. And it is not always at the forefront of consciousness. Sometimes unhealthy guilt is so ingrained that it takes professional psychotherapy to flush it out.

Dr. Gunn gives the example of a former client, a young man with a talent for swimming who joined the Navy to become a frogman, but who experienced severe anxiety attacks when he embarked on solo scuba dives. In therapy it came out that at age 5 or 6 he loved swimming, but his parents were terrified of the water. His mother suffered from a heart condition and repeatedly implied that if he swam alone and needed to be rescued by her, it would result in her death. At age 25, his unexplained fear of swimming alone was as intense—although inappropriate—as it was at age 5. "If something is wrong at age 5, it is not necessarily wrong at age 25," says Dr. Gunn. It's a variation of a theme that surfaces repeatedly in his private practice. He counsels many women who feel guilt about their healthy sexual appetite, mostly because they were so warned against sex decades earlier.

Tracking and Treating the Cause

Unconscious guilt—the kind experienced by the would-be Navy frogman—is always manifested indirectly. So when you don't consciously admit your guilty feelings, you find yourself having unexplained problems. You may feel depressed. You may find work piling up that you somehow aren't able to accomplish. You may feel tense. You may have sleepless nights. You may lose your interest in socializing. You may lose your temper.

It may be a matter of not being aware of the guilt or it may be a matter of your not owning up to it. Say you get "called on the carpet" by your superiors at work for continually making errors. You are told your job may be in jeopardy if you don't improve. You arrive home that evening feeling down on yourself, feeling threatened, feeling that you've lost the confidence of your boss and that you may also lose your job. You may not realize it, but you also may feel guilty—about not performing well and about not being secure in your ability to support your family.

So when you walk in the door, your son enthusiastically asks you to review his homework. You find two errors and immediately lash out at your child. "How can you make these errors?" you demand. "You've been watching too much television. Starting tonight, the TV goes off at 7:00." You are unconsciously repeating what went on at work. You are bringing your guilty feelings and feelings of self-defeat home.

The smartest method for determining whether guilt is behind such a scene may be to engage in some reflection, alone or with the support of others. It helps to blow off some steam with a spouse. In the process, you may find yourself striking upon the real issue at hand. Or discuss the symptoms with a friend you trust. You may ask them if they've noticed that you haven't been your real self lately. Tell them how you've felt: withdrawn, lazy, anxious. A session with a counselor or therapist may get you to notice how guilt translates into problem symptoms and may offer suggestions about what to do. It may be a matter of telling yourself—even aloud—that you're not feeling good about something and that you've got to guard against overreacting.

To Punish or Not to Punish

In his popular self-help book *Feeling Good*, David D. Burns, M.D., implores readers to examine the distortions that sometimes govern guilt. One possible distortion is the belief that your behavior is "bad." He writes, "Is the behavior you condemn in yourself in reality so terrible, immoral or wrong? Or are you magnifying things out of proportion?" Another possible distortion is that your behavior makes you a "bad" person.

Dr. Burns explains how the concept of "badness" distinguishes guilt from what he describes as the healthier feeling of remorse. "Remorse stems from the undistorted awareness that you have willfully and unnecessarily acted in a hurtful manner toward yourself or another person that violates your personal ethical standards. Remorse differs from guilt because there is no implication your transgression indicates you are inherently bad, evil or immoral," he writes.

So if you're experiencing remorse, you feel bad about your action, but you don't feel that *you're* bad.

Dr. Burns and other cognitive therapists ask clients to explore these potential distortions as well as a few others, among them the notion that they are inappropriately assuming responsibility for problems they did not cause. "If a person has a poor self-concept, not a normal amount of self-esteem, they'll seize upon any situation where they did something wrong," says Dr. Didato. "A counselor can get to the more fundamental issues and strengthen the personality and enhance the self-esteem."

More Warning Signs

Here are some other signs that you may be wallowing in unhealthy guilt.

- Feeling vaguely guilty, even when there's nothing to feel guilty about.
- Feeling guilty about being happy, or about something good that's happened.
- Turning your guilt into anger because it's easier to express anger than to admit guilt.
- Experiencing guilt over an incident that occurred 20 years ago.

How intense are these feelings? Are you virtually immobilized by some cruel statement you made to your spouse last week? And what kinds of behavior does the guilt cause? To explore that behavior, ask yourself:

- Does it get you into more difficulties?
- Does it cause you to lose friends?
- Does it cause people to reject you, to withdraw their love from you?
- Does it cause you to have self-critical feelings and attitudes?
- Does it diminish your drive for engaging in constructive behavior such as working and socializing?

Owning Up and Letting Go

Many therapists suggest that guilt is best dealt with quickly and efficiently. Once you realize you're feeling guilty, you should analyze the situation that triggered the guilt and decide whether your guilty feelings really are appropriate.

If you decide the guilt is appropriate, *own up to it.* Take responsibility for your actions by apologizing to a person you've wronged or resolving to change if it's yourself that you've failed.

And then let go of the guilt.

"It's better to let go and try to do better next time," says Julian Marder, M.D. He explains how people who cannot rid themselves of guilt often back themselves into a corner. Take the example of a person who said something to his wife that he regrets. He hangs on to the guilt feelings so that the guilt is a constant burden. Because of it, he may feel caged by the relationship. He becomes angry about the incident, about the guilt and about the burden. And his anger may cause him to repeat his behavior.

"He can't forgive himself. He can't take responsibility. There's no way out," says Dr. Marder. "In its own way the guilt reinforces the bad behavior. It becomes a vicious cycle."

So try to understand your guilt and let it go. And remember, says Dr. Marder, that we all make mistakes. After all, we're only human.

Chapter 22

PERFECTIONISM

Are you a perfectionist? To find out, take the quiz below.

1. Do you believe that to be a worthwhile person you must be at the top of everything you try?
2. Do you overlook your accomplishments and concentrate on your failings?
3. Once you accomplish something, do you prefer to look at the next challenge instead of experiencing the rewards of your accomplishment?
4. Do you procrastinate at any task or project that will be judged by others?

Well, nobody's perfect.

Simple words of wisdom, true, but if you're among the folks who answered yes to the questions above, you probably won't find it so simple to incorporate that bit of wisdom into your life.

"Perfectionism is the world's greatest con game," writes David D. Burns, M.D., in his popular self-help book, *Feeling Good*. "It promises riches and delivers misery." Like many con games, you don't know you're playing until someone points out the ways you're getting cheated.

In a study of more than 700 men and women, Dr. Burns discovered that perfectionists experience distress and dissatisfaction with their careers and personal lives. And he found no evidence that they were more successful than their nonperfectionist peers.

The Harder You Strive, the More Disappointed You Get

Here's the con. For any one of a number of reasons, a perfectionist is convinced that total failure lies ahead unless everything is done *perfectly*. But perfection is an illusion. And the harder one strives for perfection, the worse the ensuing disappointment will be—because perfection is unobtainable.

The first step you should take to stop playing the game is to recognize your stress-inducing behavior.

Recognize that you're never satisfied with what you do. "Perfectionists can never rest on their laurels, never tell themselves they did a good job," says Asher Pacht, Ph.D., a professor of psychology at the University of Wisconsin.

Recognize that you're a procrastinator. People often procrastinate at tasks and projects because they're afraid of being judged on results that may be less than perfect.

Once you've identified your perfectionist behavior, systematically learn how to expect less from yourself. We're not suggesting you slouch off at everything, not work to the best of your ability or not set high standards for yourself. But don't judge yourself so harshly if you fail to meet your lofty goals.

Be selective. "Choose one or two things you really want to do well at, and concentrate your best efforts on those activities," recommends Don E. Hamachek, Ph.D., a professor of counseling and educational psychology at Michigan State University.

Give yourself permission to be imperfect. "It's important to recognize that 100 percent is unattainable, and that if you continue to shoot for that goal, you're likely to always feel under a lot of stress, depressed and anxious," says Dr. Pacht. "Settle for 90 percent and recognize that it's a pretty damned good accomplishment."

Choose at least one activity you can do without self-criticism. Dr. Hamachek runs three or four miles each day and is proud that he doesn't care how long it takes him to do it.

Change Your Thinking

Begin to identify those thought patterns that lead to built-up stress and cause postperformance judgments or depression. Perfectionists tend to indulge in several varieties of self-defeating thinking.

They may overgeneralize. ("I didn't get up to snuff. I'm really falling down and I'm no good.") They may engage in dichotomous thinking. ("I'm really good at some things and I'm a failure at others.") They may engage in selective thinking. ("Once I accomplish something, that accomplishment becomes insignificant.")

Why do perfectionists torture themselves so? Because, in an odd sort of way, it makes them feel good, too.

Become aware of the gains that *you* get out of being a perfectionist. Sometimes people are able to change their stressful self-dialogue when they realize they may be telling themselves, "I am a special person because I'm tough on myself," says John C. Barrow, Ed.D., a psychologist at Duke University's Counseling and Psychological Services.

Then develop new ways of thinking. If you're so anxious about the outcome of a task that you can't concentrate on it, put your mind on the task as opposed to the consequences.

Adopt what Dr. Barrow calls a "coping dialogue." His examples? "Here I go again. I'm already worrying about the future. Let me settle down and do my best." Or, "This task is important, but I have a lot to do in a limited amount of time. Hang on, there are only 24 hours in a day."

Learn Why You're Like That

Challenge the basic assumptions about yourself and what makes you feel like a worthwhile human being. A professional therapist may help you understand that your self-worth is based on gaining the approval of everyone who is important to you, says Dr. Pacht. Or that your self-worth is based on your ability to perform. Or that being perfect will not bring you love and a great sense of well-being.

It's easy to understand how people convince themselves otherwise. As San Francisco psychologist Debra White, Ph.D., says, "The obsession with being perfect infiltrates families and is passed on from one generation to the next. A child in a perfectionistic home soon learns that worth is defined by performance."

In such homes, simply "being" is not good enough, she says. "Standards for what is 'good' and 'bad' are set from the outside, not from within, and have clear demarcations: a letter grade of 'A' is acceptable, a high 'B' is failure. There is nothing in between. Spontaneous and creative expression becomes risky and is muffled out of fear of disapproval."

If your anxiety over being perfect is disrupting your life, taking a physical and psychological toll, remind yourself that nobody's perfect. Try to recognize the underlying causes of perfectionism and begin to accept yourself as you are.

Chapter 23

PHOBIAS

Fear is natural. Some people are afraid to walk through dark alleys late at night. Others fear vicious dogs, killer bees or rabid bats. Still others are afraid to skydive, race Indy cars or stand under tall trees during thunderstorms. Those are reasonable, appropriate fears.

A phobia, by contrast, is irrational and inappropriate. It's the dread of being trapped in a place or circumstance that wouldn't upset most people. The most common phobia treated by therapists is agoraphobia, or fear of venturing out into open spaces, which includes fear of public places like stores, restaurants or theaters, fear of public transportation, especially when traveling alone, and fear of being away from a safe place, person or object.

Other common phobias include:

● Social phobias, such as a fear of speaking, writing or eating in public.
● Simple phobias, such as fear of dogs, cats, birds, insects, spiders and snakes. (Animal phobias can become serious if you're so afraid of cats, say, that you never leave the house for fear one will cross your path.)
● Blood/injury phobias, such as fear of medical procedures like getting an injection.

A person with intense phobias will rearrange their whole life to avoid what triggers the fear, and they'll do almost anything to avoid confronting that fear.

If you have a phobia, you have lots of company—13 million other phobics, according to the Phobia Society of America. Some doctors say phobias (and related anxiety problems) are the most prevalent mental health problem in the United States, rivaling depression and alcoholism. Yet until recently, most phobias were dismissed with glib comments like "It's just nerves," or "What you really need is a long vacation," or the sufferers were handed a prescription for tranquilizers.

97

A Special Kind of Fear

Phobias rarely materialize out of nowhere. Usually a stressful situation sets off the first panic attack, then the fear of the panic attack itself takes on a life of its own. You fear having a panic attack if the situation recurs. (See chapter 44 for more information on panic attacks.)

A panic attack—and the apprehension and dread associated with it—is pretty terrifying. Typical symptoms include shortness of breath, palpitations, chest pain or discomfort, choking or smothering sensations, dizziness, vertigo, unsteady feelings, feelings of unreality, abnormal or strange feelings, hot and cold flashes, sweating, faintness, trembling and shaking.

"The initial phobic experience . . . is often an unforgettable panic attack, which may occur when the person is under unusual physical or psychological stress," explains Robert DuPont, M.D., in the book, *Phobias and Panic: A Physician's Guide to Modern Treatments.* "Typical prephobic stresses include getting married or divorced, the birth of a child, the serious illness of a loved one, moving away from home, a personal illness, a serious accident or a surgical operation. Any major life change can be stressful and may, in a vulnerable person, precipitate a panic attack."

"Phobic people are usually bright, energetic, successful, otherwise healthy and above average in many ways," says Jerilyn Ross, co-founder and president of the Phobia Society of America. "On the surface, they're strong, able to remain calm in a crisis and even to pull others together." Then one day, driving their car or standing in a checkout line, they suddenly feel as if they'll become unglued.

The first time a panic attack happens, the person often believes he or she is having a heart attack, going "crazy" or losing control. If the episode recurs within days or weeks—as it often does—the person begins to fear panic itself and tries to reduce the risk of panic by avoiding what they believe triggers the attacks.

And in fact, phobic attacks are the classic "fight-or-flight" response to stress—with the emphasis on "flight."

"Often, the fear hits them in an area with which they previously had no problems—driving or performing, for example," says Ross. "They wonder, 'What went wrong? Am I going crazy?' Then they make excuses to get out of doing things or going places without letting on why. A young mother who became phobic about driving would get out of carpooling by saying she had a headache, or other appointments—anything to avoid driving. Then she'd feel loss of self-esteem and guilty about lying or not fulfilling her obligations."

The worst fear is the *anticipation* of what might happen, says Dr. DuPont, with most of the pain and disability occurring before actual exposure to the stressful experience. The phobic lives in a constant state of "what if," fearfully avoiding activities previously pursued without anxiety. Often, stress—a new job, a separation or childbirth, for instance—heightens sensitivity to phobic feelings. So a phobia is almost as much of a cause of stress as a reaction to it.

Where to Go for Help

If you have a phobia (or phobias), don't panic. There are more than 1,000 phobia and panic disorder specialists in North America. To receive general information about phobias and panic disorders and how to find effective treatment, as well as information about the services and activities of the Phobia Society of America, send a business-size, self-addressed envelope bearing *two* first-class stamps to the Phobia Society of America, Department R, 133 Rollins Avenue, Suite 4B, Rockville, MD 20852–4004.

Take a typical case, a man who is afraid of elevators. Outside of elevators, he's fine. But if he has to ride an elevator, he becomes panicky and dreads stepping into the car even though he knows that millions of people safely ride elevators every day. What he's really afraid of isn't the elevator or what will happen inside it, but how he will feel inside the elevator. He fears he will have a panic attack and be so overwhelmed with anxiety that once again he will "lose it."

Why Avoidance Doesn't Always Work

People who are afraid of elevators usually can take the stairs. People who are afraid of flying can take buses, trains, boats or cars—or stay home. People who are afraid of being trapped can stay out of stores, restaurants and theaters.

And at first, avoidance works because it relieves anxiety and gives a sense that the situation is under control. But deep inside, phobics feel like closet cowards, and because they know their fears are irrational, their self-esteem suffers. Over the long term, avoidance tactics can undermine the quality of both life and health. Agoraphobics may become housebound—so afraid of going out that they sever all ties with the outside world, becoming prisoners of their phobia.

When fear of medical or dental procedures results in avoidance, it can prevent a person from obtaining routine health care. They may ignore minor ailments, letting things go until emergency medical treatment or surgery is the only recourse "One woman put off going to the dentist so long that when she finally did go, half her teeth had to be pulled, they were so bad," says Ross.

Drug Therapy—and Fear of Drugs

Certain antipanic drugs like Tofranil, Elavil, Sinequan, Adapin, Ludiomil, Desyrel, Parnate and Nardil can help reduce feelings of panic. More potent drugs, like alprazolam, can block a panic attack in phobic people. But like any other stress-management drugs, anxiety-reducing medications have certain drawbacks. (For more on drug treatment of anxiety-related disorders, see chapter 88.)

But here's another hitch: Many phobic people are also afraid to take any kind of mood-altering drugs, for fear that they'll lose control under the influence of medication.

If medications worry you, tell your physician. He or she should be able to prescribe the lowest dosage needed for the shortest period of time. For further reassurance, discuss possible side effects with your physician and be on the alert for slurred speech, cloudy thinking or other signs of toxicity. Lowering the dosage or changing to another type of medication may help.

"It is also reassuring . . . for the physician to give the patient a phone number at which he or she can be reached at any time of the day or night," says Dr. DuPont. Most people find they never use the phone number: Having an emergency phone number at hand, "just in case," is usually reassuring enough to prevent an attack.

In any case, it's worth a try to get used to what scares you—even before you resort to drugs.

Anti-Scare Tactics

"We teach people how to deal with the anxiety itself, so they learn not to fear the fear," explains Ross, who overcame a height phobia. "Using rational arguments to try to convince a phobic that they shouldn't be afraid just doesn't work. Telling someone who's afraid of flying or driving or riding in elevators that nothing will happen is like saying to someone about to step into a lion cage, 'Don't worry, he hasn't eaten anyone today.' For a phobic, the fear is very real, it feels like a matter of life or death."

Exposure therapy (also called *in vivo* desensitization) consists of gradual, supervised exposure to the frightening object or experience. You'll go on a number of "field trips" to encounter the real-life situation—swimming, driving a car, riding a plane or elevator, shopping, speaking in front of people or whatever creates anxiety. Treatment usually involves one or two sessions a week for 8 to 20 weeks under the direction of a psychiatrist, psychologist or other therapist and sometimes others who share your phobias but have learned to overcome their fear. The following tools can help overcome a phobia.

Ride out the wave of anxiety. "Few phobics have stayed in their phobic situations long enough to realize that the anxiety will subside without their having to leave the situation if they wait a minute or two," says Dr. DuPont. They tend to flee before giving themselves a chance. "Most panic attacks last about 20 seconds," says Ross. "So instead of saying, 'Oh, my God, here it goes again' and working yourself into a panic, say to yourself, 'As bad as I feel, this will pass.' And it will."

Give yourself an "out." "Except for animal or insect phobias, which usually arise out of a traumatic experience during childhood, most phobias are based on the fear of being in a situation where you believe you're trapped. And once trapped, you might have a panic attack. And during that attack you feel a loss of control, you fear embarrassing yourself, going crazy or dying," says Ross. "But you can reduce that fear by arranging for a possible means of escape, *if* you need one. If you're afraid of crowded theaters, for example, and your spouse gets tickets for a show, make an agreement that if you start to feel uneasy during the performance, you can leave immediately. (Obviously, support from your spouse or other close associates is important, too.) Knowing the escape is there, you may not need to use it.

"Similarly, if you're afraid you'll freeze up or lose your composure should you have to speak in front of a group, tell yourself that you'll plead a sudden attack of the flu and excuse yourself *if* things get bad," adds Ross. "It's a game you play with yourself. Anything that gets you in is an acceptable out."

If you dread sitting still for dental work because you're afraid you won't be able to let the dentist know whether you're in pain or need a breather, arrange to use hand signals to tell him to stop.

"Just knowing you have an 'out' will allow you to put yourself into the situation," says Ross.

Cut down on alcohol and caffeine. "Say you're afraid of flying," says Ross. "While one drink might calm your nerves, if you drink heavily, you'll probably feel more vulnerable, helpless and out of control and therefore *more* likely to panic. Also, caffeine triggers the release of adrenaline and has been linked to panic attacks. So if you're going to give a speech, try decaf. You're less likely to get the shakes."

The goal of exposure therapy is to enable the phobic to live a normal life without serious limitations because of his or her fear. And many do live happily ever after. With proper treatment, 90 percent of phobics can obtain relief.

Chapter 24

RISK-TAKING

Which is riskier:
(a) scuba diving in shark-inhabited waters or (b) signing a mortgage?
(a) skydiving or (b) parenting?
(a) downhill skiing or (b) changing careers in midlife?

The right answer is (a). Or (b), depending on who's answering the question and who's taking the risk.

Exciting activities such as scuba diving, skydiving and downhill skiing are examples of what Ralph Keyes categorizes as Level I risks in his book, *Chancing It: Why We Take Risks.* Keyes defines Level I risks as highly stimulating, often dangerous activities that seldom last long. Besides thrill sports, Level I risks include performing in public, running for public office, wearing offbeat clothes to work or trying new, unfamiliar foods on a restaurant menu.

Major commitments such as signing a mortgage, having children and changing your career are Level II risks, according to Keyes. These are less dramatic but last far longer and may actually be more stressful than thrill sports or other Level I risks. Taking a Level II risk can jeopardize financial security, relationships or careers. Other Level II risks include getting married, continuing your education or buying stock in public utilities.

Risk Is in the Eye of the Beholder

Most of us take both types of risks sometime in our lives but lean toward one type over the other. People who find routine not only tedious but agonizing seek novelty and excitement. They get a thrill out of taking Level I risks. Relaxation is not in their vocabulary. Risking death and disability is not nearly as daunting as the risk of a major commitment like marriage. In contrast, people for whom change and unpredictability are very stressful shy away from thrill sports and tend to be more comfortable with Level II risks, involving major commitments.

"Risk is in the eye of the beholder," says Keyes, who conducts seminars on productive risk-taking for corporate employees. "Take one skier I know. He confronted what he considered his greatest fear by skiing down a mammoth glacier. Afterward, I asked him, 'Is there anything you're afraid of now?' He said, 'Nothing.' I said, 'What about marriage?' He admitted, 'Well, yeah, that scares me.' What about having kids? 'Hey, let's not get carried away!' he replied."

In other words, risk-taking can take two forms—Level I and Level II. Few people are strictly Level I or Level II risk-takers. Most end up taking both

---

The Do's and Don'ts of Risking

To help reduce the stress of taking risks, psychiatrist David Viscott, M.D., offers the following guidelines:

Don't risk out of fear, anger, hurt, guilt or depression. These feelings should be resolved on their own, not through a risky act.

Don't risk just to prove yourself. This, too, is hazardous risking.

Do have a goal. A risk without a clear purpose is in trouble from the start.

Don't combine risks unnecessarily. To try to take more than one risk at a time compounds the loss and therefore the anxiety.

Do know the loss involved. If you don't expect the loss, you don't understand the risk.

Do list everything that can go wrong—and why. You'll detect problems sooner because you'll be looking for them.

Do ask questions. It's better to appear a little stupid than to make a big mistake.

Don't rush. Take enough time to know what you are doing. Prepare beforehand.

Do make a timetable. A schedule can be strongly persuasive because it gives direction and reinforces the belief that your plan is working.

Don't pretend you're not afraid if you are. Only fools do not fear danger. If the fear won't go away, maybe you're risking too much.

Do act decisively. Once you have decided the risk is worth taking and the time is right, you should act.

Don't ignore problems. They will not go away on their own.

Do take time to correct mistakes. Even when the act of risking is under way, mistakes still can be fixed.

Don't give up too soon. Have patience and perseverance.

Don't hold on forever. If you know you've lost, let a bad situation end. Don't prolong it.

Adapted from *Risking*, © 1977 by David Viscott, M.D. Reprinted by permission of Simon & Schuster, Inc.

kinds of risks. There are plenty of downhill skiers who are married, have children, are paying off a mortgage and engage in other long-term commitments. Conversely, many settled, responsible and wise individuals get a thrill out of traveling to exotic or unfamiliar locations, driving speedboats, hunting wild game, or other stimulating activities.

The Rewards of Productive Risk-Taking

Why take Level I risks at all?

Many people are quick to assume that those who engage mostly in Level I risks—the thrill-seekers—have more pluck than brains. (Some probably do.) But let's take a closer look. What lessons can be learned from the daredevil personality—the go-for-it, sensation-loving thrill-seeker? Plenty. Thrill seeking is a form of risk-taking behavior that can act as a "dress rehearsal" for dealing with major and minor stresses.

How can sailing a boat through pea-soup fog relate to making managerial decisions back at the office? How can diving into 100 feet of water with lead weights strapped to your body make you better able to handle the stress of parenting?

"By mastering new situations, people are better prepared to meet unexpected challenges," says Bessel van der Kolk, M.D., director of the Trauma Clinic, Massachusetts Mental Health Center, Harvard Medical School. "And life certainly presents a number of challenges—getting a job, keeping a job, getting married and so forth.

"Psychologists call that 'stress inoculation,' " continues Dr. van der Kolk. "Once you become accustomed to finding solutions to difficult situations—and accumulate feelings of mastery—you will be better able to meet new challenges."

Frank Farley, Ph.D., has carefully studied thrill-seekers' psyches, although he labels risk-taking personalities differently than Keyes does. The University of Wisconsin professor of educational psychology calls people who seek excitement and stimulation wherever they can find or create it—Type T or Big T (for Thrill) personalities. At the other end of the continuum are people whom Dr. Farley calls Little T personalities—people who prefer to avoid risks and cling to the familiar. (As with Ralph Keyes's categories, most people are not full-blown Big T's or Little T's, but a combination of both. But Dr. Farley's labels are useful for understanding human behavior—and why some people enjoy risking.)

"While most people are uneasy with uncertainty, the Big T personality *thrives* on uncertainty," remarks Dr. Farley. "And what is risk-taking but engaging in something with an uncertain outcome?"

Echoing Dr. van der Kolk's remarks, Dr. Farley believes that Big T's—people who test their own mettle again and again—handle crises better than Little T's, who avoid risks when they can.

To Risk or Not to Risk

Even the most conservative and stable among us are faced, sooner or later, with circumstances that prompt some risk-taking.

Should you buy a house–or continue to rent?

Should you quit your job–or stick it out in spite of the boredom?

Should you ask your sweetheart to marry you–or keep your feelings to yourself?

Should you have your gallbladder out–or hope the pain subsides on its own?

To evaluate risks, a little introspection can be a big help. David Viscott, M.D., author of *Risking*, suggests people ask themselves the following questions when considering a risk. "The object," says Dr. Viscott, "is to help you break through some of the bonds that now keep you from seeing your risk clearly, approaching it decisively and following through successfully."

- What feeling am I trying to express in taking this risk?
- Is this risk necessary?
- What do I need to know before taking this risk?
- Who can tell me what I need to know?
- Can I reach my goal another way?
- How much can change because of this risk?
- What can I lose by taking this risk?
- Is the potential loss greater than the possible gain?
- What can I do to prevent losses or harm from occurring?

After assessing your situation in this thoughtful way, you can decide whether to bet the kitty or fold.

"The Big T personality has less fear and anxiety relative to other people and would experience less stress in unavoidable crises," says Dr. Farley. "That enables them to keep their cool and make the right decision under pressure."

"What's more, Big T's are self-motivated–they like to make up their own minds," says Dr. Farley. They're more creative. And one major facet of creativity is embracing novelty and uncertainty. So they do well in unprecedented situations that require creative solutions."

Substituting Good Risks for Bad

That doesn't mean it's "creative" to drag race on icy roads or bet the family farm on the turn of a card. The risk should be positive–what Dr. Farley calls a T-plus risk that will relieve the anxiety and agitation that comes from too little stimulation. *Productive* risk-taking can lead to outstanding achievements in business, sports, science and the arts, according to Dr. Farley. *Destructive* risk-taking behavior, on the other hand, is an unsuccessful way of handling the stress of feeling trapped matrimonially, occupationally, financially or geographically. Negative risks (Dr. Farley calls these T-minus risks) include heavy drinking, reckless driving, experimenting with drugs, cheating on one's spouse, gossiping, gambling, shoplifting and other antisocial or unhealthful pursuits.

"Getting people to realize why they take negative risks is a tremendous help," says Dr. Farley. "Stress often results from a mismatch between your personality and the level of risk, arousal or stimulation you get from your job or environment. Suppose you are a Little T personality but you find yourself in a job that has a high arousal level—a noisy, unstructured work environment, open-ended or constantly changing expectations, many conflicts—in short, lots of uncertainty. You would probably find that very stressful and prefer more routine work. The opposite applies to a Big T personality, who is likely to feel stressed by a highly routine, predictable job because his or her biological need for stimulation is not being met."

Physically, your body can't distinguish between a "bad" thrill and a "good" thrill. Thrill-seekers, psychologists say, can satisfy their need for stimulation by participating in more positive extracurricular activities such as competitive sports, long-distance running, dancing, skiing, scuba diving— anything that boosts their arousal to a level comparable to the stimulation generated by fast driving, hard drinking and stirring up trouble.

"I would also recommend weekend adventuring, camping and creative mental activities such as writing, acting, music and art as outlets," says Dr. Farley. The key is to match the activities to your personality. Remember, what makes downhill skiing exhilarating for one person may terrify another. So choose activities you honestly enjoy. Otherwise, the activity may cause more stress than it relieves.

"I must emphasize that thrill-seekers aren't stress-seekers," says Dr. Farley. "I've spoken to many world-class adventurers—balloonists, skydivers, rock climbers, round-the-world sailors—and I get the impression they're seeking fun, excitement, challenge and risk, but not stress. Sigmund Freud would have said these people have a death wish, but the opposite is true: They have a powerful *life* wish."

A Fear of Living Dangerously

What about Little T personalities? Should people who aren't natural risk-takers adopt a daredevil attitude?

"Not necessarily," says Dr. Farley. "There are plenty of Little T individuals who lead perfectly happy, deeply satisfied, highly fulfilled lives. No thrills, no spills, you might say. Risk-taking may not be good for them if they don't get much out of taking risks. Don't forget, the more risks you take, the greater your chances for failure, which could be very stressful—even devastating—if you don't relish risk."

In other words, don't set out to become a motorcycle stunt driver just because it seems glamorous or to prove yourself to someone who thinks you're too conservative. But if you feel the stress that comes from a dead-end job, a hopeless marriage or any unrewarding or frustrating situation, you may relieve the tension with a little positive risking.

Chapter 25

TYPE A BEHAVIOR

Do you get antsy when you have to wait in line at a bank, movie theater or supermarket?

Do you honk the horn, mutter or swear when a car ahead of you is going too slowly?

Do you feel that others are to blame for most of your troubles?

Does your spouse frequently tell you to slow down, take it easy or just plain cool it?

If you answered yes to those questions, you may live in a continual state of annoyance (or perhaps even fury)—a key factor in the "Type A behavior pattern." And chronic anger (where you react to every minor incident as though it were a major crisis) often goes hand in boxing glove with chronic hostility (an outlook that considers people and events as "the opposition").

Type A behavior is easily provoked by deadlines, overwork, competition for jobs and promotions, or the mistakes (real or imagined) of others. And for complex reasons, Type A people tend to react to these stresses by trying to accomplish more and more in less and less time. The result is a potentially deadly game of one-upmanship—with themselves.

Are You a "Hot Reactor"?

In the 1960s, a study of more than 3,000 workers (predominantly in white collar jobs) suggested that people who respond to environmental stressors with hostility, impatience and aggression are more than twice as likely to develop heart disease as people who were labeled Type B's. Of 1,013 heart attack patients recruited for a later study, 97.5 percent exhibited Type A behavior.

Over the years, the link between Type A behavior and heart disease has become generally accepted. In 1981, the Review Panel on Coronary-Prone Behavior and Coronary Heart Disease of the National Heart, Lung and Blood

Institute concluded that Type A behavior is as hazardous to your heart as other proven hazards like smoking, high blood pressure and high cholesterol. And while a few dissenters remain, most doctors now accept the link between Type A behavior and heart disease.

Heartfelt Hostility

How do your arteries know you got furious when someone cut in front of you in traffic? And why should it make any difference? No one is certain. But some researchers suspect that competitive, time-driven, mistrustful Type A's spend a lot of time in a tense, unsettled state. With the nervous system on red alert all the time, norepinephrine and other stress-related hormones are discharged into the body, which in turn triggers production of blood fats that cling to the artery walls, reducing the amount of oxygen reaching the heart.

"Say someone runs a stop sign and just misses your car," says Virginia A. Price, Ph.D., a psychologist who's worked with Type A coronary survivors for ten years at the Meyer Friedman Institute in San Francisco. "Norepinephrine [the "struggle" hormone] skyrockets momentarily. If you prolong your rage and continue to relive the incident all day, you might as well have taken a drink from a bottle of poison stashed in your glove compartment. The effects are that toxic.

"The evidence suggests that anger temporarily reduces the amount of oxygenated blood flowing through coronary arteries," says Dr. Price. "In that respect, each angry outburst is the equivalent of smoking a cigarette."

Another theory says that emotional stress raises blood pressure, which may over time cause damage to the artery walls.

Downshift to Live Longer

Realizing that your attitude can set you on a collision course with disaster is the first and most important step in stemming heart-hurting behavior. Yet relaxation exercises alone won't do the trick. Changing your beliefs and learning new, healthier ways to react to and cope with stress are essential.

Skeptics may wonder if the Type A behavior pattern is so ingrained that taming a hostile attitude is like taming a grizzly bear. But apparently, people *can* change if they want to, says Meyer Friedman, M.D., one of the cardiologists who first identified Type A behavior in 1959. Some of Dr. Friedman's research, published in the *American Heart Journal*, indicates that behavior counseling can reduce Type A behavior. Only 12.9 percent of the type A's who changed their behavior had a second heart attack within 4½ years. In comparison, 28.2 percent of the Type A's who did not undergo counseling to change their behavior suffered a second heart attack. In conclusion, Dr. Friedman calls

Type A behavioral counseling "powerful protection" against a second—and possibly fatal—heart attack. Other studies have reported similar results.

Attitude Adjustment

"The key to improving the way you react to stress is to change what you can change, avoid what you can avoid and begin the process of accepting what you can or can't change as reality," says Dr. Price. "Take a situation that occurs so often: A Type A man and his wife are supposed to go out for dinner at 6:00 P.M. At 6:07, she's not ready to leave yet—as usual—and he acts as though it's a capital offense—as usual. But yelling at her to hurry up hasn't worked for 25 years, and it isn't going to work this time. So the only thing the husband can change is his reaction.

"Since most things that annoy us can't be changed, changing the way we react to stressful events is the only alternative," Dr. Price continues. "You can make an obscene gesture to the guy in the pickup truck who cut in front of you in traffic, but what does that change? Learn to shrug it off."

A good time to start practicing Type B behavior is while driving in traffic, says Dr. Price, since driving seems to trigger Type A behavior so readily. One common drill "prescribed" to Type A's is to force themselves to drive in the slower, right-hand lane on highways.

Here are some steps to practice in other situations.

Avoid situations that provoke you. If you can't stand to wait in line at the bank, use the automatic teller machines. If you hate crowded stores, shop during off-peak hours. "Rearrange your schedule to minimize the number of provocations." says Dr. Price.

Lighten up on commitments and obligations. "Type A's have trouble saying no to both demands and opportunities," says Dr. Price. "They like to be in charge of things. And they make an all-out effort at everything they undertake. Such ambition may be very useful in school and early in your career, but it can destroy your marriage, your friendships, your relationships with your children—and your health. Time management and delegating to others are indispensable skills for reform. Use them," says Dr. Price.

Get rid of the battle armor. "Replace 'AIAI'—anger, impatience, aggravation and irritation—with 'ASAS'—acceptance (of trivial mistakes), serenity, affection and self-esteem," says Dr. Price.

Don't expect perfection—from yourself or others. "Type A's typically enter every situation looking for things to criticize, partly to bolster their own self-esteem," says Dr. Price. "And they feel compelled to prove themselves again and again. Learn to appreciate yourself for who you are, not what you can accomplish."

Learn to relax. People who've been addicted to adrenaline all their lives often do not know what it feels like to relax, says Dr. Price. But it's a skill that, like any other, can be learned with practice. "Walk more slowly. Talk more slowly. Don't interrupt others midsentence. Learn the Relaxation Response or another technique. Then use it to control your anger and impatience when something happens that could rile you."

Don't sweat the small stuff. Adopt this motto when faced with traffic delays, minor screw-ups and other annoyances. ("And remember," says one cardiologist, "it's almost *all* small stuff.")

Healthier and Happier

A new attitude may cut your risk of heart attack in half—and double your happiness.

Many Type A's assume that an aggressive attitude is necessary for success. But chances are, successful Type A's got where they are in spite of their disposition, not because of it.

"Constantly finding fault and interrupting others isn't going to get anyone promoted, is it?" remarks Dr. Price. Likewise, the excessive self-involvement typical of achievement-oriented Type A's rarely makes for good "team players." Many reformed Type A's report that they became *more* successful after modifying their counterproductive behavior.

Your family, friends and co-workers, too, will probably welcome the change. It's not easy to live and work with someone who wakes up coiled for battle and stays that way all day, throwing a temper tantrum at the slightest provocation. Countless Type A's have told Dr. Price that learning to back off from stress was worth the effort, and not only because it cut their risk of heart disease. They finally found peace.

Chapter 26

WORRY

Worrying is like a rocking chair—it will give you something to do but it won't get you anywhere.

Baseball may be the nation's favorite sport, but worry seems to be our true national pastime. If we live in California, we worry about earthquakes and freeway backups. If we live in New York, we worry that the IRT express at 14th Street will be stalled in the station again. In between, we worry about our kids' tonsils and our own chances of breast cancer. We worry about money and friends—about not having enough of either.

In his research on worrying, the Pennsylvania State University psychology professor Thomas D. Borkovec, Ph.D., estimates that 15 percent of the population are chronic worriers, those who have spent more than eight hours a day during the last six months worrying. Nonworriers, those who report worrying less than an hour and a half a day and who do not consider worry to be a problem, comprise 30 percent of the population. The majority of folks are moderate worriers and fit between those two extreme groups. They worry between 10 percent and 50 percent of each day and may or may not be troubled by their worrying, according to Dr. Borkovec.

That's a lot of agonizing.

Worries reflect your attempts to mentally cope with your concerns and fears. You can view it as the thinking part of anxiety. While you await the results of your son's college board exams or your own blood test, you experience a sinking feeling in your stomach. Your muscles tighten. And ruminations have taken over your mind, replacing all the unimportant thoughts.

Making Worry Work for You

Worrying can be useful if it helps make you more vigilant or if it helps you take steps to prevent something negative from happening, says Roxane L. Silver, a professor of psychology at Canada's University of Waterloo. So worrying is not a stressful waste of energy if it gets you to quit smoking, have a breast examination or replace your brakes.

And worrying can help prepare you for a dreaded event or outcome. In *Through the Looking Glass,* the Red Queen advised Alice to do her worrying in advance. That way, said the Queen, when the real trouble came along, she would be ready to deal with it calmly. That's roughly what one retired psychology professor reasoned. In *The Work of Worrying,* Irving Janis wrote that worrying lets you rehearse negative possibilities and allows you to prepare for the experience. You'll cope better because you worried.

Some psychologists suggest that instead of worrying in the abstract, you plot out how you'll cope if you do, in fact, fail. Instead of just sobbing over the possibility of not qualifying for a mortgage, for example, you can put your energy into developing alternative housing plans. Planning helps you to take some control. And James W. Pennebaker, Ph.D., a professor of psychology at Southern Methodist University who has conducted studies on worriers, recommends you don't get angry with yourself because you're worrying. Don't beat up on yourself for having negative thoughts, he says, although he admits that's not always easy.

When Your Worry Troubles You

There comes a point, however, when worrying becomes counterproductive—not to mention stressful. It's fruitless to worry when there is no way to prevent your worries from becoming reality, or when the worrying is so pervasive that you are immobilized.

How do you stop these troublesome thoughts? Don't try to simply set them aside, says Daniel M. Wegner, Ph.D., a psychology professor at Trinity University in San Antonio, Texas. In extensive research, Dr. Wegner learned that if you make a point of trying to forget a random thought—much less a worry—it'll return again and again. "In trying repeatedly to avoid a thought, the person processes the thought frequently. As you try to get rid of it, it'll keep coming back," he says. Unconsciously, you're rehearsing the thought and making it more accessible to your conscious mind.

"It's the impulse to set it aside that may create the problem," says Dr. Wegner. Instead, he recommends you *express* your worries. Think them through very carefully and discuss them with friends.

Dr. Pennebaker instructs worriers to write out their concerns. In his research he asked participants to spend a regular part of four or five consecutive days writing about their most upsetting traumas. He found that the writing had a positive impact on their health. It increased the immune functions and, over time, reduced blood pressure.

Psychologically, writing about your worries is likely to help you assimilate them. The writing forces you to organize your thoughts and fears. Dr. Pennebaker says writing for 20 minutes a day is probably sufficient. And don't expect instant results. It may take days or weeks for your worries to ease.

Besides the writing, he suggests you talk about your concerns with someone you trust. And find a creative outlet to take your mind off your woes. Draw, or play a musical instrument, or dance.

The Worry Period

But if you find that strategy doesn't work, you may get some relief by trying a little trick suggested by Dr. Borkovec. Schedule a worry session into your day. Dr. Borkovec reasons that because you are free to worry at nearly any time or place, worrying becomes associated with many situations. So to reduce its frequency, you can limit the conditions in which you allow yourself to worry. Eventually, you will learn to associate it only with limited circumstances. His self-control strategy involves five steps.

1. Establish a half-hour worry period to occur at the same time and place each day. "It may just be a trick," says Dr. Borkovec, "but if you know you have a special time during which you will worry, you may be able to postpone it for that time. If you simply try to postpone it forever, the worries might keep cropping back up."
2. Monitor your worries during the day, identifying as soon as possible the beginning of any episode. "Most worriers don't know they've been worrying until they're well into it. But the earlier you pick up on it, the easier it is to change," says Dr. Borkovec.
3. Once you notice yourself worrying, make the decision to postpone it. Let go of the worries until your worry period.
4. Dislodge the worrisome thoughts by focusing your attention on the task at hand. If you're driving, focus on the environment—the billboards, the cars, the beauty of the landscape. Or try to concentrate on skillful driving.
5. Use your prescheduled "worry period" to work intensely on your woes. You can do one of two things: You can worry, or you can problem-solve. Problem-solving might involve sitting down with a pencil and pen, listing your worries on one side of a sheet of paper and on the other side listing possible solutions that would reduce the source of your worry. If you're worried about taxes, your solution might be to schedule time to work on them (or a list of conceivable sources of money to pay them).

As part of problem-solving, force yourself to take a look at the bottom line on your worry. Ask yourself, "What's the worst thing that can happen?" "Is it survivable?" "What's the probability of that happening based on past evidence?"

If you're worried about the possibility that you won't make any friends in a new town you're about to move to, look to your past experience to get your mind back on track. Remind yourself that you've done okay before and that there's little reason to worry about meeting people in the future. If there *is* reason to worry, if you don't have a strong record of making friends easily, you can spend your worry period figuring out a strategy for making friends—drawing up a list of groups to join or activities to explore.

Dr. Borkovec suggests you determine which worry period activity—worrying or problem-solving—is best for you. Neither is better than the other, he says.

To study the effects of his worry-postponing strategy, Dr. Borkovec tracked a group of chronic worriers who followed his advice during a four-week period and kept careful note of the hours they worried. By taking regular worry breaks, they reduced their overall worry time by an average of 35 percent.

Part 3

MEETING THE CHALLENGE OF LIFE'S MAJOR STRESSORS

Chapter 27

CHANGE

Changes are our only constant. And we are told that even the best of them—marrying the person of our dreams or obtaining the world's best job—are loaded with stress. Everyone is familiar with the numerous symptoms—anxiety, depression, physical illness—that can accompany *negative* changes. But it's not so easy to recognize how those same symptoms may accompany a *positive* event.

So let's take a look at a positive change, moving to a new dream house, to discover what happens behind the scenes.

While moving is voluntary, it involves lots of small events that are now out of your control.

Will the movers damage your treasured possessions?

Will the painters at your dream house arrive on time and do a decent job?

Will the new addition be completed by the holidays?

"No matter how positive it seems, there are aspects of it that are stressful, and you can't foresee every event," says Alex J. Zautra, Ph.D., a psychology professor at Arizona State University who has extensively studied people's responses to life events.

In addition to those out-of-one's-control events, there may be nagging doubts about the decision to move, albeit to a dream house. And there may be remorse about leaving your old neighbors behind, leaving a neighborhood that, in Dr. Zautra's words, "provided a meaningful context."

Managing Positive Change

There's a strategy for managing the stress of such positive changes as the long-awaited move. First, recognize that there will be events that are out of your control. It's an inevitable consequence of any change. So realize that you'll encounter some problems and that any time frame you set for yourself to have odds and ends accomplished or to adjust will likely be overly optimistic.

"People need to know that change in and of itself is intrinsically stressful. It's a shock to the system," says Eric Margenau, Ph.D., a New York psychologist. "Obviously, some change is more traumatic than others, and the stress is proportionate to the degree of change."

The stress of traveling from one place to another, for example, is not as stressful as changing from one job to another. And changing from one job to another is not as stressful as changing from one wife to another.

The important thing is to anticipate the problems and the stress. The stress will be less onerous if you expect it, says Dr. Margenau. And give yourself time and space to make the adjustment—as much as you need.

To gain some control, devise strategies for solving problems that may crop up. If you're moving to your dream house, spend some time developing a good contract with the movers. Make alternative arrangements in case your addition isn't completed by the holidays. Plot a strategy for making friends with your new neighbors.

And recognize the loss—as well as the gain—that you are likely to experience as part of the move, suggests Dr. Zautra. "Arrange to maintain relationships with your old neighbors. Do something special for them. Take the time to say your goodbyes."

After you've acknowledged the stress, don't be critical of yourself because you're experiencing its symptoms, says Dr. Margenau. "Talk about and share the feelings that come about as a result of the stress. That doesn't mean you have to go to a shrink if you're moving or changing jobs, but talk about your new situation with someone. Share your concerns."

Changes beyond Your Control

Changes beyond your control are likely to be more stressful than those you direct. If your apartment house is sold and you are forced to find a new place to live, you'll feel the stress more than you would if you made the decision to move on your own. If you are reassigned to a new job because of a corporate merger, you'll probably feel the stress more than if you chose a reassignment. "If you understand that difference, it tends to mitigate the effect of the change," says Dr. Margenau.

"From a stress standpoint, you're better off making a choice and having it turn out to be the wrong choice than to have the choice made for you, even if it's right. It's much better to make a wrong decision than to be paralyzed by making decisions," he says. But there's a trap: If you make a choice that doesn't work out, don't keep blaming yourself. It intensifies the stress.

And if you face a change for the better that you didn't initiate—say you get promoted when your boss quits his job—don't expect the promotion to necessarily do wonders for your psychological well-being. In his research, Dr. Zautra found that positive life events didn't necessarily have a positive effect on mental health if they were caused by an outside agent.

Avoid "Awfulizing"

Arthur J. Lange, Ed.D., an Irvine, California, psychologist who runs stress-management workshops for organizations, recommends what he calls a "cognitive-attitudinal" (thinking and perspective) approach to managing the stress that accompanies changes.

On the one hand, he says you'll do best if you avoid "awfulizing" (viewing your situation as a catastrophe) or "shoulding" (placing needless demands and blame on yourself or on others). On the other hand, it helps if you avoid the opposite extreme, which is rationalizing (telling yourself you don't care).

Say you get a job promotion. You've got excitement, a new challenge and financial gains. But you've also got the stress of establishing a relationship with a new group of people and the need to perform at a new level.

Dr. Lange recommends you avoid telling yourself that you've "got to" succeed. Instead, tell yourself, "I like getting the promotion. I'm going to do everything I can to succeed. But if it doesn't happen, I'm not going to make myself miserable by worrying about whether I meet the demands." By repeating those words, and by living them, you are putting the situation in perspective, he says.

But he warns you not to go so far that you rationalize. "Don't tell yourself it doesn't bother you to fail if it certainly *does* bother you," he says.

The coping strategy Dr. Lange recommends is the same if your change is a negative one. Say you're fired from your job. Don't make yourself miserable by telling yourself that you "should" have been more diligent or that you "should" have taken steps to prevent being fired. And don't devote endless energy to blaming others. And don't take a vacation. It doesn't help to walk away from the problem, pretending that it doesn't matter to you.

Instead, he suggests you repeat the following "functional thinking," as he calls it.

"I'd like not to have lost my job."

"I'd like to get a new one."

"I'd like to make a smooth transition, but I'm not going to berate myself, put myself down, if it doesn't work."

Dr. Lange says that people "awfulize," "should," and rationalize thousands of times a day. You may be able to counter the effects of those destructive thought patterns by repeating the functional thinking so frequently that it eventually becomes your natural response.

The Most Stressful Changes

On the oft-referred-to scale of measuring stress (Holmes and Rahe's "Schedule of Recent Life Events"), 43 life events are ranked in order of their approximate level of stress. At the top of the list is "death of a spouse." Anyone who has lost a spouse will agree to the impact of such a trauma, but Dr. Zautra draws the distinction between deaths that are anticipated and those that are not. "In the case of older adults, a death is not always unexpected, and older people who anticipate a death often recover relatively quickly. It's the untimely deaths that are often the most difficult," he says.

In either case, Dr. Zautra says you should not rush the grieving process. Don't set a date by which you'll be over it. And take small steps to fill the void in your life. No one can replace your spouse, so you may be setting yourself up for disappointment if you look for a substitute. But others certainly can fill some of the roles your spouse played in your life. And have faith in yourself to endure the grieving, he says, even if your relationship was full of conflicts and you are burdened by guilt feelings and remorse that you can't tell your partner you are sorry. "Human beings are marvelously adaptive creatures. We can put our lives and our past in perspective," says Dr. Zautra.

And while friends and family can help you weather such a major change, you can't rely exclusively on them. "Lack of support can hurt when missed," writes Dr. Zautra in a study on the subject. "[But] its presence does little to help. The underlying active agent in coping with stress is the person and not the support network."

Predicting How You'll Cope

When psychologists talk of "transitions," they are referring to the movement from one stage of life to another. How one is able to cope has less to do with the transition itself—it could be the birth of a first child or the decision to retire—than it does with how much the transition alters the person's roles, relationships, routines and assumptions, according to Nancy K. Schlossberg, Ed.D., a professor in the Counseling Department of the University of Maryland and author of *Counseling Adults in Transition.* A transition can even be a nonevent such as realizing you'll never get promoted or realizing you'll never get pregnant.

Dr. Schlossberg says that how well you handle a transition may be determined by the resources and deficits you have in four areas. She calls them Situation, Self, Supports and Strategies. She suggests you take advantage of your resources in those areas and shore up the deficits.

Situation involves whether you see the transition as positive or negative, expected or unexpected; whether it came at a good or bad time; whether it was voluntary or not; whether it is at its beginning, middle or end; and whether the transition is personal or a reaction to someone else's.

Self involves your previous experience in coping with transitions, your belief in the existence of options, and your optimism (or lack thereof).

Supports can be both financial and emotional, and from friends, family or co-workers.

Strategies can be for changing the situation or the meaning of the situation, or for managing the stress.

In an article for *Psychology Today,* Dr. Schlossberg wrote, "By systematically sizing up transitions and our own resources for dealing with them, we can learn how to build on our strength, cut our losses—and even grow in the process."

One of the methods Dr. Schlossberg suggests is developing a ritual around transitions, even those that involve nonevents. So she has already planned her strategy for one such transition in her own life. If Dr. Schlossberg fails to find a publisher willing to accept her book on transitions after a few years of trying, she plans to throw a "nonbook" party. "People throw book parties when they *get* their books published. I would throw one if I *never* get it published. That would make it an official nonevent, closing it forever," she says. "It's my way of dealing with the transition."

Chapter 28

DIVORCE AND SEPARATION

According to one widely consulted stress rating scale, only the death of a spouse ranks higher than divorce and marital separation as a major cause of stress. No wonder. After all, what is divorce but the death of a relationship, triggering not only a sense of emotional loss but the added burdens of guilt, depression, anger and feelings of betrayal? And, much like the death of a spouse, divorce catapults one into chaos, necessitating a change in living arrangements, income, standard of living and access to children—all stressful adjustments.

Nothing seems routine after divorce. Marital breakup is destined, it seems, to turn life into a melodrama fraught with uncertainty. What part do you play? Good guy? Rat? Martyr? What's going to happen next?

No divorce is stress free. If you initiate the break, the guilt can devastate you. If your spouse initiates the divorce, hours of shock and disbelief give way to weeks of anger, which, in turn, can stretch out into months—and sometimes years—of bitterness and depression. Even the death of a loved one does not pummel the ego the way divorce can. When your marriage dies, the part of you that was Mr. or Mrs."John Doe" dies, too.

Digging Out from under an Avalanche of Stress

"Divorce can cause more stress than the death of a spouse," says Constance Ahrons, Ph.D., associate director of the Marriage and Family Therapy Program at the University of Southern California in Los Angeles, "because if your spouse dies, you have the immediate and often continued support of family and friends. Your self-image doesn't suffer. But with divorce, the stress *escalates* with the chain of events and circumstances that evolve." If you and your ex-spouse fight over child custody, for instance, or try to get the "best" deal in divorce court, stress becomes even more intense. And divorce, like the death of a spouse, all too often causes or coincides with other stressful life events, leading to what Dr. Ahrons calls "stress pileup."

"Take a middle-aged woman whose husband leaves her for a younger woman," says Dr. Ahrons. "Like a widow, she feels the stress of living alone, possibly combined with feelings of growing old and watching her grown children leave home. She may also have to face new career demands. But combined with all that is the added humiliation of being publicly rejected for another."

Not unexpectedly, this stress pileup takes a considerable toll on health. "There is a growing body of evidence that marital disruption (separation or divorce) constitutes a severe stress and that the consequences of that stress can be seen in a surprisingly wide variety of physical and emotional disorders," say Bernard L. Bloom, Ph.D., and his colleagues in an article published in *Psychological Bulletin.*

All told, the cost of divorce, in terms of money, emotions and health, can be devastating. What do you do when not only the rug but the floor and the foundation are pulled out from under you?

While separation and divorce are never easy—unless there wasn't much of a marriage to begin with—you can survive with your self-esteem intact, without going bankrupt emotionally or financially. Coping strategies begin early on, when you find yourself entertaining thoughts of divorce or when you first realize that your marriage is not only in trouble but finished. Psychologists we consulted had plenty of practical advice for coping with the stress of divorce proceedings—and for helping yourself recover emotionally when the divorce is final.

'Til Death Do Us Part (Maybe)

Divorce doesn't just happen; it evolves. For many couples, legal separation merely finalizes an emotional split that occurred months or years earlier. For some, divorce is unquestionably the way out. They're convinced that life apart couldn't possibly be worse than life together. But for many, the decision to divorce isn't so clear-cut.

"Sexual differences, change in finances, loss of a job, a career move, changing leisure interests can all stress a marriage," says Dr. Bloom, who's headed several studies of why marriages fail. "Some couples end up divorced, others stay married."

Agonizing over whether or not to break up your marriage can be—and usually is—pure hell. Wrestling with ambivalence—and your conscience—may be the worst part of separation. To decide *if* you should get a divorce, it helps to think about *why* you are considering divorce.

Judith S. Wallerstein, Ph.D., executive director of the Center for the Family in Transition, Corte Madera, California, has found that the decision to divorce usually falls into one of four categories.

Divorce as a rational solution. That is, divorce that is undertaken to undo an unhappy marriage considered unlikely to change, representing the culmination of years of visible unhappiness in which divorce had long been considered.

Divorce as a stress-related response. "Divorces occur in families where marital unhappiness had not been a special source of concern to either partner," writes Dr. Wallerstein in her book, *Surviving the Breakup: How Children and Parents Cope with Divorce.* "Rather, the decision to divorce followed some stressful experience outside the marriage which was profoundly upsetting to the person who then initiated the move toward divorce. The response to the external stress, in other words, ricocheted into the family arena." Examples of outside stresses that can influence divorce include the death of a grandparent, the diagnosis of a life-threatening illness, or a crippling accident to a child, says Dr. Wallerstein.

Why do events that mobilize some families, drawing members together in mutual support, rupture others?

"The psychological mechanisms that lead from such stress to divorce can be explained by the stressed person's need to take flight to ward off the depression that threatens to overwhelm him or her," explains Dr. Wallerstein. "One or both parents escape from each other and run from the marriage in a desperate effort to avoid the unbearable memory of the tragedy and so avert the threatened depression."

Impulsive divorces. Some divorces are initiated without really considering the consequences. A good example is the spouse who sues for divorce in outrage and jealousy in order to punish a partner who's been unfaithful or to secretly win back the partner. More often than not, says Dr. Wallerstein, the strategy fails, leaving the aggrieved partner raging for years.

Decisions encouraged by others. If marital distress is obviously to blame for physical symptoms or emotional distress, psychotherapists or physicians suggest divorce, says Dr. Wallerstein.

Generally, though, only you can decide whether you're better off unhappily married or unhappily divorced—undoubtedly one of the hardest decisions anyone can face in life.

"Yes, seeking divorce is a very emotional decision," says Dr. Ahrons. "You can start by asking yourself, 'Am I divorcing the person or the marriage?' Many young adults, married only a year or two, for example, split up because they realize they made a wrong choice—either they chose the wrong mate or married life wasn't for them. The mistake may become obvious rather quickly and they decide to get out before investing more time in the marriage or having children."

For people who've been married longer, the decision is usually harder. "Motivation to continue is the key to whether a marriage will end or not," says Ann Leahy, a social worker and co-owner of the Marriage and Family Institute, a private clinic in the Washington, D.C., area. "Making the decision comes down to asking two questions: 'Am I interested in continuing this relationship or not?' and 'Are there enough positive benefits to enable [me] to live with the problems?' Those kinds of questions take a lot of self-knowledge, but the answers help people to decide whether to stay married or to split up."

Mediation Is Less Stressful than Confrontation

Once the decision to split has been made, more practical questions arise. Who will live where? Who gets the kids, the good car, the stereo? If you and your spouse take the customary, adversarial approach, you hire lawyers and square off over division of property, child custody and support, parental visitation rights, spousal support, tax considerations and responsibility for debts. Sad to say, money and children become the emotional currency of adversarial divorce. You find yourself caught up in a no-turning-back-now legal power struggle in which each spouse fights bitterly for all he or she can get. Adversarial divorce can make the unhappiest of marriages look like a picnic by comparison.

Few couples realize they have any choice, so they don their armor and sally forth, prepared for all-out war, when in fact there is a rational, humane alternative to adversarial—i.e., lawyer-negotiated—divorce. Mediation is a process of creative bargaining, facilitated by a neutral third party, by which divorcing couples work out a mutually agreeable legal arrangement that's fair and equitable to both sides.

Unlike adversarial divorce, in which spouses are instructed to not speak to each other, spouses themselves negotiate their needs. The mediator is not the legal representative of either party but rather a trained professional (family counselor, psychologist, social worker or attorney) who sugggests various available arrangements to be explored. These arrangements are based not so much on emotion-fueled demands but on the legitimate needs and resources of each spouse.

As yet, only 3 to 4 percent of the divorces in this country are settled through mediation, but experience shows that, conducted in good faith, mediation minimizes the tension and crossfire generated by a legal power struggle. Mediation focuses, instead, on constructive problem-solving, leaving fewer battle scars for all concerned.

In their book, *Parting Sense: A Complete Guide to Divorce Mediation*, attorney Jack J. Shapiro and family therapist Marla S. Caplan point out six advantages of mediation over adversarial divorce.

It is less costly. Mediation runs roughly between $500 and $1,000, compared with $3,000 to $5,000 for an adversarial divorce involving children along with accumulated property and other encumbrances.

It is less time-consuming. Mediation can take as little as two or three months, versus six months to one or two years for full litigation.

It is confidential. Neither party is forced to blame the other for divorce, and you don't have to air your unpleasantness in court.

It causes less wear-and-tear on children. Mediation avoids the emotional blackmail of a long, drawn-out custody battle. "It also reduces the traumatic period of time between the child's first recognition that his or her family is being torn apart and the moment when he or she can begin to see how it will be put back together again," say Shapiro and Caplan. "That reassuring moment comes only when custody agreements are clear, living arrangements are established and the child can begin to predict his future."

It eases financial hardship and distress. More often than not, divorce leaves both parties poorer, but surveys show that women over 40 who've never worked full-time outside the home are hardest hit. Shapiro and Caplan have found that mediation creates the foundation for easier and more organized financial planning, especially for the spouse with the lower income. What's more, statistics indicate that absent parents are more apt to adhere to mediated agreements regarding child support than those that result from adversarial agreements. "Millions of dollars each year are not paid and spouses are spending large sums of money on attorney fees to collect these unpaid support obligations, often without success," say Shapiro and Caplan.

It forestalls future problems. "Couples are more apt to adhere to a mediated agreement which they, not lawyers, made, and are less likely to return to court, time and again, to modify the settlement—and modify the modifications," say Shapiro and Caplan.

If you and your spouse couldn't get along during your marriage, you may have trouble imagining yourselves sitting down during divorce mediation and calmly discussing such highly charged subjects as finances and child rearing. But like the Geneva Strategic Arms Limitation Talks, mediation works when both sides are aware of the unpleasant alternatives.

"It's not a question of getting along," says Shapiro. "It's a matter of being able to sit in the same room and talk to each other through the mediator, in a neutral environment. Together, the mediator and the environment facilitate communication in ways the couple could never hope to communicate before.

"Also, knowing the alternative—what adversarial divorce involves and the enormous amount of time, money and emotional strain they're saving themselves—is a *big* incentive to cooperate," says Shapiro. If emotions are running too high to permit productive discussion in the same room together, you can try shuttle mediation, in which the mediator meets with the husband, then the wife (or vice-versa) and so forth.

No marriage ends painlessly, but Shapiro and Caplan say that mediation clearly reduces the conflict that is otherwise present in adversarial divorce. "Mediation has enormous emotional and practical advantages over adversarial divorce," they write, "and is available to any couple who can resist the temptation to use divorce as a means of recrimination and punishment."

Marriage counselors can sometimes recommend a divorce mediator. Shapiro and Caplan suggest that when considering a mediator, couples should look for someone with a strong professional background in either law or social sciences and substantial mediation experience. "Ask how many divorces he or she has mediated and whether any previous clients are willing to discuss their mediation experience. Also, it's in the interests of each party to have the settlement agreement reviewed by a legal attorney before signing."

A Bright Tomorrow, but What about Today?

Mediation may address your economic needs, but what about your emotional needs? Like the death of a spouse, divorce can leave you feeling lonelier than you've ever felt in your life. But loneliness is only one of many emotions triggered, for divorce is a hydra-headed antagonist. You're probably also feeling resentful, scared, depressed, hostile—and paralyzed with anxiety and tension. Motivation evaporates. Preparing meals once shared with a spouse may turn from a source of inner satisfaction to a task done simply to survive. Activities once pursued together no longer seem worth doing. Why think about taking a vacation if you can't share it? Why plant the garden this spring if no one is nearby to enjoy it? Why get out of bed at all? Death may result in loss of a spouse, but divorce results in loss of a dream.

Your task, if you are to survive with your self-esteem and sanity intact, is to grapple with the emotions one at a time. Only then can you leave your divorce behind and get on with life.

First-Aid for Divorce Trauma

Don't wait until your marriage is officially over to start nursing your bruised psyche back to health. But deal with one emotional problem at a time, as they strike.

Friends make good shock absorbers. The first reaction to sudden loss is disbelief, shock, numbness. Like a steelworker suddenly learning that the factory is closing, you may find yourself moving trancelike through the day—or putting yourself into a funk with alcohol or drugs.

"How you cope with divorce is related to how you cope with other crises," says Dr. Ahrons. "If somebody routinely reacts to stress by turning to alcohol or drugs, that's how they tend to react to divorce. But if they usually turn to close friends in a crisis, that's how they cope with divorce."

In fact, confiding in others is a legitimate way to deal with the initial feelings of I-can't-believe-this-is-happening-to-me.

"First of all, it's important to realize that divorce no longer carries the stigma it once did, mainly because so many people go through it," says Dr. Ahrons. "Knowing that makes it easier to turn to friends for support."

Don't get stuck in the "anger" phase. "If you hang on to anger and keep it alive longer than necessary, what you are really doing is masking or delaying depression," says Dr. Ahrons. "Granted, it's easier to be angry at a target—your ex—than to review your life together and give in to feelings of sadness and loss. Anger can keep you going but you won't adjust. Eventually, you have to deal with sadness to come out with a balanced view of the breakup. If you negate the sadness, you negate a big part of yourself."

Grieving is normal—and healthy. "Bereavement entails the work of emotionally disengaging yourself from your marriage partner, whether separated by death or divorce," explains Dr. Ahrons. "The person who initiates the divorce goes through this bereavement beforehand, while contemplating his or her decision. For the person left, bereavement is similar to mourning for a deceased spouse—with one big difference: The 'dearly departed' is still around and may have to be dealt with during the divorce procedure and possibly later, especially if you share child custody. So your grief is reactivated again and again.

"Allow yourself to feel pain," says Dr. Ahrons. "Divorce is painful enough; trying to deny the pain only makes it worse."

Don't pretend your "ex" doesn't exist. "If you've been married for 20 years you may be feeling angry, but chances are it wasn't all bad. You share a lot of experiences, memories, family and kinship ties that aren't severed with the divorce.

"What's more, it's not healthy to try to sever all ties," continues Dr. Ahrons. "We have a stereotypical idea that says divorce cuts all ties between two people. But in my experience, divorced people continue to have some kind of relationship, especially if children are involved. I see a pattern: People relate to their ex in much the same way they relate to other significant people in their past. People who maintain friendships with old suitors or high school classmates tend to continue to relate to their ex in some new way, despite the anger and conflict that broke the marriage.

"You almost have to build a new relationship, if only in your mind," says Dr. Ahrons. "It's unhealthy to have been married to someone and to have children together and then pretend they don't exist. Denying the relationship is like tearing 20 chapters out of the middle of your life and throwing them away."

Give yourself time. Divorce takes longer to get over than a bad haircut. Give yourself a couple of years to heal, says Dr. Ahrons. "I've found that it takes people an average of two years after a divorce before people start to feel excited about life and regain a sense of wholeness. Don't rush yourself."

Use divorce as an opportunity to improve your life. "For some, getting divorced is a growth period, a time to explore various options and take steps to make changes in your life that perhaps you should have made anyway," says Dr. Ahrons.

Resist any temptation to leave town, quit your job or make other rash decisions. Moving takes a lot of energy and would put extra strain on your already disrupted life. "Resist the urge to 'run away,' " says Dr. Ahrons. "If you move, you'll be anonymous. Stay where you are, where you have friends, where you know who the reliable dry cleaners, hairstylists and auto mechanics are, to maintain what continuity is left in your life."

Don't rush into a new relationship. "Work out your bad feelings about the divorce before you rush into a new relationship," advises Dr. Ahrons. In other words, resolve one relationship before getting entangled in another.

Consider counseling if you feel you can't go it alone. Surveys indicate that separated or divorced individuals seek mental health care more than single or married folks—usually within the year surrounding separation.

"Psychological counseling isn't always necessary after divorce, but it can certainly help, especially in finding out what went wrong with the marriage, what part each played in the breakup," says Dr. Ahrons. "Divorce is rarely one-sided, even when it seems to be.

"Once their anger has subsided, some ex-spouses go into counseling together, especially if they still have to confer over children." Think of divorce counseling as post-mortem, to find out what killed the relationship and prevent future heartbreak.

In fact, counseling can reduce the emotional stress generated by divorce during mediation, as each issue is grappled with, says Shapiro.

"Sometimes counseling is imperative," says Dr. Ahrons. "If you're depressed for more than six months, if you're abusing alcohol or drugs or having suicidal thoughts because of divorce, you may need professional help to work things out.

"Like it or not, divorce is now a normal part of life," says Dr. Ahrons. "Yet it's important to realize that divorce is not the same for everyone. Divorce means different things at different stages of a marriage or at different ages. An early divorce is far easier to survive than a midlife divorce," she says, "mainly because it's easier to resume a single lifestyle if you've only been married a year or two. But midlife divorce is quite complex. We lose not only a partner but a whole way of life. We have to allow ourselves time for recovery."

Chapter 29

ELDERLY PARENTS

People—*parents*—are living longer. That's fact. But not all seniors become wards of their children, or anyone else. Some are entirely capable of handling their own affairs throughout their lives.

But when responsibility for parents does fall on members of the family (typically female members), experts say there are ways of handling—and sharing—this added responsibility to keep the stress to a minimum.

Don't take on needless responsibility. Even if your parents are aging and ill, they still might be perfectly capable of taking care of themselves, says Lillian Troll, Ph.D., a psychologist in San Francisco. "Too many adult children feel they have to make decisions for their parents," she says.

"I've often had 20-year-olds in my classes who wish to study gerontology because they want to take care of their parents—and their parents turn out to be only 40 years old," says the professor emeritus from Rutgers University, who is currently with the University of California.

Attributing such zeal to "a culture that makes younger generations feel superior to older generations," Dr. Troll advises you take on the role of caregiver only if absolutely necessary.

Define your responsibility. If caregiving is necessary, don't panic, says Nancy Schlossberg, Ed.D., professor of counseling at the University of Maryland. She says the stress that often comes with caring for one's parents is largely anxiety about entering an unknown world.

"We have no norms in our society for this," says Dr. Schlossberg, because past generations rarely had to deal with the "problem" of parents living into their seventies, eighties and beyond.

Dr. Schlossberg suggests the first thing you do, should you find yourself in the caregiver role, is to go through what she terms "the four S's"—Situation, Self, Supports and Strategy.

First, look at the *Situation:* Just how much care does your parent need? Is he mobile? Can he dress? Then consider your *Self:* How much free time do you have? How well do you generally cope with stress? Are you going through

131

other transitions in your life right now? Next consider your *Supports:* How much money is there? Will brother and sister help out? What help is available in your community? Only after you've answered these questions can you begin to really plan a *Strategy.*

Dr. Schlossberg believes that as you brainstorm through the four S's—and get as many friends and relatives as you can to brainstorm with you—your stress will dissipate as you begin to discover options for your aging parents, some of which you may never have known existed.

Enlist the help of others. You've decided your parent needs help getting by. Whether you decide to bring him into your home, to hire a professional caregiver or to find a retirement community or nursing home, the key to keeping your sanity, says Louise Fradkin, co-founder of Children of Aging Parents, is "not to try to do it all yourself."

Fradkin cares for her 91-year-old mother, but not alone. From 7:15 in the morning, when the bus picks her up, to 4:30 in the afternoon, when the same bus drops her off, Fradkin's mother is cared for at a professional adult day care center. She sings, does arts and crafts and exercises, while Fradkin is free to pursue her own life.

"As a caregiver," says Fradkin, "you have to create your own job description."

Fradkin's option to use an adult day care center (one may or may not be available in your community) gives her free time and gives her mother something to do. In other words, she beat two of the greatest parent-care stressors—full-time caregiving and an idle, bored parent—in one step, according to Steven Lovett, Ph.D., coordinator of the Caregiver Project, Center for the Study of Psychotherapy and Aging at the Veterans Administration Medical Center in Palo Alto, California.

Take a break. "Caregivers often don't take enough time out for themselves," says Dr. Lovett, "and that's a real risk because there's then nothing to offset the stress they're bound to feel." He suggests the most important thing you can do to alleviate the stress of caregiving is "to make sure you get out of the house, and stay involved in the activities you were involved in before."

Counter boredom. Similarly, Dr. Lovett believes it is extremely important for your elderly parent to have activities, too—for *your* peace of mind. He says that some elderly parents can become difficult, either nagging you about your housekeeping all of the time or reminding you ten times a day how much you loved broccoli as a kid.

"Nagging and living in the past can be products of boredom," says Dr. Lovett. So can "televisionitis." He cautions, however, that before pushing mom into a physical activity, you should explore why she is so inactive. "Her not being active may be due to something like bunions, which can be treated," he says.

Assistance at Your Fingertips

Most experts agree that the most stressful thing for you as caregiver is to try to shoulder the burden alone. You don't have to.

A Parent Is Not a Child

"Caring for a parent is a lot different than caring for a child," says Lillian Troll, Ph.D., author of *Family Issues in Current Gerontology*. "Caring for a parent is imbued with family history."

In other words, if there were family troubles when you lived together 40 years ago, they may still be there today—perhaps magnified through time. Dr. Troll says we should be open to seeking professional family counseling should ancient bugaboos crop up.

Thelma Rutherford of Washington, D.C., is herself an aging parent (grandparent and great-grandparent). She is 79. Although still very much in charge of her own life, years as a social worker and the experiences of her contemporaries have given Rutherford insight into how elderly parents should be cared for. She advises:

• Don't make company out of your parent. If your mom lives with you—and she's physically able to work—put her to work.

• Don't remind your parents how much they once did for you. Tit-for-tat talk will make them feel you are caring out of obligation, not love.

• If a parent nags, complains or reminisces too much, let it go in one ear and out the other.

• Remember that you, too, will grow old. Be patient. Your parents are used to being independent. As stressed as you feel at times, consider how stressed they feel with their new-found dependence.

Children of Aging Parents, based in Levittown, Pennsylvania, can give you seasoned advice and help you set up a local support group for sharing your problems with other caregivers. Call (215) 945-6900, or send a business-size, self-addressed, stamped envelope with two first-class stamps to Children of Aging Parents, 2761 Trenton Road, Levittown, PA 19056.

Many churches, civic groups, companies and local governments offer varying kinds of assistance for the elderly. Check with your friends, colleagues, neighbors and local librarian. (Your librarian can also refer you to books offering legal and medical advice for proper caregiving.)

The American Association of Retired Persons (AARP) in Washington, D.C., can also be very helpful. Call (202) 728-4300, or write AARP, 1909 K Street NW, Washington, DC 20049.

If you live in one part of the country, say Miami, and your aging parent lives in another, say Niagara Falls, consider contacting American Aging Network Services, a referral service for "care managers"—people who live near your parent and who, for a fee, will do everything you can't do from 3,000 miles away. Fees range from $30 to $60 an hour. Call (212) 675-2135, or write American Aging Network Services, 62 Pierrepont Street, New York, NY 11201.

Caring for elderly parents while managing kids and perhaps a career may always make you feel a little sandwiched, but you can learn to hold down the stress.

Chapter 30

GRIEF

Our world is studded with monuments to grief. One of its most beautiful buildings, the Taj Mahal, was built by a grieving maharajah in memory of his young, dead wife. The sun never sets on the numerous memorials Queen Victoria dedicated to her beloved Albert. In our contemporary culture, however, grieving is considered a somewhat overblown emotion—even a waste of time. Rather, we tend to admire the stoicism of mourners who don't shed tears at funerals and people who "get on with the business of life" despite all sorts of personal trauma. Recent research suggests, however, that we should not be so quick to dispatch our grief. Psychologists say our cultural mind-set makes losing a loved one, for example, even more stressful than if we allowed ourselves to grieve, and places added burdens on bereaved people.

"Formal psychiatry suggests that 'uncomplicated bereavement' should be over and done with in two months. That's ridiculous," says Gerald Koocher, Ph.D., chief psychologist at Children's Hospital in Boston and an expert on the emotional repercussions of grief. "A person can grieve continuously for a loved one for as long as two years, and intermittently for many years after. There is nothing wrong or unhealthy about it."

"In our society, we think a person who isn't 'back to normal' four to six weeks after a loss is somehow sick or wallowing in self-pity," says Stephen Goldston, Ed.D., a psychologist who has carried out a great deal of research on bereavement. "This places a burden on grieving people, who then think they should 'snap out of it' after a few weeks. But people just can't recover from a major loss that quickly. And when they don't, they are made to feel abnormal or guilty about experiencing normal, understandable emotions. In fact, it takes most people a full year to resume life after bereavement, and it can take as long as three. They find ways to cope with a loss themselves, at their own pace. In fact, that is really the only way to handle grief."

134

The Spectrum of Grief

"Because we deny death and grief, most people don't know that bereavement unleashes a whole spectrum of emotions," notes Dr. Goldston. Feeling lost, sad and lonely during bereavement doesn't surprise most people. Feeling angry and guilty does. But these emotions too are part of grief."

"Many people are trapped by the myth that you must not speak or think ill of the dead. They feel tremendous guilt about being angry with the dead person for leaving them, or jealous that they have found peace, or oblivion, from worldly cares," says one psychologist. "Or they become obsessed with memories of little injustices they did to the dead person while they were alive. These are normal reactions. They happen when you are so wrapped up in your loss you can't think of anything else. With time, most people regain their sense of proportion, and realize the dead person didn't leave them on purpose, or to punish them."

One phenomenon that alarms grieving people terribly is aural or visual hallucinations of the dead person. "You'll be sitting in a room and imagine you hear the dead person's voice," says Dr. Koocher. "Or drive down a familiar street and think you see them. Bereaved people can be terrified that they're going crazy. They're not. This phenomenon is normal and common."

Pain that mimics the final illness of a loved one also can frighten a bereaved person and send them to the doctor convinced they, too, are dying. "Chest pains when a husband died of a heart attack, or abdominal pain when the person succumbed to colon cancer are frequent occurrences," reports Dr. Goldston. "A sensitive physician will discuss this with a bereaved patient before launching into a full-scale medical investigation. On the other hand, an examination can reassure a person that they are in fact healthy, and let them deal with their grief without worrying about placing a new burden on their family."

In the past decade there has been much research into the impact of bereavement on the immune system, but the findings are preliminary and tentative, according to Dr. Koocher. Some studies have indicated that people who lose a spouse are more likely to develop serious illnesses themselves in the year after their loss. "Does bereavement itself cause a depression of the immune system? Or is it the stresses associated with dealing with illness, death and its aftermath, like settling the dead person's estate, that cause these illnesses? Right now, there is no clear answer," he says.

Even if the exact reason for illness in bereaved people is unknown, there are still good arguments for taking extra good care of yourself after the loss of a loved one. Eat regular, nourishing meals. Exercise is a proven tonic for depression. Don't attempt to drown your sorrows in alcohol or blur them with drugs. A report on bereavement done in connection with the National Research Council says many experts recommend caution in prescribing minor tranquilizers, sleeping pills, antidepressants or other similar medications for people who have suffered a loss. The researchers noted that there have been no studies or other scientific evidence of the effectiveness of medication for coping with normal grief, and the danger of developing a dependence is very real.

Seeking Support

A person in mourning needs emotional support. It is vital not only immediately after a death but also in the months that follow. Both Dr. Koocher and Dr. Goldston have conducted studies in "grief intervention" which suggest the crucial time in bereavement is about two months later, when the shock has worn off and people are making their first tentative steps back into the world. Ironically, this time comes just when others who have extended their sympathy assume their support is no longer required. Those who have suffered a loss may need to ask for help, or may need someone to talk to. Often the best help comes from others who have experienced a similar tragedy.

One self-help and support source is the Widowed Persons Service program run by the American Association of Retired Persons (AARP). The AARP trains widowed volunteers of both genders and all ages to be "outreach" volunteers. Once back in their own communities, they contact widowed people and offer their support. Although the focus of the program is one-on-one, there are also group meetings.

For more information about the Widowed Persons Service, call the American Association of Retired Persons at (202) 728–4370, or write AARP, 1909 K Street NW, Washington, DC 20049.

Bereavement is a time to open or strengthen communications within your family. "People avoid talking about a dead loved one or how they feel about a loss because that usually causes tears, and that is perceived as stressful," says Dr. Koocher. "But talking and crying are helpful in coping with grief."

Some Guidelines for Coping

Although there is no pat formula for dealing with the stress and grief that come after the death of a loved one, the experts agree there are steps to take that can help people to cope.

"It is possible to prepare for bereavement," says Dr. Goldston. "A mature person realizes that life is a series of attachments, losses and reattachments. Accepting that can help you face a major loss without overwhelming despair." To further prepare, Dr. Koocher urges people faced with an imminent death to say the things they have always wanted to say to the dying person.

Afterward, they emphasize, don't expect to get over the experience quickly, even though society expects that you should. It is very important not to isolate yourself. Realize that you need support and seek it, from family, friends, clergy or self-help groups. Don't be ashamed to cry—tears provide emotional release and may even wash away some of the chemicals that stress builds up in our bodies. Expect to have overwhelming flare-ups of grief— holidays, birthdays and anniversaries can bring back powerful memories. Resume your daily routine when you feel up to it. Making a productive contribution to the world can be a source of comfort by helping you realize that life is going on. Recognize the signs of needing professional help, such as severe or prolonged depression, suicidal thoughts, an inability to find pleasure in anything, smoking or drinking too much, persistent pains or illnesses.

A Time to Cry, a Time to Grow

At some time, everyone faces the bleakness of bereavement. And for that we should be grateful, because if we grieve, it means we loved. The death of one who is dear opens up a black pit of emptiness that can seem inescapable and everlasting. By taking the time to grieve and by acknowledging death, we can become reconciled to our loss. With that accomplished, we then can move on to a full and happy life.

Chapter 31

HOSPITALIZATION AND ILLNESS

A few days before his 60th birthday, Joe had a heart attack. Not a massive one, but cause enough for hospitalization. His wife, children and grandchildren—not ones to let a little matter of heart disease get in the way of a family celebration—persuaded an understanding nurse or two to look the other way while they smuggled birthday cake and party hats up to Joe's room. Counting five grandchildren and a patient with a broken leg in the next bed, 21 people helped Joe celebrate his birthday—and forget about his ailing heart for the time being.

No one would be so naive as to imply that hospitalization can always be turned into a party. Treatment for illness or injury is inherently stressful. But a stint in the hospital doesn't have to be all doom-and-gloom, either.

How to Take the Fear and Anxiety Out of Your Hospital Stay

"Much stress experienced by hospital patients is caused by feeling a lack of control," says Lynda Denton Lane, R.N., a clinical nurse specialist in the Department of Cardiovascular Physiology, University of Texas Health Sciences Center, Dallas. "But there are a number of ways to restore some control, thereby relieving much of that stress."

Learn about your medical problem and its treatment. A number of studies have suggested that the more psychologically prepared you are for hospital treatments, the less traumatic the experience. In one study, published in the *Journal of Stress*, a psychologist divided 80 women who were undergoing minor gynecological surgery into three groups: One group received rou-

138

tine care and nothing more, one received routine care and read a booklet briefly describing hospital procedure, and one received routine care and a highly informative booklet. Women in the third group experienced less fear and anxiety before the operation. Their heart rate and blood pressure were also lower. Plus, they reported less postoperative pain and recovered faster in the hospital. They also were able to resume normal activities sooner than the other women.

Similar studies have found that candidates for hernia repair, cardiac catheterization and other nonemergency procedures who received information, emotional support and psychological counseling experienced less distress or needed fewer painkillers or sedatives than those who did not.

"Patient education is the key to de-stressing medical and surgical procedures," says Lane.

Ask questions. If you don't understand what is being done for you or why, don't hesitate to speak up.

"In the past, if a patient questioned anything—'Why do I have to use a bedpan?' 'How much medicine am I taking?' or 'Why won't you tell me my temperature?'—the nurse simply stated, 'Doctor's orders' and that was that," says Elizabeth Hahn Winslow, R.N., Ph.D., assistant professor of nursing at the University of Texas at Arlington School of Nursing. It was very much a parent/child sort of relationship.

"One big change in medical care is that nurses now view themselves as patient advocates rather than simply physician assistants," says Lane.

"The squeaky wheel gets the grease—or in this case, reassurance," quips Dr. Winslow. "The more assertive a patient is, the better able they'll be to take care of themselves."

Find out what the procedures you're about to experience will feel like. A number of studies have suggested that knowing what to expect reduces fear, anxiety and pain. "If a nurse says she's going to give you a shot, ideally, she should prepare you for what to expect by saying something like, 'I'm going to wipe your skin with a cool cotton swab; then you'll feel a burning sensation that will last a second or two,' " says Lane. "If it makes you feel better, prompt the nurse for the information."

Also, the less anxious you are before surgery, the less anesthesia you may need.

Less Pain, Less Stress

One of the biggest fears patients have is that they will suffer unrelieved pain after surgery, waiting hours between doses of pain medication. They also worry that doctors or nurses won't believe them if they say their pain medicine isn't helping. Rest assured, though: Pain relief is a mutual goal for doctors, nurse and patients alike.

If necessary, ask for an adjustment in your pain medication. "Nurses are governed largely by doctor's orders, but there is some degree of flexibility," says Lane. "Nurses *can* make you more comfortable. Giving aspirin or Tylenol in addition to Demerol, for example, can make pain relief more complete and longer lasting."

Ask your doctor about "patient-controlled analgesia." In many hospitals, doctors allow postsurgery patients to control their own painkillers—without risk of overdose—by means of a specially designed dispenser attached to an intravenous line.

"The nurse sets the IV [intravenous] pump to deliver a certain amount of painkiller per hour, based on the doctor's prescription," explains Cynthia Pastorino, R.N., clinical nurse specialist at Methodist Medical Center, Dallas. "If a patient feels the medication wearing off, all he or she has to do is push a button to release more.

"This alternative method of pain relief has some definite advantages," says Pastorino. "The patient is in control; the IV delivers the medication instantly, without the delay of calling the nurse, asking for more medication and waiting until she unlocks the 'medicine chest' and returns with the medicine; best of all, blood levels of painkillers are more consistent, without the peaks and valleys of relief experienced with injections given at conventional intervals." (In fact, studies have found that self-medicating patients end up using *less* medication than those who rely on injections from a nurse.)

"The best time to ask about patient-controlled analgesia is when you and

Are Bedpans and Sponge Baths Obsolete?

Anyone who's served time as a hospital patient is probably familiar with two time-honored hospital rituals: using a bedpan and taking a sponge bath. Both foster dread and loathing. As if being sick isn't stressful enough, using an awkward receptable in place of a toilet adds insult to injury. And trying to wash and rinse from the same basin of water only leaves you shivering, soggy and disgusted.

Added to the sheer awkwardness of trying to relieve yourself and bathe in bed is the worry that a visitor will walk in on you. If you're not allowed to get up to go to the john, how are you supposed to get up and draw the curtain?

Doctors don't prescribe bedpans and basin baths just to be sadistic, though. For one thing, most have never used either one and don't realize just how disgusting they are. Rather, they assume that getting up to use the john or take a shower is just too much work for many patients, especially cardiac patients.

Well, it's high time to retire the bedpan and basin—or at least use them only when absolutely necessary, say two nurses who conducted research at the University of Texas Health Sciences Center in Dallas.

your doctor decide on surgery," says Pastorino, "so that he or she can incorporate it into the hospital orders."

Practice "slack-jawed" relaxation. Anxiety sharpens the perception of pain. Consequently, relaxation tends to lessen the perception of pain. Toward that end, researchers at the College of Nursing, Wayne State University, in Detroit, Michigan, taught jaw-muscle relaxation to patients admitted for gallbladder surgery, hernia repair and hemorrhoidectomy. Their goal was to relax the link between the brain and the mouth, to rest the speech mechanism. Patients then used the technique as they first ventured out of bed to walk across the room and back, six to eight hours after surgery. Compared with surgical patients not taught relaxation, they reported less incisional pain and bodywide distress and needed less pain medication during the 24 hours after surgery.

Here's how to practice the technique. Drop your lower jaw slightly as though starting a small yawn. Let your tongue rest motionless in the bottom of your mouth. Let your lips go slack. Breathe easily and deeply—inhale, exhale, pause. Avoid thinking or forming words.

A Smooth Recovery for Body and Soul

Doctors and nurses have long noted that the more relaxed a patient is going into surgery, the more relaxed he or she is coming out. The rationale is,

Authors Elizabeth Hahn Winslow, R.N., Ph.D., and Lynda Denton Lane, R.N., measured oxygen consumption, blood pressure and heart rate in heart patients, other medical patients and nonhospitalized people. They discovered that except for a relatively few patients who are immobilized or severely debilitated, using a bedside commode is less stressful and more convenient and practical than using a bedpan or urinal. Their studies, published in the *American Journal of Nursing* and *Journal of Cardiac Rehabilitation,* also found that showering and tub bathing generally didn't cause any more physical stress in patients than the basin bath, and most patients preferred it.

If you're hooked up to a cardiac monitor, however, you may have no choice. But the nurses feel that many hospital patients should be permitted to bathe and relieve themselves in the least stressful ways possible.

"It's no wonder these rituals are stressful," says Dr. Winslow, now assistant professor of nursing at the University of Texas at Arlington School of Nursing. "As a child, you're trained *not* to urinate in bed. Now you have to try to do what you've avoided all your life. It's basic things like this that make hospital patients feel helpless and powerless."

Now, if only hospitals would replace those dismal hospital gowns!

the more you know about what to expect, the less panicky you are afterward. Here are some suggestions to further smooth recovery.

Try to get up and around as much as your doctor allows. "The untoward effects of bedrest are horrible," says Dr. Winslow. "Studies have shown that patients who are allowed to get up and sit in a chair do better, physically and psychologically, than patients who lie in bed feeling helpless and powerless. Bedridden patients are susceptible to a variety of physical problems, including faintness, muscle atrophy and constipation, as well as depression."

Let family members help you. "Hospital patients are often too sick to verbalize their wishes, so they need a 'protector' or 'advocate' who knows and understands them to express their wishes to the health care team," says Dr. Winslow. If you need an extra pillow or blanket, ice water or more pain medication, it helps to have an attending friend or relative who can speak up for you.

Nurses also encourage interested and able family members to help a patient eat, wash or get to the bathroom. "Because so many hospitals are short on nurses, patients benefit tremendously from family helpers," says Dr. Winslow. Most patients also feel less self-conscious being bathed and assisted by their spouse or family. Plus, taking an active role in patient care alleviates some of the powerlessness that family members feel at seeing their loved one confined to an alien setting, she says.

With visiting hours stretching from morning until night in many hospitals, bedside helpers can be available to tend and comfort you for most waking hours. "That also gives nurses more opportunity to answer questions about postoperative care and teach the patient and his or her family the survival skills they will need to recuperate at home, after discharge," says Dr. Winslow. "That's especially important now, with so many patients admitted for short-stay treatment. We see them during the most acute phase of their condition only, then they're discharged," says Dr. Winslow. "The patient and his or her family are more or less on their own."

Get discharge instructions in writing. "Patients and their families are told when to change dressings and so forth, but they're under so much stress they may not remember everything," says Dr. Winslow. "So we give them booklets or written instructions clearly explaining what signs and symptoms to look for, and when and if to call the doctor."

"From the moment you put on that hospital gown, you feel vulnerable, and the entire hospital experience puts you in a passive role," says Dr. Winslow. "So the whole idea is to make the hospital stay as homelike as possible."

Chapter 32

MARITAL CONFLICTS

The object in marriage, according to myth, is to wed a mate who blends perfectly with your personality and temperament. Presumably, once this miracle occurs, you can set your marital cruise control on automatic and live in complete harmony happily ever after.

In reality, though, conflict and discord are bound to arise some time after the wedding cake is sliced. And it doesn't necessarily take a major calamity (like loss of a job) or a staggering blow (like infidelity) to strain a relationship. Everyday stresses can create considerable friction and fireworks, especially if you and your spouse can't discuss the most trivial of issues without acrimony.

"All stressors do not lead to conflict, but many do, particularly those that have to do with money, sex, children and shared responsibility in the family," writes Dolores Curran in her book, *Stress and the Healthy Family.* And when these stresses reach a high level, they can damage the marriage, unless the couple has the skills needed to resolve conflict.

Bickering and Your Blood Pressure

Poorly handled, marital conflict can also jeopardize your physical health. Researchers in the Department of Psychology at the University of Michigan and School of Public Health studied 696 men and women for 12 years and concluded that an inability to express anger combined with marital stress can *double* the risk of death for people with high blood pressure. Apparently, *how* married people cope with anger makes quite a difference, say the researchers. "Anger-In" (suppressing your feelings) and "Anger-Out" (venting your anger on the spot) escalate internal stress, while "reflective coping" (waiting for the anger to subside and then rationally discussing the conflict) is easier on your health. The reflective coping style appears to be the healthiest choice because it restores a sense of control over the situation and helps solve the problem. (For more information on dealing with anger, see chapter 19.)

Further analysis showed a strong link between marital stress and higher blood pressure among women aged 30 to 44, who were more likely to either suppress their anger or feel guilty if they express it. The highest levels of blood pressure were found in women aged 45 to 69 who reported greater marital stress and were more likely to suppress anger. The researchers speculate that women who suppress their anger store up dissatisfaction and resentment.

Keeping your cool on the domestic front may boost your immunity and foster good health in general, according to a study of marital stress and immunity conducted by psychologist Janice Kiecolt-Glaser, Ph.D., and Ronald Glaser, Ph.D., professor of microbiology and immunology at the Ohio State University College of Medicine. Blood tests indicated that married women who rated their marriage as poor had weaker immune systems than those who said they were happily married.

How to Stop Arguing—for Good

When your spouse says or does something that makes you angry, do you: (a) swallow your fury and try not to "make waves," (b) tell him or her immediately—and quite vocally—how annoyed you are, (c) give your spouse the cold shoulder for two weeks, (d) take a few minutes to think about the situation, then raise your concerns calmly and rationally.

If you chose (d), give yourself a gold star: You probably resolve most of your difficulties without too much acrimony. The other options usually escalate stress levels.

Marriage counselors say that in many cases of marital conflict, the real problem is not the topic under discussion—money, sex, work, time or children—but poor communication style.

"Certain communication styles—blaming, placating, deciding by decree and dismissing issues or avoidance—don't solve problems but perpetuate conflict," says Lori Heyman Gordon, director of the Family Relations Institute, Falls Church, Virginia.

In contrast, "the couples best able to deal with everyday stresses are those who develop workable ways of solving their disagreements and a fat supply of coping skills," says Curran.

You can turn your arguments into constructive problem-solving discussions by learning to spot negative communication styles and correcting your course accordingly, suggests Gordon.

"Blaming is typical of the 'Virginia Wolfe' type of marriage, where one person is very judgmental—always nitpicking, a constant critic or chronic complainer," says Gordon. "Blaming alienates a person and attacks their self-worth so that they end up either defending themselves, launching a counterattack or just tuning out the critic instead of dealing with the issue at hand."

Placating, or accommodating, your spouse is an easy way out that can eventually backfire, say marriage counselors.

"Saying everything is fine when it isn't leads to a situation where the placater just collects injustices until, much to his or her spouse's surprise, he or she just leaves," says Gordon.

Ignoring or dismissing feelings—either your own or your spouse's, also dead-ends a discussion.

"We call these people 'super reasoners,' " says Gordon. "They say things like, 'That's not the way you're supposed to feel, so I will ignore your feelings.' Or they will decide by issuing a decree or by deferring to higher authority, with statements like 'This is the way my parents always handled it and this is how we are going to do it.' "

Still other people are avoiders who simply refuse to deal with the underlying problem. "It may seem easy just to make believe that what's happening isn't happening, to put your head in the sand like an ostrich and hope that when you look up again, the trouble will be gone," says Gordon. But it won't. (And it may get worse.)

Scratching the Marital Itch

Poor communication styles, like other bad habits, evolve over time and can often be traced back to earlier conflicts in life that condition us to react the way we do.

"You don't have to spend years in psychotherapy to realize that you may be reacting to your spouse the way you dealt with parental criticism," says Gordon. "Poor communication may be related to the psychological age of the person you're dealing with. If one or the other or both of you are stuck in the adolescent stage of 'Don't tell me what to do,' that person may hear a legitimate concern as an effort to treat them as a child, and react accordingly.

"Also, if you had a parent who deceived you, you may not trust your spouse and may question his or her honesty even if they are being truthful," points out Gordon. "I call that an 'emotional allergy.' We are programmed by early experience to react one way to certain similar triggers, like breaking out in hives when you wear any kind of perfume."

The key to reducing marital tension, then, is to modify your communication style.

To blamers, Gordon says, "Think about how you're going to be heard. Speak your mind without placing blame on the other person. Instead of saying, 'You are wrong' or 'You made a mistake,' say 'I feel bad when . . .' or 'I am hurt when. . . .' "

To placaters/accommodators, Gordon says, "Your spouse can't read your mind and will have no way of knowing what's bothering you or what you expect them to do if you don't tell them. Does it bother you, for example, that your husband waits until the last minute to buy you a birthday present and then ends up spending more than your budget can afford? If you don't act overjoyed, he'll be confused because he honestly thought he was doing something nice."

To super reasoners, the 'Mr. Spocks,' Gordon says, "Use your logic and reasoning powers to create solutions and solve problems the best you can, but also think about the impact of your reasoning on the other's feelings."

To avoiders, Gordon says, "Allow yourself a temporary cooling-off period, if necessary, but don't ignore a problem indefinitely in the hope that it will go away. Make plans to solve it."

More Tips for Peaceful Coexistence

"Many people avoid confrontation of any kind because they are very uncomfortable with the tension of conflict itself," says Curran. "And sometimes, avoiding conflict is appropriate. But generally, compromise and collaboration are better. Over time, couples find that the more they resolve, the better they get at it. But the less they resolve, the worse things get."

Curran offers two additional tips for resolving conflicts peaceably.

First, separate the issue from the person, so that you don't habitually think: If you disagree with me, you don't love me. "Disagreement is a normal part of life," says Curran. "We disagree with co-workers and still manage to get along. Why not at home? Couples need to establish early in the relationship that they can disagree, whether it's over where to spend Christmas or who to vote for in the next election, and not stop loving each other."

Second, fight respectfully. "That means don't attack one another's weaknesses or bring up past trangressions or unpleasantness," says Curran. "And no name calling."

"What all this boils down to," says Gordon, "is, speak in your own behalf, but also care about how the other feels and work toward a mutually beneficial solution. Because if your conflicts always have to have a winner and a loser, then you both lose."

Chapter 33

MONEY WORRIES

The evolution of piggy banks into automatic teller machines may have changed how we save our money, but how we *feel* about money is the same—stressed. Asked which emotions they most often associated with money, 71 percent of the 20,000 people responding to a survey that was conducted by *Psychology Today* listed anxiety. Fifty-two percent listed depression and another 51 percent, anger. (More than one response was allowed.)

Those most troubled by money—and they were not necessarily poor— complained of more fatigue, headaches, insomnia and other stress-related complaints than those least troubled by money.

And in researching her book, *Stress and the Healthy Family*, Dolores Curran found that when asked to list their troubles, "the number one stress reported by respondents has to do with economics, financing and budgeting."

What makes money so stressful? Mainly the fear of what will happen without enough of it. Inflation, taxation, single parenthood and even increased longevity all threaten financial security. So no book on stress would be complete without some guidelines for gaining better control of your financial life and reducing the stress of economic uncertainty.

Breaking Financial Free-Fall

Are you going broke at the speed of light? No matter how hard you try to shake off debts, do bills seem to stick to you like Velcro? To bring your situation under control—and diffuse a lot of unnecessary worry—take some time to decide where you stand financially, where you want to stand and how to get there. Here are some suggestions to help you do that.

Make a budget. Say "budget" and most people immediately think of financial austerity—no steak, no movies, no fun. But a budget is simply a way to better meet both your needs (food, clothing, shelter, transportation) and

147

your wants (restaurant meals, designer clothes, a spacious house and a luxury car).

"Sound personal planning has no more to do with belt tightening and crash budgeting than dieting has to do with self-starvation," say David M. Brownstone and Jacques Sartisky, coauthors of *Personal Financial Survival.*

Besides presenting a more realistic idea of what you can and cannot afford, a written budget can reveal where your oh-so-disposable money goes—those Bermuda Triangles of finance that swallow up hundreds of stray dollars every year. In that way, a carefully thought-out budget can relieve the stress of wondering why you always seem broke no matter how hard you work.

"Control is the key word," says Patricia Elder-Jucker, Ph.D., psychologist at the Temple University Counseling Center in Philadelphia. "A budget helps people feel that they control their money and that money doesn't control them."

Make a five-year plan. "To further avoid the anxiety of not knowing where you stand or where you're headed, decide on a goal," says Dr. Elder-Jucker. "Do you want to buy a house? A second car? Start a retirement plan? Then make a written plan of action stating how you will achieve your goal or goals."

Hold family business meetings. Most businesses, large or small, hold regular business meetings to evaluate their finances. Since a household is another form of small business, regularly reviewing household finances makes fiscal sense. "Regular, planned discussions about household finances take the sting out of the conversation, preventing conflict and blame," says Dr. Elder-Jucker.

Consider professional advice. If you need help establishing a budget or managing your debts, consider an accountant, banker, financial planning adviser or other person trained and equipped to deal with finances. Financial advice columnist Sylvia Porter also recommends the Consumer Credit Counseling Service, a nonprofit, community-sponsored group whose services are confidential and low-cost or free (depending on your income). To locate the office nearest you, consult your area telephone directory.

Brownstone and Sartisky caution against seeking financial advice solely from insurance sellers, stockbrokers or others who may have a financial interest in your decisions. Look for a financial advisor who will pay attention to your needs, goals and desires, not dispense broad financial advice, they recommend. "You expect such concern from your medical physician—it is not too much to expect from your 'financial physician,' " say the authors.

How to Deal with Budget Breakdowns

Do you live from crisis to crisis? Do inevitable but surprise expenses like new tires, clothes for the kids and a broken water heater leave your "budget" shaken, to say nothing of your composure?

The key to coping? Expect the unexpected.

Establish an emergency fund. Dolores Curran advises putting a share of each paycheck into savings for unexpected repairs, replacements, trips and medical bills, *separate* from long-range untouchable savings for your child's education or your retirement. "When families have a cushion, they don't fall apart when something out of the ordinary happens," she says.

Other psychologists agree. "Sure, unexpected crises like job loss or car repair create anxiety," says Dr. Elder-Jucker. "But having money put aside to take care of them reduces the anxiety created."

Consider automatic payroll deduction. "An . . . excellent way to save is to authorize your bank to deduct a specified percentage from your paycheck when you deposit the paycheck in your checking account and to transfer this percentage to your savings account," says Sylvia Porter in her book, *Sylvia Porter's New Money Book for the Eighties*. "Make it 10 percent, if you can manage, or 5 percent—but make the transfer automatic and regular. The automatic, regular feature is the secret."

Weathering the Worst

Should the bottom fall out of your financial plan due to a major, disabling illness, accident or legal difficulties, you can still land on your feet. There are some strategies you can use to survive the stress of a financial catastrophe.

Don't blame yourself. "Many things are beyond our control," says Dr. Elder-Jucker. "So when catastrophe strikes, it's okay to feel sad. But it's also important not to blame yourself or feel guilty or ashamed. Don't torture yourself by thinking, 'If only . . .' or 'I should have. . . .' "

Negotiate your bills. "Most doctors and hospitals are willing to discuss a workable payment schedule for unanticipated medical or dental bills," says Lisa Astor, administrator with the Health Benefits Research Center in New York City. "That reduces strain on family members who are already under considerable stress caused by hospitalization or illness."

Know your rights. Until you get back on your financial feet, bill collectors may start nipping at your heels, adding to your aggravation. To protect consumers from harassment, the Fair Debt Collection Practices Act prohibits debt collectors from contacting you at unreasonable times (before 8:00 A.M. or after 9:00 P.M.), bugging you at work or otherwise hounding you about money owed. For a copy of the law, contact the Division of Credit Practices, Federal Trade Commission, Washington, DC 20580.

Reducing Social Insecurity

Sometimes, even financially secure people don't seem to have enough money and find themselves driven to earn more and more money, creating a different kind of stress.

"For many, money—and what it buys—is a barometer of how they're doing," says Dr. Elder-Jucker. "But money is a precarious and inaccurate measure of self-esteem, since finances can change. Find something else in your life besides dollar signs to measure your worth."

Nonmaterial rewards—reaped through friendship, community work, teaching—can help balance financial concerns in your self-esteem ledger.

Chapter 34

MOVING

Whether you're moving cross-country to a dream house or across town to a more affordable apartment, relocation is stressful.

"Trust in one's surroundings is the foundation of people's sense of security," explains Joan Costello, Ph.D., psychologist on the staff at the University of Chicago. "Moving creates stress because it disrupts the predictable elements of our lives—where to find things, who our friends are, what dry cleaners are reliable and countless other familiar rituals.

"But moving, like other major changes such as marital separation or loss of a spouse, also triggers a sense of loss," says Dr. Costello. "Don't be surprised if you feel depressed, disappointed or discouraged that things will never be the same after you've moved.

"You may also feel angry and irritable," she adds. "You might complain that the vegetables in the supermarket aren't as fresh as you used to buy back home or otherwise romanticize about where you lived before. If you grumble to the grocer, that probably won't hurt, but if you lash out at your spouse, whose new job may be the reason behind the move, marital stress can result."

In fact, relocation often follows *other* stressful life changes, such as a new job, divorce or retirement. Clearly, there's more to the stress of moving than worrying that your good china will get chipped.

"Most people concentrate on the logistics of moving—packing, forwarding their mail and renting a truck, for instance—and neglect the emotional strain of being uprooted and transplanted," says Kenneth I. Howard, Ph.D., head of clinical psychology at Northwestern University in Evanston, Illinois. And coping with the internal stress of moving is as important as organizing and packing the outward trappings of your life.

You *Can* Take It with You

"The conventional approach to moving is to simplify your possessions and discard old or unused belongings cluttering up the attic, basement or closets," says Dr. Costello. "And economically, that's smart. Why pay to have all your junk moved? But to maintain a certain amount of continuity and cushion the effects of change, take familiar things with you, too. It might be better to hold on to your old couch, for example, than to buy brand-new but unfamiliar furniture for your new living room.

"Don't regard your possessions on the basis of their monetary or aesthetic value alone," she says. "Sure, that couch may look like it's weathered one television season too many, but if you've lived with it and loved it for years, it's become part of the family. Take it along.

"I remember one child who clung to an old chair as it was carried off during a yard sale his mother held in order to pare down the household goods before moving," says Dr. Costello. "Ever since he was very small, the child used to sit in that chair and watch his mother do the laundry. The chair was old and worn, but it symbolized home and security to him."

Another way to cushion the shock of moving is to do it gradually. "Just as plants need to be pampered when transplanted outdoors after living in the shelter of a greenhouse, people need to acclimate to a new environment," says Dr. Howard. "If you can, move a few things ahead of time. Install your plants or a few clothes or a couple of small pieces of furniture, for example. Take a walking tour of the neighborhood. Visit your new community for a weekend or two before the actual move.

"And don't get so wrapped up in the tasks of packing and unpacking that you ignore the psychological preparations," he continues. "Save some energy for getting to know a little about your new destination, just as you would on any other trip."

Help for the Moving-Day Blues

"The kitchen is often the last room of the house people pack up to move and the first to be unpacked when they reach their new quarters," says Dr. Costello. "For many, the kitchen is the focal point of the household and, somehow, putting old familiar pots and pans in new kitchen cabinets fuses the past with the future. But if you and your family don't mind take-out food for a day or two, you might want to settle another room instead. If you have children, for example, your first priority may be to outfit their rooms with their beds, bureaus and toys—all the familiar props they need to feel safe. Kids get restless and need to be able to retreat to familiar surroundings as soon as possible.

"Different things help different people feel at home," she says. "For some, unpacking the towels and bed linens is a high priority. Twenty-year-olds typically plug in the stereo before anything else."

You can cut moving-day stress considerably by not trying to get everything unpacked and reorganized immediately. In fact, you may save yourself work in the long run by putting off unpacking nonessentials.

"Personally, I don't like to do things twice," says Dr. Costello. "So I leave boxes unpacked until I've had time to figure out exactly where the contents are going to go. But many people feel they have to unpack everything, even if it's just to stash it all, willy-nilly, in the closets or attic."

Which strategy is least stressful for you? "Think about how you go about settling into your lodgings when you travel or vacation at the beach," says Dr. Costello. "Do you unpack immediately and put everything in drawers? Or do you put off unpacking until after you've had time to look around? Vacations are mini-moves that can give you some idea of what's comfortable and efficient for *you*."

Allow Plenty of Time to Adjust

The aftershocks of moving linger long after your toothbrush is hung, the china is unpacked and your mail catches up with you.

"It takes six months to disengage from your former home and two years to fully adjust and feel at ease in your new location," says Dr. Costello. "So while you shouldn't sit around pining, you can expect to feel 'homesick' for some time."

"Sports and hobbies make great connectors between your former and prospective home," says Dr. Howard. "If you play tennis, for example, find a club near your new lodgings. You'll make new friends all that much sooner. Also, if you belonged to a church or temple, join a nearby house of worship."

Think of moving as an adventure and a challenge. "The up side of moving is that it opens doors and offers new opportunities," says Dr. Costello. "It's fun to discover new stores, explore new restaurants and so forth. But it also takes energy."

Chapter 35

RETIREMENT

Your Golden Years.

In theory, retirement does sound golden. You've got freedom, glorious freedom to do as you please. No alarm clocks, no bosses, no kids to raise. And for some folks, years in retirement—which can comprise as much as one-third of your life—are indeed the most enjoyable.

But for others, retirement is unrelenting stress. It is 50 extra hours of free time with nothing to do. It is a loss of self-esteem, an unexpected emptiness. It is guilt over being unproductive or guilt over not really wanting your grown-up son to move back home. It is insecurity about money and insecurity about health.

Even retirement humor emphasizes the dual nature, the mixed blessing of the situation. The nicely framed needlepoint maxim: "Retirement—twice as much husband, half as much money" hangs on the living room wall of Bernice Guy, a widow from Smith Island, Maryland. A friend gave it to her years ago, about the time her husband, Fred, a crabber, reached retirement age. (Like many people, he never could find happiness in retirement. Instead, he continued crabbing right up until the day before he died.)

"I married you for better or for worse, but not for lunch," is another humorous saying that describes a problem two otherwise happily married people suddenly have to face. Once, lunch may have provided a much-needed break from the day's work and an opportunity to socialize with friends or colleagues. After retirement, however, the simple meal can symbolize a couple's new struggle to make their marriage work. Must the wife forfeit her friends and daytime activities to make lunch for her husband every day now that he's going to be home?

Despite the inevitable stresses, some folks manage to thrive after retirement, while others are devastated by it. There are several factors that may determine how well an individual will handle retirement. "The more flexible a person is and the more options they have, the easier it will be to adjust to any change," says Robert Atchley, Ph.D., director of the Scripps Gerontolgy Cen-

154

ter at Miami (Ohio) University. The most likely candidates for a successful transition, he says, are those in good health, those with enough money to enjoy a comfortable lifestyle and those who maintain a good attitude toward human development.

Retirement Planning

Other experts add a fourth group of likely candidates: Those who plan. Several years ago a committee of the American Medical Association released well-publicized statistics to the news media that indicated that the average man dies within three years of retirement. Not pleasant news for those facing retirement. But further investigation revealed how erroneous—and irresponsible—the statistic was. It had been based on the facts that male life expectancy at birth was an average 68 years and that most men retire at age 65. In reality, average life expectancy for a man who reaches age 65 is about 14 years. That means you won't drop when you stop.

"It's not true that retirement has an adverse effect on health," says Thomas Wan, Ph.D., professor of health administration at the Medical College of Virginia and author of *Well-Being for the Elderly: Primary Prevention Strategy.* In fact, if you retire from a job because your health is poor, you may find your health *improving* in retirement. But if you have trouble coping with the stressful events that retirement often brings, you may experience a wide range of physical ailments as well as such psychological problems as depression and anxiety, according to Nan Lin, Ph.D., professor of sociology and public health science at State University of New York, Albany.

The way to counter retirement stress—and its possible health problems—is *planning.*

"Long-range planning is the key. You can start ten years in advance," says Dr. Wan. If you wonder why some people experience tremendous stress in retirement, consider that it's not uncommon for people to spend more time planning for a two-week vacation than they spend planning for the rest of their lives.

Part of the problem is that when you sit down to make retirement plans, you may be dealing with all sorts of nagging insecurities. You are forcing yourself to look into the future—into possible financial woes, into ill health and into your own mortality. These anxieties often lead to immobilization.

Many psychologists agree that you can start to shake those fears and anxieties by plowing ahead into retirement research: collecting data on retirement locales, working with a financial consultant, discussing your hopes (and fears) with friends and family.

Another way to decrease your retirement anxiety is to know what to expect. Many therapists suggest you take up new interests *before* you retire. Take a course to prepare yourself for a part-time job or craft that may enable you to supplement your income. Practice living on your retirement income.

Openly discuss with your spouse the possibility of engaging in a few separate activities. Or, if you are one of the 30 percent of retirement-age people who live alone, spend some time investigating group housing alternatives—if you think you'd enjoy that option.

Such advice is prominent in *Planning Your Retirement*, a preretirement planning booklet published by the American Association of Retired Persons (AARP). For a free single copy, send a postcard to AARP, P.O. Box 2400, Long Beach, CA 90801. This 20-page booklet may do wonders for dispelling the negative myths and stereotypes about life in retirement.

Financing Your Retirement

What greater fear can there be than the fear of growing old in poverty? True, the Social Security Act of 1935 was a big step in helping people finance retirement. But realistically, it is at best a supplement to savings, a pension or other income. The average monthly Social Security retirement benefit check amounts to only $488 for an individual retiree or $833 for a retired couple. True, the advent of Medicare in 1965 enabled retirees to dispel fears that they could not afford medical treatment or hospital care. But in reality, Medicare covered on average only 74 percent of retirees' hospital care bills and 54 percent of doctors' bills, according to a study published in 1984 by *Consumer Reports*. Most retirees need supplemental insurance.

The average person will need about 75 percent of his or her preretirement income to maintain the same standard of living in retirement, according to Lewis J. Altfest, Ph.D., a financial adviser whose clients include many retirees. He says it varies widely, depending on such factors as whether the person lives in the high-cost cities of the Northeast or moves to the low-cost Sunbelt. Among the least expensive areas, he says, are areas of Florida and Arizona where businesses cater to older people, offering such benefits as early-bird dinner specials for senior citizens.

A complete understanding of your finances will influence virtually every retirement decision you make. Don't make decisions before you've taken a careful account of your financial situation. "People under stress often restrict themselves unnecessarily in the choice of activities and lifestyles in retirement, frequently because they fear that they will not have sufficient funds," writes Robert K. Kinzel in his book *Retirement: Creating Promise Out of Threat*. But examine your options. There may be more money than you think.

If you will receive a pension from your employer, you may have the option of taking it in a lump sum or getting it in the form of a monthly annuity for the rest of your life. Your decision is important, and it must be based on such factors as taxes and the availability of conservative investments. If you don't feel comfortable making the decision on your own, seek the help of a financial adviser, preferably one who operates on a fee-only basis. (Financial advisers who make their money on a commission basis may steer you in the direction of investments in which they earn commission.) You may need only a one-hour consultation with a financial adviser. The cost could be $100, but it may turn out to be well worth the expense.

And make yourself familiar with the intricacies of Social Security. Write for information that will tell you when to apply and what benefits you will receive. (Write to the Office of Public Inquiries, Social Securities Administration, 6401 Security Boulevard, Baltimore, MD 21235.) If you have no additional income and have no prospects of earning extra income with a part-time job, give some thought to sharing your home—or moving in with another retiree. Taking the steps to investigate such a move will probably help dispel some of your biggest fears of financial insecurity.

If you've constructed a savings cushion to help in retirement, make sure you know how much you can withdraw each month before the principal is depleted—or how much you can withdraw indefinitely through interest accumulations. If your nest egg is $10,000 invested at 7 percent compounded quarterly, you can withdraw $59 a month indefinitely or $116 for ten years, according to the AARP's *Planning Your Retirement*. Your banker should be able to help you with the calculations.

And learn what Medicare covers and what it doesn't cover. (Write to the Health Care Financing Administration, 6325 Security Boulevard, Baltimore, MD 21207.) Is the group health insurance your employer provides guaranteed to be convertible to an individual policy to bolster Medicare? If not, Dr. Altfest recommends you at least buy catastrophic insurance for large illnesses that could zap your savings. But he warns that too many retirees overinsure themselves to the point that they become insurance poor.

The earlier you start your financial planning for retirement, the better off you'll be. "People come to me two years from retirement and they have no funds," says Dr. Altfest. Ideally, preretirement planning should start ten years before retirement—five years at the very least. The first step, for those who have no funds stashed away, is to invest in a pension plan such as an Individual Retirement Account (IRA).

It may ease your mind to study two brochures published by AARP: "Money Matters" and "Take Charge of Your Money." To obtain them, free of charge, write to AARP Fulfillment, P.O. Box 2240, Long Beach, CA 90801. Above all, remember that unscrupulous individuals may be out to take your hard-earned money. "I would caution people against giving anybody any money without knowing what they're going to get in return," says Katie Sloan, the AARP's consumer advisor. "Have a contract. Understand the refund constraints. Older people very easily get sucked into financial scams. So you've got to know who you're dealing with."

The Second Career

Here are some seemingly contradictory facts: More Americans than ever are taking early retirement. Yet more Americans than ever over 65 are still in the workforce. The explanation, of course, is that retirees are pursuing second careers in retirement, either on a full-time or part-time basis.

Among the many luxuries retirement affords is the possibility to explore a new career. Those who succeed in these second careers frequently are people who were deeply involved in an interest that easily carried over into retirement. But it's possible to pursue something totally new: the purchase of a small business, the training for a new skill that's sellable. Whatever the case, the transition from old job to new will be easiest if you lay the groundwork for a second career before you retire.

If you are the neighborhood Mr. Fix-It, helping your neighbors repair appliances, it may be wise to set up your basement business *before* leaving your job, so you can work out the kinks while you still have an income. If you're an accountant and plan to help friends and neighbors complete taxes, it's advisable to smooth the transition by drumming up the clients before you leave your firm.

Just as the process of starting a business is fraught with problems for 35-year-olds, it can be disastrous for retirees, regardless of expertise, enthusiasm and energy level. One option available to retirees: Purchase a franchise of anything from a doughnut shop to a gift-wrapping business. The required investment is generally smaller than that needed to open and operate a comparable independent business. And you don't have to worry about how to run the business. The same franchisor who sells you the doughnuts or wrapping paper also teaches you the ropes and will give you management assistance if you need it.

But that's not such a good idea if you dislike having someone else give the orders—the same way your boss probably did before you retired. Also, franchisors quick to make a sale often underemphasize the amount of work involved in running one of their businesses. If you want to get a handle on the amount of time you'll have to put into the operation, talk to other franchisees of the same organization before buying your franchise.

And despite a relatively high rate of success among legitimate franchise operations, the industry still has a substantial sleaze factor. Unscrupulous franchisors love to separate retirees from their life savings. So before buying a franchise, check with the International Franchise Association (202–628–8000). In addition, carefully go over the franchise papers with a lawyer and talk with others who have franchises with the particular company.

Many community colleges offer free or reduced-tuition courses to retirees. That education can be a virtual gold mine for anyone interested in developing a skill or learning a craft that may lead to a second career. If you've got the interest, don't let your age discourage you. Continuing to work won't necessarily make you rich, but it can help you finance your retirement.

Barbara Newcombe is an Oakland, California, retiree who started a second career in retirement and is already looking forward to a third. Two years ago she left her job as the librarian for a major metropolitan newspaper in the Midwest (it was a career she had begun in her fifties) and moved to California to be closer to her children and grandchildren. She wanted to go into business for herself doing indexing for publishers. So she bought herself a computer, learned how to use it and began gathering customers for her service. Her volunteer work at the Center for Investigative Reporting may translate into a major source of income for her business.

Meanwhile, she anticipates the day when she can leave indexing behind to pursue a career in archives and geneology, fields she enjoys. "I find it boring to stick to one thing," she says.

If you want to return to the workforce in the same profession you left behind, there's an important thought to keep in mind as you hunt for work: You probably have a lot to offer a prospective employer. So don't approach a job interview as if the employer will be doing you a favor to hire you. Be confident. And if you don't get hired, look elsewhere—or think about what kind of career you'd like to pursue next. Heed the advice of retirement author Kinzel when he writes, "Be honest with yourself. If it is unlikely that you can continue to practice your vocation, it is better to acknowledge it now so that you can search properly for an alternative style of life."

When Retirement Shatters Your Self-Esteem

Retirement can be toughest for those who define themselves in terms of their work—or at least derive a great deal of their self-esteem from the job they left behind. Take the case of the executive or manager with considerable power, who suddenly finds that selecting the proper golf club is the biggest decision of the day. A big-shot businessman is now an average Joe. Former librarian Newcombe, who so successfully made the transition into a second career—and in a new community—remembers the early stress she experienced when "people were no longer calling me because I was the person listed as the head of a large department for a large organization. That position made a difference in how people regarded me. Suddenly I became almost a non-person." Psychologists suggest you realize just how powerful the loss of prestige can be.

"The shock for many is not only great but also bewildering," writes Leland P. Bradford, who, with his wife, Martha, wrote *Retirement: Coping with Emotional Upheavals.* "Events are less under one's control, and the importance in others' eyes that power gives has evaporated. Must the person who has lost power continue to vie for it, or can the individual find power and importance within himself?"

Duke University psychology professor Martin Lakin, Ph.D., has worked extensively in this area of retirement and still considers that question "the $64,000 question." In his opinion, there are no easy answers for the person who placed a great value on work and career and now has neither. Most of the activities in senior citizens' centers are loathed by them. "They see it as child's play," he says.

"It's a matter of making the best of a bad situation in a society that values work," he says. People who were specialists in highly technical fields are in a good position to regain some sense of importance through their value as consultants. At the very least they can maintain a connection to their preretirement life through professional organizations. Others, he says, should "try to find volunteer programs that have meaning for them. Some people find it satisfying to work with younger people in their area of expertise; others are satisfied working with Meals on Wheels." One bit of advice, he says, is to seek out others in the same situation—former colleagues, for instance—and talk over your dilemma. "Shared troubles are sometimes eased," he says.

Some people derive satisfaction from jobs that make them feel more knowledgeable than anyone else, says Sheila Miller, Ph.D., a professor at the Scripps Gerontology Center. She suggests such folks get involved in an organization or issue where, once again, they will know more than anyone else.

But those who want to beat the stress of suddenly being a nobody can take another approach: Learn to derive pleasure from other things in life, suggests Dr. Miller. It may not be easy, but it may be necessary in order to manage the stress of retirement. If you haven't yet retired, do a bit of self-analysis and try to determine your needs and activities that may satisfy them. Do you enjoy the physical nature of your job? Take up hiking and stick to a planned daily regimen. If you're already retired, there are a host of activities that may help you overcome your feelings of emptiness and uselessness—or the guilt you experience from being away from "work."

Meaningful Activities

Two mornings each week Robert Kennedy, 74, hikes up a steep block-and-a-half hill from his home in the Pittsburgh suburbs to Avalon Elementary School. And when he makes his way into a second-grade classroom, he is barraged with cheers of delight. Kennedy, a retired salesman, is a grandfather-in-the-classroom, sharing his knowledge, experience and friendship with a generation of youngsters.

He helps them with their vocabulary lessons or listens as they discuss the important issues in their lives. For Kennedy, it is a rewarding activity that he hopes to pursue "as long as I can make that hill." He misses the chance to nurture his own grandchildren—they live out of state—so the classroom volunteer program helps fill a void in his life.

As America's elderly population grows, an increasing number of programs are being formed that link retirees and youngsters. Although it is a relatively new phenomenon, the National Council on Aging knows of several thousand intergenerational activities. In western Pennsylvania alone, a program at the University of Pittsburgh named "Generations Together" brings retirees together with as many as 20,000 youngsters. Program director Sally Newman says a national study of retiree participants indicates they feel more satisfied with life and continue to grow mentally by volunteering in these meaningful activities.

But to chat with the retiree volunteers is to learn the true value of working with youngsters. Retired payroll accountant Mark Narr, 67, wanted "to give back something to the community," so he volunteered to work two afternoons a week at a school for youngsters who are disabled or retarded. He calls his volunteering "the most important thing I've ever done." Artist Ann Sawyer Berkley, 72, volunteers as a once-a-week artist-in-residence at the Pittsburgh High School for Creative and Performing Arts. Being around the students "makes her young," she says. She also gains pride from the fact that young black students view her as a role model.

And in Philadelphia, an improvisational acting troupe, "Full Circle," comprised of both retirees and adolescents, tours the region's senior centers and high schools. Its 18 members perform highly improvised scenes that deal with problems facing the young and old. Only one of the performers has had any previous acting experience, and none of them has had any professional training. It is just something they've always wanted to do.

If you'd like to do something meaningful in your retirement, there are more options than you can imagine.

Redefining Your Marriage

In addition to financial planning and finding a creative outlet, a third important facet of life is affected by retirement, and that is marriage. How well a couple weathers retirement may depend on the health of their relationship.

Redefining your relationship after retirement takes a lot of work, says Miriam Galper Cohen, a psychotherapist who has led preretirement workshops and has worked extensively with older people. Remember, you don't have to spend 24 hours a day together, seven days a week. Many retirement counselors say it's a good idea, sometimes even crucial, to pursue some separate interests. And if your home is big enough, stake out and maintain separate turf. It may be the garden for one spouse and a basement workshop for the other.

Do you feel guilty separating yourself from your spouse for some private time? In their book, *Coping with Your Husband's Retirement*, authors Roslyn Friedman and Annette Nussbaum offer a script.

First, the "Don't" script ("Asking for Permission"):

YOU: Honey, do you mind if I meet my sister for lunch and the symphony tomorrow? She has an extra ticket.

HE: Well, I thought we'd do something. But if you'd rather be with her . . .

YOU : Oh, I'm sorry, I didn't realize . . . okay, I'll call and tell her to get someone else (guilty).

HE: No, go ahead. Do what you want.

YOU: No, I'll stay home (angry and frustrated)—or—Okay, I'll go (guilty, guilty, guilty).

Now the "Do" script ("Giving Yourself Permission"):

YOU: Honey, I have a date for lunch and the symphony with my sister tomorrow. I want you to know that I'll be gone most of the day.

HE: I thought we'd do something.

YOU: I'd love to do something with you. Why don't we plan a day together on Friday?

Authors Friedman and Nussbaum say they aren't suggesting that you aggressively demand time of your own but that you simply "recognize your need as being equal to his."

But, like many women who entered the workforce late in life, you may be the one who is busily working while your husband retires. If that's the case, psychologists say it's important to recognize that his needs to play are equal to yours to work. They suggest you encourage him to find suitable outside interests that he can pursue alone or with friends.

AARP's *Planning Your Retirement* preretirement booklet poses another scenario: You're both retired and you resent the fact that your husband spends five afternoons a week on the golf course. Possible solutions to consider? Don't hesitate to discuss your concerns with him. He may not be aware of how his golf is affecting his marriage. Or you can take up golf yourself and accompany him once or twice a week.

Communicate and compromise. "People ought to talk to one another about what their expectations are. It's good if they approach the process of developing mutual expectations with the spirit of give and take," says gerontologist Dr. Atchley.

Your relationship with your spouse may not be the only relationship that needs to be redefined in retirement. What about your connection with your kids? In retirement, you may not be able to afford to continue playing your role as party host to your children and grandchildren. And you may not want to be viewed as a convenient babysitter. In retirement, you may want to enjoy yourself by yourself—and hesitate to invite your grown-up son or daughter to move back home after living away for several years.

If that's the dilemma you're facing, Dr. Atchley suggests you be "real straight" with your son or daughter. "There are certain times when you have to grin and bear it. If somebody just got divorced and doesn't have a job, you've got to say, 'Come on home, we'll give you support for a while, but after six months we expect you to dust yourself off and have a new place.' That sort of understanding is good to have in the beginning," says Dr. Atchley. "They have to respect your agenda."

Making and Keeping Friends

Whether you are retired and married or retired and single, you can reduce stress by being part of a social network. A study headed by Carl I. Cohen of the Department of Psychiatry at State University of New York-Downstate Medical Center tracked 133 elderly New York residents and found that social networks reduce physical symptoms of stress by buffering the effect of increased levels of stress.

That's a fact to consider if you plan to move after retirement. Will your new home offer you access to people of similar interests? And if so, are you the type of person who can seek them out?

The importance of friendships can't be overplayed. In fact, a social network may be better than family in helping you weather the stress of retirement. "An older person with one good friend is better able to cope with the later years than a person with a dozen grandchildren but no peer-group friends," says sociologist Zena Blau in her book *Aging in a Changing Society.* And Dr. Atchley says that among retirees, a social network is a better magnet than a good climate.

If you can maintain old friendships or make new ones, you've got an antidote to the loneliness that sometimes overpowers retirees. If you're a shy person but would like to make friends, your solution may exist in the form of a social skills group. These are therapy groups designed to help you overcome shyness. Hundreds of them exist throughout the country. You can find out about them from the psychology department at any major university.

There are a surprising number of good retiree groups to join if you take the time to look. In Washington, D.C., a club called "The Fossils" has been bringing retired men together for 40 years. Some 400 men belong to the nonsectarian, nonpolitical, nonprofit organization whose only requirements are that members be retired and male. The group holds a monthly business meeting at a church in Chevy Chase, Maryland, at which the speaker could be a noted historian or a retired athlete. There are biannual luncheons and an abundance of groups within the organization: a camera group, a bridge group, an investment group. There's a duckpin bowling group that meets weekly; its members include a 92-year-old and a 96-year-old. In fact, one team accepts only those over 90!

Remember, the more time you spend with people of similar interests, the more friends you're likely to make. If you enjoy traveling to distant shores but you don't want to do it alone and have a limited budget, nothing beats a passenger-carrying freighter trip. The voyages can be as short as 30 days or last several months, and you're never totally certain of every place you'll visit. It depends on the cargo. You may wind up in Casablanca one day, Marseilles a few days later. You always have a place to sleep and eat onboard. You always have a group with which to tour the port of call. The trips are particularly popular among adventurous retirees. (For free information on freighter travel write to Pearl's Freighter Tips, Suite 303, 175 Great Neck Road, Great Neck, NY 11021, or phone 516-487-8351.)

For $15 a year, you and your spouse can join the National Senior Citizen Sports Association and participate in or become a spectator at special events in golf, tennis, bowling and other sports. Write the organization at 317 Cameron Street, Alexandria, VA 22314, or phone (703) 549-6711.

And then there's Elderhostel, a network of more than a thousand colleges, universities and other educational institutions that host week-long programs on campus for people who are 60 or over (you can bring a companion who is under 60 if you wish). Participants live like college students while they take noncredit courses in everything from Shakespearean literature or marine biology to cross-country skiing or human sexuality. Groups are limited to 40 participants, so there's ample opportunity to get to know fellow classmates. And a week-long program often includes field trips, concerts, plays and movies. For a catalog, write to Elderhostel, 80 Boylston Street, Suite 400, Boston, MA 02116.

Retired Philadelphians Larry and Sylvia Miner schedule two Elderhostel trips each year—one in the spring and one in the fall. They spend six weeks each winter in Florida and spend most of their summer days at a swimming and tennis club. And when Larry—who underwent heart bypass surgery several years ago—rattles off his regimen of activities, it's easy to believe him when he says, "The only stress in retirement is being too busy."

At age 65 he is an avid trader of old photography equipment and antique photographs; he plays tennis twice a week during the indoor season and more frequently during the warmer months. The couple belongs to two book discussion groups and a social group, and Larry is a member of a "semiamateur" therapy group named "Dynamics of Growing Old," where the issues of the aging are discussed and dealt with. He participates in a Pritikin support group, rides a stationary bicycle three times a week and does 25 minutes of stretching exercises each morning. He makes the rounds of flea markets, plays his guitar twice a week, lunches with friends and former colleagues from his years as a school administrator and plays computer games with his three young grandchildren every chance he gets.

All of this on top of the regular household routine. The retirement schedule has made the Miners so busy that they've decided to set aside a day each week to loaf by themselves.

Chapter 36

UNEMPLOYMENT

Lose your job, and you lose much more than a regular paycheck.

"It's like bowling," says Barrie Greiff, M.D., an occupational psychiatrist in Boston and visiting professor of occupational psychiatry at Harvard Business School. "Your job is the kingpin. Knock that over, and everything else falls with it."

"Everything" includes friendships with co-workers (a major component of social life), a big chunk of your identity ("And what do *you* do for a living?") and a reason to get out of bed in the morning (it's amazing how much you miss that alarm clock when it doesn't ring anymore). And not least of all, your job gives you something to talk about—even if all you do is gripe about the incompetents in the next department.

"Talking about where you work is one of the most common pastimes in America," remark Robert Levering, Milton Moskowitz and Michael Katz in their well-known book, *The 100 Best Companies to Work for in America.*

"Most of all, though, losing your job tells you that someone or something else is in control," says Jeanne Curran, Ph.D., professor of sociology at California State University-Dominguez Hills at Carson, California. "And it's lack of control that makes job loss so stressful, especially for people who feel that as long as they work hard and try their best, they can control their fortune."

Some people feel *better* after losing their job, usually because it frees them from on-the-job stress. One man who worked for a major steelmaker and survived wave after wave of massive personnel cutbacks for years experienced great relief when his number finally—and inevitably—came up. But he's one of a small minority. Most people are upset after they're "terminated," as employers like to say. And getting the gate seems to be stressful even if you didn't like your job.

"For many, losing their job is like being raped: Their sense of control over life has been violated," says Dr. Curran. "The people who break down are the ones who thought they were in control."

So while it's financial insecurity that worries jobless workers the most,

165

money is not all that matters. And stress tends to increase the longer you sit on the bench, leveling off at about six months.

Why They Called It "The Great Depression"

Lose your job and you're apt to feel anxious, depressed—or just plain apathetic. Perhaps you find it hard to concentrate or make decisions. You may also find yourself drinking, smoking or eating more than usual or acting a bit surly toward your spouse and kids. Sex becomes a chore—or a memory. Parties leave you feeling like an outcast. Movies are out—you hate to spend the money. You dread Christmas.

If you feel really down, don't be alarmed. In effect, you're mourning the loss of your job, and that's normal. In fact, family therapists are struck by how similar a family's response to unemployment is to bereavement over loss of a loved one, another major stress in life. One study of plant closings, for example, found that workers experienced a classic grief reaction to losing their jobs, including a spate of various physical complaints, just as they might after the death of a loved one.

"The first stage is a shock: Nobody believes that it is going to happen to him," says Richard Smith, assistant editor of the *British Medical Journal,* in a series of articles on the health of those who are unemployed. "The next phase is one of denial and optimism, the 'holiday feelings,' but within a few weeks this gives way to anxiety and distress. In this stage, [people] seek work with great energy, but repeated failures drive them to resignation and adjustment. But this is not a healthy adjustment; rather, time drags, the day is empty and [his or her] personality and relationships are corroded."

Losing Your Job Can Be Hazardous to Your Health

Job loss leaves many people more susceptible to colds or other infections, because unemployment, like other major stresses, lowers immunity, according to research.

The physical aftershocks of unemployment are not to be taken lightly. If you have borderline high blood pressure, for example, unemployment could also nudge blood pressure into the hazardous zone. Rising cholesterol levels can increase your risk of heart attack. All this when your paid medical coverage is about to expire! Talk about adding insult to injury.

Middle-aged workers—who often have heavy commitments like college tuition and other large debts to pay, or are too young to retire—suffer more than younger or older workers, according to one source.

"No one handles the loss of a job smoothly—*no one*," says Dr. Curran. "But the people who suffer the most are the ones who don't show their distress or ask for help," she adds. "Outwardly, they may look cool, but underneath they're scared to death—and they may pay for it later with a heart attack or ulcers."

So take a deep breath and start "resetting your pins," one by one.

Your immediate instinct after losing your job will probably be to tell your family. But wait: First, take some time to process the news yourself and prepare for their reaction.

"There's no point in hiding the fact that you're now out of work," says Dr. Curran. "But telling them is never an easy or pleasant chore. And you can automatically transfer your anger at yourself or your company to them. So the best thing to do is vent your feelings *before* breaking the news, away from home.

"Go to a bowling alley and knock down pins. Rail at a sympathetic friend. Do *something* to recognize and deal with your anger on your own, before you tell your spouse," says Dr. Curran.

"Then, couched in words that say, 'I feel bad and I need your help,' break the news. But don't be surprised if you look for support and get anger instead," says Dr. Curran. "The full effect of the shock wave will hit them the same way it hit you, and if they don't handle the news too well, you have to allow them to feel and act devastated without taking it personally," she says. "The spouse is bound to hurt, and you both need protection. But if you don't recognize that need, you may end up whimpering to each other like a couple of two-year-olds trying to say, 'Take care of me!'"

Swamped with Anxiety? Send an S.O.S.

Panic or despair is hard to hide. But if you're entertaining suicidal thoughts, try to resist blurting them out to your spouse. "Call your minister or rabbi, call a counselor, call a crisis hotline, so you can enlist these people to help you with your spouse," says Dr. Curran. Your husband or wife has too much at stake to be able to help you work through your despair the way a trained professional can. "*I'm* a trained professional, and I've called hotlines myself for personal problems," adds Dr. Curran.

"Job loss is a terrible blow, and it can strain a marriage at a time you need each other more than ever," says Dr. Curran. "Both spouses need time to adjust, and sometimes counseling can help."

"Group counseling may be helpful for people who avoid social gatherings out of embarrassment, but still need someone to talk to," says Margaret W. Linn, Ph.D., director of social research at the Veterans Administration Center in Miami, Florida, and professor of psychiatry at the University of Miami

School of Medicine. "If interpersonal or emotional problems contributed to job loss, full-fledged counseling may be in order.

"Talking about your feelings can help you get over the difficulties and raise your self-concept, especially if you need help convincing yourself that you're not to blame for losing your job," says Dr. Linn.

A study conducted by Dr. Linn and others on the effects of unemployment found that men who had a supportive family and other social contacts

---

Spouses of Job Hunters Feel Stress, Too

If your husband or wife loses their job, you may feel as angry, upset and scared as they do. How do you cope with *your* feelings without making your spouse feel even more depressed and humiliated?

"The spouse of the unemployed may not suffer the loss of self-esteem that the out-of-work partner does," says Margaret W. Linn, Ph.D., director of social research at the Veterans Administration Center in Miami, Florida, and professor of psychiatry at the University of Miami School of Medicine, who's studied the effects of unemployment on mental and physical health. "But the situation is equally stressful in other ways."

"Everyone sympathizes with the jobless spouse," says Jeanne Curran, Ph.D., professor of sociology at California State University-Dominguez Hills, Carson, California. "But the partner of the unemployed spouse is under stress, too.

"Say a man and wife both work and she loses her job," says Dr. Curran. "The husband of an out-of-work woman gets little sympathy, even if she earned as much or more than he did, because people still assume he is the main provider.

"If the wife does not work at a paying job outside the home and her husband suddenly loses his job, she will feel stressed by the fact that she's thrust into the supportive role, which can endanger the relationship," says Dr. Curran. "Her husband, in turn, may feel hostile toward her in her new role, which wasn't in the marriage bargain."

Sometimes the spouse of someone who's unemployed can find help in applying the old adage "Misery loves company."

"Talking to husbands or wives of other unemployed workers can also be helpful to an anxious spouse," says Dr. Linn. "Spouses need to vent their feelings with sympathetic listeners who are going through the same thing. They also need to get out and recharge their batteries at times.

"By all means, though, don't avoid talking to your husband or wife about unemployment," says Dr. Linn. "The unemployed spouse needs to feel understood. And so do you."

to rely on weathered the emotional and physical effects of unemployment better than those who did not. Evidently, feeling that others care and are at least willing, if not able, to help plays a critical role in salvaging your professional life as well as your pride and self-esteem.

A Cure for the Out-of-Work Blues

Keeping in mind that social support is the key to surviving unemployment with your self-esteem intact—and to landing a new and possibly *better* job—here are some tactics for success.

Get out of bed in the morning. This seems to be simple enough advice. Yet Dr. Linn's study found that those who lost their jobs spent nearly five times as many days in bed during the first six months as men who continued to work.

Look for a job elsewhere within your company. Surprising as it may seem, getting booted out of one department doesn't necessarily mean no one else will want you. They may even welcome you. One advantage here is that you can hang on to valued friendships in the workplace—and your place on the company softball team.

Or, consider applying for a job at a competing company or one with which your former company had a business relationship, such as a supplier or producer of essential goods.

Line up allies. "Make a checklist of people who can help you," says Dr. Curran. "Include friends and colleagues outside of work who can support you objectively, without feeling the guilt of having survived a job that you didn't. Ministers and rabbis, too, are often good at helping people regain their sense of control over their lives."

Dr. Linn says that keeping in touch with people you used to work with and feel close to can help in some cases. "Retirees do it all the time," she says. "Who knows? They may end up helping you locate another job."

Cast your net wide. Include relatives, friends, schools, professional societies and employment counselors on your list of contacts, says Dr. Greiff.

"Look to people in your church or synagogue, or on community service committees, in the Kiwanis club—any organization—not to ask them to hire you but to find out what they know," says Dr. Curran.

In researching their book, *The 100 Best Companies to Work for in America*, authors Levering, Moskowitz and Katz asked all sorts of people for leads: executive recruiters, management consultants, market researchers, public relations counselors, business school teachers, newspaper reporters, magazine editors, radio and TV news staffers and others in close contact with the job market. There's no reason why you can't tap into the same network to track down job openings. (Many job openings never appear in the help-wanted ads.)

Make looking for work a job in itself. One of the ironies of unemployment is that even though you have oodles of free time, you can't seem to get nearly as much done as when you were employed. That's because the unemployed lose what psychologists call "traction."

"[When you're employed] the structure of your work pulls you along," explains Smith. "Something that you quickly achieve when you are busy and working can somehow fill your day when you have nothing in particular to do."

Job hunting with zeal serves two purposes: It increases your chances of landing a job and keeps time from hanging heavy on your hands.

"Pursue work with a sense of purpose: Work at it every day, between nine and five, like any other commitment," says Dr. Curran.

Log all your applications and job inquiries on a calendar. And let the kids help. "That helps you keep a quantitative record of your efforts, but more important, it keeps the kids from getting scared, because they see that their parents are doing something," says Dr. Curran. "Otherwise, they'll sense that you feel powerless, and they'll feel powerless—and scared." Making the job quest a family project also helps prevent family members from feeling alone and anxious about the future.

Consider volunteer work. "This has several benefits," says Dr. Curran. "It gets you out of the house every day. It looks good on your résumé. And it tells prospective employers that you're not depressed. And any useful, meaningful work helps restore your sense of control."

Maintaining Morale over the Long Haul

Statistics say that the average period of unemployment is 19 weeks. But jobless workers have little use for statistics. (As the saying goes, "When everybody else loses their job, it's a recession. When *I* lose my job, it's a depression.") If weeks drag into months and you still haven't found a job, it's easy to get discouraged. It's also okay to feel a little frayed around the edges.

"You can't expect to cope well all the time," says Dr. Curran. Still, you want to sustain hope. Otherwise, depression and poor health may interfere with your efforts (or desire) to find new work, completing the cycle of joblessness and despair.

Step up your exercise program. Unemployment is a great opportunity to get serious about an exercise program. Exercise reduces stress, counteracts insomnia and other physical complaints associated with the out-of-work blues *and* helps you look good for job interviews. So take up the exercise you always put off for lack of time.

"Recent studies have shown that unemployment lowers immunity," says Dr. Linn. "Activities like exercise, which have a positive effect on the immune system, would certainly be a good way to feel better and maintain resistance to certain kinds of illness."

Keep in touch with your old friends—but look for opportunities to

make new ones. "Fraternizing with members of your bowling team, church or a community group can fill the gap often left by friendships made on the job," says Dr. Linn.

Treat yourself—you deserve it. Some people are reluctant to spend money on movie tickets when the mortgage is due, school is about to start and the tires are bald. "But if you can possibly allow for some form of leisure and recreation in your budget, you should," says Dr. Linn. Sports (like jogging) and hobbies (like sewing or carpentry) are excellent because they give you a sense of accomplishment.

Stay current in your field. Keep up on technical matters and continue your association with professional groups.

Think positive. "If you were good enough to get your last job, you're good enough to get another one," says Dr. Greiff.

The Hidden Benefits of Losing Your Job

"It may sound corny, but the up side of all this is that you may very well end up with a better job than you had before," says Dr. Greiff. "I don't necessarily mean better in terms of money, position or other tangible benefits, but better in terms of finding a job that fits you better, so to speak."

Some management styles, for example, may suit you more than others. If you found it stressful to work for a rigid taskmaster, a new job may provide an opportunity to work for a coach, not a controller.

One man took up painting after he lost his job and said it had become more important to him than his job had ever been. Another was equally passionate about gardening. And one survey of young unemployed parents found that in 14 cases the fathers were grateful to have more time to be with their children.

"Losing your job may give you an opportunity to reevaluate your standards and expectations of where, how and if you want to work—a luxury few people ever have," says Dr. Greiff.

Part 4

PREVENTING AND TREATING PHYSICAL PROBLEMS

Chapter 37

BACK PAIN

It's definitely back there. The dull ache just above the hips. The biting twinge at midback. The soreness around your shoulders that's moved in like an invasion of termites—and seems about as likely to leave. Eighty percent of us have a backache at one time or another, and for 70 million Americans that pain is as regular as the mail.

What's in back of it all? Rarely disease or a structural problem. A big scientific study says that 83 percent of all back pain is caused by muscle problems. The muscles may be weak because of a desk job or a constant slouch or extra pounds or careless lifting. And if your back pain is of that variety, it probably has another ingredient in its recipe: stress.

Your muscles don't like emotional stress, explains Hans Kraus, M.D., author of *Backache, Stress and Tension.* They tighten up, and if they are forced to make a sudden movement, those rigid muscles can cause a spasm, which in turn can cause a knot that primes the muscles for *more* spasms. And tight muscles can work against you in other ways.

"Over a period of time, a chronically tensed muscle may lose its stretch and become shortened," writes coauthor Lawrence W. Friedmann, M.D., in *Freedom from Backaches.* This, he says, may "lead to awkward, jerky movements, which may make the muscle more susceptible to injury."

Ways to De-stress Your Back

Several of the stress-management techniques described in this book may help prevent you from turning stressful situations into back pain. Many people respond well to massage (see chapter 69) as a means of relieving pain. According to Dr. Friedmann, a light, stroking massage at home can relax muscles and relieve spasms.

Certain relaxation techniques, if practiced properly and routinely, can work to eliminate muscular tension. For example, the use of deep breathing techniques (see chapter 58) is being accepted as part of relaxation training in some pain clinics. One method suggested by James E. Loehr, Ed.D., and Jeffrey A. Migdow, M.D., in their book, *Take a Deep Breath,* may be especially helpful to release the tension that contributes to your back pain. They call it "The Controlling-Pain-with-Imagery Breath."

1. Keep your eyes closed throughout.
2. Begin abdominal breathing (breathing with your belly instead of your chest).
3. Imagine tension leaving your body, like a vapor or stream of color, with each exhalation.
4. Imagine relaxation coming in with each inhalation.
5. Move parts of your body as you breathe, if it helps to release any general tension.
6. Imagine your incoming breath traveling to the area of pain and filling it with calmness.
7. Imagine the pain flowing out with each exhalation.
8. Allow yourself, through crying or sighing, to release any emotion related to the pain.
9. Continue steps 5 through 8 for five to ten minutes.
10. Feel the movement of your breath again.
11. Stretch your arms and legs.
12. Open your eyes when you feel better.

All these techniques are good—but using two or more of them in combination may be better. Robert G. Addison, M.D., of the Center for Pain Studies at the Rehabilitation Institute of Chicago and author of *Living with Your Bad Back,* says that people who suffer from stress-aggravated back pain should use a variety of stress-reduction techniques. In addition to physical techniques and exercise, people might consider using relaxation, exercise tapes *and* biofeedback, for example.

Dr. Addision also says people with chronic back pain should "examine what is causing the stress." Or who. According to one study, family conflict was often the cause of low back pain. In the workplace, lack of a feeling of camaraderie with co-workers was cited as one cause of the problem. And the person who's stressing your life may be you. Another study concluded that people with chronic lower back pain tend to have a negative self-concept. In that case, a professional therapist may help you improve how you view yourself—and get you back to normal.

Chapter 38

COLITIS

When it comes to life-disrupting ailments, colitis can be among the worst.

The most prevalent version of this disease is known as ulcerative colitis—inflammation of the colon lining. And as structural abnormalities go, this one takes quite a toll. Not only are its symptoms painful, but when flare-ups occur, regular day-to-day activities scarcely can go on as normal. For one thing, you spend most of your time enthroned on the nearest toilet.

A 46-year-old Philadelphia woman recalls her agony: "On two separate occasions I spent almost a year of my life in bed. I spent all of my time—that's *all* of my time—either in the bedroom or the bathroom."

In the acute phase of the disease, you have severe diarrhea, usually with blood, and up to 24 stools a day. Your inflamed bowel makes it difficult to absorb the nutrients in your food, so you may experience nutritional deficits—and possible weight loss. If you lose too much blood, you may become anemic. On top of that, there is abdominal pain—usually *lots* of it. And fever.

According to the National Foundation for Ileitis and Colitis, between one and two million people suffer from the ravages of Crohn's disease (or ileitis) and ulcerative colitis. These are often baffling—and sometimes genetically inherited—diseases.

At least ten times as many people are afflicted by a less severe condition that may be confused with colitis. It is called irritable bowel syndrome, or IBS, but it has been known by other names, too. (Sometimes IBS is referred to as spastic colon. And because its sufferers may pass mucus, it was once poorly termed mucous colitis.) "IBS is not a form of colitis," says Richard Johannes, M.D., a gastroenterologist at Johns Hopkins University School of Medicine, Baltimore, Maryland.

IBS, which hits 50 to 75 percent of us at one time or another, involves the alternating symptoms of diarrhea and constipation. And as its sufferers know well, there are abdominal pains. The mystery about IBS is that there's no known cause or associated disease responsible for producing the annoying symptoms (unlike colitis, where colon inflammation is the source of the problem).

What is known, however, is that the symptoms can be aggravated by stress. "It's not too uncommon that the symptoms are worsened with physical or mental stress," says Sidney Phillips, M.D., professor of medicine and gastro-enterology at Mayo Medical School, Rochester, Minnesota. He adds that "stress makes it less easy to tolerate the symptoms."

And while doctors prescribe everything from anti-inflammatory agents to antidiarrheal drugs to iron medication to dietary changes to treat the symptoms of colitis and IBS, there is a movement to treat patients through stress management.

Stress Management to the Rescue

And why not? Here's a look at some of the evidence that stress management helps keep these ailments in check.

First, colitis.

In a study conducted by faculty members at the University of British Columbia School of Nursing, Vancouver, researchers determined that a stress-management program can greatly boost the physical and psychosocial well-being of colitis sufferers. Of 80 people in the study, half participated in a stress-management program and half were designated as a control group. The stress-management group attended 18 hours of classes that combined autogenic training (see chapter 54) and Progressive Relaxation. Also, they were taught communication skills such as assertiveness training and active listening in a group setting. And they were given instruction in personal planning skills—worry control and time management.

"Worry control was important because when you have a condition like this [ulcerative colitis], you become worried about recurrences and about coping when you're in an acute episode," says Barbara Milne, R.N., an assistant professor of nursing at the University of British Columbia School of Nursing and one of the study's authors. (The participants used some of the worry-control techniques outlined in chapter 26.)

Time management also is crucial. If you've got colitis, chances are you're not going to get around to doing everything you want to do. And the resulting pileup of chores and commitments can overwhelm you and contribute to your symptoms.

That's a lesson learned by one colitis sufferer, who said, "Over the years I realized that when I had so much to do, so many commitments to fulfill, I would get sick so that I had an excuse not to do them. Later I learned that my life would go on if I say no to commitments. I can relax and free my mind of the worry of not doing them."

In the Canadian study, the group that practiced stress management watched happily as their disease activity dwindled. They also discovered a boost in their mental health. For the other group, there was no reported change.

Hypnotherapy May Help

A separate study showed that hypnotherapy may help colitis sufferers. Edward Taub, Ph.D., a professor of psychology at the University of Alabama at Birmingham, and Alan Ginsberg, M.D., director of the gastroenterology clinic at George Washington University School of Medicine in Washington, D.C., tracked 25 patients from that clinic. The patients underwent eight hypnosis sessions that searched for the events that triggered colitis flare-ups. Under hypnosis, it also was suggested to the patients that they could handle the illness and its symptoms. The hypnosis also included some suggestions for relaxation, according to Dr. Taub. The results? There was a general reduction in symptoms among half of the patients receiving hypnotherapy.

There's also hope in massage and deep breathing therapies. Both of these techniques helped colitis patients to cope with their plight. In a study of 15 people by Gloria Joachim, R.N., an assistant professor of nursing at the University of British Columbia School of Nursing, a majority were able to get to sleep more quickly and feel they had some control over pain. They also discovered ways of quickly calming themselves.

Experts suggest that a colitis sufferer find a stress-management program he or she can live with. "The point is to develop a personal plan that gives the body a break and helps relieve the stress for a certain time every day," says Milne. "The best stress-management technique is the one you can do every day and can incorporate into your lifestyle." Adds Dr. Phillips, "If you can make some modifications in your lifestyle so that physically and mentally you may be under less stress, it's a useful thing to add."

An important first step may be to learn all you can about colitis. For information, write to the headquarters of the National Foundation for Ileitis and Colitis, 444 Park Avenue South, New York, NY 10016. And if you've got colitis, keep this important fact in mind: Patients with colitis have a higher-than-normal risk of developing cancer of the colon or rectum. So you should be examined regularly to detect early treatable cancers.

Self-Help Groups for IBS

New Jersey psychologist Rosemarie Scolaro Moser, Ph.D., works with a lot of IBS sufferers and has built a repertoire of sound advice.

Education. Very often people with IBS are convinced they have the more serious colitis or—worse yet—cancer. Dr. Scolaro Moser advises that if your doctor diagnoses IBS, you should learn all you can about the disorder. The knowledge that you're suffering from a problem, not a dangerous disease, will go a long way toward reducing anxiety. That in turn may help reduce flare-ups. (To learn more about IBS, write to the American Digestive Disease Society, 7720 Wisconsin Avenue, Bethesda, MD 20814, or phone 301-652-9293.)

Groups. Wouldn't it be great to discuss your ailment without embarrassment? Self-help groups for IBS sufferers, while hard to find, can provide support and maybe a few coping strategies. Imagine laughing with friends who suffer from the same discomfort. To start a group, contact your gastroenterologist and ask to post a notice in his office. You may want a professional psychotherapist to lead the group. If your physician can't recommend someone, try your local mental health agency or the psychology department of a nearby university hospital. (For more information on self-help groups, see chapter 80.)

Relaxation techniques. Virtually any relaxation technique that works for you will help you manage your IBS, says Dr. Scolaro Moser.

Therapy. Don't get the impression that all IBS sufferers need to pour out their souls to a shrink, but if your IBS is out of control, a therapist might guide you to the proper stress-management technique. A cognitive behavior therapist may show you how cognitive restructuring—such as learning to challenge the belief that you have to be perfect—can help alleviate IBS.

Chapter 39

CORONARY ARTERY DISEASE

You probably won't be surprised to know that coronary artery disease is the major health problem in the industrialized world today. Yet the five biggest risk factors—high blood pressure, high cholesterol, diabetes, overweight and smoking—fail to explain half of the worldwide cases of coronary artery disease. Stress accounts for a good portion of the rest.

Is heart disease the price we pay for living with 20th-century stress?

"We have the bodies of our ancestors, yet we are living in a world they never dreamed would exist," says Robert Eliot, M.D., director of the cardiovascular unit of the Swedish Medical Center in Denver, Colorado. "Mankind has been around for 1,600 generations, 1,300 of which we spent in caves. The major stresses were physical and triggered physical reactions, including higher heart rate and blood pressure. Today's stresses are more often mental than physical: We face 30 or 40 mental 'saber-toothed tigers' a day that may trigger the same sort of physical reactions. So those who interpret mental stress the same way as a physical threat are activating out-of-date ancestral responses that can be suicidal," says Dr. Eliot, author of *Is It Worth Dying For?*

Like most people, you probably assume that a sudden, overwhelming shock can send your heart into a dither—and you into the nearest coronary care unit. And a major upset can trigger a heart attack. But what you may not realize is that *chronic* stress also threatens your heart in other, less obvious but equally threatening ways, either directly or by increasing risk factors such as cholesterol levels.

What Gets Your Goat, Gets Your Heart

Did you know, for example, that nervous tension can raise your cholesterol levels as easily as eating a ham and cheese omelet? Or that giving up in

180

the face of a stressful event is as bad for your blood pressure as getting fighting mad? What's more, a low-cholesterol, low-salt diet doesn't cancel out the effect.

One of the most significant effects of the acute stress response is the damage it can wreak on heart muscle fibers. "[The stress reaction] actually takes bites out of the heart muscles," says Dr. Eliot. "It can overcontract the small muscle fibers until some of them rip." This leaves the heart vulnerable to arrhythmias—heart spasms that can cause sudden death.

Pulling the Plug on Stress

The difficulty in overcoming this problem is that different types of stress affect different people in different ways at different times. "That's why there is no objective definition of what a stressful event is or how many events add up to 'too much' stress," says Dr. Eliot, who also directs the National Center of Preventive and Stress Medicine in Phoenix, Arizona, and serves on the Prevention Committee of the American College of Cardiology.

"Identifying the sources of stress in your life is simple," says Dr. Eliot. "Just ask yourself, 'What three things bug me the most?' Right off the bat, most people say it's something like traffic, deadlines or a relationship. Once you identify and deal with the Big Three, you can uncover—and deal with— less obvious secondary sources of stress."

Dr. Eliot compares stress with overloaded circuitry. "If you have six or seven appliances plugged into an electrical outlet and unplug three, you lighten the load considerably."

Another simple way to assess your stress levels and therefore your heart disease risk, according to Dr. Eliot, is to ask yourself, "Am I working, or am I struggling?"

"A famous physiologist from Sweden, Dr. Bjorn Folkow, discovered that when animals struggle and perceive they can't win, their metabolism changes and they roll over and die," explains Dr. Eliot. "Similarly, if you work hard yet feel you're getting somewhere, you'll feel fulfilled, your blood pressure will usually be fine, your immune system will coast along smoothly and you'll be okay. But if you struggle and don't feel you're making any headway, you could be in big trouble. Being caught in the 'struggle/defeat syndrome' is a tough way to get through the day, let alone your whole life.

"In other words, if you feel that deadlines will kill you, they probably will. But if you feel they're unreasonable yet probably won't kill you, they probably won't," says Dr. Eliot.

Mastering Stress

Sometimes, life seems to be just one big "in box" for stress. Here are seven ways to manage that stress—and your reaction to it.

Don't overreact. Some people call it "making a mountain out of a molehill." Dr. Eliot calls it "burning a dollar's worth of energy for a dime's worth of trouble." Call it what you will, chronic overreaction grossly overworks your heart and arteries.

Talk yourself down from the brink. Psychologists use a technique known as cognitive therapy that deals with "self-talk" to help people cut down on self-induced stress when things don't go their way. Suppose you're waiting for friends to pick you up for dinner, for example, and they're 15 minutes late. Irrational, negative self-talk—thinking "People should always be punctual" or "Lateness shows that a person doesn't care how you feel"—creates unnecessary stress. Positive self-talk, on the other hand—thinking "That's okay—I'll use the time to finish a project I'm working on"—is a positive, less stress-producing reaction.

"The most important conversations you'll ever have are with yourself," Dr. Eliot quips. "So watch your language!"

Stand back and consider all your options. According to Dr. Eliot, managing stress actually means managing the anger and anxiety you feel in a stressful situation so that, rather than being overwhelmed, you can see options available—and solve the problem.

Learn to say no. Dr. Eliot says "no" is the most lifesaving word in the English language, especially for heart attack candidates, who tend to try to do more than is realistically possible.

Set realistic expectations for yourself and others. "Much self-induced stress—especially guilt and perfectionism—arises from expectations that cannot be met," says Dr. Eliot. "So ask yourself, 'Am I asking more of human performance than can be expected?' Aim for excellence, not perfection. After all, not even machines are always perfect."

Make friends. "The data are definitely in: Social support reduces the impact of stress on the heart," says Dr. Eliot. "And that includes having a spouse and friends you can confide in or count on in the face of uncertainty. So ask yourself, 'Do I know someone who would lend me money if I needed it? Who would give me a lift if I needed a ride? Who would let me spend the night at their place if I had nowhere to go?' With friends in the wings, you'll survive."

Find a relaxation technique that suits you, and practice it daily. "Relaxation methods are like music: We all like different kinds," says Dr. Eliot. "Most people can learn and use deep breathing, for example, but not everyone can do visualization. So try various methods, and adopt the ones you like best."

And remember, says Dr. Eliot, that learning to control your emotional responses to everyday stress—just like learning any skill—takes practice.

A Prescription for the 21st Century

Small adjustments in coping style can make big differences in heart health. "Like aiming for any target, one small adjustment can determine whether you hit the bull's-eye or miss the target entirely," says Dr. Eliot.

"People who've completed our preventive program can control their blood pressure without medication," says Dr. Eliot. "Their cholesterol levels drop. They feel less anxiety, hostility and depression. They have fewer arguments, headaches, backaches or sleep interruptions. In short, their physiology cools off, even among people in high-pressure, commission sales jobs. What's more, their incomes have risen anywhere from 40 to over 200 percent—yet they work an average of 50 hours a week instead of 70."

The benefits, to your heart and to your quality of life, are tremendous. No wonder one doctor calls Dr. Eliot's prescription "medicine for the 21st century."

Chapter 40

FATIGUE

Everybody feels tired once in a while. Jet lag, shift changes, late nights and other schedule deviations can cause even the sturdiest of us to drag through a day—or two or three. But too often folks complain of feeling fatigue that has no clear cause.

Frequently it's stress alone—either an abundance or a lack of it—that can lead to this feeling. But your fatigue also may be a symptom of a physical ailment, your diet, your mental health or your sleep habits. Here's a checklist that can help you figure out what's causing your fatigue, and then work up a strategy for treating and preventing it.

Check Your Physical Health

Fatigue can be a symptom of disease. So if you find yourself dragging without apparent reason, first check with your doctor. Make sure you're not suffering from diabetes, kidney or liver diseases, anemia or any of the other illnesses that cause fatigue.

If illness isn't causing your problem, take a hard look at your physical condition. You've heard the saying "Fat folk fade fast." It takes extra work to carry around extra pounds. Begin a daily ritual of exercise. Your doctor can help tailor a routine to suit your physical condition and needs, but you can make the first step by taking a daily walk.

A lack of exercise ages the body and can contribute to fatigue. William M. Bortz, M.D., of the Palo Alto Medical Clinic in California, says that even though disuse is the opposite of stress, both produce the same impact: aging and the feelings of tiredness, weakness and feebleness. Dr. Bortz goes so far as to estimate that exercise is a 40-year age offset. "A fit person of 80 is as fit as an unfit person of 40," he says.

Check Your Diet

In addition to a lack of exercise, a nutritional deficiency also can cause fatigue. Some adults (particularly women in their childbearing years) barely satisfy the daily minimum requirement for iron, a mineral that maximizes the oxygen-carrying capacity of the blood. If you have only the minimum in your system, you can become deficient should you lose blood for one reason or another. People who regularly take aspirin lose blood from their stomach, menstruating women lose blood, nosebleeders lose blood, peptic ulcer sufferers lose blood. The Recommended Dietary Allowances (RDAs) for iron are 10 milligrams for men and 18 milligrams for women—although some distinguished nutritionists believe the RDA may be too low, particularly for women.

Even stress itself can deplete you of some important nutrients—enough to wipe you out, according to Ray C. Wunderlich, Jr., M.D., a physician who practices preventive and nutritional medicine in St. Petersburg, Florida.

The cause of stress can be something very serious—childbirth, divorce, a court case—or just a dressing-down by your boss, but the response is the same. The event sends you into that adrenal overdrive of the fight-or-flight response. You initially experience a burst of energy as your hypothalamus signals the pituitary gland and then the adrenal glands to release stress hormones into the blood. But if you don't have the nutrients or adrenal sources to resupply those hormones, you may lapse into fatigue.

Dr. Wunderlich suggests you protect yourself from fatigue by building up the stores of such nutrients as thiamine (vitamin B_1), vitamin B_6, pantothenate, vitamin C, chromium, manganese, selenium, potassium, calcium and zinc in appropriate amounts. Your physician can help guide you.

Check Your Sleep Habits

Fatigued during the day and don't know why? Maybe you're not getting a good night's sleep. To ensure that you get sufficient sleep, practice what sleep experts call "good sleep hygiene." Stick to a regular bedtime and a regular wake time. Avoid substances such as caffeine or alcohol that interfere with your sleep. Don't spend too much nonsleep time in bed.

Set aside enough time to get the right amount of sleep for you. "Don't underestimate the amount of sleep you need. You may need ten hours of sleep a night and feel sleepy during the day if you only get eight," says Timothy Monk, Ph.D., a psychologist at the University of Pittsburgh's Western Psychiatric Institute and Clinic. And keep in mind that not everybody can supplement a bad night of sleep by taking catnaps. "People often believe they can 'snack' in their sleeping the way they 'snack' in their eating," says Dr. Monk. Don't cheat yourself of sleep.

Check Your Emotions

Sleep is very sensitive to our physical and emotional well-being. If something is bothering you, it can cause insomnia that results in next-day fatigue. David F. Dinges, Ph.D., co-director of experimental psychiatry at the University of Pennsylvania, estimates that psychological problems contribute to at least 60 percent of all insomnia. But it's not always easy to determine whether the sleep disorder is causing the stress or is *caused by* stress.

Just as you examine yourself for physical problems, look for evidence that your emotions may be keeping you in a state of fatigue. Donald Norfolk, a British osteopath and author of *Farewell to Fatigue,* writes, "Don't let emotional conflicts fester or allow doubts to lie unresolved. Take action. Face up to your fears, resolve your doubts, banish your hang-ups, conquer your inadequacies and make peace with your conscience. Learn to give vent to your emotions—frustration, laughter and tears—in socially acceptable, purposeful ways. Setting your mind at rest, you'll find, is an essential part of putting your body to rest."

Check Your Arousal Level

According to one theory, anxiety improves performance until a certain optimum level of arousal has been reached. Beyond that point, performance deteriorates as higher levels of anxiety are attained. How does this theory relate to fatigue? Dr. Norfolk writes that many sufferers of chronic fatigue have either too little or too much arousal. On the one hand, they may "have nothing to tap their energy stores or arouse their latent powers," he writes. "If they are to overcome their lethargy they must live more adventurously, be more competitive, take on extra responsibility, pursue new hobbies and tackle fresh challenges." On the other hand, there are those who have passed their peak of arousal and "need a temporary relief from stress to help them regain their normal vigor."

His advice: If you're bored, inject more variety and challenge into your life. If you feel tired from overstress, step back and slow down for a while. Learn your personal warning signs that you've overstepped your limits of stress arousal. They may be headaches, backaches, tooth grinding, increased consumption of alcohol or an escalation in your willingness to yell at your kids.

Dr. Dinges says that much fatigue is caused by three factors: The quality and quantity of our sleep at night, the state of our internal clock and how long we've been trying to work on a difficult task.

In fatigue, the brain loses some of its ability to function. When that happens, says Dr. Dinges, we become more dependent on our environment for stimulation. So if we're already fatigued—and at the same time our environment offers little stimulation—we're bound to be dragging. But when we're wide awake, there's no reason why we would fall asleep during a boring lecture or a long dull drive, he says.

With good diet, regular exercise and a solid night's sleep behind you, even stress won't rob your energy.

Chapter 41

HEADACHES

Headaches are symptoms, not diseases. Although they can be related to a physical ailment like a hangover or an allergy, many chronic, recurring headaches are brought on by stress, according to Seymour Diamond, M.D., author of *Advice from the Diamond Headache Clinic* and other books on the topic.

Among the varieties of headaches that have been isolated by experts, muscle contraction headaches are the type most directly caused by stress. More commonly known as "tension" headaches, this type of headache afflicts people when they transfer their tension to their muscles. What happens is relatively simple: As you meet your day-to-day challenges, frustrations and disappointments—watching your child dump a jar of jelly on the freshly scrubbed kitchen floor, having your boss make an impossible demand—the muscles in your head and neck begin to contract. As a result, they constrict blood vessels, the action that is believed to be the main cause of the discomfort, according to Dr. Diamond.

To escape from the grip of tension headaches, the most obvious solution is to pay attention to the sources of your stress and observe how your body reacts to them. For some people, the discovery that it's stress and not something physical that causes the headaches is enough to help prevent them from recurring. So before reaching for an over-the-counter headache remedy, determine if you're doing all you can to release the tension in your muscles, where the headaches begin. (However, if the headaches become increasingly frequent and more severe, you should seek a doctor's help right away.)

The Electronic Headache Detective

You can use biofeedback techniques to discover which muscles contract to cause your tension headache and then designate a strategy for relaxing those muscles. Joel Greenspoon, Ph.D., a professor of psychology at the University of Texas at Odessa who has conducted research in the area of headaches, relies on biofeedback to help clients focus on the activity of their muscles to predict when a headache is likely to occur.

Dr. Greenspoon attaches electrodes to various muscle groups of a headache sufferer and measures the electrical activity in terms of microvoltage. In a trial-and-error manner, he tries to pinpoint the muscle groups most affected. If he sees the normal limits of electrical activity are surpassed in a particular area, it's a good bet that those are the muscles involved. Most of the time, he says, it's the *frontalis* muscle (the muscle across the forehead) that tenses first. But it can also be the muscles in the back of the neck or in the jaw, with the headache eventually working its way up to the head.

But once a person realizes where the headache starts, he can engage in one of several strategies to relax the particular muscles. Dr. Greenspoon's clients employ Progressive Relaxation, deep breathing (see chapter 58) or autogenic training exercises (see chapter 54). For some, a warm bath works to eliminate tension (see chapter 55). For others, stretching exercises (see chapter 83) loosen muscles in the neck or jaw.

Think Your Headache Away

Kenneth A. Holroyd, Ph.D., a professor of psychology at Ohio University, relies on cognitive therapy to help clients prevent and treat tension headaches. He instructs clients to keep daily records of headache episodes and to record the thoughts, feelings, activities and environmental factors that precede or accompany the pain. Once the clients understand how their thoughts and underlying beliefs contribute to headaches, they begin the task of changing those thoughts and beliefs.

So you get a tension headache every time your boss makes an impossible demand? Dr. Holroyd would have you determine whether the *perception* of the demand is impossible or whether the demand itself actually *is* impossible. If you determine that it's your perception that's creating the difficulty, Dr. Holroyd's next question is: What is the source of that perception? (Your own fear of failure, for example.) Another thought he has you ponder: How much of your perception is a reaction to something else about the boss? These new perspectives are a first step in changing the way you think and feel when a demand is made, and the first step in taking control of the stress—and the headaches.

Avoid Your Migraine Triggers

Migraines, by their nature, are more dramatic than muscle contraction headaches. They are technically considered *vascular* headaches. In vascular headaches, the blood vessels or arteries inside and outside the skull dilate or expand; thus, the walls of the blood vessels apply pressure on the nearby nerves and cause pain. Unlike muscle contraction headaches, which usually are felt on both sides of the head, migraines are often felt on one side or the other.

While migraines tend to run in families, there's no evidence that the problem is inherited genetically. "People have predispositions to migraines the way some people have predispositions to ulcers," explains Jack Hartje, Ph.D., a professor of psychology at the University of North Florida, who treats migraine sufferers with biofeedback.

Migraines occur when a person with such a predisposition is exposed to a trigger, such as certain foods or a stressful situation. As Dr. Hartje explains, the trigger activates the stress response. One result is that the carotid arteries—which supply blood to the brain—constrict. When the brain senses it isn't getting enough blood, it releases neurochemicals to dilate the carotid arteries back to normal. The problem is that migraine sufferers experience an overreaction: The arteries overdilate. Sensitive pain receptors that are wrapped around the arteries are stretched—which is what causes all that pain.

Physicians suggest migraine sufferers understand their physical or emotional triggers. Avoiding a food or substance that triggers the migraine is often the best way to control attacks. If emotional triggers are causing migraines, a therapist may be able to help you recognize the triggers and learn to avoid them or deal with them in a different way. According to one study, stress may play a role three or four days prior to the onset.

While many of the stress-reduction techniques outlined in this book may not cure you of your migraines, they may help you prevent them. Biofeedback, combined with various relaxation techniques (see chapter 56), has been successful in training patients to suppress attacks.

Chapter 42

IMMUNITY

People who've gone through tough times sometimes get sick. Take Jessica. She sold her beautiful old home and moved into an efficiency apartment. She auctioned off lots of furniture that "just wouldn't fit," but even with the extra cash, she had trouble paying the moving company. After only three days in her new home—with curtains still to be hung and china to be unpacked—Jessica developed a thunderous cough and a fever. She'd come down with bronchitis, and her illness may very well have been related to the stress of moving.

Over the years, researchers have noticed that respiratory illnesses such as colds, laryngitis and bronchitis often occur in the aftermath of a stressful situation. It is a widely held belief that stress plays a role in herpes attacks, although the evidence isn't quite as solid.

"The argument is not that stress produces an infection," say John B. Jemmott III, Ph.D., of Princeton University, and Steven E. Locke, M.D., of Harvard Medical School, Boston, in an exhaustive review of the medical evidence linking stress and physical illness that was published in *Psychological Bulletin.* "But it impairs immunologic functioning and makes the person, if exposed to an infectious agent, more likely to develop the disease than he or she would have been if not under stress."

Stress: The Last Straw?

This intriguing new branch of medicine is called psychoneuroimmunology (the interrelationship between the mind, the nervous system and the immune system), and it goes something like this.

The immune system is one of the most complicated systems in the body, serving to defend the body against infection and disease. If all goes according to plan, the "bug" is destroyed.

But this surveillance system doesn't work independently. The immune system changes and is influenced by many factors: heat, cold, what you eat, the genetic blueprint you inherited from your folks, your age, race and sex, your circadian rhythms—and possibly stress.

One theory suggests that the perception of stress prompts the brain to trigger the nervous system, which in turn releases hormones (including cortisol, epinephrine and norepinephrine) that can jam your immune system. Increases of cortisol secretion, for example, lead to production of weaker lymphocytes, cells that are important for immunity.

One study, supported in part by the National Institutes of Health, dug up evidence that the mind plays a role in physical health. Scientists at a University of Texas health center in Houston found that stress-related hormones (specifically epinephrine and norepinephrine) appear to block the ability of immune cells to kill cells infected with herpes simplex viruses such as genital herpes.

So yes, germs, poisons and other invaders can and do trigger illness. But evidence strongly suggests that a life steeped in stress weakens the immune system and can leave us more vulnerable to illness, including upper respiratory tract diseases, allergies, hypertension and even cancer. The role of stress helps to explain why, when exposed to certain disease-producing agents, some (but not all) of us get sick—and then only some of the time.

The link between stress and immunity is complex—and hard to study. Scientists can't inject hundreds of people with so many units of positive thinking, separate out various other factors in their lives and measure their immunity as easily as they can measure their blood pressure. For one thing, people vary greatly: Two people experiencing the same event at the same time for the same duration may vary in how much stress they endure, depending on their attitude and coping skills. Some, called "racehorses" by stress pioneer Hans Selye, even thrive on stress and seek it out.

Despite such limitations, the bulk of evidence favors the existence of a powerful link between mind and immunity. At the University of Toronto, for example, researchers studied stress symptoms and immune function (such as T-lymphocyte levels) in 21 accountants. Anxiety, depression and other signs of distress were highest in April (a peak stress period for accountants), while immune function was suppressed. "These results suggest that chronic occupational stress may increase susceptibility to disease," conclude the researchers in *Psychosomatic Medicine*. In a similar study, researchers noted an increase in anxiety and depression—and a corresponding drop in immune function—among high-stress subjects taking an important exam. In fact, many other studies have revealed a similar pattern: When stress increases, immunity decreases.

The Best Offense Is a Good Defense

The collective implication of such studies is that certain states of mind and feelings can produce powerful biochemical aftershocks strengthening the link between the mind, brain and immune system.

By learning to deflect or diffuse stress, you may *also* deflect or diffuse disease. At Albright College in Pennsylvania, college students were randomly assigned to a control group or to one of four 20-minute relaxation methods— the Relaxation Response pioneered by Herbert Benson (see chapter 76), guided visualization, massage (see chapter 69) or lying quietly with eyes closed. Antibody activity in the students' saliva was measured both before and after they relaxed. No matter which method of relaxation they used, the levels of disease-fighting activity rose. Levels did not change, however, in students in the control group.

Other methods to help "vaccinate" you against the harmful effects of stress include cognitive therapy, exercise, friendship, laughter, meditation, prayer, time management and other coping techniques discussed in part 6 of this book.

Chapter 43

INSOMNIA

Way back around midnight you tried counting sheep. You couldn't muster anything more imaginative, like chronologically naming all the vice presidents of the United States. At 1:00 A.M. you got up and drank some warm milk. The only result? A scorched pot to clean tomorrow. An hour and a half later you poured yourself some Scotch. That knocked you out for a while, but it's now 3:30 and you're wide awake once again.

This is torture by sleeplessness, and even though the spouse beside you sleeps like the proverbial rock, you've got plenty of company if you ever suffer from insomnia. Some 30 to 35 percent of all Americans have trouble sleeping at least once a year. Among all symptoms reported to doctors, insomnia ranks second in frequency; only headaches are more common.

So what can you do?

First, stop doing anything.

If you're putting intense pressure on yourself to sleep, you may be contributing to the problem, says Edward Stepanski, Ph.D., director of the insomnia clinic at the Henry Ford Hospital Sleep Disorders Center in Detroit. The harder you try to sleep, the more aroused and more tense you are likely to become, he says. He offers some suggestions for folks who are light sleepers or who have periodic bouts of insomnia.

Stop trying to sleep. Get up and do something that relaxes you. Read. Watch the late, late, late movie. You may eventually fall asleep. But even if you don't, you'll set the stage for future sleep-filled nights by denying yourself sleep tonight.

Try a relaxation exercise. It just may work, particularly if your problem is stress or presleep anxiety. Try deep breathing (see chapter 58), autogenic imagery exercises (see chapter 54), progressive muscle relaxation or baths (see chapter 55).

Don't hit the bottle. While alcohol may relax you, even enough to knock you out, it produces what sleep disorder researchers call "fragmented" (read: bad) sleep. You'll awake more frequently.

194

Don't try late-night vigorous activity. That, too, makes things worse. "Rigorous exercise tends to make the muscles more stimulated. It can lead to more fragmented sleep," explains Dr. Stepanski. And if all that tossing and turning woke your partner up, don't think you'll be sedated by a round of sex. For many sleepless folks, the arousal that comes with making love only worsens the situation. "Don't do anything that is physically or cognitively stimulating," suggests Dr. Stepanski. These rules, of course, apply only to those who have trouble sleeping. "People who sleep well could do anything they want," he says.

Don't raid the refrigerator. Your body might get used to the idea of eating cold pizza at 3:00 A.M. It may crave food the next night at the same time, and you could be setting yourself up for long-term sleep trouble.

Don't build any "awake" activities into sleep time. Don't pick up that report you need to finish. Don't work on your income taxes. You may be setting a bad precedent for your body, says Dr. Stepanski. If you can't sleep, you can at least try to relax.

Start Relaxing Beforehand

Charles Dickens, the noted insomniac/author, suggested that one would sleep better if the bed faced north to take advantage of the pole's magnetic attraction. Benjamin Franklin recommended that insomniacs get up, remake the bed, walk around nude until they are thoroughly cold and then return to bed. More modern-day sleep researchers offer somewhat more believable tips.

Try some mild exercise between two and four hours before your bedtime. "Take a walk, a swim—nothing too strenuous," says Ernest Hartmann, M.D., a professor of psychiatry at Tufts University School of Medicine in Medford, Massachusetts, and author of *The Sleeping Pill.*

Whether you exercise or not, set aside time to begin the process of relaxing toward sleep in the two or three hours before your bedtime, suggests Dr. Stepanski. That process can involve reading, watching TV—again, anything that will not overstimulate you.

If you're having trouble sleeping at night, avoid caffeine after noon and sugary snacks at night. Eat conservatively in the evening. Your body will be working overtime if it has to digest a big meal, and it could contribute to your sleeplessness.

Some physicians recommend pharmaceuticals to overcome temporary insomnia, either over-the-counter sleeping aids, which consist of antihistamines, or prescription drugs such as Valium. Pills may produce side effects—the dreaded next-day drowsiness, for example—and ordinarily are suggested only for short periods of time.

Those who have trouble sleeping because of temporary stress or emotional disturbances will often return to normal sleep once the stress disappears— when the check finally arrives in the mail, when the crucial exam is finally taken. But if the stress is not of a temporary nature, a vicious cycle can begin, according to Richard R. Bootzin, Ph.D., a professor of psychology at the University of Arizona, Tucson. "The stress may cause insomnia, and the resulting lack of sleep may make it less likely that the person will have the resources to deal with the factors causing the stress," he says.

Because your insomnia may be the symptom of a serious medical, neurological or psychological problem, check with a doctor if you can't trace your sleeping difficulty to some specific emotional stress or physical cause. "The most important thing to remember about insomnia is that it's a symptom, not a disease," says Dr. Hartmann. "The question to ask is not what you can do for it but why you have it in the first place."

The Sleep Restriction Approach

Some chronic insomniacs are treated through sleep restriction therapy. It's a method that often works in cases of situational insomnia as well. Simply put, you establish a rigid schedule of denying yourself sleep.

The sleep restriction approach stems from the notion that chronic insomnia is perpetuated by several possible causes, among them irregular sleep/wake schedules, worrying about sleep, taking drugs and alcohol and spending too much time in bed. Arthur J. Spielman, Ph.D., a psychology professor at City University of New York's City College, has researched sleep restriction therapy and he explains how it works.

He has patients keep a log of the average amount of time they sleep each night and the average amount of time they spend in bed each night for five nights. If someone reports sleeping an average of 5 hours but spending an average of 6½ hours in bed, Dr. Spielman advises spending only 5 hours in bed each night. The point is to restrict the time in bed to what is ordinarily sleep time.

If a patient spends little enough time in bed, he or she eventually will increase the percentage of time spent asleep. When the sleep portion comprises 90 percent of the time in bed, Dr. Spielman permits the patient to increase, in 15-minute increments, the time in bed. The scheduling continues and more bedtime hours are added until the insomnia is treated.

Stimulus Control Instruction

Sleep experts Dr. Bootzin and Perry Nicassio, Ph.D., developed some instructions to help the insomniac acquire a consistent sleep rhythm. The instructions strengthen the bed as a cue for sleep and weaken it as a cue for activities that might interfere with sleep.

1. Lie down with the intention of going to sleep only when you are sleepy.
2. Do not use your bed for anything except sleep; that is, do not read, watch

television, eat or worry in bed. Sexual activity is the only exception to this rule. On such occasions, the instructions are to be followed afterward when you intend to go to sleep.
3. If you find yourself unable to fall asleep, get up and go into another room. Stay as long as you wish and then return to the bedroom to sleep. Although you should not necessarily watch the clock, you should get out of bed if you do not fall asleep immediately. Remember, the goal is to associate your bed with falling asleep quickly. If you are in bed more than about ten minutes without falling asleep and have not gotten up, you are not following this instruction.
4. If you still cannot fall asleep, repeat step 3. Do this as often as is necessary throughout the night.
5. Set your alarm and get up at the same time every morning, regardless of how much sleep you got during the night. This will help your body acquire a consistent sleep rhythm.
6. Do not nap during the day.

Older People Need Less Sleep

As we get older, our sleeping patterns change: We sleep lighter and require fewer hours. Between the ages of 20 and 50, deep sleep is reduced by 60 percent, and the number of arousals in the night doubles. Keep in mind that it's normal to sleep less as you age. You're not suffering from insomnia unless your sleep patterns have dramatically and persistently changed or if you are experiencing such symptoms as lethargy, irritability, poor coordination and lapses of attention. If that's not the case, enjoy the news that your body needs less sleep. Physicans often tell older people to forget the myth of the required eight hours. Find pleasant activities for the extra waking hours you so rightly deserve.

In some parts of the country, you can even join an insomniac tour. In Baltimore, for instance, there's an Insomniac's Tour by the Sea, an Insomniac's Preakness Tour and a Halloween Insomniac Tour that includes a reading of "Annabel Lee" at the grave of that famous insomniac, Edgar Allan Poe.

Chapter 44

PANIC ATTACKS

It's as if the symptoms jump you from behind without warning. Your heart begins to beat wildly, your forehead is suddenly wet with perspiration, your hands tremble, your throat dries and swallowing is almost impossible. Your mind races to grab control of your body, but even as you tell yourself, "stay calm," it happens. You look for the nearest door, any door, so you can run away, far away, because that's the only thing that seems to help.

If this scene sounds familiar, then you know what it's like to be gripped by a panic attack. It's estimated that anywhere from 1 to 6 percent of the U.S. population suffers from panic attacks or other anxiety disorders. Panic attacks are far more severe than phobias, general anxiety or butterflies in the stomach. The attacks often start in early adulthood and, although the condition can be debilitating, it is not usually life-threatening.

It's now felt by many that panic attacks have a biological basis. They can be triggered by a number of things. People with diagnosed physical problems, such as asthma, hypertension or a heart condition, can suddenly fall victim to a panic attack when they believe they are about to experience another round of their physical illness. The fear of the future and the feeling of being unable to handle the pressures of responsibilities also can trigger an attack. In other cases, panic episodes can be an offshoot of a psychological disorder, such as depression, alcoholism or agoraphobia.

To gain control of panic when it arises, you'll find the support of others—family, friends and perhaps professionals—makes it easier. You'll also need some basic tools, the main one being breathing. "By changing your breathing pattern during an anxious episode, you can reverse your body's panic-provoking symptoms," writes psychologist R. Reid Wilson, Ph.D., in his book *Don't Panic: Taking Control of Anxiety Attacks.*

When faced with a stressful situation, your upper chest lifts upward and outward, and you take breaths that are shallow and rapid. By consciously changing to diaphragmatic breathing, you fill the lower part of your lungs with air so that with each breath, your stomach seems to be expanding and

198

contracting. This slow, deep breathing will help you relax and become more calm.

When you notice the first signs of panic, Dr. Wilson advises that to calm yourself you take a long, deep breath and then exhale slowly while silently saying the word *relax*. Take ten natural, easy breaths, counting each exhale silently, starting with ten. Notice any tensions, perhaps in your jaw, forehead or stomach, and imagine them loosening. When you've counted back to one, slowly return to whatever you were doing when you felt the panic coming on.

If you suddenly find yourself in the grip of a panic attack, use the deep-breathing technique to disrupt the negative, self-critical, hopeless thoughts. Then, if possible, find some neutral or pleasant task to occupy your mind. "As you gain control of your breathing and thoughts, reinforce your will to overcome the panic by repeating some supportive statements, such as 'I can be anxious and still perform this task,' 'I can manage these symptoms,' 'I can take all the time I need to feel safe and comfortable,' 'I've survived this before and I'll survive this time, too,' " suggests Dr. Wilson in his book.

If you're prone to panic attacks, stay away from caffeine. Research at the Yale University School of Medicine, New Haven, Connecticut, has shown that when people with anxiety disorders were given caffeine, there were significant increases in anxiety, nervousness, fear, nausea, palpitations, restlessness and tremors. The researchers found that people who suffer from panic attacks appeared to be more sensitive to the anxiety-causing effects of caffeine.

As for medication, several drugs have shown promise in research trials, but there's an ongoing debate within the medical community about side effects. "It's something each patient has to decide," says Redford B. Williams, M.D., professor of psychiatry at Duke University, Durham, North Carolina, and head of the university's Behavioral Medicine Research Center. "In severe cases, where a person's fear of having an attack is so paralyzing that he won't leave his house, the advantages of using medication and resuming a normal life may outweigh the chance of side effects."

Two other factors that may help are a proper diet and exercise, says clinical psychologist Sue Breton, a victim of panic attacks. "Research has shown that just as there is a definite connection between diet and physical illness, so there is between diet and mental illness."

The key, she says, is to improve your vitality by avoiding foods with added sugar, caffeine, alcohol, salt and artificial additives. Instead, eating more fresh fruit and vegetables, whole grain breads, and lean meat and fish will help you feel "more alive and energetic than you did before, and less susceptible to anxiety."

Being in good physical shape also enhances your ability to cope, she adds. Exercise "replaces the symptoms of stress and fear by providing a natural physical response. Physically fit people who take regular exercise will testify to feeling mentally invigorated afterward, yet at the same time having a sense of calm and well-being."

Chapter 45

SEXUAL DYSFUNCTION

Stress can have a major impact on your sex life. In fact, it's the culprit behind as many as 80 percent of the erection problems suffered by men, according to Harvey Caplan, M.D., a San Francisco psychiatrist. A lot of it has to do with the fear of failure and with a man's self-esteem. Here's how a problem can develop.

A man has a fight with his wife. The resulting anger and loss of esteem from being criticized creates erection problems.

He may identify his manhood with success at work, so a missed promotion causes him to believe he'll be a failure in the sack.

And then there's the trauma of experiencing one of the not-so-subtle signs of aging. Suddenly an unprecedented failure comes from out of the blue and a man believes something is wrong. He can't satisfy his woman. He can't stack up to other men. He develops anxiety about it. Each time he gets into bed, as he sweats over the issue of achieving an erection, his anxiety compounds the problem.

The Snowball Effect

Meanwhile, the woman involved is blaming herself for the man's erection troubles. In addition, she also feels rejected and hurt. The feelings snowball so much that when and if her lover does achieve an erection, her autonomic nervous system responds to the stress by failing to produce vaginal lubrication. And she may find herself losing her ability to achieve an orgasm.

According to Dr. Caplan, 80 percent of all secondary orgasm problems (those among women who have achieved orgasms through intercourse but who no longer can) are stress related. "It may be from some trauma, such as a death in the family, but it can also be the result of suppressed anger that she can't deal with. The discovery that her partner is having an affair. The stress of feeling frustrated that her partner can't please her. If the man pulls back emotionally because he can't get an erection, she feels frustrated. This leads to her closing down," he says.

There's hope, however. The first step: Stop making yourself miserable. "The important thing is to see this as a health problem, not as a statement about your worth," says Richard E. Berger, M.D., a Seattle urologist and coauthor of *BioPotency: A Guide to Sexual Success.*

Most males experience stress-related impotence at some time in their lives. So realize that your visions of James Bond being capable of lovemaking during a firefight are based on fiction.

And understand that most age-related changes in potency aren't a problem at all—not if you know what to expect. Your change in desire can elevate your sexual relationship to one that is more pleasure oriented and less performance oriented.

"When the wife is loving, accepting and sensitive to the changing needs of her husband and is free of sexual problems herself, while her husband is fundamentally secure and connected enough not to base his self-esteem on the physiological functioning of his genitals and is mature enough not to blame his partner for his problem, there is no midlife crisis," writes noted sex expert Helen S. Kaplan, M.D., Ph.D.

Remember: Even if you have a long-term erection problem, there's a 90 percent chance you can treat it, according to Dr. Berger.

Blame Bad Habits and Stress

Your problems are not likely to be of a physical nature (and therefore, treatable) if you can achieve erections outside of intercourse—if you can sustain a full, firm erection when you masturbate or if you have normal erections upon awakening. Or if you haven't suffered any injuries to your pelvic area or nervous system.

Before you rush to a sex therapist, try some self-help. Get rid of any negative factors that may be causing the problem. Smoking can sabotage your potency. Nicotine constricts blood vessels, including those in the penis. Dr. Berger estimates that one-third of all middle-aged men who have erection problems could end them if they stopped smoking. If you give up tobacco for three weeks and your erections don't return, it's not smoking that's causing the problem, he says.

Alcohol is another factor. "Heavy consumption of alcohol can ruin potency in the short term. And in the long run, too much alcohol can shrink a man's testicles, reduce or remove sexual desire and render him impotent," writes Dr. Berger. Medications you may be taking can also affect you sexually. Check with your doctor about possible sexual side effects of the contents of your medicine chest.

After you've eliminated the negative environmental factors from your life, take a look at your stresses. The second stage of Dr. Berger's self-help therapy is to tackle anxiety. To do that, you need to learn how your body works and how your anxiety is transmitted into the fight-or-flight response that affects your sexual performance. "People are not surprised when they're under stress and their stomach is upset, but they don't realize that erections can be affected by the same things," says Dr. Berger.

When you're experiencing stress, blood flows toward your muscles and away from your penis. In addition, your nervous system acts differently. The sympathetic part of your autonomic nervous system preempts the parasympathetic part. The parasympathetic part of your system is the part that helps you in getting an erection. It relaxes artery walls in the pelvic area, so they dilate and blood flows in faster than it flows out. For men, the increased blood volume produces an erection. In women, it produces vaginal lubrication and swelling of the vulva, clitoris and vaginal walls.

Under ordinary circumstances, the sympathetic system—the part that increases your heart rate—kicks in as your sexual excitement mounts. But physical or psychological stress can upset the critical balance and cause it to take over from the parasympathetic system earlier. It will increase your heart rate and make the arteries in your penis constrict. It can keep an erection from occurring or, if one has occurred, it can make it go away.

A Moratorium on Intercourse

What Dr. Berger and others advise is to learn to relax with your partner. Instead of clamming up on the topic, discuss your erection problem freely. "Get her to understand the factors that cause the stress," says Dr. Caplan. Be kind to each other, cooperate, approach the problem as a team. Remember, this is a health problem and no one is at fault.

To get back on track, start by putting intercourse temporarily off-limits. One strategy sex therapists recommend is for a couple to have affectionate caressing of each other—but without intercourse. "Without the need to have an erection, he won't have the stress of trying to produce one or the belief that she is thinking she wants one," says Dr. Caplan. The couple is challenged to develop new skills in communicating and caressing. The couple expands what its sense of sex is. The focus is taken away from the genitals and orgasm as a proving ground. With the stress taken away, the genitals may start working again and orgasm may happen.

For the first three weeks of an intercourse moratorium, Dr. Berger recommends couples schedule half-hour lovemaking sessions, five times a week, in which they refrain from touching either genitals or breasts. "The idea is to relax and enjoy the pleasure of being close without any expectation that intercourse will take place," he writes. In the following three weeks, genital and breast touching is permitted but intercourse is still to be avoided. After that, the couple may enjoy intercourse if erections have returned. If not, they return to caressing—or consult a professional therapist for direction.

Support Groups

There are support groups for men with erection problems and their partners.

Impotents Anonymous (for men) and I-ANON (for partners) have chapters throughout the United States. Write to 119 South Ruth Street, Maryville, TN 37801–5746 and include a stamped, self-addressed, business-size envelope, or phone (615) 983–6064.

Recovery of Male Potency (ROMP) has chapters in several states. Phone (800) Tel–ROMP; Michigan residents phone (313) 966–3219.

To attempt to prevent erection problems before they occur, Dr. Berger suggests men do anything possible to avoid the onset of diabetes or circulation problems: Keep blood pressure down; stick to a low-fat, low-cholesterol diet; exercise; and keep weight down.

Women without Orgasms

Stress plays a role in several of the sexual problems experienced by women. Vaginismus, involuntary spasms of the vaginal muscles that come from the fear of intercourse, is often stress induced, according to Dr. Caplan. Sometimes women respond to stress by developing yeast infections.

Stress is sometimes, but not often, the reason that certain women have never experienced an orgasm, says Lonnie Barbach, Ph.D., a San Francisco sex therapist. It is more of a factor in secondary orgasm problems (suffered by women who have experienced orgasms but who now have trouble) or situational orgasmic problems (suffered by women who experience orgasms only through means other than intercourse).

The first thing for women to do in these situations is to identify the stress and its causes. If it isn't an illness or physical ailment that's causing the problem, determine if there's a connection to other stressors. Make the connection between the anger at your partner, your boredom, your fatigue, your depression and your sexual problems. "Question what it is that is making you feel so under stress," says Shirley Zussman, Ed.D., a sex therapist in New York and co-director of the Association for Male Sexual Dysfunction.

"If you do feel stress plays a part, question in what way the stress can be reduced," suggests Dr. Zussman. "Sex therapists advise you to make love only when you feel like it. Do it when you're relaxed and feeling good about each other, not when it's merely convenient. And don't rush. Allow as much time as you need to enjoy your sexual experience."

In addition to working out the stress, Dr. Barbach advises you to pay attention to your thoughts and feelings during lovemaking. "Notice when your mind is wandering and bring it back. Focus on the feelings in your body, where your partner is touching you, and focus on what you're doing to your partner. Or move into a fantasy," she says.

The advice for impotent men can be heeded by nonorgasmic women: If you're worried about succeeding, you probably won't. "The anxiety about the fact that you're not having an orgasm pretty much rules out that you will," says Dr. Zussman.

Discuss your problem with your partner—taking his feelings into consideration. If resentment builds up, if your sexual dissatisfaction spills over into other areas of your relationship, it may be the time to seek the help of a professional sex therapist. For the names of sex therapists in your area, contact the American Association for Sex Educators, Counselors and Therapists, Suite 220, 11 Dupont Circle NW, Washington, DC 20036; (202) 462-1171.

A professional sex therapist may want to help you overcome your sexual dysfunction not by treating the symptoms but by attacking the cause. There's the chance that your therapist will devote a great deal of energy in getting you to understand—and deal with—the underlying anxiety that is causing your problems in bed.

Chapter 46

ULCERS

Kibby and Aphrodite, dolphins on display at the National Aquarium in Baltimore, Maryland, developed stomach ulcers. They were sent to a natural environment training center for dolphins in the Florida Keys for R and R, where their ulcers were treated with Maalox and Tagamet (standard medicine for ulcers in humans, their fellow mammals). The ulcers healed, only to recur when Kibby and Aphrodite returned to the aquarium. Apparently, swimming around and around in a concrete tank day after day while thousands of people stared at them through Plexiglas windows was stressful for the dolphins.

Dolphins share three things with people: Relatively few are susceptible to ulcers, reactions to stress may be connected to ulcers in some way, and once healed, ulcers will recur if the aggravating factors persist.

Ulcer, Ulcer, Who's Got the Ulcer?

Lots of people in the United States have ulcers. Are they all ambitious, hard-driving, "go-getter" executive types?

Forty or 50 years ago, doctors thought so. But subsequent research has since dispelled that myth: There is no "ulcer personality." Ulcers can and do affect anyone—white collars, blue collars, clerical collars, or—counting students, homemakers, retirees and the unemployed—no collars at all.

Enter myth number two: Stress causes ulcers. Animal studies showed that stomach ulcers in rats (personality unknown) can be brought about by psychological stress. But that idea was shelved when studies revealed that people with ulcers experienced no more stress in their lives than others. Consequently, research to find an ulcer treatment focuses primarily on physical factors, such as a way to control the secretion of gastric acid (digestive juices that break down protein) or to prevent the deterioration in the sticky, protective mucous lining of the digestive tract. Those two forces can create a

205

craterlike sore on the inner wall of the digestive tract. (Gastric ulcers occur in the stomach. Duodenal ulcers occur in the duodenum, pronounced *doo-oh-DEE-num*, the part of the small intestine nearest the stomach.)

This hole in your stomach feels like—well, like a hole in your stomach.

"Classic ulcer symptoms are burning or gnawing [upper to mid abdominal] pain, which occurs one to three hours after meals and often awakens [you] at night, about two hours after retiring," says Grace Elta, M.D., in the journal *Modern Medicine*. "Pain [comes and goes] and is relieved by foods or antacids." Other symptoms include belching, bloating and intolerance of fatty foods, according to Dr. Elta. On the other hand, some ulcer patients feel no symptoms whatsoever.

Okay, now you've got it straight: Ulcers are a purely physical problem and doctors treat them as such. Well, that's *almost* the truth, because in the last few years doctors have found that the physical causes aren't as clear-cut as they thought: Ulcers occur in some people who secrete *less* acid than normal, but do not occur in others who secrete *more* acid than normal. Taking a look at psychological factors, they found that people with ulcers do not necessarily experience more potentially stressful events than others. What they did find, however, is that, as a group, people with ulcers differ from others in the way they *react* to events. Ulcer patients seem to experience more anxiety and fear than others when things threaten to disrupt their lives. And those emotions can fuel the fires at your core.

Despair and a Weak Stomach Lining

"Some, but not all, ulcer patients under stress experience an increase in acid production," says Charles T. Richardson, M.D., of the Dallas Veterans Administration Medical Center. "In those who develop ulcers, emotional distress may lead to a breakdown in the way the stomach and duodenum protect themselves against acid secretion. In other words, stress—or specifically, the physiological reaction to stressful events—may interfere with the defense mechanism in some way."

In an important study, published in the journal *Gastroenterology*, Mark Feldman, M.D., and others at the University of Texas Health Sciences Center and the Dallas Veterans Administration Medical Center examined various psychological and social factors in 49 men with ulcers, then compared them with men being treated for kidney stones or gallstones (which have no readily apparent psychological component) and with healthy men. All experienced roughly the same number of potential stressors.

While all ulcer patients didn't fit one narrow stereotype, they did differ from the control group in a few significant ways. Most notably, ulcer patients were more likely than healthy people to view life events like a job change or relocation as negative. Many tended to be hypochondriacal (expressing over-emphasis of bodily concern), overly pessimistic (expecting the worst, feeling threatened by low-risk situations) and overly dependent (tending to rely on people more than is healthy). They average lower scores than control groups on something psychologists call "ego strength," or the ability to bend, not break, under stress.

At the same time, the men with ulcers reported a higher average level of alienation than a control group, with slightly fewer friends and relatives whom they felt they could rely upon in times of crisis. And they were more anxious and depressed than men without ulcers.

Relax—Your Stomach Will Thank You

If a defeatist outlook can leave etchings on your stomach's wall, can a sunny outlook smooth them over?

Doctors are beginning to ask this question. Pamela Walker, Ph.D., a medical psychologist who worked on this study, stated, "Some studies suggest that certain stress-management techniques, practiced in conjunction with medical treatment, may help people with ulcers make life easier on their sensitive stomachs.

Education. If you've read this far, you may already have taken one important step in preventing a repeat ulcer attack. "One early study suggests that intensive education of how stress affects people physically—specifically the gastrointestinal system—along with learning ways to change habitual thinking patterns that create worry, seemed to help. This education appeared to prevent ulcer recurrence in 29 out of 32 patients, which is unusual because ulcers tend to recur," says Dr. Walker.

Cognitive therapy. Also called self-talk, self-affirmation or cognitive restructuring, cognitive therapy may be another promising approach to consider for improving an ulcer sufferer's perception of stress. "Say you're given more responsibility at work," says Dr. Walker. "A negative reaction would be to automatically think, 'I can't handle it. What if I fail?' A healthier, positive reaction would be, 'Gee, that sounds like a real challenge, let's see what I can do.'

"Or say you have to move to a new city," continues Dr. Walker. "Rather than think, 'This is terrible, it's a whole new place, I won't know my way around, I'll be lonely because I don't make friends easily,' try to look forward to the move as an opportunity to discover exciting new places and meet interesting new people.

"Cognitive therapy may be a positive approach for ulcer patients because positive self-talk improves self-confidence, whereas negative self-talk tends to undermine one's ability to cope," says Dr. Walker.

"Also, negative thinking tends to be a self-fulfilling prophecy," she continues. "If you expect things to go wrong, your thoughts and actions may influence events in countless small ways to help determine the outcome. So if you think things will go wrong, you may be more likely to do things that lead to failure.

You've got to break the cycle at some point, and cognitive therapy does the trick. It also gives the responsibility for control back to the individual, a basic principle of stress management."

Assertiveness training. "Dependent people often have trouble expressing anger appropriately. So they may either internalize it or communicate it to others indirectly," says Dr. Walker. This is counterproductive, because their behavior may end up alienating the very people who could help in a crisis—friends, family and co-workers. "Assertiveness training encourages people to express their feelings appropriately, ask for what they need and get along better with others, giving them better access to social support." (The importance of social support in stress management is discussed at length in chapter 63.)

Relaxation training. "Meditation or other relaxation techniques may be useful for people experiencing stress-related symptoms, because relaxation is the opposite of the stress response," says Dr. Walker. She adds that ulcer patients who practice relaxation or any other stress-management technique should continue to seek appropriate medical treatment.

Dr. Walker, Dr. Feldman and Dr. Richardson emphasize that there are many unknowns in the link between stress and ulcers. Studies such as theirs have not proven stress to be a cause of ulcers, although researchers continually seek to better understand that relationship. They also are investigating the developing area of stress management in order to determine how its techniques may be used to help people who are suffering from ulcers, as well as other stress-related illnesses.

Part 5

COPING TECHNIQUES THAT CAN BACKFIRE

Chapter 47

ALCOHOL AND SUBSTANCE ABUSE

Of all the reasons people drink alcohol, "unwinding" often tops the list.

"Shifting gears from the responsibilities and high energy level of the day to a slower and easier evening mood is a very common purpose of drinking," state Roger E. Vogler, Ph.D., and Wayne R. Bartz, Ph.D., in their book, *The Better Way to Drink*.

Yet the brief and vivid sense of relaxation produced by alcohol is quite temporary. Over the long haul, alcohol abuse *escalates* stress. Drink too much too often, and your body produces an excess of hydrocortisone and other stress-related hormones. But even a moderate intake of alcohol has a curious effect on a bluish area of neurons in a part of the brain called the locus coeruleus. Apparently, inhibiting these locus coeruleus neurons sets off a chain reaction that activates other brain cells, increasing arousal. After hitting a blood alcohol level of about 0.05—half the usual legal standard for intoxication—relief from stress usually ends and anxiety generated by additional alcohol begins.

For many people, drinking tends to increase whenever the overall level of stress increases. Divorce, unemployment and other losses generate severe stress and the need for relief. (Among problem drinkers, women are more likely to date the onset of their drinking to a particularly stressful event, such as divorce, whereas men date the onset to job-related or legal problems.)

"Your health, your job, your financial and marital situations may all get worse . . . from an overreliance on alcohol to relax," say Dr. Vogler and Dr. Bartz.

Are You Abusing Alcohol?

Dr. Vogler offers the following guidelines to determine whether you are abusing alcohol as a means of stress relief.

Do you drink every day? Occasional use of alcohol to enhance a good time is okay; relying on alcohol is a bad habit.

Do you drink enough to push your blood alcohol levels higher than 0.05? On those occasions when you drink alcohol, do you consume less than one drink an hour? Regardless of weight, your rate of alcohol consumption should not be greater, because the body cannot metabolize alcohol any faster. Keep in mind that a "drink" is defined as 12 ounces of beer, 4 ounces of table wine or 1¼ ounces of liquor.

"If you drink more than that or drink every day, you will grow tolerant to alcohol and need more and more to achieve the calming effect usually experienced after a glass or so," says Dr. Vogler.

Does drinking alcohol trigger negative behavior? Do you become abusive—verbally or physically—no matter how little or how infrequently you drink? Do you unleash hostility behind the wheel of your car? Do you neglect your kids or tune out your spouse?

Do you also abuse other substances (tranquilizers, sedatives or amphetamines) to relieve, for example, anxiety and depression? Alcohol abuse is often only one of various poor coping techniques.

Substance Abuse: Overdosing on Stress

Cocaine. Many users start out looking for relief from tedium or tension (or both). Eventually, though, they end up as stress personified: nervous, irritable, angry, paranoid, anxious and depressed.

Cocaine's instant, euphoric high is replaced by less pleasant feelings, which seem to last longer and longer over time. But people keep chasing the once-certain high, all in a frenetic search for more relief, more fun, until they are financially and emotionally bankrupt, according to Joanne Baum, Ph.D., author of *One Step over the Line: A No-Nonsense Guide to Recognizing and Treating Cocaine Dependency.*

"When they do come for help, they are once again looking for relief," says Dr. Baum, who practices in the San Francisco Bay Area and specializes in the treatment of chemical dependency.

At the very least, your self-respect—a precious commodity in stress resistance—evaporates.

If any stress-reducing chemical—be it cocaine, alcohol, marijuana or tranquilizers—plays too significant a role in your life, you may need professional help to regain control. Consult the blue pages of your local telephone directory for the location of Narcotics Anonymous or other drug dependency treatment centers in your area, or call the National Clearinghouse on Drug Abuse, located in Maryland, at (301) 443-6500. This group will refer you to organizations in your residential area at no charge.

If you've answered yes to any of these questions, it may be time to stop and evaluate the role alcohol plays in your life.

How to Step Out of the Alcohol Rut

"As tranquilizers go, alcohol is legal (for adults), relatively inexpensive, widely available and works fast," says Dr. Vogler. But drinking for relief from tension or stress is the use of alcohol for self-medication, not for enjoyment.

"We tend to get into comfortable ruts and then deviate very little from our routine, which quite often results in an overreliance on alcohol." Here are some suggestions to limit stress-induced drinking.

For a few weeks, keep a written record of your drinking habits. "Describe the settings and circumstances," says Dr. Vogler. "Think about your feelings. If you can identify the people, places and moods that provoke excessive drinking, you can get a pretty good handle on how much you drink, how often and why. By recognizing these situations, you can learn which you need to control and which you may have to avoid," he says.

If you're a woman of reproductive age, note whether or not you tend to drink more often during your menstrual period. In one study, nonalcoholic women reported significantly more bad moods, more frequent drinking to relieve tension or depression and more frequent solitary drinking during menstruation.

Take concrete steps to resolve conflicts or worries. "Stresses will always exist," say Dr. Vogler and Dr. Bartz. "And being tuned out by alcohol may mean that you avoid dealing with the stress-producing situation. In the long run, that can only mean more stress and more need to escape—a vicious circle."

Substitute nonalcoholic beverages for your customary drinks. "The alcohol in the evening cocktail does not alone account for the shift in mood," explain Dr. Vogler and Dr. Bartz. "Just sitting comfortably away from a stressful environment, sprawled in an easy chair and forgetting about work, leads to relief of stress."

"Stock your fridge with other fun beverages such as imported mineral water or guava juice," says Dr. Vogler. "Near beer and dealcoholized wine are fine, too. Then make your first drink nonalcoholic and sip it while you get out of your work clothes or whatever. That 15-minute decompression period buys you time, helping you to shrug off a layer or two of tension. After 15 minutes, you may find you need only one beer instead of several to finish unwinding. Or you may not want any alcohol at all."

Find alternative ways to dissipate stress. Walking, tennis, swimming, reading, drawing, listening to or playing music, gardening and meditation are just a few of the many satisfying ways to deflect stress. Dr. Vogler and Dr. Bartz suggest people make their own lists, based on individual preferences and abilities.

If you try those tactics but still find yourself overusing alcohol when stress looms, do yourself a big favor and consider professional help.

"Counseling can provide the direction you need to make changes that will minimize or help you handle stress better," says Dr. Vogler. Also, self-help groups such as Alcoholics Anonymous and Women for Sobriety can provide opportunities to meet people who have learned to deal with stress without relying on alcohol or other drugs.

Chapter 48

COFFEE

Coffee is amazing stuff: A cup or two energizes some somnambulating java lovers the way lightning brought Frankenstein's monster to life. It's just the charge many people need to get up and go.

Coffee owes its energizing powers to $C_8H_{10}N_4O_2$—a compound better known as caffeine (also found in tea and some soft drinks). Many people believe coffee gives them the edge they need to delve into complex problems, cram for exams or plough through piles of repetitious work. Others, however, just get edgy. For them, coffee is the last thing they need in the middle of a stressful day.

All Wound Up and Nowhere to Go

"Coffee does help people feel slightly more alert and able to concentrate—but at a price," says Kirby Gilliland, Ph.D., associate professor of psychology at the University of Oklahoma in Norman. He has studied the effects of caffeine on a group of undergraduate students and found that "coffee drinkers *also* felt considerably more anxious, frustrated and depressed. And the more they drank, the worse they felt."

People who drank five or more cups a day fared worse than people who drank four or fewer, reports Dr. Gilliland. "And as with any drug, caffeine affects some people far more than others. But for some, even small amounts of caffeine add a layer of anxiety to their mood. What's more, these 'background' levels of anxiety and depression build up slowly over a period of time, so many people never connect their anxiety with their coffee intake."

Caffeine plus Stress Jacks Up Blood Pressure

When you drink caffeinated beverages—like coffee, tea or cola—while you're under stress, your blood pressure also may rise. A study by Gwendolyn

A. Pincomb, Ph.D., and other researchers in the Behavioral Sciences Laboratory of the Oklahoma City Veterans Administration Medical Center found that drinking a caffeinated beverage *and* preparing for exams raised blood pressure considerably higher than either consuming caffeine or studying in themselves. What's more, the effect of the caffeine lingers, raising average blood pressure for at least two hours. This effect may become more pronounced as you get older, since many people's blood vessels tend to become less "elastic" with age. So people who have high blood pressure (or who are at risk for high blood pressure) should be aware that too much caffeine may add even more pressure on already-stressed blood vessels.

If drinking coffee when you are in an already stressful situation seems to jack up your blood pressure or your anxiety level, it makes sense to cut back on both coffee and stress.

Here are some tips to help you cut back on caffeine.

Drink decaffeinated coffee. In taste-tests of unlabeled brews, coffee drinkers can rarely distinguish between decaffeinated and regular.

Switch to herbal tea. With so many perk-me-up flavors around, you'll probably find at least two or three you really like.

Chapter 49

COMPULSIVE SHOPPING

Everyone does it occasionally. You feel blue, so you buy a new pair of shoes. You have an argument with your kids—or your mate or your boss or your mother—and a new sweater makes everything better. Taken too far, though, shopping as a means of stress reduction can backfire.

Some people get high when they buy—and can't stop. Like binge eaters or alcoholics who find solace in food or drink, when anything goes wrong in their lives, "spendaholics" go shopping. Buying can generate an adrenaline rush, and purchases serve as tranquilizers.

"It's normal to get excited when you buy a new stereo or car or similar indulgence," comments Hank Berman, a marriage and family counselor in San Francisco. "You can feel your heart beat faster and your palms begin to sweat. But compulsive shoppers experience that same kind of 'high'—like a gambler betting on a racehorse—whenever they shop. The problem is, no matter how much they buy, compulsive shoppers never think they have enough. So they continue to spend, whether they can afford it or not."

Clothes are the biggest weakness among compulsive shoppers (more than likely due to the boost in self-esteem they lend), followed closely by shoes, restaurant meals, vacations, cars and electronic equipment. The crash comes when compulsive shoppers get home and look at the price tags. Or when they realize they earn good money but have nothing to show for it. Feeling guilty or remorseful, they tell themselves they'll never do it again.

But they know they will. Compulsive shoppers (most but not all are women) have little control over their behavior. Any sort of stress can trigger a plastic-powered shopping frenzy.

In not-so-rare cases, compulsive shopping leads to bankruptcy, mortgage foreclosure, theft from friends and relatives, embezzlement of company funds to support this habit—and, not surprisingly, marital friction. The real problem with this "buying disorder," though, is not so much the debt incurred but the behavior itself—and the reasons for it.

The Surprising Reasons Why Overspenders Live to Shop

What drives people to overspend?

One is tempted to blame easy availability of credit, the glut of mail-order catalogs with round-the-clock toll-free telephone order numbers and the influence of ads, ads, ads for the epidemic of overspending. (Total consumer credit debt for 1986, the latest year for which figures are available, was $600 *billion*.) And, to a fair degree, unlimited credit and rampant commercialism heavily influence our buy-now-pay-later psychology. But those factors alone don't account for compulsive spending. Like compulsive eating, compulsive shopping can often be a self-destructive response to handling stress—tension, boredom, anxiety, anger and rejection. Binge buyers just use money and credit cards instead of food. (Actually, many abuse both credit *and* food. Psychologists report that many binge buyers are also binge eaters.)

Stressful circumstances—and the emotional waves they create—are behind many episodes of compulsive shopping. An aspiring opera singer, for example, spent as much as $200 every time she auditioned for a part. After each tryout—and rejection—she trooped into an expensive store and bought new shoes.

"I've noticed that people are more likely to overspend and shop compulsively when they're feeling despair," says Judy Barber, a San Francisco psychotherapist specializing in the psychology of money. "Often they'll say to themselves, 'Oh, well, I'll never be able to afford a new car or a big house or whatever, so I'll buy this $100 blouse.' In effect, they're buying themselves a consolation prize."

One woman's shopping sprees at ritzy boutiques in New York, for example, were based on the unfulfilled fantasy of being married to a famous multimillionaire who had the power and funds to afford her anything she wished. Shopping provided momentary gratification against the disappointment that life didn't turn out the way she'd hoped.

If you have a sneaking suspicion you would be a good candidate for the Overspenders Hall of Fame, take the quiz in the box on page 219.

How to Beat the Urge to Splurge

Recognizing you have a problem is the first step toward gaining control of your buying habits.

"To control spending binges triggered by stress," says Barber, "you have to cope with the stress itself, whether it's changing jobs or going to a marriage counselor or whatever, and at the same time take concrete steps toward setting realistic goals that become as important to you as the immediate gratification of overspending."

Abstinence from shopping is virtually impossible. Eventually, you will have to shop to replenish your supplies of food, clothing and other essentials, at the very least.

Experts on compulsive shopping offer these suggestions for curbing chronic splurges.

Cut up your credit cards. It's a big step in breaking away from compulsive shopping, says one expert.

Avoid shopping when you're feeling lonely, deprived or otherwise stressed. "Anniversaries of a loss—a separation, divorce, death of a loved one—can be triggers for spending," says Berman.

Don't use shopping as recreation. Do you often spend your lunch hours cruising the local stores just to escape the office? Do something else instead. Take a walk in the park or write letters to friends. Do you head for the mall just to pass the time? Substitute work, sports, hobbies, reading—anything—for recreational shopping.

Always shop with a list—and a limit. "To cut down on spending binges, shop with specific goals," says Barber. Know exactly what you want and how much you can reasonably afford to spend before you head for the store.

"When considering a purchase, ask yourself, 'How much am I really going to wear—or use—this item?' " says Barber.

Allow yourself a "cooling off" period. To further escape the pressure to buy, Barber suggests leaving the item on the rack and, if you still think you really need or want the item, returning for it a day or two later.

Set an overall, long-term, reachable financial goal. "If you have a clear-cut dream to save for—a vacation, a second home, your child's education—you're less likely to spend out of despair," says Barber.

You Don't Have to Go It Alone

Knowing that others share your dilemma—and that they are learning how they control *their* spending urges—can be an enormous help. A self-help group for compulsive shoppers usually operates along much the same principles as Alcoholics Anonymous and Overeaters Anonymous. It can help put you in touch with former overspenders who can offer both encouragement and practical solutions. One such group is Shopaholics Limited, 135 Willow Street, Brooklyn Heights, NY 11201 (phone: 212-484-0998).

If there are no self-help groups for compulsive shoppers in your area, you may want to start your own support group. An alternative is the "buddy system." Link up with a close friend who shares your problem—or at least

---

Are You a Compulsive Spender?
Take This Quiz and Find Out

1. Do you have trouble leaving a store without buying something? _____

2. Do you buy things you don't need or want because they are on sale and, as a result, have closets full of unused items? _____

3. Do you buy things on credit that you would not buy if you were paying cash? _____

4. Do you insist on paying the restaurant bill or collecting cash from others with you, then put the bill on your credit card? _____

5. Do you often divert money from legitimate responsibilities in order to shop? _____

6. Do you always have to charge expenses for emergencies—flat tires, sick pets, unexpected company? _____

7. Do you only pay the minimum balance on your accounts each month? _____

8. Are you always trying to beat your checks to the bank? _____

9. Do you believe that having more money would solve most of your problems? _____

10. Are you preoccupied by thoughts of money, or do you have trouble imagining life without credit cards? _____

11. If you have money left at the end of a pay period, are you obsessed by having to spend it quickly? _____

12. Do you feel defensive about your money situation and debt with family or friends to whom you owe money? (Do you, for example, hide new purchases from your mate or feel others would be appalled if they knew of your spending habits?) _____

If you answered yes to five or more of the above questions, you may be a compulsive spender.

Adapted with permission from SpenderMenders, Box 15000-156, San Francisco, CA 94115.

---

sympathizes. Agree to call each other whenever the urge to spend seems overwhelming. "The 'buddy system' can help to discharge the tension that accompanies preoccupation with shopping—or manage the tension that triggers a spree," says Berman.

For help with financial problems in general, see chapter 33.

Chapter 50

NERVOUS HABITS

When it comes to nervous habits, the first-place prize goes to nail biting. More than half of us at some time in our lives have been persistent nail nibblers, according to Nathan Azrin, Ph.D., coauthor of *Habit Control*. Nail biting, like other nervous quirks, by nature occurs most frequently when we are anxious; that may explain why puberty is the hottest time for it. Holding second place among nervous habits are the facial tics. This response is particularly awkward because practitioners can't always tell they're doing it. What takes third? The nervous ritual of pulling hair. And not only pulling hair on the head but also pulling out eyelashes, eyebrows and beards.

These responses can be broken if you embark on a well-planned strategy. First you become intensely aware of the times the habits occur, then you develop a *competing* reaction. It also helps to reduce the tension that causes the habits in the first place, therapists say.

Sometimes the habits can be broken by the person doing the biting, facial twitching or pulling. Sometimes it takes the assistance of a trusted friend. And if that doesn't work, a professional behavioral therapist can come to the rescue. In any event, there's hope.

Overcoming Nail Biting

You don't bite your nails because of their flavor or because you like the way it makes them look. You probably bite them as a negative way of handling stress. So the first step in breaking yourself of the bad habit is to become painfully aware of how often you engage in it and what events, behavior or emotions trigger it. One of the simplest methods is to carry around a tiny notebook or a three-by-five-inch card and make a little slash each time you catch yourself biting your nails. (You can divide the notebook or card up into days of the week and hours of the day to track when you tend to bite and how you're improving.)

After you catch yourself biting, stop for a moment and take a quick survey of what's happening and what you're feeling. Are you anxious? Angry? Afraid? Did your boss just demand the impossible? Did your kid just dump a jar of jelly on the floor? Jot that down.

Or maybe you are waiting in a slow-moving bank line. "People engage in nervous habits when they're under a good bit of stress, but we also find people do it when they're waiting. If they get busily involved in something, their nail biting drops to virtually zero," says R. Wayne Fuqua, Ph.D., professor of psychology at Western Michigan University and coauthor of a study on nervous habits.

Establish a Competing Reaction

The next step in controlling the habit is to establish a competing reaction. "Engage your hands in a position that's incompatible with biting," says Dr. Azrin. Clench your fist, grab a book, telephone, chair edge—anything to get your hands away from your mouth. Do this immediately after you realize you've been biting your nails or as soon as you become aware that you're in the "danger zone" that precedes nail biting.

"The events that trigger the habit are very specific to individuals," says Dr. Azrin. "Some people do it when they are about to speak in front of a group, others do it when they're driving in their car." And the bodily signals that you are about to start nibbling vary from individual to individual—it might take a trusted friend or even a professional behavior therapist to point them out to you. If you deliberately practice your habit in front of a mirror, you may begin to detect preliminary movements, such as rubbing the nail with other fingers, almost to prepare it for biting, or moving the hand up to the face and allowing it to linger there.

Self-Destruction to Self-Beautification

"Carry around an emery board to fix your nails immediately after you have bitten them," says Dr. Azrin. Then engage in this competing reaction for another three minutes. The point of fixing up your nails is to help change your orientation from one of self-destruction to one of self-beautification. Most nail biters avoid wearing nail polish, rings or bracelets—anything that draws attention to their nails. Dr. Azrin suggests you become proud of your nails—even wear jewelry.

And find an appropriate method for handling the source of stress that leads to the nervous habit. If your diary indicates that you find yourself biting your nails every time your boss makes an impossible demand—and you can't stand up to him—maybe assertiveness training (see chapter 53) is appropriate. If it's tension that's bringing on the nail biting, you might try using the

Relaxation Response (see chapter 76) or relaxation tapes (see chapter 77). Once you become aware of what leads you into a "habit situation," you can learn to assert yourself, relax, or do whatever is appropriate, instead of nibbling.

Facial Tics and Hair Pulling

There are a variety of reasons why you engage in facial tics (which include eye and shoulder twitches). Experts technically refer to them as repetitive nonfunctional muscle contractions. Sometimes they are associated with a neurological problem and sometimes they are a reaction to stress. If you have trouble telling when and why you tic, you can engage the help of a friend who will signal you (raising one finger or giving you a code word) when they see you do it. A behavioral therapist may be able to train you to note it yourself. In either case, therapists suggest you keep a diary of the habit.

If your diary indicates that you twitch even when you aren't under stress, there may be a neurological problem, so you should consult with a neurologist or neuropsychologist. If it happens primarily when you're under stress, there are competing reactions to employ. "You have to identify the specific muscle group and engage in isometric tensing of the opposing muscles," says Dr. Azrin. "If the tic involves raising of the shoulder, then engage in a strong two-minute tensing of the muscles that pull the shoulder down," he says.

It may be wisest to refer to a behavioral therapist who can help you find the proper muscles for a competing reaction—and to aid in tackling the source of stress. (For the names of behaviorial therapists in your area, write to the Association for the Advancement of Behavior Therapy, 15 West 36th Street, New York, NY 10018.)

The advice for hair pullers is basically the same as that for nail biters. Keep a tally. Find a competing reaction such as hand clenching. Work to reduce the anxiety, tension or whatever you discover that causes you to pull your hair in the first place. And carry around a comb or small brush—or an eyebrow pencil if you pull at your eyebrows. Immediately repair your damage. Then repeat the hand clenching for three minutes afterward.

Foot Tappers, Finger Drummers

If your nervous habit is foot tapping or finger drumming, you're not likely to get much pressure to change from others, says R. Gregory Nunn, coauthor, with Dr. Azrin, of *Habit Control*. These are not socially unacceptable habits, so there's little chance you'll get feedback from those around you. But if you want to change, keep your diary and find a competing reaction. For foot tapping, apply slight pressure against the ball of your feet so you'll be aware that your feet are flat. Maintain the pressure for two or three minutes. For finger tapping, grab hold of something convenient and maintain the grasp for the same amount of time. If you're writing with one hand and tapping with the other, hold on to the edge of the paper with your free hand. If you're reading and tapping, grab the book. Again, you engage the competing reaction when you catch yourself tapping or as you feel yourself enter the "habit situation" that precedes the nervous habit.

Chapter 51

OVEREATING

You're tense and harried. Suddenly, you crave food. What do you reach for? A cookie? A candy bar? Anything you can get your hands on?

Do you stop after a nibble or two? Or do you, like many people, go into a double-fisted feeding frenzy that leaves you feeling overstuffed and guilty?

Diagnosis: The "Eat, you'll feel better" syndrome. And you're only doing what you've been programmed to do, Pavlovian-style.

"It's no mystery why I eat when I'm upset," says one woman. "Whenever I skinned my knee as a child, my mom would give me a Band-Aid, a kiss and a Popsicle. And I still associate food with comfort."

Food, especially sweet, sugary foods like ice cream, cookies and candy, is hypothesized to have a calming or soothing effect as well. One theory, based on animal experiments, proposes that eating sweets prompts the body to secrete endorphins, natural opiatelike compounds in the brain that dull pain. (Not surprisingly, they therefore also have the potential to buffer stress.) Other evidence suggests that high-carbs increase the production and release of serotonin, a nerve messenger that eases anxiety and tension.

Regardless of the mechanism at work, we almost seem destined to reach for the sweets under stress. "Studies show that stressed animals eat more sweets than do nonstressed animals," says Dean Krahn, M.D., director of the Eating Disorders Program at the University of Michigan Medical Center in Ann Arbor. "What's more, they go for exactly the kinds of comfort foods that people do. Rats *love* Oreos. And hardly anyone who eats under stress reaches for vegetables or other healthy food."

If one Oreo is good, does that mean the whole box is even better? No such luck. While seeking solace in food isn't nearly as deadly or dangerous as other stress-provoked habits such as smoking or tranquilizer abuse, "eating away your troubles" won't do anything to resolve what's causing the stress in the first place. What's more, habitual food overdoses show up as unwanted pounds, which translate into guilt—and more stress.

Even if you don't gain weight or feel guilty, "stress eating" can contribute to heart disease or nutritional problems, since many of the foods people like to eat under stress tend to be high in fat and sugar, according to Dr. Krahn.

What's Eating You?

Perhaps you eat under stress but don't realize it. Food wolfed down in a frenzy may disappear so fast you honestly don't remember having eaten it.

"I find it helps for people to keep a log of what they eat and when and where they eat it—like a diet diary," says Dr. Krahn. He also suggests diary-keepers note what they were thinking when the urge to eat hit ("The boss is a jerk") and how they felt ("I'm angry").

"After keeping a diary for a while, it occurs to them that eating doesn't do anything but make them feel guilty," says Dr. Krahn. "They still have a boss who's a jerk, and they might start to think they're not doing a good job. But if they think things through instead of trying to 'eat their troubles away,' they might conclude that they *are* doing a good job and otherwise deal with the issue."

Keeping track of stress-induced feeding frenzies is just the start. To avoid eating too much and too often under stress, Dr. Krahn also gives the following advice.

Eat regular, nutritious meals. Most people who eat under stress are people who restrict what they eat the rest of the time, according to Dr. Krahn. "Dieters—people who deprive themselves of food and get too few calories—set themselves up for binging under stress," he says.

Distract your attention. "Diverting activities are very useful," says Dr. Krahn. "Take a walk, play the piano, read a magazine, then ask yourself, 'Do I still feel like eating?' If you do, go ahead. But the urge for food, like the urge for sex, tends to come and go."

Expect relapses. "The biological urge to eat under stress is no different than the urge to urinate," says Dr. Krahn. "We can only control the urge up to a point. It's naive to think will power has anything to do with it. Coupled with a wide availability of highly palatable foods never before seen in human history, we are almost predestined toward a certain amount of 'stress eating,'" he says. "It's not only okay but more realistic to give in to the urge occasionally, when it's most overwhelming."

Don't let yourself feel guilty. "That will only leave you feeling more guilty —and vulnerable to further relapses," says Dr. Krahn.

Some behavioral scientists speculate that another reason we eat under stress is for the oral gratification provided by chewing and sucking, a hold-over from infancy. And animals do gnaw on nonnutritive objects under stress.

But Dr. Krahn hesitates to suggest that people who eat under stress chew gum, suck on a straw or crunch ice cubes to satisfy their urge. "For one thing, chewing by itself seems to stimulate appetite," he says.

If you must nibble but don't want to gain weight, judicious snacking on crunchy, low-calorie foods such as air-popped popcorn, pretzels and bite-size shredded wheat cereal may supply what you need to calm you down.

Chapter 52

SMOKING

People smoke for many reasons. Stress relief is one of them. "Nicotine [the active ingredient in cigarettes] releases opiatelike substances called endorphins, chemicals that give you a pleasant, mellow feeling and protect against stress," explains David B. Abrams, Ph.D., assistant professor of psychiatry and human behavior at Brown University and associate director of the Division of Behavioral Medicine at the Miriam Hospital in Providence, Rhode Island.

"Nicotine is a mood-altering substance that will help you cope with loneliness, anxiety and stress—it makes life more bearable. *And* it improves concentration and accuracy," adds Dr. Abrams. "I think that's why people in very high-pressure jobs—air traffic controllers, nurses, newspaper reporters—tend to smoke.

"In any situation that produces stress—that is, whenever you are strained beyond your limits in the face of a demand—nicotine and other chemicals in cigarette smoke can reduce fatigue and transform an unpleasant mood into a pleasant one," says Dr. Abrams.

Smoke and Stress: Double Trouble

But the instant stress relief afforded by cigarettes has a dark side. Every year, scientists add to the list of health problems fostered by smoking; it now includes prematurely aged skin and poor hearing along with the more serious problems like emphysema, lung cancer and heart disease. But the threat of bad health is rarely enough to prompt people to quit. In fact, just *thinking* about the damage caused by cigarettes can make you so edgy you need a light!

The problem is, cigarettes are the last thing an already stressed-out heart needs. A study at the University of Pittsburgh School of Medicine found that smoking and stress combined raised blood pressure and heart rates higher

227

than either smoking or stress alone. The combined effects of stress and nicotine may well trigger heart disease in some smokers, say the researchers.

But here's the catch: Trying to quit smoking is stressful, too. It's breaking an *addiction*.

"Nicotine is one of the most addictive substances known," says Dr. Abrams. "In terms of its effects on brain chemistry, nicotine is similar to cocaine or heroin, but in much smaller doses.

"Plus, cigarettes are legal, relatively inexpensive compared to other addictive drugs, and convenient to use," says Dr. Abrams. "But a big reason nicotine is so addictive is that you can dose yourself so precisely. By either taking a tiny puff or inhaling deeply, by smoking frequently or infrequently, or buying low-nicotine or regular brands, you can tailor the dosage to maintain just the right blood levels that produce pleasurable effects. It's unlike cocaine or heroin, where one injection produces a tremendous rush followed later by a crash. And nicotine doesn't slow reaction time or interfere as much with performance, like alcohol does."

Smoking also is very habit-forming because it's associated with many other everyday habits. "Smoke even a pack a day or less," says Dr. Abrams, "and you end up smoking while you're on the phone, driving in your car, waiting to pick up your kids, watching television and so forth. In the course of a year, your brain has made thousands of connections between all those everyday situations and smoking.

"So like Pavlov's classic experiment with conditioned responses in dogs, smokers tend to light up whenever the phone rings, whenever they get into the car or have to wait, and so forth, to the point where their brain thinks something's wrong if they're on the phone without a cigarette in their hand."

How to Quit—for Good

What enables some people to kick the habit for good, while others pick it up again?

Dr. Abrams thinks one important key to kicking the habit once and for all is learning to cope with stress. He and some colleagues studied 44 smokers and ex-smokers to try to find out why some eventually resumed the habit after quitting.

"Social situations like parties, where others smoke, accounted for a lot of relapses," says Dr. Abrams. "But the people who seem most vulnerable—and most likely to smoke again—are those who don't know how to cope with stressful feelings like anxiety, anger, loneliness, boredom, depression and fatigue. In stressful situations, they feel they'll go nuts if they don't have a cigarette. If any cigarettes are available, they'll light one (or they'll seek one out)."

You can survive stressful situations without cigarettes, though. Here's how.

Stressed out? Sit it out. "The feeling that you can't go another minute without a cigarette—and the fear that that feeling will get *worse*—is irrational," says Dr. Abrams. "Stress, depression, loneliness and fatigue come and go—and so does the need for a cigarette. If you wait a few minutes, you will feel better."

Talk yourself out of it. "As with an irrational fear—like agoraphobia or obsessive-compulsive behavior, for example—rational thoughts and phrases can get you through the misery," says Dr. Abrams. "Instead of thinking, 'I can't possibly get through this without a cigarette,' say to yourself, 'Wait a minute. Slow down. Stop. I *can* survive without a cigarette.'

"We encourage people to confront situations without a cigarette," says Dr. Abrams. "The anxiety begins to wear off as the old patterns die away and your body adapts to the new situations."

Use your imagination. "Imagine yourself skiing over a snow-covered mountain," says Dr. Abrams. "Your craving for a cigarette is the mountain. Conquering that mountain is scary and thrilling, but you make it to the bottom and feel good. You say to yourself, 'I thought I was going to crash and fall, but I made it.' "

Pleasant imagery also acts as a distraction, taking your mind off cigarettes until the urge passes. "Activate a pleasant image the minute you begin to feel the urge to smoke—in the middle of a busy day, during a hassle with your kids, or after a desperate call from a friend, for example," says Dr. Abrams. "Think of this technique as a fire drill: Have a list of stressful situations that have given you the urge to smoke in the past. Then by identifying such high-risk situations ahead of time, you can use the imagery under pressure."

Reduce stress overload. "Set realistic goals and deadlines, don't take on more tasks than you can comfortably handle, and rearrange your day to allow for hobbies or exercise," says Dr. Abrams. "Good time management is common sense, especially for someone who wants to quit smoking."

"Keep Smoking while You Learn to Quit"

That's the motto of Smokenders, a nationwide program that combines social support, behavior modification and relaxation therapy. It's an approach that might be just the ticket for people who smoke under stress, because you don't have to give up cigarettes (at least not at first).

"Enrollees meet once a week for six weeks," explains Judith Brodsky, a former Smokenders group moderator. "Smokers are allowed to continue to smoke for the first four weeks, during which they gradually cut down by learning to deal with trigger situations and downshifting to low-nicotine brands. When the 'cut-off day' arrives, their bodies harbor approximately 85 to 90 percent less nicotine than when they started."

Here are a few of the techniques employed by Smokenders.

Deep breathing. "When you smoke under stress, you inhale differently than when you're relaxed," says Brodsky. "If you're watching television, for example, you might absentmindedly take a few light puffs. But if you're under tension, you'll take a good, hard pull and exhale slowly. And smoking in that manner does in fact cause a feeling of relaxation. So we teach smokers a deep breathing exercise that can achieve the same feeling of relaxation without the cigarette."

To practice deep breathing, stand up, bend forward from the waist and breathe deeply for 15 or 30 seconds, or however long it takes to fully expel air from your lungs, says Brodsky.

Take a break. When you feel overwhelmed—if you have 12 million gizmos to assemble or your "in box" looks like the Eiffel Tower—and you feel an urge to smoke, take a brisk walk for the length of time it would take to smoke a cigarette. Or get a cool drink from the water cooler. "Do something to repattern your behavior," says Brodsky.

Think about *why* you smoke. "Does smoking make you any better able to deal with your problems? Does it help you get caught up on your work? Probably not," says Brodsky. "Smoking is like thumb-sucking, but for adults. You associate smoking a cigarette with feeling better, so you reach for one under stress."

Free at Last

"The best quitting strategy is to use whatever technique is best for *you*," says Dr. Abrams. "We recommend that people experiment with different strategies—deep breathing, relaxation therapy, biofeedback or other ways to cope with anxiety and stress. If rational thinking doesn't work for one person, for example, thinking about a cool lake might. So there is no general prescription.

"Also, the only way to finally kick the habit is to accept the fact that for three to six months you will crave cigarettes very intensely," he says. "We encourage people who have very strong cravings to isolate themselves from smoking for a whole day, perhaps in a hospital setting, to prove to themselves that they can go without a cigarette for several hours, that the craving they think won't subside does in fact go away, and to teach them that quitting will get easier as time goes on.

"After six months of talking on the phone without lighting up a cigarette, you will begin to unlearn the habit," says Dr. Abrams. "After six months to a year, a ringing phone—or other stimulus—will no longer trigger an urge for a cigarette."

If you go six months without a cigarette, you might be out of the woods. "But don't get complacent," says Brodsky. While people are smoking, it's the nicotine that keeps them hooked. But after they've quit, it's the psychological moods, circumstances, events and other reminders that trigger the urge to smoke. "So you must remain vigilant and resist the temptation," warns Dr. Abrams.

Part 6

COPING TECHNIQUES THAT WORK

Chapter 53

ASSERTIVENESS TRAINING

Picture this: You bought a curling iron that fails to curl. You do one of three things.

1. You stay home and fume about the inferior quality of modern appliances.
2. You storm back to the store, demand to see the manager, scream and yell about how you're tired of getting ripped off. You insist on getting your money back and you march out of the store.
3. You return to the store, calmly ask to speak with the manager and, in a very earnest, straightforward manner, explain that your curling iron isn't working satisfactorily and that you would like either to have your money returned or the iron replaced.

Now which of those situations produces the most stress?

If you're the stay-at-home-and-fume type, you're probably too passive for your own good. If you're the screaming-demanding-storming type, you may be too aggressive for your own good. Option number three, of course, is to be assertive: to know your rights and to respect the rights of others, and to have polished skills in effectively communicating your message, without hostility.

Let's look at another situation: You're at a party where you know very few people. You want to mingle, so what do you do?

1. You hang around on the fringes of other folks' conversations, waiting for them to include you.
2. You burst into a group and dominate the conversation. One by one the members wander away, and when each one does, you shout, "Hey, you're missing a golden opportunity!"
3. You approach a group with an effective opening line, such as "How do you know the host?" or "Are you enjoying the party?"

232

Again, which solution appears least stressful?

From a stress-reduction point of view, the assertive behavior wins hands-down over the passive or aggressive solution. The trouble is, too many folks have been programmed to respond in business, social or intimate relationships in a manner that makes most psychologists cringe. Girls are generally reared to be too passive. Boys sometimes are treated as if aggression is a birthright. On top of that, we haven't grown up learning from people who exhibit calm, clear assertive behavior all that much.

Without the benefit of either upbringing or role models, the only way to learn this behavior may be assertiveness training. It's a method of unlearning habits that professionals call an "anxiety response" to other people's behavior. With the help of assertiveness training, the passive or aggressive find themselves becoming assertive in a matter of weeks. They know what they want and learn how to go after it in a healthy manner. They become more open with themselves and with others. And they understand the consequences of their actions. As a result, relationships improve and life becomes generally less stressful.

Who Needs Assertiveness Training?

Most experts agree that assertiveness training is not for everyone. But if you've learned how *not* to stand up to others, if you're fearful of rejection and emotional situations, if you're helpless and depressed, you may be a prime candidate.

"If your general fear of what other people think inhibits your self-expression, you may be causing yourself a great deal of stress, and you should consider assertiveness training," says Joseph Wolpe, M.D., professor of psychiatry at Temple University School of Medicine in Philadelphia and a pioneer of assertiveness training. And Eileen Gambrill, Ph.D., a professor of social welfare at the University of California at Berkeley says the form of behavior therapy is for those who find themselves generally dissatisfied with the course of their relationships. "Just ask yourself: 'Am I satisfied with my social life?' 'Am I satisfied with my relationships?' "

Advises Jean Baer, author of *How to Be an Assertive (Not Aggressive) Woman*, "Systematically survey the problems you face, the things that make you feel bad, the situations that make you frustrated, the things that you'd like to have different about yourself and your life situation. Do these relate to the area of assertiveness?"

Some of the telltale signs that professional assertiveness training may help are unwanted feelings—depression, frequent outbursts of anger, frequent feelings of helplessness and frustration and of being pushed around by others.

But you may have been plagued with these problems for so long that it may not be easy to recognize your lack of assertiveness, your unrecognized inhibitions, as the culprits behind all that stress. So here's Dr. Wolpe's profile of the assertiveness training candidate, a person who is inhibited from performing "normal" behavior because of fear. Do you recognize yourself?

"He may be unable to complain about poor service in a restaurant because he is afraid of hurting the waiter's feelings; unable to express differences of opinion to his friends because he fears that they will not like him; unable to get up and leave a social situation that has become boring because he is afraid to seem ungrateful; unable to ask for the repayment of a loan or to administer a legitimate reproof to a subordinate because he is afraid of losing his image as a 'nice guy'; or unable to express love, warmth, admiration or praise because he finds such expression embarrassing."

If that sounds like you, here's some advice: *You have a perfect right* to your opinions and feelings. *You have a perfect right* to express yourself honestly—without stepping on others' toes, without trying to hurt others.

Learning to be assertive can make those words, your personal bill of rights, come alive for you. You will also learn the varying degrees of assertiveness and the appropriate times to assert yourself. Sure you have a perfect right to feel your boss is a dimwit, but it won't improve matters to tell him so. Assertiveness training can help you gain good judgment.

It's all designed to increase the effectiveness of your social behavior so that you get more positive feedback and less critical, punishing responses from others. It is based on the idea that by changing your actions, you change your attitudes and feelings about yourself. The result will be a new feeling of self-esteem—in many ways, a brand-new you.

Your local mental health organization or the psychology department at a nearby university can put you in touch with assertiveness training professionals.

A first decision is whether to opt for a group therapy workshop setting or to go it alone. "A group lets a person realize that they're not the only shy one. It gives people a chance to see the way other people do things successfully. It offers a 'buddy system,'" says Dr. Gambrill. "You get to practice what you're learning," adds David C. Diffendale, Ph.D., a psychologist in Clearwater, Florida, who runs assertiveness training workshops.

On the other hand, you may prefer the individualized attention of one-to-one therapy. "This is particularly good for people who are not going to be aggressive enough to get what they need out of a group," says Dr. Diffendale.

Either way, you will first learn clearly the differences among assertive, passive and aggressive behavior. A therapist or group facilitator can provide endless examples of each type of response.

A second step may be to evaluate your own response to specific situations. Also, you determine which relationships you would like to single out first for improvement. "You want to find out which areas you're assertive in and which areas you are not. Some people are assertive at home and not at work, and vice-versa," says Dr. Diffendale.

The lack of assertiveness at work is a major source of stress. Say your boss tells you he is dissatisfied with a major project you spent months completing. Many women in that situation would simply burst into tears, says Marion R. Frank, Ed.D., a psychologist who works with individuals and groups in assertiveness training. "They feel overwhelmed and put down and respond with tears. It's a passive response and it's totally inappropriate in the workplace." Turning on the waterworks won't get you what you want.

On the other hand, the employee may respond with expressions of anger, aggressively shouting back at the boss or lashing out at others. But you can be angry and behave assertively, not aggressively. "Instead of blowing up, you can say 'I'm having trouble with this,' " says Dr. Frank. "The proper assertive response is to ask for specifics of what your boss doesn't like about the project, without being defensive." You need to be calm and clear, have direct eye contact, good posture, and a well-modulated voice. Easier said than done, it's true. But everyone can learn with practice.

Working Up a Script

Once you've determined where your assertiveness skills need a boost, you may be asked to draw up sample scripts of assertiveness in action. How best to communicate the message that you don't want to visit your husband's parents every Sunday, without causing hard feelings. How best to communicate your displeasure when your husband comes home from work late and inebriated—without calling to warn you.

Then you'll be asked to complete tasks that set you on the road to assertiveness. If it's shyness you're overcoming, you may be instructed to strike up one conversation a day with a fellow passenger on the bus. For those who have trouble saying no, therapist Albert Ellis, Ph.D., suggests an assignment in his book, *Anger:* "Risk saying no or refusing something yourself. Pick something that you don't usually want to do but that you do in order to please others—such as going out to eat, having sex in a certain way or carrying on a conversation for a long period of time—and deliberately take the risk of refusing to do this thing."

For those with trouble asking for things, Dr. Diffendale often assigns people to ask for something they want but don't ask for, such as asking the person next to you not to smoke or simply asking your spouse to get you a glass of water while in the kitchen.

A final step may be to examine how your nonverbal behavior communicates nonassertiveness, and to learn to change.

It's Not Just Your Words

Yes, your weak gestures (fingers spread apart) may suggest passiveness or your forceful gestures (a clenched fist) may indicate aggressiveness. Assertive behavior includes many components that are easy to overlook. From

Your Perfect Right, a manual of assertiveness training by Robert E. Alberti, M.D., and Michael L. Emmons, here's a checklist of some of the things you're likely to focus on in assertiveness training.

Eye contact. Look directly at the person you're speaking to and it will help communicate your sincerity and help you get your message across directly.

Body posture. You'll add assertiveness to your message if your posture is active and erect.

Gestures. You'll add emphasis, openness and warmth if you accentuate your message with appropriate gestures. If your movements are uninhibited, you will suggest openness, self-confidence and spontaneity.

Facial expression. Let your face mirror your message. You're sending mixed signals if you smile while delivering an angry message.

Evaluating Assertiveness Training

Dr. Diffendale says you should find yourself challenged by assertiveness training, but not at a level that overwhelms you. For some people, the therapist or group leader is too easy-going and the person winds up not being stretched and doesn't learn any new behavior. That's no good because any learning you do in assertiveness training *should* be tough, he says. On the other hand, he points out that some therapists or group leaders push so hard that people feel overwhelmed by the challenge. They get frightened and drop out.

In group settings, a good trainer will start out by helping people tackle situations that are not particularly threatening or emotionally intense, says Dr. Frank. This is when you learn to ask your spouse to get you some water if he's going into the kitchen (and hope it comes in a glass). She adds that after training progresses and skills are honed, it's time to deal with emotionally laden issues.

How can you tell if the assertiveness training you choose is effective? Among the items on a consumer checklist drawn up by Dr. Gambrill and Cheryl A. Richey, Ph.D., a professor of social welfare at the University of Washington, are:

- Participants select their goals.
- Long-term as well as short-term consequences of changed behavior are considered.
- Personal and social goals selected are individually tailored for each person.
- Goals pursued are achievable.

Beyond that, ask yourself if you are aware of using new skills outside of the classroom in situations that would have otherwise had you hooked. Do you know your rights and how to enforce them?

Chapter 54

AUTOGENIC TRAINING

Imagine being able to simply tell your body to relax—and having it respond! That's the goal of autogenic training, a form of self-hypnosis that is among the best and most complete reducers of stress.

"Autogenic" means self-regulation or self-generation. It's a technique developed by Johannes Schultz, M.D., and Wolfgang Luthe, M.D., early in this century. Autogenic training is a combination of their medical research (particularly hypnosis) and Yoga. The result is a series of self-instructions that can help the body to rid itself of such diseases as high blood pressure, headaches, chronic pain, allergies, ulcers and general anxiety. It also can induce deep relaxation.

You tell yourself what you want ("My heartbeat is calm and regular") and you produce the desired physical results. As you practice the training on a regular basis, you'll discover it becomes easier to instruct your body to reply. Part of what's happening is that you get relaxed to the point where your body's self-regulating systems take over. Says Martin Shaffer, Ph.D., a clinical psychologist who runs the Stress Management Institute in San Francisco, "It's not the verbal cue but the relaxation that brings about the physical change."

There's a variation of the process that's perfectly suited to relieve stress: autogenic relaxation. It may take weeks or longer to use autogenic training to achieve a desired physiological result (such as increased thyroid production). But if you practice the method for relaxation, you're likely to get satisfaction in the first session.

How to Do It

As with other relaxation techniques, you do this one in a quiet room. Turn the lights down low and wear loose clothing. You should sit in an armchair that comfortably supports your head, back and extremities. Or you can lie down comfortably with your head supported, feet slightly apart, and arms at your side but not touching your body. You should be free of tension.

As Dr. Shaffer outlines in his book, *Life after Stress*, here are the basic instructions for using autogenics to produce relaxation.

In your comfortable position, close your eyes and slowly recite the following instructions. Breathe deeply and evenly, and recite the verbal cues to yourself as you exhale.

1. "My hands and arms are heavy and warm" (5 times).
2. "My feet and legs are heavy and warm" (5 times).
3. "My abdomen is warm and comfortable" (5 times). (Omit this step if you have ulcers.)
4. "My breathing is deep and even" (10 times).
5. "My heartbeat is slightly calm and regular" (10 times). (Use of the word *slightly* in this step can help prevent the reaction of a rapid, irregular heartbeat some people experience when that word is omitted.)
6. "My forehead is cool" (5 times).
7. "When I open my eyes, I will remain relaxed and refreshed" (3 times).

Perform the following sequence of body movements.

1. Move your hands and arms about.
2. Move your feet and legs about.
3. Rotate your head.
4. Open your eyes and sit up.

All of this should be done with an attitude of passive concentration. Observe what's happening to your body, but don't consciously try to analyze it. By all means don't criticize yourself for having distracting thoughts. If your mind wanders, simply bring it back to your instructions as soon as possible.

Dr. Shaffer advises doing two-minute autogenic training sessions ten times a day. "If you spend ten little times a day bringing your tension level down, it's unlikely to get up that high," he says.

Unexpected Results

You may experience "autogenic discharges." These can be tingling or other body sensations, involutary movements, pain or even a desire to cry. These feelings may be pleasant or unpleasant, but they will pass as you progress. "When that happens, simply do nothing," says Dr. Shaffer. "Tell yourself this is a normal discharge of tension in your body. What's happening is that your brain is dumping tension through your motor system."

Some people lie back, begin their autogenic ritual, but instead of feeling relaxed lapse into a panic of anxiety. "That happens with people who need tension as a defense," says Dr. Shaffer. "They're getting rid of their tension and up comes anxiety. Things they've not paid attention to are coming up to the surface." His initial advice: Let it pass and continue the autogenic formula. His secondary advice (if the agitation continues): Seek professional therapy to get to the root of your anxiety.

Because autogenic training produces physiological changes, it's not something to take lightly. If you have high or low blood pressure, diabetes, hypoglycemic conditions or heart conditions, you should consult with your physician before you even start. Those with severe mental or emotional disorders are discouraged from trying autogenic training. If you find yourself feeling restless during or after autogenic sessions—or if you suffer disquieting side effects—practice only under the supervision of a professional autogenic training instructor.

Bidding Migraines Adieu

Some professional therapists hook up people to biofeedback machines, so they can monitor the physiological changes that occur in autogenic training. It's a first step in learning to voluntarily control certain functions. This combination of autogenics and biofeedback can be a powerful tool to get rid of migraines. At the Menninger Foundation's Biofeedback and Psychophysiology Center in Topeka, Kansas, patients use the autogenics/biofeedback duo to learn to short-circuit the onset of migraines. (For more information on biofeedback machines, see chapter 56.)

A biofeedback unit is attached to a patient's finger to measure skin temperature. The patient repeats an autogenic phrase ("My arms and hands are heavy and warm"). After about 20 minutes, he looks at the printed record of temperature changes and writes down a summary of his feelings, emotions and thoughts during the session. The point is to perceive body changes without having to rely on a biofeedback machine, says Steven Fahrion, Ph.D., co-director of Menninger's voluntary control program.

After practicing this method with a home machine twice daily for about a week, the patient begins to replace the autogenic phrases with personal visualizations designed to make hands turn warm—visualizing burying one hand in warm sand, for instance.

How does this prevent migraines?

The stress response causes a constriction of the body's arteries, among them the carotid arteries, which supply blood to the brain. When the brain senses it isn't getting enough blood, it releases neurochemicals known as neurokinins, which cause the carotid arteries to overdilate. The arteries are wrapped with pain receptors that are stretched; that's what causes the pain.

Some migraine sufferers get a warning—such as blurred vision—that a migraine will soon occur. By warming their hands as soon as they get that warning, they can use autogenic training to halt the painful sequence of events and stop the migraine. But most migraine sufferers get no warning. Those folks are often taught to keep their hands warm all the time, to keep the stress response in constant check, says Jack Hartje, Ph.D., a professor of psychology at the University of North Florida who trains therapists to use biofeedback. One practical method is a daily session of autogenic training until the hand-warming becomes second nature.

Chapter 55

BATHS

If they ever made bathing an Olympic event, Dana Horwitz would be a contender for the gold. The pleasant Scarsdale, New York, homemaker has devoted a chunk of the past several decades perfecting her technique.

Not only does she have a daily training schedule, but she sneaks in extra practice every chance she gets. For example, when she wakes up early, rather than reading, putting up coffee or folding socks—diversions her neighbors prefer—Horwitz climbs into the tub for 10 or 15 minutes of luke-warm soaking. "I find it wakes me up," she says.

And it's the last thing she does every night. Her P.M. bath, she explains, prepares her for sleep. "How can people say they relax in the shower?" she asks. "Standing on one's feet can't be relaxing when you could be lying down."

In between the occasional morning splash and the requisite evening splash, Horwitz finds time to bathe prior to luncheons or important dates with friends. She sometimes takes an impromptu afternoon bath as a respite from her two kids. "Once I'm in the tub I can't be interrupted. If the kids fight, I can't do anything about it.

"My baths are just another method of coping with tension," explains Horwitz, and experts agree that bathing can indeed be a stress-management technique akin to meditation or Progressive Relaxation.

Not Too Warm, Not Too Cold . . .

You probably feel you're an expert at this technique, having developed your style in a Bathinette and perfected it during the ensuing decades. The fact is, if you've got stress reduction in mind, you may be doing it all wrong.

So grab your thermometer and keep reading.

"If you're stressed and want to relax, you want to bathe in water that's about the same temperature as your skin," says Jens Henriksen, M.D., medical director of the Greater Chattanooga Pain Center in Tennessee. For most people, that's between 85° and 93°F, depending where on your skin you measure it. (Skin temperature is somewhat lower than body temperature.) You can buy a battery-run electric thermistor at a medical supply house to take your skin temperature. But without one, you'll be safe if you keep the water between 90° and 95°F, says Dr. Henriksen. Only a thermometer can tell you when the water's fine, so keep one handy.

If you make the water too cold, say 70°F, it will be unpleasant. Worse than that, it will stimulate, not relax, your tense muscles. And it can also be unpleasant if the water's too hot. Bath water at 100°F is likely to cause perspiration—precisely what you don't want if you're trying to relax. (Dr. Henriksen warns that you should avoid hot baths if you are pregnant or have high blood pressure, heart disease, nerve impairment or diabetes.)

To prevent the water temperature from dropping while you bathe, keep the tap dripping slowly at a temperature slightly higher than what your water should be.

Stay in the bath for 20 to 30 minutes. Take along an air-inflated plastic pillow to support your head. And take the phone off the hook.

If you're bathing to help you get to sleep, Dr. Henriksen has a simple, effective strategy. Take your bath, get out of the tub, dry off, put on your sleepwear—and march straight to bed. Don't read, don't watch the late movie. Just close your eyes and drift away.

The Jet Set

Delightful as they are, hot tubs and whirlpools are not for everyone. If you have any one of the physical conditions that dictate you should avoid hot baths, you should also stay out of those trendy little tanks.

Even for those who can take the heat, a hot tub session should never last more than ten minutes. And if you like to stew in one after an exercise workout, wait until your body cools down.

In a hot tub or whirlpool, you get the added benefit of a body massage. Those throbbing jets produce the same effect that you get when a massage therapist gives you a rubdown. "It promotes circulation and brings more oxygen and nutrients to your muscles," says Donald Johnson, M.D., medical director for Sentry Insurance, Stevens Point, Wisconsin. And hot tubs or whirlpools produce the same psychological benefits as a massage, adds David I. Abramson, M.D., former head of the Department of Physical Medicine and Rehabilitation at the University of Illinois College of Medicine in Chicago. You feel great when you step out.

A Word about Saunas and Steam Baths

In Finland, land of the midnight sauna, researchers recently disclosed that, according to scientific evidence, you shouldn't feel relaxed in saunas—which produce dry heat—or in steam baths, their wet-heat counterparts. They reported that the process elevated concentrations of nervous system stimulants in the blood. Also, in the confines of those heat chambers, your body has to work harder to get rid of the heat, says Dr. Abramson, who therefore hesitates to recommend hot baths for older people.

Why then, do you feel so good after a sauna or steam bath? With tongue planted firmly in cheek, Dr. Abramson told the *Journal of the American Medical Association* that the sense of well-being a person experiences after leaving a steam bath "could be compared with the great feeling of relief experienced by the patient who has been suffering from severe pain and suddenly finds that he has become free of symptoms."

Experts may bicker over evidence for and against the benefits of saunas or steam baths, but people whose sweat glands don't need the permission of a Ph.D. to work may still want to give them a try. (Of course, those with the health conditions mentioned previously should avoid them.)

"Anything that's relaxing for a person may help with stress," says Edward R. Eichner, M.D., a professor at the University of Oklahoma Health Sciences Center, Oklahoma City. "Even though it may increase the secretion of stress hormones while you're in it, the net effect might be positive after you get out."

If you're going to take a sauna or steam bath, here's the "classic" approach, according to Dr. Henriksen. Start with three sessions of five minutes each—interrupted by cold showers—and end with a cold shower or plunge in a pool. (Or do it like the Finns: After a session in the sauna, lower yourself into a frozen lake through a hole cut in its surface or jump into the snow.)

You'll bake best in a sauna temperature of 180° to 200°F. For steam baths (where humidity reaches 100 percent, a bit like Savannah in the summer), the temperature should never exceed 130°F, advises Dr. Henriksen.

Chapter 56

BIOFEEDBACK

Want to know exactly how much you're sweating?

You probably don't. But maybe you should. Because if you hook yourself up to a GSR 2—an inexpensive, hand-held biofeedback machine that emits a pleasant hum in response to tiny decreases in the perspiration levels of your fingertips and a near-whistle when your skin becomes more moist—you'll know exactly when you're stressed and when you're not. And you'll be able to do something about it.

That's the principle of using a biofeedback machine. It reports on one or more of the physical functions that increase with stress: heart rate, breath rate, muscular tension or the moisture produced on your skin. Once you're aware of stress, you can reduce it. And there's no question about that reduction or its lack. Your body can't lie!

Just a Tool

But don't think a biofeedback machine is a relaxation robot you can command to de-stress you. You've got to practice a relaxation exercise (such as any of the techniques described in this book) until the gadget indicates that you're relaxed. After enough experience, you'll begin to get a clear sense of when you're relaxed and how much of what technique gets you there.

A biofeedback machine, whether a hand-held model or the elaborate doctor's-office variety, is only a tool. "People may have an exaggerated expectation of what they can accomplish with biofeedback," says Alan Glaros, Ph.D., a psychologist at the University of Florida, Gainesville, who uses biofeedback in conjunction with other methods for stress management in his practice. "Some people think biofeedback, with the stroke of a magical wand, will transform their daily, troubled existence into a Cinderella-like fairy tale. The reality is that it takes work."

Even though you may get yourself to stop sweating, he says, that's only a first step. You still have to examine and understand the stress factors that bring on the sweating.

That's why the biofeedback patient has to become a personal scientist, says John Corson, Ph.D., a professor at Dartmouth Medical College in New Hampshire. "Biofeedback allows you to collect data on your psychological strengths and weaknesses, on what upsets you and what calms you down."

Hum, Sweet Hum

The advent of hand-held biofeedback units opened up biofeedback therapy to do-it-yourselfers. No longer do the overstressed have to rely on $50 to $100 sessions in the office of physicians.

Let's tune in to one person's experience with home biofeedback, as reported in the "Regenerative Living" column of *Prevention* magazine.

"A couple of months ago a package came in the mail from a company called Thought Technology. Inside was a hand-sized piece of machinery with the enigmatic label 'GSR 2.' It was a biofeedback unit.

"'The GSR 2 biofeedback unit,' explained a doctor I asked about the product, 'monitors the skin's perspiration level and emits a tone, which rises in pitch as more moisture is produced or drops as the skin becomes drier.'

"The actual unit fit easily in my hand and had a small elastic band that held my fingers snugly against two smooth metal plates. Upon contact, a small earphone began humming softly in my ear. I closed my eyes and started purposefully thinking about a stressful situation: my next deadline. Sure enough, within three seconds, the tone started climbing the scale until it resembled the high-pitched whine of a mosquito. No doubt about it, I was definitely worked up.

"Bringing the tone back down took a little more work. Over the next two weeks, I practiced regularly with the unit while listening to a tape of relaxation exercises that came with the package. Soon I had the unit humming a low complacent tone that was a virtual one-note hymn to relaxation. If I heard the tone rise, I stopped and examined my thoughts to see what was bothering me. In this way, I not only learned correct relaxation techniques, I also discovered hidden stressors that I never realized were upsetting me.

"If you're thinking of giving biofeedback a try, be prepared for some serious work. To start, you've got to find a good relaxation technique and really concentrate on making it work. 'The unit itself only tells you how you're doing, not what to do,' says the doctor. I put in a good half hour a day at feedback. But the doctor says even 10 to 20 minutes daily, done regularly, can have a beneficial effect. 'Besides the promise of daily relaxation, I've found that biofeedback in conjunction with stress-management training often delivers other bonuses, such as better sleep and relief from stress-related high blood pressure,' he says.

"Eventually, when you've learned proper relaxation techniques, you can wean yourself from the feedback unit. But again, to make it work, you still must practice your exercises regularly. Otherwise your body will forget everything you taught it. 'Occasionally it's a good idea to go back to the biofeedback unit to make sure your skills are in good order,' says the doctor."

Professional Help

The ease of home biofeedback doesn't mean you should overlook the role of professionals. Physicians or professional therapists who are certified by the Biofeedback Certification Institute of America can give you direction and clear-cut goals in your stress management. They can tell you what to reasonably expect and can help you figure out what some of the other factors are that contribute to any stress-related ailments you may have. They can offer suggestions or remedies.

If you decide to go the at-home route, here are the addresses of two companies and descriptions of the units they manufacture.

Thought Technology, Ltd.
R.R.1, Route 9 North #380
West Chazy, NY 12992
(800) 361–3651

Or in Canada:
2180 Belgrave Avenue, Suite 693
Montreal, P.Q. Canada H4A 2L8
(514) 489–8251

1. The GSR 2. GSR stands for "galvanic skin resistance," a measure of your perspiration and resistance of skin to electrical flow. The tiny unit described above costs $49.95 (and comes with a relaxation cassette). For $79.95 you get the unit, four cassettes and a 48-page stress-control workbook.
2. GSR/Temp 2. It's the GSR 2 with the added ability to measure the temperature of your fingers to within $1/20$ of a degree Fahrenheit. (Stress causes cold and clammy hands. The temperature measures the cold, the GSR measures the clammy.) The unit is designed so that you don't have to hold it in your hand. A meter registers temperature changes. Cost: $99.95.
3. Calmset 3. In addition to GSR and temperature functions, this unit has an electromyograph that registers your level of muscular tension. You listen in on headphones. Cost: $249.

A note for lovers of computers. All of the above can be hooked up to a computer via a software program named Calmpute. That way you can check out your responses in patterns or bar graphs on your computer terminal.

Thought Technology also sells an electronic gadget named Calmtone that lets you connect any of these biofeedback units to your stereo. Your favorite music will get louder or softer in sync with your relaxation.

Bio-Feedback Systems, Inc.
2736 47th Street
Boulder, CO 80301
(303) 444–1411

1. EDR–002. This unit measures skin conductance, which may help determine your level of stress. Metal contacts on two Velcro strips wrap around your fingers. A cable connects your fingers to the unit, which is the size of a hand-held calculator. You check out your conductance level on a digital display. Cost: $150.
2. Mini-Relaxometer. If you prefer to *hear* how well your skin conductance changes, this unit monitors your conductance and tells you what's happening via earphones. Pulse/clicks increase in speed when you get sweatier, slow down as you get dry. Cost: $110.
3. DT–002. Similar to the EDR–002, this machine checks out your temperature and displays the news in Fahrenheit on a meter. Cost: $150.
4. PE–020. Want to keep track of your muscle tension? Attach the electrodes from this unit to your lower back, forehead or any other muscle area that tends to tense up. This unit provides both visible and audible feedback. Cost: $345.

Chapter 57

COGNITIVE THERAPY

Picture yourself in a crowded elevator. Someone is standing on the back of your shoes. You're wondering who this obnoxious person is, and you're getting angrier and angrier by the second. Suddenly you turn around and see that it's a blind person, complete with sunglasses and a white cane.

Instantly, your anger subsides. You *thought* that person was intentionally abusing you, and your distorted thought produced a negative feeling.

That one simple example illustrates the basic principle of cognitive therapy, explains Fred Wright, Ed.D., of the University of Pennsylvania in Philadelphia. The principle is that thoughts determine feelings. And *negative* thoughts, or cognitions, almost always contain gross distortions. If we can identify our distorted negative thoughts, we can learn to change them. And if we can learn to change our distorted negative thoughts, we can change the bad feelings they produce. While thoughts aren't alone in creating bad feelings, they certainly have a major impact.

Dr. Wright, the educational director for the University of Pennsylvania's Center for Cognitive Therapy, explains that the way we interpret events has a powerful impact on the way we feel and the way we behave.

"If, when I hear a siren, I simply say to myself that a fire truck is passing, I'm not going to cause myself any difficulty," he says. "But if I say to myself that a fire truck is passing and my house may be on fire, that's going to have a strong emotional impact. So in cognitive therapy, we look for distortions in people's perceptions. Assuming that your house is on fire because you hear a fire truck siren is a distorted way of looking at something," he says.

Dangerous Assumptions

Carry the example a bit further. Every time your boss indicates he wants to see you in his office, do you jump to the conclusion that he's about to fire you? Your heart pounds and your stomach sinks. Every time you attend a party, do you assume that everyone will be criticizing your taste in clothes? You end up being defensive and critical—in advance—and get invited to fewer and fewer parties. Every time your daughter is late from a date, do you expect the worst—and find yourself fuming and infuriated, when there always seems to be a legitimate reason for her tardiness?

By using cognitive therapy, people can learn to be more objective and thus more realistic in the things they say to themselves. Cognitive therapists train us to sift through the rubbish that floats around in our minds, especially those thoughts that upset us and cause us to get into problems with our behavior.

Think how much better you'd feel if, each time your boss told you to come into his office, you thought, "I don't know what's going to happen, but it'll be new and different." Or if you went to parties thinking, "Some people may not like my taste in clothes and maybe some people do not like me, but people won't dislike me simply because they don't like my clothes. Also, there are lots of people who like me—and some of them will be at the party." And when it comes to your daughter arriving home late, wouldn't life be less stressful if you could say to yourself: "Well, my daughter's been late before and there always has been a reasonable excuse. Maybe I should explain that it's best to call, no matter what the hour is, if she knows she's going to be late. I've never told her how much I worry about her."

Your Cognitive Distortions

The cognitive therapists teach skills to identify, monitor and replace distorted thoughts that make you unhappy. The first step: When you are having negative feelings, look for the thoughts that may be lurking in the background. When you find your mood changes, when you suddenly discover that you are angry or anxious, do an instant replay. What was going through your mind, what were you saying to yourself that could have caused the change in mood? Says Dr. Wright, "Ask yourself if there is anything you could be saying to yourself that could possibly be a distortion or a dysfunctional thought, one that isn't serving a functional purpose."

We'll explain how you can answer those questions for yourself, but first you have to see what sorts of distortions may be reigning over your feelings. Which of the following are your personal favorites?

All-or-nothing thinking. Either the situation is right or it's wrong and there's nothing in between. If your careless driving results in a car accident, you blame yourself as being totally incompetent. If you lose your job, you blame yourself as being a total failure. It's unrealistic—not to mention stressful—to view the world in such black-and-white terms. It works the same way with your feelings. You may say you're stressed to the max and it's awful and terrible and you can't stand it, or you may say you don't have a care in the world. In reality, anxiety exists in varying levels all the time.

Jumping to conclusions. You have one bit of evidence (your car won't start, for instance), and you jump to the conclusion that the day is going to be a never-ending pattern of bad events. The results of your crucial lab test are held up by the hospital, and you jump to the conclusion that you're in for catastrophic news. In reality, the lab technician never showed up for work.

Mind reading. In this type of distortion, you assume you know what another person is thinking about you, and you almost always assume those thoughts are unkind. Take the following stressful situation: A waiter delivers a steak to a dissatisfied customer and is told to take it back to the kitchen. The waiter can make this stressful situation even more stressful by saying to himself, "The person at the table thinks I'm an idiot because I didn't get his order right."

"Catastrophizing." You take a situation and you blow it out of proportion. You grossly exaggerate the importance of a single mistake, saying, for example, "I forgot to mail the monthly payment. The bank is going to auction off my home." Think how much easier life would be if you said to yourself: "Okay, so I forgot to mail the mortgage payment; I'll take care of it right now."

"Awfulizing." "I'll never be able to make new friends in the new city and that will be awful."

Mental filtering. You take an experience, filter out the positive things about it and let only the negative things through. You focus on the fact that your son forgot your birthday (for the first time) and feel he is an ungrateful louse. You overlook his good qualities and all the nice things he's done for you over the years.

The tyranny of "shoulds." Also called "the fallacy of fairness," this distortion is based on the belief that things should be fair. "My boss shouldn't treat me that way." "My sister's kids shouldn't take advantage of her so often."

Overgeneralizing. "All of the neighbors don't like me all of the time." Just because one neighbor doesn't like you—or even several neighbors don't like you—doesn't mean they all feel that way about you, and that all your friendships will be doomed. It's unrealistic to think you're locked into a never-ending pattern of defeat.

"Crystal-balling." "I know I'm never going to be happy in my new job." "I know the group will elect my opponent to be chairman." "I know our vacation will be a disappointment."

A Systematic Approach

Now that you know some of the major distortions, hunt them down in your thinking. You may find it difficult to become aware of how your vague, negative thoughts are producing feelings. So if you're feeling down in the dumps, for example, or if you're experiencing some of the physical symptoms of stress (the old butterflies-in-the-stomach syndrome, for instance) drag out some paper and a pencil and jot down three things:

Your situation ("My friend hasn't called").

Your feeling ("Sadness").

What you're telling yourself at the time ("He doesn't like me anymore. I'm worthless").

This little exercise will get you into the habit of understanding the connection between thoughts and feelings. The next step is to determine whether what you're telling yourself is true. In this process, you may suddenly remember that your friend told you he was planning to be out of town this week. Or you may realize that your friend often is out of touch with everybody, not only with you.

Now you have to challenge your way of looking at the situation. That doesn't mean you should simply replace negative thoughts ("I'm worthless") with ones that are just as distorted, albeit positive ("I'm tremendous"). Accept that your worth as a human being doesn't depend, in this example, on hearing from your friend.

To get into the routine of answering negative thought patterns, divide another sheet of paper in half. On the left side, write out your negative thought ("I'm miserable because I'm never going to make friends with my daughter-in-law"). Then give it some serious thought and jot down a constructive answer. ("That doesn't mean I'm an unworthy person. I've got lots of friends. Besides, my daughter-in-law is overwhelmed in a new job and has two infants to care for.")

If you find that by arguing with your negative thoughts you are reinforcing them and becoming more anxious, you may be overdoing it, says Gary Emery, Ph.D., a Los Angeles cognitive therapist and author of *Rapid Relief from Emotional Distress*. If that's the case, he suggests you stop arguing. "Let the negative thoughts go and try to concentrate on what will produce a good feeling," he advises.

You can still work distorted negative thoughts out of your system, he says. "I'd have people buy a golf counter and every time they have a distorted thought, they click it and let go of the thought. Or make a mark on a three-by-five-inch card. And let go of the thought. Something about the counting allows you to distance yourself from the thought. And it reinforces that it's just a thought," he says. Another idea: Write down what your thoughts are and, when you're in a better mood, look at those thoughts and realize that they have no basis in reality.

When Negative Thoughts Are True

But your negative thought may turn out to be true, in which case you must look next at the realistic consequences and possible solutions.

Put things in their proper perspective. You may be disappointed that your daughter-in-law just plain doesn't want to be your friend, but it's not the end of the world.

If possible, try to problem-solve. Most therapists suggest you take small steps. Try to understand the daughter-in-law. Listen to her. And if the reality is that you won't be friends, accept the reality.

Finally, whether what you are saying to yourself is true or false, you must consider the disadvantages of continuing to say it. Examine the long-range impact on your feelings and behavior. The Pygmalion Effect dictates that people tend to get what they expect. "If someone tells you that a person you're about to meet is really bright, you'd tend to notice the bright things they say in a conversation," says Dr. Wright.

So if you're anxious and think you'll be awkward in a social situation, that will make you more anxious and you will be more awkward. If you expect the worst in any situation, that may be what you'll notice. Advises Dr. Emery: Focus on the positive, on what you want to see happen.

Chapter 58

DEEP BREATHING

Ever notice how a newborn baby breathes? Deep and slow and rhythmic. A baby's tiny abdomen is relaxed, and he pulls air into his lungs easily and fully.

Now how do you breathe? Chances are your breaths are shallow, and it's your chest that rises and falls with each breath, not your gut. Sorry, but after all these years you've forgotten how to breathe in a way that will increase your oxygen supply and revitalize your body's tissues and organs—and keep you naturally relaxed and at ease.

Stress takes a long-term toll on your breathing. "Under stress, rather than extending all the way down to your abdomen, your breath becomes short and shallow," says Jeffrey A. Migdow, M.D., Lenox, Massachusetts, holistic physician and coauthor of *Take a Deep Breath*. Your breath probably only goes as far as your upper chest and then stops. Or you hold your breath. Or you do panting breaths.

Even if you were perfectly calm to start, such breathing automatically produces stress and reinforces stress. And what's worse, you become used to it.

Dr. Migdow says that when you breathe shallowly, the oxygen level of your blood drops and the carbon dioxide level takes a jump. To get rid of that carbon dioxide, you feel the need to breathe harder. But stress tenses up your breathing apparatus. "As the diaphragm tenses, abdominal and intercostal [between the ribs] muscles constrict and you lose the ability to inhale deeply and naturally at the very moment you need it most," he says.

If you don't believe it, try breathing with quick, shallow breaths for a minute and see how tense you feel.

The Abdominal Breath

So before we offer some special breathing exercises for the times you feel stressed, let's give you a simple refresher course on how nature intended you

253

to breathe all the time. It's called "abdominal breathing," and it's so simple a newborn can do it. Here's how Ronald Dushkin, M.D., of the Kripalu Center for Yoga and Health in Massachusetts teaches the method.

1. Start by sitting in a relaxed position with your spine straight and shoulders back (but down and loose) to allow your lungs to expand. Rest your hands on the arms of your chair or in your lap. Put your feet flat on the floor.
2. Breathe in slowly through your nose as you expand your abdomen. Imagine that you have a balloon inside your abdomen and, as you inhale, you're slowly inflating it, causing the abdominal area to swell.
3. Breathe out slowly through your nose. Pull your abdominal muscles in as you press all the air out of your lungs.
4. Continue breathing in and out as your abdomen rises and falls. Establish a natural rhythm. (Hint: Place your hands on your abdomen just above the navel with fingertips pointing toward each other and just touching. If you're breathing correctly, your hands will rise with your abdomen as you inhale, and your fingertips will separate. As you exhale, they'll touch again.)

Eventually, you'll get in the habit of breathing that way all the time. And you will find yourself more relaxed and pleasantly energized. But for those moments of high stress, take the time to reverse the fight-or-flight response with some special deep breathing exercises from *Take a Deep Breath*.

The cleansing breath. This is a good, quick exercise you can practice anytime you want to release tension.

1. Inhale deeply through your nose.
2. Exhale through your puckered mouth, as if you were blowing out a candle.
3. Repeat steps 1 and 2 three times.
4. Issue a few sighs. Inhale deeply, then sigh. Again. Again. With each sigh, drop your chin to your chest and droop your shoulders. Think of yourself as a tire letting all its air out. Think of the tension you are releasing.

The stress-discharging breath. Allow more time to do this exercise. It's perfect for after work.

1. Make sure you will not be disturbed.
2. Get into a comfortable position, lying down or sitting in a favorite chair. Loosen any constricting clothing.
3. Start relaxing with several abdominal breaths; breathe in to the count of four, then breathe out to the count of eight.
4. Take a deep breath through your nose and hold it. Tense your feet as long as you can. (Warning: If you have a history of heart disease, high blood pressure or stroke, consult your physician about this technique. He or she may suggest a modified version, with little or no breath-holding.)

5. Relax your feet as you exhale with a sigh through your mouth.
6. Take a few abdominal breaths with each count, as in step 3.
7. Breathe in deeply through your nose. Hold it. Tense your calves.
8. Relax your calves as you breathe out with a strong exhalation.
9. Repeat the sequence for each area of the body, working from the extremities to the center: feet, calves, thighs, buttocks, abdomen. Next, the upper body: fingers, forearms, upper arms, shoulders. (Hunch your shoulders up to your ears.) Don't forget your face; it may hold much tension. Work it in three stages: Pull your jaw back so your mouth looks funny; scrunch up your nose; furrow your brow.
10. Take a few minutes to relax and let go.

The waiting (in line) peacefully breath. Banks and post offices should print copies of this exercise on index cards and distribute them to customers. It works!

1. Do the slow, deep abdominal breath with long, relaxed exhalation. Feel impatience drifting away. (In a traffic jam, don't breathe too deeply.)
2. Continue the abdominal breath. As you relax, realize that impatience will not get you to the head of the line any faster. Impatience only makes the time seem longer.
3. See those around you as fellow human beings also waiting and working to the best of their ability.
4. Hum or sigh to yourself for a while.
5. Imagine how pleasurable it would be if everyone around you were also relaxed and trying new ways to be patient and efficient.

Chapter 59

DELEGATING

Carol hates grocery shopping, but her family has to eat. So until recently, Carol would drag herself to the supermarket once a week and grudgingly push her grocery cart up and down the aisles.

Carol's 12-year-old daughter, Ann, loves to shop. She says supermarkets are "real neat." Ann also loves to search through newspapers, magazines and mail fliers for coupons to clip, organize and file.

Guess who does the grocery shopping at Carol's house now? Ann, with Mom's shopping list in hand and with Dad in the driver's seat. Carol discovered a way to get the shopping done—and done right—without doing it herself. She *delegated* the job—and relieved herself of the associated stress.

Why a Woman's Work Is Never Done

Whether you're managing a household of two, a small business or a major division of a large corporation, delegation not only increases your control but also takes a load of stress off your shoulders. Yet while the workplace is usually set up for delegating, the household may not be, leaving work distributed unevenly. And all too often, mom carries the lion's—or lioness's—share of the load.

"Many women who are very capable at their paid jobs know how to delegate responsibility in the workplace, but they don't use those skills at home," says Kathleen V. Shea, Ph.D., a psychologist at Northwestern University in Evanston, Illinois. "If you don't delegate, you can dig yourself into a big responsibility hole."

"Evidence shows that in families where one spouse works, the other spouse (usually the wife) averages 8 hours of housework a day, and the working spouse (usually the husband) puts in 1.6 hours," says Ann Crouter,

256

Ph.D., associate professor in the Department of Individual and Family Studies at the Pennsylvania State University. "In households where both spouses work at jobs outside the home, however, the wife averages 4.5 to 5 hours of housework a day, yet the husband's time remains unchanged at 1.6 hours."

In other words, a lot of working wives are working time-and-a-half. There are limits to what even the most highly organized person can do. Yet many people try to defy the laws of time management and do it all.

How to Delegate without Distress

Many people would like to delegate but don't know how. Here are tips on how to delegate effectively, whether you're a business executive, a home executive or even the Chief Executive.

Decide which jobs you can unload. Make a list of routine tasks like watering the houseplants, walking the dog, folding socks and packing lunches, then decide what you can delegate. The idea is to delegate what you can (like household chores or office paperwork) so that you can devote your efforts to tasks that are too important to delegate (like hiring new employees for your company or interviewing full-time babysitters to take care of your children while you work).

Think beyond housework. Obligatory tasks like balancing the checkbook or sorting the mail can be a nuisance—unless you enjoy doing them. "Brainstorm about what has to be done, then decide who wouldn't mind doing it," says Dr. Crouter. One woman delegated to her teenage son the job of tracking birthdays and buying and sending cards. Another asked her husband to address the Christmas cards to his substantially larger side of the family, thus significantly flattening the stack of cards she had to write during the hectic preholiday season.

Give clear, complete instructions. You wouldn't give someone the responsibility of going to the supermarket for you unless you gave them a list of what you needed. By the same token, you'll be more likely to get satisfactory results if you tell people as precisely as possible what you want them to do. Just *how* specific your demands should be will depend on the age and experience of your helper.

"Rely on others' judgment somewhat," says Dr. Crouter. "You don't want to treat adults like very young children. With children, the older they are, the more discretion you can give them. For a teen, for example, cooking supper is more of a big deal if they can surprise you with what they've selected than if you given them explicit, connect-the-dots instructions."

Set a deadline. "A project will almost always be completed sooner if it has a deadline than if it hasn't," says R. Alec Mackenzie, author of *The Time Trap*.

Don't be a dictator. "Allow a reasonable amount of leeway," says Dr. Crouter. "It's one thing to say, 'Clean your room once a week,' and another to say, 'You must clean your room on Saturday mornings.' Let your delegate do the job when it's convenient, within reason. You have to be willing to relinquish a certain amount of power, because if you set too-strict requirements, you're only delegating halfway."

Offer encouragement, not ridicule. Many people resist delegating because they are trapped by the feeling that no one could do the job as well as they could. Or they criticize their spouse's or children's first efforts at a task, then complain because they don't get enough help.

"Being too critical is counterproductive," says Dr. Crouter. "Accept the fact that errors and mistakes are bound to occur. Instead of criticism, give positive reinforcement. Rave about the meals your spouse cooks when they're good, for example, and don't say much when they aren't. No one is going to continue to do something if you belittle his attempts," she adds.

"At our house, for example, my husband does all the shopping and cooking, which relieves me of the responsibility," continues Dr. Crouter. "But it also means that I eat whatever is put in front of me, as graciously as I can. Similarly, if you ask a four-year-old child to sweep the walk—something a four-year-old can probably do without hurting anything—be sure to follow up with words of praise, like, 'Wow! Look who swept this sidewalk clean!' "

Make work fun. "If someone likes the task they're assigned, they're more likely to continue to do it," says Dr. Crouter.

"Does your teen like hamburgers? When you plan a cookout assign him to grill," says Dr. Shea. "Or get everyone into the kitchen together as a team: One person peels the potatoes, the other mashes them. The next thing you know, they'll *want* to help with dinner."

Rotate unpopular jobs. There are bound to be certain tasks that nobody wants to do. So take turns. "Children especially have to learn that sometimes we have to do things we don't like," says Dr. Shea.

Don't feel guilty. By delegating, you are teaching others self-sufficiency, not imposing on them. "Many parents, particularly mothers, feel guilty about working outside the home and try to compensate by performing at super-human levels—doing all the shopping, cooking and laundry, for example," says Dr. Shea. "That encourages dependency in your children or spouse, when in reality they will be better off if they can manage for themselves."

"Without delegation, you have sad circumstances, such as when a husband, having depended on his wife to do the all the laundry throughout his adult life, enters widowerhood not having washed a shirt in 40 years—and not knowing where to begin," says Dr. Crouter. (By the same token, wives are better off if they have some experience in traditional male tasks like checking the oil in the car or filing a tax return.) So by delegating, you are not only absolving yourself of the sole responsibility for getting a job done, you are also teaching your whole family valuable survival skills they may need sooner or later. And the sooner they learn, the better.

Chapter 60

DOODLES AND DIARIES

Cathy Guisewite created the stressed-out cartoon character "Cathy" from random doodling. Like her creation, Guisewite once worked in an advertising firm, under a constant onslaught of creative demands and deadlines. In addition to occupational pressures, Guisewite was prey to other stresses: dieting, overeating, guilt, conflicts with her mother, more guilt, compulsive shopping, insecurity over romance and other tribulations common to single women in their twenties and thirties.

Alone at night with her anxiety—and a supply of chocolate eclairs for solace—Guisewite found herself reenacting the stressful circumstances of the day in cartoon doodles. She invented imaginary conversations between her alter ego and her boss, co-workers, boyfriend, mother and others to express her alter ego's hopes, fears and apprehensions.

At her mother's urging (okay, *harping*), Guisewite submitted her "doodles with dialogue" to Universal Press Syndicate, which began to publish them as a comic strip that is now widely syndicated in newspapers and magazines around the country.

Draw Out Your Frustration

You, too, can doodle away your troubles. Janie Rhyne, Ph.D., psychologist and art therapist at the School of Social Work, University of Iowa, calls doodles such as "Cathy" a "visual conversation with oneself" or a "doodle diary." Basically an exercise in visual thinking, the doodle diary is a more structured version of random doodling—aimless squiggles you find yourself drawing during meetings or while talking on the telephone. In her workshops, Dr. Rhyne instructs students or clients to keep a five- by seven-inch spiral

259

notebook in which to draw doodles based on everyday events and write a few accompanying words about the feelings they experience—annoyance, anger or happiness, for instance.

"Doodle diaries relieve stress," says Dr. Rhyne, "because bringing your feelings to the surface and expressing them in picture form both clarifies how you feel and acts as a cathartic. Pictures serve as a visual language that helps you see and acknowledge how you function in the world."

Diaries Are Good Therapy

A written diary works on the same principle—putting your feelings on paper helps to both vent and resolve bad feelings triggered by stressful events and situations.

"Keeping a diary of innermost thoughts and feelings is especially useful as a technique for dealing with problems that, for one reason or another, you can't easily talk to anyone about," says James W. Pennebaker, Ph.D., a professor of psychology at Southern Methodist University in Dallas. "People are less likely to confide in others about certain subjects—sexuality, embarrassment, failure, things that make them look bad. But they can write freely about these subjects without fear of rejection. Some people benefit from keeping a journal; others talk into a tape recorder. The effect is the same."

Writing or taping your thoughts has a definite edge over simply thinking about a problem.

"Translating your feelings into language forces you to slow down, organize your thoughts and give the problem structure," says Dr. Pennebaker. "Writing about a problem also makes it more concrete. Once it's on paper, you no longer have to dwell on it—in much the same way that making a list of things to do takes the effort out of trying to remember them all.

"These techniques are especially beneficial to people who don't readily open up to others. Men generally have more difficulty than women in sharing their inner feelings," he says.

And, as Dr. Pennebaker's research indicates, therapeutic writing works well for dealing with trouble rooted in the past as well as current turmoil.

"If you are going through a divorce, writing and talking about it should help some," explains Dr. Pennebaker. "But you will continue to have pain. The person who benefits most from writing about divorce trauma is one who was divorced two or more years ago but is still suffering from it on a day-to-day basis."

Another psychologist, Ira Progoff, Ph.D., of New York City, who conducts intensive journal workshops across the country, says that starting a journal *before* stressful events occur establishes a framework within which you can work out problems when trying times arrive.

"Yelling on Paper" May Boost Immunity

Diaries are more than a way to blow off steam for the moment; they may also counteract one of the harmful physical effects of stress. It's well known that stress can lower your immunity. A study conducted by Dr. Pennebaker and his colleagues indicates that putting your troubles in writing may boost resistance to infection.

The researchers, including Janice Kiecolt-Glaser, Ph.D., and Ronald Glaser, Ph.D., selected 50 college students at random and divided them into two groups. One group wrote about superficial topics for 20 minutes a day on four consecutive days. The other group used the same time to write about highly traumatic events in their past. Blood samples taken and analyzed before the study began, immediately after the experiment and six weeks afterward showed a fascinating pattern.

"Inhibited students who wrote about experiences that weighed heavily on them showed an increase in lymphocyte response, which is a measure of the body's ability to fight infectious agents such as bacteria and viruses," says Dr. Pennebaker. What's more, the boost in immunity lasted for six weeks, according to the blood tests.

"The students in this experiment wrote about a wide variety of problems, both past and present, including conflicts with parents and boyfriends or girlfriends, problems of adjustment to college life, past sexual trauma and suicidal thoughts, among others," says Dr. Pennebaker. "Those who wrote about things they had avoided talking about showed the greatest benefit."

A diary can often reveal clues to the causes of stress-related illnesses such as headaches, backaches, stomach troubles, colds and flu. "I've asked people to make two graphs: One charting a history of illness over the past five years, another charting major problems with a spouse, parent, at work. You'd be surprised at the number of people for whom the stressful events and health complaints coincide," Dr. Pennebaker says.

How to Use Your Pocket Therapist

To use a diary most effectively, psychologists interviewed offer these guidelines.

Begin at the beginning. Start your diary with an account of the "stepping stones" of your life—how you got where you are now. "That's particularly helpful to refer to later, when you feel drawn this way and that," says Dr. Progoff.

Write when you feel the need. "Like painkilling medicine, diaries are best used 'as needed' rather than on a fixed schedule," says Dr. Pennebaker. "Whenever you find yourself dwelling on a problem and have no one to confide in, write it down."

Put yourself in the right frame of mind. Before beginning to write or record, meditate or perform some other relaxation exercise for a few minutes. A relaxed state lowers your inhibitions and helps your thoughts flow more freely, says Dr. Pennebaker.

Seek out and acknowledge your deepest thoughts and feelings. "A diary should be self-reflective," says Dr. Pennebaker.

Ask yourself why you feel the way you do. "It's not enough just to say that you feel like stringing up your boss," says Dr. Pennebaker. "You have to explore why you feel angry or frustrated."

Record both good and bad experiences. "Good fortune can be stressful, too," Dr. Pennebaker reminds us. "Say you get a promotion but for whatever reason you can't share your good news with your friends. Or you're madly in love but for whatever reason can't let it be known."

Invent dialogue. Write an imaginary script between you and others who play a part in your life but to whom, for some reason, you can't speak directly: a spouse who has died, a close friend whom you no longer see frequently or someone who has wronged you. "Dialogue is a means of saying what is in your unconscious, what you know but cannot articulate," says Dr. Progoff.

Keep your diary private. Write anonymously. Or discard what you've written (or erase the tape) once it's served its purpose. "If you're worried about what might happen should your spouse or roommate or friends find your diary, you'll be too inhibited to let your thoughts flow freely, defeating the purpose," says Dr. Pennebaker.

And don't worry if you feel you aren't a born writer. "Even people who say they freeze up when they have to write find that it's easy to write about important parts of their life," concludes Dr. Progoff.

To help get started, see the Appendix, Keeping a Stress Diary, on pages 376–84.

Chapter 61

EXERCISE

As you move through your day, chances are you'll have more than one opportunity to get angry. It might be a chance encounter with an infuriating person, a near fender-bender in heavy traffic or an overcharge on your electric bill. If the rage subsides almost as fast as it came, you're probably no worse for the experience. But if your rage continues and you don't vent some steam, a part of your body is pumping out a potentially toxic substance called noradrenaline.

Along with adrenaline, noradrenaline is a hormone triggered into action by your brain when you sense trouble. The problem is, if you stay angry and don't vent the hostility, the brain continues to trigger noradrenaline, which threatens the heart and may hamper the immune system.

"Everyday stressors can cause the release of this hormone," says Redford B. Williams, M.D., professor of psychiatry at Duke University, Durham, North Carolina, and director of the university's Behavioral Medicine Research Center, who has studied the hazards of hostility. "In lab experiments, we've found that noradrenaline can be released when people are given a difficult math problem to solve. This hormone is very easy to discharge, especially in today's society, where there are so many potential irritants."

It's also easy to deal with.

"If you blow up and vent your feelings, then you're releasing your anger and, in most cases, everything inside will go back to normal and the hormonal release will stop," says Dr. Williams. "Any physical expression that uses up calories, such as exercise, burns up the hormones instead of allowing them to get to the stage in the body where they can do harm. In this case, physical exercise is actually relaxing."

"Exercise also may induce a kind of 'Relaxation Response' by flooding your body with endorphins, natural opiatelike painkillers released by the brain and other organs," says Daniel M. Landers, Ph.D., of the Exercise and Sports Research Institute, Department of Physical Education at Arizona State University, Tempe. "That theory is still under debate, however, because researchers aren't sure whether endorphins relieve tension directly, by traveling back to the brain, or indirectly, by slowing down your breathing."

The "Feel-Better Phenomenon"

Still another theory suggests that exercise relieves tension by taking your mind off whatever is bugging you—that exercise may be no different than such nonphysical diversions as reading. To test that hypothesis, Dr. Landers and Stephen Boutcher, Ph.D., measured anxiety levels in experienced runners and nonrunners before and after a vigorous run, then before and after a quiet reading session. The experienced runners felt less anxiety after running than after reading. They also felt less anxiety after running than the nonrunners did. Reading didn't seem to significantly reduce anxiety for either group.

"These data suggest that hard physical activity and a quiet reading session are not equally effective in reducing anxiety," conclude the researchers. "Thus, the effects of running may be more than just a 'time-out,' and physiological changes associated with recovery after exercise may also influence anxiety reduction."

Swimming has the same mood-elevating effects as running, say Brooklyn College physical education researchers. The researchers asked beginner and intermediate swimmers about their levels of tension, anxiety, depression and anger, then compared their answers with those of a group that didn't swim. The swimmers consistently reported better moods just after a swim.

Regardless of how exercise reduces tension, though, most researchers agree: People who take part in vigorous physical activity consistently report a dramatic increase in psychological well-being. They feel good not only after exercise but in general, saying they have feelings of mastery, patience and a capacity for change. In fact, some doctors refer to this exercise effect as the "feel-better phenonmenon."

Fit People Handle Stress Better

That heightened sense of peace and well-being can carry you through wave after wave of stress. "Increasing fitness may be a way of diminishing the effects of unavoidable stress," according to David L. Roth, Ph.D., and David S. Holmes, Ph.D., psychologists at the University of Kansas in Lawrence. They base that statement on a nine-week study of the moderating influence of physical fitness on the impact of stressful life events among 112 individuals.

First, the people being studied listed the stressful events they had experienced in the preceding year. The researchers then measured their physical fitness by recording their heart rate and estimating their aerobic capacity (an index of the amount of oxygen the body burns up as you exert yourself) while they rode on a stationary bicycle. For the following two months, the people studied kept a record of their physical health, depression, anxiety and general psychological distress.

The results: Among people who reported the most "bad experiences" over the year, only those who were physically unfit reported a significant number of health problems. In contrast, similar bad experiences seemed to have had little effect on the health of physically fit people. Physically fit individuals also reported less depression.

"With those people who cannot avoid or reduce life stress, increasing physical fitness may be an effective means of reducing the deleterious effects of stress on physical and psychological health," conclude the researchers.

A similar study, published in *The Physician and Sportsmedicine*, concludes, "Physical fitness is often associated with a feeling of well-being and reduced anxiety . . . regardless of the subject's age."

You Never Outgrow Your Need for "Recess"

You already may have experienced the "feel-better phenomenon" without realizing it. Remember elementary school recess? After drilling you on spelling and arithmetic all morning, the teachers released you and your classmates out into the schoolyard to play tag, kickball and hopscotch. That playtime helped you and your fidgety friends expend nervous energy and revitalized you for the afternoon lessons.

We never outgrow our need for "recess." Granted, it's rarely practical to go off and swim a few laps when you are straining to meet a deadline. Neither can you leave the scene to bicycle or shoot a few baskets every time toil and trouble bubble. But you can plan your activities to precede or follow anticipated stress, when exercise can do the most good. Schedule a workout for your lunch hour, after work or after you pack the children off to school in the morning.

The Exercise Prescription: How Much, for How Long

Researchers report that, generally, the best kinds of exercise for counteracting stress are continuous, rhythmic aerobic activities such as running, walking, cycling, swimming and cross-country skiing. Stop-and-go activities such as tennis, racquetball and basketball are less potent stress aids but are still worthwhile, if you enjoy them. Or, as one doctor put it, "Most anything that makes you sweat should work." (See the table on pages 266–67 to find out how other popular forms of exercise stack up.)

Stress-Reducing Potential of Various Forms of Exercise

Some activities are better at diffusing stress and generating a feeling of relaxation than others. Daniel M. Landers, Ph.D., of the Exercise and Sports Research Institute, Department of Physical Education at Arizona State University in Tempe, has selected a number of popular activities (listed below) and rated them for their approximate potential for reducing tension. Ratings range from 1 (minimally effective) to 5 (very effective).

Activity	Rating when performed at 70% or higher of maximum heart rate*	Rating when performed at approximately 30–40% of maximum heart rate†
Aerobics	5	2
Badminton (stop and go)	3	1
Basketball (stop and go)	3	1
Bowling	1	1
Calisthenics	4	2
Canoeing	2	1
Circuit training	5	3
Cross-country skiing	5	3
Cycling	5	3
Dancing	2	1
Frisbee	2	1
Golf (foursome, pulling clubs)	2	1
Hiking	3	2
Hiking (with 10-pound backpack)	4	3
Ice skating	3	2
Martial arts	3	1
Racquetball, handball, squash	3	1

Activity	Rating when performed at 70% or higher of maximum heart rate*	Rating when performed at approximately 30–40% of maximum heart rate†
Roller skating	3	1
Rope skipping	4	2
Rowing	5	3
Running	5	3
Softball	3	1
Swimming (crawl stroke)	5	3
Table tennis	3	1
Tennis (singles)	3	1
Tennis (doubles)	2.5	1
Volleyball	3	1
Walking	4	2
Water skiing	3	1
Windsurfing	2	1
Yoga	4	3

*By well-conditioned individuals.
†By less conditioned individuals.

To get the optimum Relaxation Response from exercise, you should work out a minimum of three times a week, for at least 20 minutes, at a moderate or vigorous level (that is, 70 to 80 percent of your maximum heart rate, which is roughly 220 minus your age). Check with your doctor before beginning any exercise program.

How soon after you begin an exercise program can you expect to feel a noticeable decrease in tension levels? That depends, in part, on your age and fitness level at the starting line.

"A healthy 20-year-old may begin to feel the effects in a matter of days," says Robert S. Brown, M.D., Ph.D., associate professor of behavioral medicine and psychiatry at the University of Virginia in Charlottesville. "People age 40 and older may not begin to feel the full effects for a month."

Attitude Adjustment

So far, exercise sounds like just the ticket for stress relief. But for many people, the mere thought of exercise can *cause* stress. Busy people struggling to meet existing demands on their time and energy may think of exercise as one more pressing obligation on an already hectic schedule. In one survey, "inconvenience" topped the list of reasons people gave for dropping their exercise program.

Other studies have shown that those who engage in sports do so because they are attracted by a variety of rewards, like improving their skills, enjoying the excitement of competition, increasing their physical fitness, feeling a mastery of the sport and gaining the recognition and approval of others. People who shun sports or drop out blame excessive time and energy demands or excessive competitive pressures, among other factors. Some are simply put off by the "suffer, sweat and grunt" image of exercise. Or they feel self-conscious about baring their out-of-shape bodies to the world.

Any prescription for exercise has to take such anxieties into account, say doctors, because if you hate to exercise, you'll defeat the purpose, which is to *relieve* stress.

"If you exercise grudgingly, you won't get nearly the boost in well-being as you would if you're enthusiastic, even if you pretend you're enjoying yourself," explains Sara Snodgrass, Ph.D., professor of psychology at Skidmore College in Saratoga Springs, New York. Dr. Snodgrass tested the effects of three different walking styles on 79 college students. Each student took a three-minute walk, taking long strides, swinging their arms and fixing their eyes ahead, shuffling along and casting their eyes downward, or with a natural gait.

The shufflers experienced far fewer of the mood-elevating effects of walking than either the normal walkers or the striders did. Dr. Snodgrass feels that her study suggests that when we feel down, we can brighten our mood by purposely walking with vigor. In other words, if you approach exercise with the attitude that you're going to feel great, you probably will feel great!

Taking the Stress Out of Your Workout

The key to stress-free exercise is to make it fun, convenient and suited to your personality.

Pick an exercise you like. "If you dread your workouts and find yourself looking at your watch every five minutes, maybe you've chosen the wrong exercise," says Dr. Landers. "To benefit from exercise—and stick with it—you have to enjoy it and feel comfortable."

Make an appointment to exercise. Experts stress the importance of scheduling exercise into your calendar. "Then you've made a personal commitment to it, and you're less likely to miss your workout," says Dan Lynch, vice president of the Executive Fitness Center, New York. For some, that means exercising first thing in the morning, before you get swept up in the day's other activities.

Don't compete if it drives you to excess. Competitive sports are especially counterproductive for hard-driving Type A personalities. Also, don't play with highly competitive teammates or opponents unless you truly enjoy the pressure. (For further information on competitiveness and stress, see chapter 5.)

Choose more than one activity. "Variety is the key to successful exercise programs," says Dr. Brown. It prevents you from getting bored and dropping out. Giving yourself more than one option enables you to stick with your program if the weather or other factors interfere with your regularly scheduled workout.

Choose relaxing surroundings. Walk or bicycle in parks and trails, for example, instead of in city traffic or on busy highways.

Give yourself the "home advantage." Pro athletes know that they play better on their home turf. You, too, will be more likely to reach your fitness goals if you find a pool, track, route, court or club in which you feel comfortable. Where do your friends work out? Familiar faces will put you more at ease than a roomful of sweaty strangers. Or you can work out to exercise videotapes in the privacy of your own home.

Pack a week's worth of exercise clothes at a time. If you stash several sets of clean socks, underwear and other workout gear in your tote bag, car or locker, you won't find yourself scrambling for fresh clothes as you rush out the door in the morning.

Exercise to music you like. Music relieves the monotony of sports activities that involve the same kind of work for extended times, week after week, such as rowing, cycling, ice skating and long-distance running. Exercising to music, according to researchers, helps you to stay interested in repetitious activities, reduces anxiety and keeps you from looking at your watch every two minutes.

By integrating exercise into your family, social and work life, you can reduce any stress it may add to your schedule.

Chapter 62

FLOTATION TANKS

A closed container dark as a cave, small as a coffin, half-filled with salty water. You lie in it for an hour, on your back, alone. And you've never felt more relaxed in your life.

Sound a little strange? That's because you're tanked—flotation tanked, that is: a high-tech, low-gravity relaxation environment that some experts say is possibly the best method for relieving mind and body of stress.

In their early days of existence, they were known as "sensory deprivation" tanks or "isolation" tanks. They were housed, for the most part, in the basements of research labs, and the act of climbing into one *was* a lot like getting into a coffin.

Today's flotation tanks often have some of the same features: a shallow tub of warm, salty water that keeps your body effortlessly suspended, sound-proofing that blocks out noise, a sealed structure that keeps out light. But for those who like the deep physical relaxation of effortless floating yet don't want to be quite so "isolated," some of the newer tanks are larger, are open or have a control panel that can engage music, soft lighting or an intercom.

In the serene atmosphere of a flotation tank, the body's borders are blurred. You are suspended weightlessly. And, free from the strain of gravity, you can feel the tension flow from your muscles. The proven stress-reducing benefits are many.

Spending an hour in a flotation tank will trigger a Relaxation Response to counter the ill effects of stress, according to Michael Hutchinson, author of *The Book of Floating: Exploring the Private Sea.*

Clearing Away Stress Biochemicals

Under stress, the body releases several biochemicals—blood cortisol, ACTH, norepinephrine and epinephrine (adrenaline)—that can produce high blood pressure and muscular tension. Tests on floaters indicate that an hour in the tank reduces the amount of blood cortisol and ACTH. Researchers believe it also lowers the levels of norepinephrine and epinephrine. Deprived of stimulation, your body seems to use its inner mechanisms to return to an optimal functioning level. Your heart rate goes down, your blood pressure goes down. And researchers believe that the capillaries that were constricted during stress become dilated, sending blood back to the extremities.

And with a lowered level of stress-induced biochemicals in the body, a floater increases his tolerance to stress after leaving the tank, says Roderick Borrie, Ph.D., a psychologist at Maimonides Medical Center in Brooklyn, New York, who is conducting tank research. The effect can last for days after a single floating session. His studies with rheumatoid arthritis sufferers indicate that two sessions a week of floating produce pain relief for three to four days. He also uses the flotation tanks in his private therapy practice as the "ultimate couch"—communicating with patients through an intercom.

At St. Elizabeth Hospital in Appleton, Wisconsin, where a flotation tank is a primary method for relaxation training, two separate studies indicated a 70 to 80 percent improvement in the treatment of a wide range of problems, including anxiety, gastrointestinal ailments, headaches and chronic pain.

Peter Suedfeld, Ph.D., a professor of psychology at the University of British Columbia, has found that the flotation tank helps sufferers of chronic tension headaches. In his test, a group of headache sufferers that used the flotation tank in addition to progressive muscle relaxation reported fewer and less severe headaches than a group that relied only on progressive muscle relaxation.

Theta Waves

Brain wave activity of floaters appears to change from the beta waves of normal concentration to the alpha waves of relaxation and to theta waves— the threshold between consciousness and unconsciousness, according to some who study the effects of flotation. In a state of theta wave production— and free of the need to process external stimulation, the theory holds—the mind can be open to vivid, dreamlike visualizations. Some professional athletes rely on tank-assisted visualizations of perfect performances to show their bodies how they can achieve perfection in an athletic contest.

If you're thinking of trying a flotation tank for stress management, Dr. Suedfeld suggests that a regular weekly float is enough to help. You can also try it when you're under high levels of stress—or are about to be.

There are more than 150 flotation tanks in the United States that you can rent for hourly use. To locate one near you, write to the Flotation Tank Association, P.O. Box 30648, Los Angeles, CA 90030–0648 or phone (213) 264–7960.

Chapter 63

FRIENDS AND FAMILY

If your monthly phone costs sometimes look like the Pentagon's budget for Star Wars, perhaps it's because that bill represents your own personal defense strategy. It may simply show that you have developed a good way to cope with stress: talking to those who are close to you.

Should your mother or father fall ill, do you automatically phone your brother or sister to enlist their support? If you get that big promotion, is the first person you call your old college roommate? (Good fortune can sometimes be stressful, too, according to psychologists.) When you're feeling out on a limb—and alone—remember that a friend is just 7 digits away (11 if you're out of town).

"People who have others with whom they can communicate about the tensions in their lives often find relief for those tensions," says Lillian B. Rubin, Ph.D., psychologist, sociologist and author of *Just Friends: The Role of Friendship in Our Lives*.

"Just knowing that you can turn to others is comforting," says Anthony D'Augelli, Ph.D., associate professor of human development in the College of Health and Human Development at the Pennsylvania State University. "And when trouble does arise, friends can help you out and prevent problems from escalating beyond control."

In fact, some psychologists go so far as to say that many people may not necessarily need professional counseling to deal with certain kinds of problems, and that a good listener and trusted confidant can serve the same purpose.

"Friends can and do serve as effective counselors," says Dr. Rubin. "Feelings of loneliness and despair, for example, can be met and assuaged by a solid network of friends with whom you share your life."

The Amigo Factor in Health and Disease

"Close, confiding personal relationships have been found to reduce or buffer the stress connected with life's major changes (deaths, births, marriages,

272

geographic moves, etc.) as well as with the cumulative effect of daily hassles," concluded a study conducted for the California Department of Mental Health.

Medical evidence indicates that people in crisis who enjoy contact and support from others tend to maintain higher morale—as you'd expect—but also suffer fewer physical symptoms than those who do not. In one study, for example, pregnant women under stress who had access to supportive, confiding relationships had one-third the complications of women who were undergoing similar levels of stress but did not have supportive relationships.

One of the largest studies of the link between social support and stress relief was conducted by the Institute for Social Research at the University of Michigan in Ann Arbor. Researchers asked 2,000 people to rate how much they confided in others (friends, relatives, co-workers, supervisor) or sought their help. The people interviewed reported that social support helped to alleviate feelings of dissatisfaction, depression or anxiety generated by various types of on-the-job stress.

Should you lose your job, sympathetic comrades and kin can be of invaluable help—even if they can't solve your unemployment predicament. One study of urban and rural blue collar workers, published in the *Journal of Health and Social Behavior*, found that people who lost their jobs but had no family, friends or neighbors to turn to for sympathy and help reported more symptoms of emotional and physical ill health than others who had people to turn to during the crisis. The people who found themselves both jobless and friendless had significantly higher serum cholesterol counts (increasing their risk of coronary heart disease), were more depressed, reported more illnesses and considered themselves worse off than those with strong social ties.

He Ain't Heavy, He's My Brother

If you belong to a close-knit family, you have an unconditional charter membership in an emotional support group wherever you roam. Many people consider close relatives—brothers, sisters, parents, grandparents or cousins—to be their oldest friends. For certain problems—especially those involving a major change or disappointment—no one is in a better position to provide a therapeutic shoulder to lean on than someone who knows how you got to be who you are, who shares many of the same childhood memories, good or bad (same house, same dog, same tuna casserole).

"The family can often be counted on to provide practical and concrete aid in times of crises—financial help, help with children, technical aid (cleaning or repairing, for example) and employment," says Cary L. Cooper, Ph.D., in his book *The Stress Check*.

"The person from a really supportive family doesn't have to go it alone," says one family counselor. "That person is part of something bigger—a family that cares enough to let him or her know he or she is okay."

"Probably the most obvious way family members can show support is by praising one another and by letting each member know how much he or she is cared for," says Dolores Curran, a family specialist, in her book *Traits of a Healthy Family.* In other words, a family who praises you when you succeed and supports you when you fail can go a long way toward helping you cope with mistakes, disappointments and other stressful events.

"Mutual support within a family in times of crisis is critical," says James J. Strain, M.D., psychiatry professor at Mount Sinai School of Medicine in New York. "Succoring one another, the family never feels alienated or alone. Instead, members feel useful, involved, in control, and able to adapt and reduce stress by pulling together."

"On the one hand, friends may be easier to establish a frank rapport with than family members because they're not as entangled in your life and can more readily adopt an objective point of view," says Dr. Rubin. "But kin still seem to most of us to offer a safe retreat, an anchor in an uncertain and unsteady world—the people who can be counted on when need is most urgent."

Family teamwork is probably one of the top ten means of reducing stress. Ask anyone whose spouse or children pitch in with dinner or chores after they've had a trying day. And never underestimate the stress-reducing power of having someone to hold your hand (figuratively and literally) through an emotionally trying time, an illness, a frightening hospital experience or other traumatic event.

(Of course, if your family resembles the Medicis more than the Waltons, your relatives may cause more grief than they relieve. If that's the case, see chapter 11.)

People You Can Count On for Better or Worse

A strong social network is too important a factor in stress control to leave to chance. Dr. D'Augelli suggests that people sit down and make a list of up to 20 people they feel they could turn to before stressful circumstances arise. Then ask yourself, "Of these people, who could I talk to about financial trouble? Marital problems? On-the-job stress? Who would be willing to give me a lift if my car breaks down? Who could I trust to pick up my child at day care if I can't get there in time? Who could help me if I got sick?"

This kind of practical help, along with emotional support, can make the difference between whether a crisis is manageable or catastrophic. And "preventive stress control"—having analyzed your support network *ahead of time*—gives you a person to call upon when trouble occurs, says Dr. D'Augelli.

When it comes to considering the supportive people in your life, quality counts more than quantity, says Dr. D'Augelli. The best candidates, of course, are people who've expressed concern and a willingness to help in the past, people whom you feel comfortable approaching again. And there are other traits common among your Who's Who of Helpers.

Good listening skills. "You need someone who will listen sympathetically but impassively, and not try to impose an answer on you or muddy up your thinking with their own views," says Dr. Rubin.

Dr. D'Augelli agrees. "Helpers are primed to rush in with advice, because they think that's what people want," he says. "To head off unneeded—and sometimes unproductive—advice, approach potential helpers by saying, 'I need to talk,' not, 'What should I do?' Ideally, the supportive friend will then help you sort out your feelings, set goals, and otherwise help you to make plans to resolve the crisis."

Open-mindedness. "Certain attitudes encourage us to open up, and others prompt us to back off, especially if we're distraught," says Dr. D'Augelli. "Judgmental, pushy or moralistic advice isn't constructive."

Trustworthiness. Needless to say, you should think twice about confiding in anyone who is apt to broadcast your troubles to others or use the information against you.

Give-and-take. Effective communication involves an exchange of both ideas and help, says Dr. D'Augelli. If you expect someone to take care of your kids at times, for example, be prepared to do the same for them.

"Reciprocity is the *sine qua non* [absolute essential] of friendship," says Dr. Rubin. "Otherwise, the person doing all the giving feels taken advantage of and will drop out of the friendship."

Shared fun. "People without a close family—whose relatives live out of town or single parents whose nuclear family has broken down—often develop a 'family' of friends with whom to share holidays," says Dr. Rubin. "Many good friends take vacations together."

Realistic optimism. Fatalistic, doom-and-gloom characters aren't likely to help you feel better or help you see possible solutions to a dilemma. "Also, people who are naive or offer simplistic solutions may mean well, but they won't really help you resolve the problem," says Dr. D'Augelli. "The best support comes from someone who has a positive yet realistic attitude."

To Make Friends, Be a Friend

Dr. D'Augelli offers two final tips for building a supportive social network.

Take the initiative. Show you care about your teammates. Look for subtle signs of distress and be ready to listen or help.

Say "thank you." Express your relief and appreciation for favors and help with a grateful word or a small gift.

Chapter 64

HOBBIES AND PLAY

"Chances are you know how to work," says Robert Eliot, M.D., a noted cardiologist who is director of the cardiovascular unit of the Swedish Medical Center in Denver, Colorado. "But you may not know how to play."

What's more, play is not optional, something to squeeze in when and if you finish all your work, or to postpone until after the kids grow up and move away or until you retire. Play is a good way to counteract stress *now.*

"The detachment provided by genuine leisure can create a fresh perspective when you reenter your work world," says Dr. Eliot in his book *Is It Worth Dying For?* "Without leisure, life lacks balance and perspective, giving stress a chance to take over."

Am I Having Fun Yet?

"Ask yourself, 'When was the last time I did things I really wanted to do and really had fun doing?' " advises Dr. Eliot. If it's been a while, you may be suffering a fun deficiency. Yet choosing a leisure pastime is too important to be left to chance.

"Some people choose an activity because it's the latest thing and everyone is doing it (like playing racquetball) or so that they can play with business clients (like golf)," says Nora Britch, director of Leisure Planning, a New York firm that conducts seminars on constructive use of free time. "Or people do more of what they do for work because they love it when they *really* need a break.

"Also, what's satisfying to others may be stressful for you," adds Britch. "Some people don't camp because they're afraid of bears. By the same token, someone else may not like to sit and crochet for hours, but it may be just what you need."

Here are some guidelines for choosing free time activities that will be relaxing and satisfying for *you.*

Make a list of what makes you feel good. "I ask people to take an inventory of the sort of things their job does and does not provide," says Britch. "Then look for a pastime that can supply elements that are important to you but missing from your daily routine—physical work, privacy, challenge, communication or leadership, for example."

Recall how you played in the past. "Think back to what you did for fun in your teens or twenties, and analyze what it was you liked about those activities," says Britch. "Were they planned or spontaneous? Pursued alone or with others? As a participant or as a spectator? Structured (like racquetball) or unstructured (like juggling)? Cooperative or competitive? Simple or difficult? Person-centered (like playing bridge) or product-centered (like making crafts)? High risk or low risk? Short term or long term? Conventional or unconventional?"

List activities you didn't like—and why you didn't. "My sister, for example, tried pottery and painting but dropped both because she doesn't like to get her hands dirty," says Britch. "But she does beautiful needlework—and loves it." If you hate to clean up messes, certain arts and crafts may cause stress instead of relieve it. "You'll probably notice that your likes and dislikes have certain things in common," says Britch.

Consider pastimes that differ from your work. "My brother, for example, is a computer whiz but in his leisure he loves to garden and build furniture," says Britch. "A woman I know who's in sales likes needlework. To some, that may suggest she isn't sociable enough to make sales, but she feels she needs a solitary activity to counteract a job that puts her in constant communication with lots of people."

Make time for play. "If you look closely at the lives of productive people, you'll find that they make time for what they need and want to do by planning it in their schedules," says Dr. Eliot.

Don't take your hobbies too seriously. "It's not the activity you choose that determines whether you're working or playing; it's your attitude toward it that counts," says Dr. Eliot. If you approach gardening with rigid perfectionism, it may start to feel more like work than play.

"Even needlepoint can get competitive in the hands of a highly competitive person," says Britch.

Do something engaging. Sitting and daydreaming can be a constructive use of spare time, says Britch. Everyone needs to pause to absorb and reflect on life. But passive activities such as watching television out of sheer boredom don't necessarily counteract stress in a positive way.

"The most satisfying leisure involves active choice," says Dr. Eliot. "Escape will help turn off stress, but it will not regenerate you to meet life's responsibilities."

Keep an open mind. "If you have arthritis or other physical limitations, certain activities may be difficult or impossible," says Britch. "But don't be overly timid or use your limitations as an excuse. Find out what you *can* do. A violinist I know who developed arthritis in her hands found she enjoyed conducting string quartets, for example."

While exercise is a bona fide stress reliever, don't assume sports are the only effective way to let off steam. "Volunteering is leisure in that it's self-chosen," says Britch.

Getting Started

To find out more about a sport, hobby or other pastime, Britch suggests you consult the *Encyclopedia of Associations*, found in most libraries. The directory lists the names and addresses of thousands of organizations that publish newsletters, catalogs and other informative materials on everything from juggling to collecting model trains. Their headquarters can put you in touch with local clubs and chapters of groups of people who share your interest. Once you have chosen your activity, here are some ways to get started.

Begin with group instruction. "One-on-one instruction is ideal, but group lessons are less expensive," says Britch. "Then, if you decide to pursue the activity further, you may decide to pay for individualized instruction."

Look into adult education classes. "Town, county or state recreation departments often sponsor low-cost programs with good instructors," says Britch.

Try before you buy. "You can usually rent or borrow whatever equipment or materials you need at first until you decide whether you want to make a commitment," says Britch.

"Along with reducing stress and making yourself emotionally healthier while you're working, finding positive ways to spend your leisure provides an added bonus: It prepares you for retirement, when 90 percent of your time will be leisure," says Britch. "We're all retirees-in-training in the sense that we're preparing for retirement all our lives. So it's good to know how to evaluate your values and plan your leisure time accordingly."

Chapter 65

HOUSEHOLD APPLIANCES

Microwaves beam our dinner onto the table. Instead of going to the movies, we have "home entertainment" systems. The latest bathroom—with water jets in the tub, a stereo system and plenty of room—is a "personal spa." And why not? What better way to insulate yourself against the pressures of the outside world than to create a low-stress oasis in your home?

You don't have to spend a small fortune on high-tech electronics to build more serenity into your home, though. Dozens of simple, affordable devices exist to reduce everyday stress in small but significant ways.

Home, Stress-Free Home

To determine how you can make life easier at home, take a "stress audit" of your house and grounds. Look for situations that foster worry and hassle—like irons you consistently forget to turn off or garden hoses tied in a Gordian knot. Then thumb through catalogs or visit hardware stores to find ingenious items that can spare you unnecessary aggravation and stress. Here are a few notable stress-saving devices to get you started.

Automatic shut-off iron. One woman spent her entire week's vacation in St. Croix worrying that she'd return to see her house burned to the ground because she felt sure she'd left the iron on when she left home. (She hadn't.) The woman has since bought a new iron that automatically shuts off after sitting idle for ten minutes, whether she's in the next room or the next county.

Light and appliance timers. By making your house look occupied while you're away—and lighting it for your return—timers serve as magical house minders. You can preset lamps, televisions, radios and stereos to turn on and off at various intervals. In hot weather, you may want to preset the air conditioner to cool the house for your return later in the day. A timer can even signal the coffee pot to brew your morning cup of coffee before you crawl out of bed!

Kitchen timer. If you've ever burned a pot roast (pot and all) because of a phone call or other distraction, a kitchen timer can save the day—and your cookware. A kitchen timer can also prevent other household disasters by reminding you to take the laundry out of the dryer, to rinse a permanent wave solution out of your hair or tend to other time-urgent tasks.

Magnetic bottle opener. Stick one of these on the refrigerator and never search through jumbled kitchen drawers again.

Heat tape. Plagued by burst water pipes whenever temperatures plummet way below freezing? Wrap exposed plumbing in heat tape and sleep easier.

Pet door. Why be a doorman for your dog or cat?

Take the Work Out of Yard Work

With the right tools at hand, yard work can be a pleasure—or at least not a pain.

Garden hose reel. No house should be without a wind-up hose reel to tame that impossibly tangled garden hose and keep it out of the path of lawnmower blades.

Long-handled grass and weed trimmer. *Popular Science* calls these trimmers "the biggest breakthrough in yard tools since the power mower." And it's no wonder: Why spend hours crouched over walkways and patio edges to groom your property when you can do it in minutes, with no aches and pains? (To further save frustration, keep in mind that the bigger your yard, the more powerful a trimmer you'll need.)

More Time- and Temper-Savers

Here are some other items you may want to consider.

Magnetic nail starter. This device holds nails in position to be hammered. Saves your thumb and your temper.

Traction mats. Even snow tires sometimes need help getting your car under way in snow and ice. Inserted under recalcitrant tires, traction mats—nylon-reinforced neoprene pads with dozens of steel grippers—can help free snowbound vehicles.

Log carrier. With a lightweight, flexible, sturdy canvas log carrier, you can tote logs to your fireplace without getting dirt and wood chips on your clothes or the floor.

Luggage or grocery caddy. The caddy takes the "lug" out of getting luggage to, from and through airline terminals. It's also handy for toting heavy bags of groceries from one point to another.

Your own shopping list of stress-reducing gadgets and gizmos will be determined by how and where you live and how you spend your time. But the whole idea is to find out which jobs you can eliminate or make easier with household aids.

Chapter 66

IMAGERY

Try this. Command your mouth to "produce and secrete saliva." Bet it didn't work. Now try, as vividly as possible, to picture yourself biting into a juicy slice of lemon. Taste its sourness and wetness. Did that work any better?

Our autonomic nervous system—the system that kicks in when we're under stress—is linked to our *un*conscious mind. While we can use verbal commands to get our conscious mind to do things, we can't order around our unconscious mind the same way. What we can do, however, is communicate with it through images. Want to raise your heart rate? Think of something fearful—being chased by a snarling pit bull terrier, for example. Want to lower it? Think of something restful—swinging in a hammock, watching the leaves overhead. This powerful technique, sometimes called "visualization," has had well-documented and broad-ranging success. It has helped many women fight the pain of childbirth. It's eased the symptoms of some cancer patients, and even helped Olympic skier Jean-Claude Killy win gold medals.

There are a variety of uses of imagery to keep stress in check. One simple method suggested by Martin L. Rossman, M.D., a physician in Mill Valley, California, is to take a brief vacation in your mind.

A Trip to the Land of Relax

First, get yourself into a comfortable position. Take about six deep breaths. Breathing deeply and slowly, completely relax your body from toes to scalp. Think of relaxing each muscle in your body and feel the tension flowing out of you. Now count down slowly from ten to one, and feel yourself getting more deeply relaxed with each number.

Now that you're relaxed, imagine yourself in a peaceful, safe and beautiful place. It could be a place you've been to or an imagined spot you'll never really get to—like floating on a cloud.

Then you recruit your senses—and scout around for as many details as possible. Are there trees or plants in your paradise? Try to see the coconut palms. What time of day is it? Where's the sun in the sky? Feel the freshness of early morning. Now, what kinds of sounds do you hear? Chirping birds? What fragrances are there? Suntan lotion? The smell of the surf?

For stress-reduction maintenance, Dr. Rossman says to take such a minivacation for about 3 to 5 minutes a couple of times each day. If you suffer from a stress-related or stress-aggravated illness, he suggests you do it for 20 minutes twice a day for three weeks. Not only will it interrupt your stress cycle, it will also accelerate your natural healing process, he says. Have fun with the method. It may be the only vacation you ever take that doesn't include luggage, crowds, traffic and sunburned shoulders.

Talking to Dogs

If you are faced with a stressful situation you don't quite know how to handle, Dr. Rossman says you should ask a dog for advice. Or a towering oak tree. Or a wise old man or woman.

Dr. Rossman uses these and other images to help patients tap into wisdom that they already possess. First, he suggests you do a relaxation exercise to get you completely settled. Once you're calm, he says to imagine a place that is peaceful, safe and beautiful. Comfortably in place, you then have a talk with a "wisdom" figure that is close at hand. If you're imagining yourself blissfully lying on that Tahiti beach, it may be a friendly dog that happens by. But you can imagine yourself conversing with almost anyone or anything.

In that blissful state, you describe the predicament that's causing your stress and ask the inner adviser what to do. The result? If you're like many who have used the method, you'll learn, often by surprise, that you have the ability to understand and cope successfully with a stressful situation. To drive home the point and to transfer the advice to reality, you should keep a diary of the "inner-wisdom" discussions. (Nobody but you has to know it's a big black retriever who helped you out.)

Mind Games to Manage Your Anxiety

You can use Anxiety Management Training (AMT) if such emotions as anger get in your way whenever you are under stress. It's a method devised by imagery expert Richard M. Suinn, Ph.D., head of the Psychology Department at Colorado State University.

First, you completely relax yourself with a relaxation technique and abdominal breathing (see chapter 58). Then you imagine a circumstance in which you were highly stressed—returning an item to a store and having a salesman give you a hard time, or walking into your boss's office and being turned down for a raise. "It must be a real circumstance that prompted a moderate level of stress," says Dr. Suinn.

While you're charged up from reexperiencing the stress, pay close attention to the emotional and physical upset you're going through. Then lower your upset by shifting to a relaxing image. You go from picturing the nasty salesperson to picturing a comforting friend. After some practice in making the shift, run through the exercise again, but this time imagine a *highly* stressful circumstance. After a period of time of working with this exercise, you should be able to shift to your relaxing scene at will.

Directing Your Own Show

While AMT is particularly useful for people who are paralyzed by emotional upset when they're under stress, others find it's their *behavior* that needs improving. In such cases there's another method that can offer help. Visual Motor Behavior Rehearsal (VMBR) relies on imagery to help you practice your coping behavior; it's much the same method used by pro golfers to visualize themselves sinking putts.

VMBR gets you to play the director of a stressful scene—let's say approaching your boss for a raise—and then test out different plots and dialogues. In this case, you'd picture yourself approaching your boss for the raise—but this time you won't be nervously entering his office. You'll be calm and self-assured. You won't blurt out your request. You'll present a well-organized case. And when he raises criticism, you'll respond with self-confidence.

You prepare yourself for every possible contingency. As a result, your reactions will be more automatic, and you'll find yourself more in control and able to be more spontaneous. "The imagery exercise reduces the chance that stress will happen," says Dr. Suinn. "And even if it does, you're better prepared to come out with the proper response."

The uses of imagery to motivate your unconscious mind are endless. By imagining something positive—that your relationships will improve, that you will see yourself as a happy person—you're taking the first step toward making your dreams come true.

Chapter 67

LAUGHTER

By 5:00 P.M., Celeste's nerves were shot. A dozen things had gone wrong—some even before noon. After that, things had only gotten worse.

All Celeste could think of on the drive home from the office was how much she could use a glass of wine—or two or three. Waiting for her in the day's mail, though, was a videotape of a childhood favorite—Road Runner cartoons—that she'd ordered weeks earlier. Celeste forgot about the wine and popped the cassette into her VCR instead.

After watching the tape—an hour of back-to-back Road Runner versus Wile E. Coyote chases—Celeste was laughing so hard her ribs ached and she could barely see or speak. And the snafus at work didn't seem to matter anymore.

Do you, too, have days when, like Wile E. Coyote, the only light at the end of the tunnel turns out to be an approaching train? Maybe you need your own "humor first-aid kit."

A Laugh a Day Keeps the Doctor Away

"Laughter can provide immediate relief from life's daily pressures," says Joel Goodman, Ed.D., director of the HUMOR Project at the Saratoga Institute in Saratoga Springs, New York, and editor of *Laughing Matters* magazine. "But it also builds up immunity to stress for the long haul."

Other experts agree.

"The ability to get a laugh out of everyday situations is a safety valve that will rid you of tensions that might otherwise continue to build and damage your health," writes Laurence J. Peter in his book, *The Laughter Prescription*.

"Laughter is not only as good a method of stress relief as a massage, a hot bath or exercise, it's *essential* to stress relief," says Steve Allen, Jr., M.D., son of comedian Steve Allen and "a graduate of the Hawkeye Pierce School of Medicine."

285

Assault with a Friendly Weapon

Playful humor (as opposed to derogatory humor) also helps to take the stress out of trying circumstances. Take the case of a couple who stopped at a roadside restaurant for lunch in the middle of a long drive from Boston to Philadelphia. After they had sat at a table for 20 minutes, the waitress still hadn't noticed them, let alone taken their order. So they toyed with the notion of sending her a postcard saying, "Having a nice time. Wish you were here." Instead of fuming, they giggled.

Slow service is only one of the many stressors that can get you riled up—if you let them. A good-natured sense of humor can make the difference.

"Situations like that aren't stressful in themselves; rather, our *perception* of adversity makes something stressful," says Katherine Ferrari, founder and president of the International Laughter Society, Inc., headquartered in Los Gatos, California. "By looking at a stressful event or situation in a new, absurd or slightly cockeyed way, humor changes our perception of the stressor and therefore can reduce tension and anxiety."

In other words, the problem hasn't changed—the waitress is still slow on the draw, the phone company still can't untangle the error on your bill, your car still needs a new muffler to pass inspection—but humor enables part of your psyche to step back and view the situation from a different perspective.

"And humor helps you move from venting frustration to inventing a solution—and preventing stress buildup," says Marjorie J. Ingram, director of the Creative Response to Stress Project at the Saratoga Institute.

Laughing, like aerobic exercise, also diffuses physical tension directly, according to gelontologists (people who study laughter).

"One theory proposes that laughing triggers a sequence of actions in which muscle tension first increases, then decreases—which explains why you can end up 'weak' with laughter," explains Dr. Allen.

At the same time, laughter seems to decrease the production of adrenaline and cortisone, the stress hormones, explains Dr. Allen, thus leaving you more relaxed. "And while it's hard to prove in the laboratory, experience indicates that these beneficial effects last."

Help for the Humor-Impaired

Caught up in the spinning vortex of life's commitments and conflicts, though, it's not always easy to stop and focus through the clear and detached lens of a Candid Camera. Even the mental health professionals interviewed admitted that they, too, need reminders to lighten up once in a while. Here are their tips.

Remind yourself to have fun. When the going gets tough, just repeat to yourself, "Life is crazy" and "It's okay to be foolish."

Keep a "silly scrapbook." Collect funny cartoons, humorous anecdotes, remarks you overheard and other items that make you chuckle with amusement, say the experts. Then leaf through the book whenever you need a fix of laughter. (Your scrapbook is also a good place for mementos, like zany photos of you and your friends.)

Head off stress with regular doses of humor. "A shot of humor is like a dose of medicine; the effects linger, dissipating gradually, over several hours," explains Dr. Allen. "Say you see an Eddie Murphy or a Woody Allen movie on Friday night. You'll find yourself thinking about the movie as you leave the theater, after you get home and often into the next day. Like medicine, at a certain point half the therapeutic effects of laughter will have been used up. Then you need another dose. So I tell people to gauge the 'humor half-life' of whatever amuses them and replenish their dosage as needed."

Take a "laugh break" instead of a coffee break. "Keep a 'humor first-aid kit.' Fill it with noisemakers, comedy tapes, a Groucho Marx disguise and other comic props to draw on when you feel the urge to be silly," says Dr. Allen, who's been known to retreat to his back office to juggle for 15 minutes if things get too hectic in his office practice.

Make a "silliness" check at 4:30 in the afternoon. "People around you need to see you smile, especially at work—we spend so much of our lives at it," says Dr. Allen. "If you haven't laughed yet, you should." A well-developed sense of humor is especially essential to avoid burnout for people in the so-called caregiving professions: doctors, nurses, teachers and writers of greeting card verse.

Lighten up. View would-be calamities through the eyes of your favorite comedian. "Say to yourself, 'How would Bill Cosby (or Erma Bombeck or Rodney Dangerfield) react to this?' " says Dr. Goodman. " 'What would he or she do in my shoes?' "

Spend time with those who help you see the bright side. "If you isolate yourself, you'll lose your perspective," says Ingram. "Get together regularly with friends to share funny stories about daily disasters with an eye toward constructive solutions."

Heat up some "canned laughter." Every so often, you'll hear someone say, "Some day you'll laugh about this." Ever feel like asking for an exact date? You know you need to laugh *now.*

"If you'd *like* to be able to laugh but can't—if you're feeling angry, afraid or grieved because of divorce, illness or other major stress, force yourself to laugh anyway; it will 'kick-start' your motor," says Annette Goodheart, Ph.D. (no kidding, that's her real name), who teaches classes in Beginning and Advanced Laughter at Santa Barbara City College in California. "Think about what's bothering you and try a 'tee-hee.' If that doesn't make you feel better, try a throatier 'heh-heh,' then a 'ha-ha' from the chest or a 'ho-ho' from the belly." (If your laughter ignition seems hard to start, think of something absurd—like George Washington in a pink tutu—to help trigger mirth.)

Practice makes perfect. "Like playing a musical instrument or any other skill, the more you practice laughing, the better your sense of humor becomes," says Dr. Goodman.

So when stress threatens to get the best of you, remember this: For every action there is an equal and opposite gut reaction. Make yours a belly laugh.

Chapter 68

LOVE AND ROMANCE

Your author has found love to be the full trip, emotionally speaking; the grand tour: fall in love, visit both Heaven and Hell for the price of one.

—Tom Robbins, *Even Cowgirls Get the Blues*

A quick take of various *grand amours* reminds us that Shakespeare was right: "The course of true love never did run smooth." Witness the distress of Romeo and Juliet. ("She loves me, her family loves me not.") Or Lancelot and Guinevere. Or Elvis and Priscilla. Or Henry VIII and Ann Boleyn. (Please, no wisecracks about a lady losing her head over a guy.)

The special mix of fantasy, hope and uncertainty that constitutes romantic love can lead you to pure, unforgettable euphoria—or to the depths of despair.

Love can generate stress on any one of various fronts: longing for someone special; unrequited love; a romance gone sour; or suspecting your honey has strayed. When psychologist Dorothy Tennov surveyed college students about their romantic relationships, most reported that they obtained great pleasure from love. But more than half said that they had been emotionally depressed, and more than 25 percent said that they had had suicidal thoughts.

Other psychologists report that people associate love with anxiety (would they be loved in return?), with emotional longing and with uncertainty, confusion and pain.

Adrenaline Makes the Heart Grow Fonder

Come to think of it, a certain amount of stress is what makes love and romance so euphoric.

"Obstacles lovers encounter in pursuit of their beloved often intensify love," say Elaine Hatfield, Ph.D., and her husband, G. William Walster, in their book, *A New Look at Love.* "The passion of wartime romances, unrequited loves and extramarital affairs is fueled—in part, anyway—by frustration."

While *some* difficulty may add zest to a relationship, though, too much emotional stress can destroy you. "If you find yourself passionately attracted to [someone] who fills your life with pain only, stay away," say Hatfield and Walster, noted authorities on love. "In the not-so-long run, such relationships lose their passionate excitement and leave a residue of ugliness and pain."

Here are some tips from "love researchers" for taking unnecessary stress out of falling—and staying—in love.

If You're Looking for a Lover, Search for a Friend

Suppose you're not in love at the moment but want to be. The quest for love can be frustrating to anyone, but people who face dating again after a divorce or the breakup of any other long-standing exclusive relationship find the prospect of romance—or lack thereof—especially daunting.

"We all need to love and be loved, yet finding and sustaining an intimate relationship can be one of life's most difficult challenges," says Harold H. Bloomfield, M.D., in *The Achilles Syndrome.*

"If you hope to find someone to love, you had better arrange your life so as to have plenty of opportunity to associate with a variety of eligible men or women on a fairly regular basis," say Hatfield and Walster. They offer these tips:

- Don't spend your time longing for the "ideal" mate.
- Initiate contacts.
- Be extra-friendly to your neighbors and co-workers. They're the people most likely to become—or at least introduce you to—compatible mates.
- Get involved in an activity you genuinely like. Being involved in such activities allows people to learn your thoughts, feelings, attitudes and goals. It's a more efficient way to meet a like-minded mate than milling about in singles bars, where people are often judged largely on appearance.

Learn to Shrug Off Rejection

Suppose you express interest in someone but get rebuffed?

"So what?" says Robert J. Sternberg, Ph.D., IBM professsor of psychology at Yale University, who is sometimes referred to as the "love professor" because of his research in this field. "Rejection is only a problem if people tell themselves it is.

"Let's put it this way: You have to take the attitude that dating is like shopping for a car or a house or anything else," explains Dr. Sternberg. "To see what's available, you expose yourself to many possible choices. Sure, you risk rejection in love. But if you don't, your chances of landing a less-than-optimal choice are higher.

"As the saying goes, 'You never know until you try.' If you try, at least you have a chance. But if you don't even try, you have no chance. And besides," he points out, "sometimes *you* will be the rejecter."

He/She Loves Me, He/She Loves Me Not

Cupid, with his unlimited supply of arrows, is bound to draw a bead on you sooner or later. And unless you marry—and stay married—to your first crush, chances are you will suffer the pangs of lost love at least once in your life.

"Feelings of loss are painful. We can accept them—we do not have to go crazy or become irrational—but they *are* painful. That is reality," says Nathaniel Branden, Ph.D., in his book *The Psychology of Romantic Love*.

"Even among mature, well-actualized individuals, love is not necessarily 'forever,' " says Dr. Branden. "As people continue to grow and evolve, their needs and desires change or shift as to emphasis. New goals and longings can emerge, causing rifts in relationships. This does not mean—or need not mean—that love has 'failed.' A union that provides great joy, nourishment and stimulation for two human beings is not a 'failure' merely because it does not last forever; it can still be a great experience that one is glad to have lived."

Even within successful, lasting marriages, passion usually ebbs eventually, its loss supplemented with highly rewarding yet less stressful companionate love—shared understanding, attitudes and interests (in short, intimate friendship). "Most couples find, happily, that a friend is really what they needed all along," say Hatfield and Walster.

Love Poison #9: What an Affair Really Means

Perhaps the most stressful kind of love is that between people who are married, but not to each other. (This is equally true for romantic infidelity outside any exclusive love relationship.) Such affairs usually arise out of a desire for novelty and excitement or a desire to assure ourselves that we are still attractive. Sometimes an individual has an affair as revenge for something his or her mate did, or out of loneliness during long but unavoidable separations. But sometimes an outside affair—or a string of affairs—serves as a painkiller, to make marriage (or an equivalent relationship) more bearable. It can serve to distract you from or buffer the stress of dealing with problems within the primary relationship.

And, hard as it may be to believe, an outside affair sometimes has nothing at all to do with the primary relationship, but instead functions as a panacea for a generalized sense of tedium or boredom, or as consolation for some frustration not in our marriage but in our work or career.

"For those who are tempted by extramarital affairs, it can be very important to ask, 'How do I imagine I would feel about my marriage if I were *not* to have extramarital affairs?' " says Dr. Branden. At that point, ask yourself, "Is it worth jeopardizing my primary relationship?"

"One thing seems clear," says Dr. Branden. "It is an error to assume that if two people 'really' love each other it is impossible for either of them to have an affair—or to desire one—with anyone else."

"There are two issues with infidelity," says Dr. Sternberg. "First, was there infidelity? and second, what does it mean? The problem is, people focus too much on the first issue and not on the second. There's a big difference between a one-night stand with someone your partner doesn't particularly care about and an ongoing relationship with someone he or she sees every day." But if the primary relationship between two people is good, they'll get through the outside affair, says Dr. Sternberg.

Controlling Jealousy before It Controls You

If your mate has strayed, it's not easy to see the philosophical aspects of a fling. Mainly, you feel sick. Hurt. Angry. Distraught. Confused. Betrayed. Trapped. Paralyzed. *And undeniably stressed.* This is because jealousy is not one emotion but a chaotic jumble of painful feelings, according to psychologists. Most agree, though, that jealousy has two basic components: a feeling of battered pride and a fear of losing something one values highly.

"Healthy jealousy doesn't stem from your own poor self-image," says Roger Callahan, Ph.D., in his book *It Can Happen to You.* "It's focused on the loss of a romantic love . . . a perfectly healthy response to a terribly stressful situation."

Tempering jealousy—and panic—from the outset can prevent a bad situation from getting worse.

"If someone you love very much has stopped loving you and fallen in love with another person, it's likely that you'll feel jealous," says Dr. Callahan. "It's healthy and natural to not want to lose things you value highly, and there's nothing more valuable than intense romantic love."

Most people respond to jealousy in one of two ways. Some try to protect their egos by berating their partners or attempting to get even. Others try to improve their floundering relationship by attempting to improve their appearance, talking things out and so forth. Men are more likely to externalize the cause—to blame the partner or the third party. In comparison women often internalize the cause—they blame themselves.

How can you relieve this stress before it devastates you?

"When you begin to feel twinges of suspicion and jealousy, the sooner you exorcise them—and get them out—the less likely they are to drive you crazy and, in the process, ruin a relationship that might otherwise be in fine shape," says Dr. Callahan.

If you suspect an affair, be sure that you have good reasons. Seeking constant reassurance from an innocent mate can destroy an otherwise sound relationship.

What if your worst fears are fact? "You will be faced with a choice of either competing and trying to win back your lover, accepting the situation and waiting for its ultimate resolution, or making the final break yourself," says Dr. Callahan.

Establish an Optimal Distance from the Start

The threat of a romantic rival isn't the sole trigger of jealousy between lovers. One may feel jealous of a mate's interest in friends, co-workers, sports or hobbies. Undue possessiveness can cause stress for both parties: One person fears being abandoned, while the other feels trapped.

If you and your mate are emotional Siamese twins—joined at the heart— you're more apt to suffer pangs of jealousy, warranted or otherwise, than people who maintain a reasonable distance between themselves.

"Many counselors have found that it's a lot easier for couples to maintain a close—while not excessively possessive—love relationship if they each maintain some separate friends and interests," say Hatfield and Walster. In other words, if you have your own identity—if you associate with others who like and admire you—you are far less likely to fear being abandoned by your partner—"and it's a lot easier to cope if you are," the researchers add.

What's more, it's unlikely that any two people—no matter how perfectly matched or how much in love—will fulfill 100 percent of each other's "minimum daily requirement" of attention. Think of your emotional needs as a pie chart. While your mate will probably fulfill the largest segment, other people are bound to contribute fair portions of affection and companionship. In fact, when one partner spends some time with friends outside the relationship, that takes pressure off the other to be the total means of emotional support.

"This is something that every couple has to work out individually, depending on their emotional needs. But expectations should be negotiated early in a relationship," says Dr. Sternberg. "Because if the road starts to diverge, it tends to continue to diverge. The longer you wait to address the issue, the more likely the other person will be to get defensive, and the harder it will be to resolve it."

Love can be stressful, yes. But falling in love needn't send you into a tailspin if you take measures to stay in control.

Chapter 69

MASSAGE

The first bit of advice: Avoid massages in places that bear flashing, neon signs. You won't be relieving any stress in *these* establishments. Instead, put yourself in the hands of a trained masseuse or masseur, who will transform your uptight, knotty body into a completely relaxed puddle of pure bliss.

Swedish massage, also called Western or European massage, is the most common method used for stress management. It was developed by Per Henrik Ling as part of a medical program designed to treat disease. For bedridden people, massage often was used to take the place of exercise and to improve a patient's circulation. That's why some of the strokes are more stimulating than relaxing. All strokes are made toward the heart, to stimulate the blood supply as well as the lymph glands. "As blood flow is enhanced to the tissues, better oxygenation and cell nutrition results and more efficient removal of waste products, such as cell debris, is accomplished," says Gail Bell, an Arlington, Virginia, massage therapist. Pain or tension may vanish.

If you're visiting a massage therapist to counter your body's response to stress, you probably will receive a blending of Swedish massage techniques and a few other, more relaxing, methods.

Swedish massage relies on five basic strokes.

Effleurage. Most commonly used, these are long and gliding strokes that relax tense muscles and stimulate circulation.

Petrassage. This is a squeezing and kneading of the muscles.

Tapotement. Using this karate-chop stroke, the masseuse or masseur hacks, taps or cups you with the sides of his or her hands or with fingertips. It's infrequently used in a relaxation massage.

Vibration. To produce this action the massage therapist rapidly taps with two fingers in either one spot or a series of spots.

Friction. This is created when a circular and rolling motion is applied to the muscle near the spine and the joints. It, too, increases circulation but in a more localized way than the other strokes.

These strokes form the basis of other hands-on therapies such as shiatsu (also called acupressure) massage, which is a finger-pressure stimulation of acupuncture "meridians," which Chinese medicine believes correspond to the flow of energy in your body. Esalen massage, developed at the New Age Esalen Institute in Big Sur, California, is a free-flow relaxation massage, often done to the accompaniment of burning incense and soft music.

What to Expect

A full-body massage generally lasts an hour and takes place on a hard table. And a good massage therapist will, in addition to doing what's necessary during the treatment, send you out the door with homework, such as suggested exercises or instructions on how to massage your legs after a run, says Gene Arbetter, a Chicago massage therapist and chairman of the American Massage Therapy Association's (AMTA) department of information and inquiry.

The best way to receive a massage is in the nude, with a sheet covering the parts of your body that a massage therapist never touches: genitals and breasts. Even a modest amount of clothing will impede a massage and will require a massage therapist to leave important muscle groups unmassaged. As a massagee, you may be told to focus on your breathing and on the parts of your body that are being massaged, and to relax. This is a time to let go of tension, and one time not to feel rushed. When the massage is over, it's often nice to lie still with your eyes closed.

When you go for a massage, the American Massage Therapy Association, the oldest and largest organization of massage therapists, recommends you check to see if the place is clean. Then ask for credentials. AMTA-certified members have completed 500 hours of approved AMTA in-class study or passed an entrance exam. A therapist who has completed an additional three years of professional work and passed another exam is a Registered Massage Therapist, or R.M.T. About a dozen states have licensing requirements for massage therapists. Check with a massage therapist to see that he or she has the proper state and, in some cases, local, licenses. Also note whether the practitioner appears confident in what he or she is doing. And finally, be sure to point out any injuries or health conditions the practitioner should be aware of. (He or she should ask you about them before beginning.)

For more information about massage, write to the American Massage Therapy Association, 1329 West Pratt Boulevard, Chicago, IL 60626, or phone (312) 761–2682.

Chapter 70

MUSIC

When young David played his harp for troubled King Saul, he acted as one of history's first known music therapists, someone who knew the magical powers of this universal language.

Modern-day music therapists categorize tunes as either stimulating or sedative. Stimulating music—like an Irish jig or disco music—gets people clapping their hands, tapping their toes or dancing. Sedative music has a much slower, easier rhythm—approximately 60 beats per minute, and as regular as your heartbeat at rest. Calming music has been used to reduce distress and pain among people in dentists' offices, childbirth centers, coronary care units and migraine headache clinics.

"The right music can take you from a highly tense state to a relaxed yet alert state in as little as 30 seconds," says Steven Halpern, Ph.D, a pioneering composer, performer and producer in the field of music as it relates to health. By a fascinating and complex process, relaxing music seems to trigger the release of endorphins, opiatelike substances in the brain that make us feel less anxious, according to Dr. Halpern.

Andante for Relaxation

Instrumental pieces—notably those performed by flute, harp, piano and string ensembles—tend to be more soothing than vocal pieces, which can distract you. Surprisingly, studies have shown that not all classical music is relaxing. Look for sonatas and symphonies played *adagio* (in a slow tempo) or *andante* (moderately slow) that approximate the heart's natural rate at rest. (Some records now offer *adagio* or *andante* selections or movements only.)

Some jazz, blues or other traditional music may also instill calmness. As for background music, surveys show that many people find "canned" music irritating.

296

Dr. Halpern (and some New Age musicians) have been composing music with no dominant melody or rhythm. These compositions are intentionally designed to induce serenity. To measure the relaxation potential of the music you usually enjoy, pay attention to how your body responds. "If you feel yourself breathing more slowly and deeply, the music is relaxing you," says Dr. Halpern. "If, on the other hand, you can feel a slight tightness in the back of your neck or your solar plexus, it's not."

Chapter 71

NATURE

*I went to the woods because I wished to live deliberately, to front only the
essential facts of life, and see if I could not learn what it had to teach. . . .*

—Thoreau

Thoreau filled a book with what he learned about the wonderfully regenerating effects of living alone in the woods.

If you too want to behold the same wonders of Mother Nature—and let go of stress—you don't have to transport your household to a log cabin by a pond. You don't even have to rent a weekend cottage by the sea or drag the family out to a picnic in the park.

The first rule for enjoying nature is to appreciate what's around you, wherever you are. Joseph Nold, director of Colorado Outward Bound School for 15 years, has spent a great chunk of his life in wilderness of the most serious sorts. But he appreciates the joys of nature virtually anywhere he goes—even in New York City. "I can recall walking across the George Washington Bridge at sunset and it being an almost mystical experience," he says.

What is it about nature that's so great for relieving stress? Scientists have studied the phenomenon, and when they report on their findings, they sound like, well, scientists.

One famous study divided the benefits wilderness vacationers enjoyed into two categories. "Health-related experiences" included "mental relaxation" and "feelings of receptivity and harmony with the environment." The other part, "aesthetic-transpersonal experiences" consisted of "awareness of beauty and flux of the natural world," "perceptual alertness," "personal insight," and "expanded identity."

Maybe a key to nature's ability to soothe lies in the simple fact that it transports us away from our chores and demands and worries.

Self-Medicating with Meadows and Clouds

"When we're overloaded with everyday concerns, nature takes us away from our problems," says David C. Glass, Ph.D., a professor of psychology at State University of New York at Stony Brook. "The break allows us to restore our energy. It could have tremendous benefits in alleviating negative feelings. And as self-medication goes, it's a lot better than the self-medication people too often engage in—smoking, alcohol and drug abuse."

Outdoorsman Nold, who now directs the wilderness program at United World College in Montezuma, New Mexico, calls it "a way of getting in touch with another reality.

"Life slows down for you in the outdoors. There's a very different view of life when it takes an hour to travel two miles than when you drive down the highway at 70 miles per hour," he says. "There's a whole different rhythm to life, and it's very different from the speed at which we usually live, which is stressful."

So you slow down. "You plod through decisions you have to make, questions you may have about yourself," he says. You put time in a new perspective.

Spend a half hour watching the waves crash onto a beach and think about how many centuries the waves have been crashing against the same shoreline. Study the layers of earth in the Grand Canyon—each layer representing a geological time period. Does that put your son's unacceptable new hairstyle in a different light? "If you're on the seas, if you're in the desert, you can't help but put your problems in perspective," says Nold.

Nature also gives you delights to look forward to. What greater encore to summer could there be than the autumn leaves? "The Japanese are very wise. They have a tradition of appreciating the changes of nature. Families go out for walks to observe the cherry blossoms when they come," says Albert Mehrabian, Ph.D., a professor of psychology at UCLA and author of *Public Places and Private Spaces.*

The Scientific Evidence

You can derive soothing benefits from nature even if you just look at a picture or a film of it, says Roger Ulrich, Ph.D., a University of Delaware geography professor who has studied the influence of the outdoors on people. In one study, a group of mildly stressed students who had just completed a two-hour exam were seated in a windowless room and asked to rate their feelings on a host of stress/anxiety measures. Immediately afterward, half of the students were shown pictures of beautiful outdoor scenes; the other half was shown pictures depicting urban scenes that lacked natural beauty. When they were retested, the "nature" group had recuperated nicely from stress. The "urban" group? They actually tested worse on certain measures of stress and anxiety, according to Dr. Ulrich.

Another study measured the physiological impact of watching a nature film. To get the subjects sufficiently stressed, Dr. Ulrich and a collaborator showed 120 volunteers a disturbing film about work accidents. After viewing the film, the volunteers watched one of six different videotapes depicting an outdoor environment. Two of the films were of nature and four were of blighted urban scenes.

When the subjects were tested for such stress indicators as increased muscle tension, blood pressure and heart rate, the findings were consistent. "Those who saw nature tapes recovered much faster and more completely than those who saw the urban tapes," says Dr. Ulrich.

Another test showed that surgery patients recovered faster if they had bedside windows that looked out on nature, as opposed to windows that fronted a brick wall.

The Adventure of Rain

Is this enough to get you racing to the nearest babbling brook or towering oak every time stress rears its head? What's that—a trip to nature would be a major interruption of your day? Keep in mind that there are near-constant opportunities to experience nature.

"You can take advantage of those opportunities even if you only spend a few moments looking out the window or checking what's going on in the garden," says Stephen Kaplan, Ph.D., an environmental psychologist and psychology professor at the University of Michigan, Ann Arbor. He adds that people should not feel guilty about taking nature breaks. "Recognize that it's a way to enhance your effectiveness."

Traditionally, religious leaders turned to wilderness for divine inspiration. You can, too, and right in your own backyard. "Sunrises and sunsets are particularly compelling," says Nold. So get up in the predawn, step outside and experience the building crescendo of a new day. No sun today? Go out and stand in the rain, recommends Nold. "You will experience yourself in a new way, an experience that is renewing."

Dr. Kaplan says it is therapeutic to "make a great adventure out of a small thing." That's a lesson Nold learns from novices who return from jaunts alone in the wilderness as part of survival programs. He says they frequently tell stories about such experiences as intently studying an ant that crawled across their arm.

You, too, can discover the universe in a grain of sand.

Chapter 72

NUTRITION

When we're under stress, our bodies use up nutrients faster and less efficiently than they ordinarily do. Just when—for our bodies' sake—we should be dining on fish or whole wheat pasta, we're often up to our elbows in chocolate chip cookies and ice cream. Seeking comfort in special treats, we're sabotaging our bodies. We're also probably unsettling our digestion, which may already be in open rebellion against the stress we're under.

This then is a formula for a nutritional deficit—a poor diet plus poor digestion, combined with an increased demand for nutrients. And this stress spawns another. "Our stress responses often consume great amounts of energy, and as our energy is depleted we are less able to respond to stress," says Derrick Lonsdale, M.D., a preventive medicine physician in Westlake, Ohio.

What to do? The obvious answer for most people—one you learned at your mother's knee—is to eat three well-balanced meals a day. The advice, however, is easier said than done.

If you're too stressed to cope with menu planning, do yourself a good turn by trying to meet your body's greatest nutritional demands at times of high stress.

You may need more B vitamins. Many nutrition experts agree that the B vitamins—probably more than any other nutrients—take it on the chin when a body is under severe stress. "They are used up in the process of becoming exhausted, physically or mentally, and they have to be restored," says Charles Tkacz, M.D., medical director of the North Nassau Mental Health Center in Manhasset, New York.

The B vitamins play a complicated role. They are required by the body for the process of turning food into fuel. They're needed to supply the brain with glucose, its energy source. With insufficient glucose, the brain begins to perform poorly, according to Dr. Tkacz.

In addition, several of the B vitamins are involved in the production of neurotransmitters, biochemicals that allow the brain cells to pass messages along their nerve pathways. Without sufficient vitamins B_6 and B_{12}, a person may experience depression, fatigue and confusion. Moreover, B vitamins enhance the body's immune mechanism and help protect us from responding to stress with illness, says Dr. Tkacz.

Foods high in the B vitamins include organ meats like liver and kidneys, whole grains, nuts, seeds and beans.

You may need more vitamin C. "Stress is a factor that steps up your vitamin C requirements," says Robert Haskell, M.D., a San Francisco physician who specializes in preventive medicine and nutritional support. "If anything helps you battle the effects of stress, it's vitamin C."

As Dr. Haskell explains, stress washes out our supply of vitamin C, so we must replenish it by eating foods high in vitamin C or taking a supplement. How much you take should vary with your size and weight, so Dr. Haskell suggests that each individual be sure to get an adequate amount for his or her needs. (Of course, don't take high dosages of vitamin C or any other nutrient without your doctor's approval and supervision.)

You may need more protein and calcium. Scientific studies show that under emotional stress, the body loses an excessive amount of nitrogen through the urine. That generally indicates protein in the body tissues is being used up, says Arline McDonald, Ph.D., a nutritionist at the Northwestern University Medical School Department of Community Health and Preventive Medicine. And protein is needed as a source of amino acids, which are necessary for growth and maintenance. These acids produce enzymes important in combating stress. B vitamins are "co-enzymes," helping the amino acids to do their work.

The answer, says Dr. McDonald, is simply to get more protein. But that doesn't mean you should throw a slab of sirloin onto your plate at each meal. During times of high stress, your stomach is not ready to handle more food. "Instead, eat a little protein at a time, distributing it over the day," says Dr. McDonald. She recommends chicken, fish, egg whites and plain old peanut butter sandwiches on whole wheat bread.

And drink milk, of course. Calcium, like nitrogen, is lost through the urine in times of high stress. To compensate, Dr. McDonald suggests you increase your intake of low-fat dairy products. Not only do they contain calcium, but they will help supplement your protein needs, too.

You don't need fats. According to Dr. McDonald, they contain little nutrition but *lots* of calories.

You don't need caffeine. "It's a stimulant to the adrenal glands that will cause all of the cells in the body to work overtime," says Nan Kathryn Fuchs, Ph.D., a Santa Monica nutritionist. "It won't let the body rest and recuperate."

You don't need much sugar. Because sugar has only minuscule amounts of some minerals, a trace of B vitamins and no protein, it can't do much to satisfy your body's hunger for nutrition. But if a slice of apple pie can help you get through an occasional crisis, use it for solace. Just be sure you wash it down with a big glass of skim milk.

Chapter 73

PETS

Mom comes home tired. The kids sit mesmerized in front of the television set, consumed by a cartoon fantasy. From out of nowhere bounds an enthusiastic collie. Affectionate paws fly. A tongue may lick. A tail wags joyfully. Who cares about demanding bosses, freeway backups or kids who ignore you? A four-legged buddy, once again, comes to the rescue.

We love our pets, all 100 million of them. We offer our pets gourmet meals, shelter them, groom them, pet them, talk to them, baby them and buy them toys. But for each ounce of care and affection we provide, our pets return a ton of benefits. They give us companionship, they make us feel safe, they make us feel calm when we touch them. They are a source of constancy in our changing lives.

By their "simple indifference to human technology, knowledge, aspirations and achievement" they protect us from our changing fortunes, say Alan Beck, Sc.D., and Aaron Katcher, M.D., authors of *Between Pets and People: The Importance of Animal Companionship*. Pets don't care if we dented the Dodge. They bring out the child in us, they give us something to care about. By insisting on playing games with us where no one really "wins," they take us away from the world of endless competition.

Long-Range Effects

True, raising a pet isn't always a bed of roses (and you can forget raising prize roses), but the payoffs seem to last long after the cat, dog, parakeet, snake or gerbil becomes a mere memory. When Michael Levine, Ph.D., a psychology professor at Bloomsburg University in Pennsylvania, compared college students who grew up with dogs or cats with those who didn't, he found that those who were raised with pets were more self-reliant, sociable and tolerant and had better social skills than those who had petless childhoods.

Men reared with dogs seem to have a stronger sense of personal worth and better social skills than those raised without dogs. Women raised with dogs are more flexible and more self-reliant.

The impact of cats? Both men and women raised with cats have a heightened belief in their personal value to society and are more socially responsible, says Dr. Levine, who owns seven cats of the rag-doll breed (Blazing Star, Digger, Boy, Benjy, Squeaker, Ariel and Jenny).

The influence on a pet owner's ability to handle stress is obvious. "If you have a better self-concept, you can learn to deal with stress better," says Dr. Levine. "You're going to be more flexible, and it seems flexibility is one of the key things in reducing stress."

There are innumerable other ways in which either raising an animal or being raised with one makes you better able to tackle stress. Another of Dr. Levine's studies indicates that people who were raised with pets, particularly cats, are better able to interpret human facial expressions. Since so many interpersonal problems are caused by communications problems—even of the nonverbal variety—such a skill could go a long way to decrease a major source of social stress.

And dog-walking makes one friendlier, according to a study conducted by Dr. Katcher, a psychiatrist at the University of Pennsylvania Veterinary School who specializes in the relationship between animals and people. When your dog starts sniffing another dog, you have an excuse (practically an obligation!) to strike up a conversation with the other dog's owner. (Dr. Katcher's seven assorted species of pets include a miniature orange poodle named Pelluche.)

There's more. When you stroke a dog and talk to the animal, your blood pressure dips to a level that's lower than when you talk to people, according to Dr. Katcher's research. And if you sit quietly and pet an animal you're familiar with, your blood pressure takes a more significant drop.

Both college students and young children experienced a drop in their stress response if a dog was present when they engaged in the stress-inducing activity of reading aloud before a group.

You'll be better prepared for a session of oral surgery if you sit and stare at a fish tank for 20 minutes beforehand. An extensive study conducted by Dr. Beck and Dr. Katcher compared the anxiety and pain levels of oral surgery patients who were prepared for surgery with five different methods: sitting quietly and watching fish; watching fish and being hypnotized; sitting quietly before a poster of a mountain scene; being hypnotized while focusing on the mountain scene; and sitting quietly in an empty room.

Based on comparisons of blood pressure level and of how frequently the patients moaned, requested additional anesthesia and showed overt postures of anxiety, the findings were clear: Just looking at fish was as good as hypnosis. This is particularly good news for those who cannot be hypnotized.

And your chances of surviving a heart attack increase if you own a pet. A study headed by Brooklyn College biologist Erika Friedman, Ph.D., revealed that heart attack patients with pets to go home to are more likely to be alive one year after their hospital release than heart attack patients without pets.

How to Choose the Proper Pet

All this is evidence that pets are great relievers of stress. But amazing as it sounds, animal lovers often overlook the obvious and select pets that increase stress, not reduce it. One young woman living in Manhattan wanted a sturdy dog for protection. She chose a lively and fearless Doberman pinscher. There was only one problem: She lived in a tiny houseboat docked at the New York Boat Basin, with barely enough room for her belongings, let alone a rambunctious canine.

So how to choose a pet that's appropriate for your lifestyle and family situation? Beth McCrave, a research coordinator at the University of Pennsylvania's Center on Interactions of Animals and Society and a counselor in clinical animal behavior, offers some practical advice.

First, the obvious question that so many pet owners fail to ask: How well will the pet fit into your home? (Will the dog need room to run that you can't provide?) Is the pet likely to get along with your toddler? How much time can you spend with the animal?

"If it's two people who each work ten hours a day, it makes sense to get two cats. It's easier to raise two cats together than to raise one cat," explains McCrave, who makes house calls to people who have problems with their pets. The cats get out their aggressive play on each other, so when the owners come home, the felines are pleasant and cuddly.

She says cats raised alone who "happen to have a high need for play" will direct their play toward the owner, and often the play gets pretty aggressive: scratching, pouncing and ambushing. The scratches or nips can break the skin, which is particularly bad for the elderly, who may have fragile skin. (She adds that if you play with your cat directly with your hands or feet, your cat will think it's appropriate to scratch you. Instead, you should use objects tied to an elasticized string or drag a shoelace on the floor to play.)

Don't buy a dog on impulse. Learn as much as you can about a particular breed and go after a dog that meets your needs—one that doesn't require much exercise if you live in an apartment or one with a placid personality if you have young children.

Don't buy a dog for its color or looks. Temperament is a better factor to consider.

And if it's a dog you're getting, shop at a pet store only as a last resort. In McCrave's opinion, the dogs in pet shops often come from "puppy mills" and tend to be sickly, not carefully bred and overstressed. "If possible, buy your dog from a reputable home breeder who knows what he's doing," she says.

Chapter 74

POSITIVE THINKING

I think I can; therefore I can.

—Not Renée Descartes

You may have heard folks say an optimist sees a glass as half full and a pessimist sees it as half empty. "The real question is, what are the odds of filling it up?" says Michael F. Scheier, Ph.D., professor of psychology at Carnegie-Mellon University in Pittsburgh, Pennsylvania. "An optimist will say, 'Yes, we can fill that glass.' But the pessimist may say, 'What's the use? It's only going to evaporate or spill.'"

And if you think life is just one spilled glass of milk after another, chances are it will be. Studies by Dr. Scheier and Charles S. Carver, Ph.D., of the University of Miami, have discovered that a tendency to view events in either a positive or negative way can affect our actions—and the ultimate outcomes of stressful situations.

More than Just Another Happy Face

"Until recently, we assumed that a positive orientation—optimism—was simply an internal perception of circumstances," says Dr. Scheier. "But we're now finding that anticipating a favorable outcome leads an optimist to do things that actually determine the final outcome. Optimists *expect* things to turn out well, but they also do things that can change the course of events." (That's fitting: *optimism* comes from *ops*, the Latin word for "power.")

Since stress arises largely from our perception of events as being harmful or threatening, whether your perception is positive or negative is pivotal in determining how you cope with stress. Primed with positive expectations, optimists regard potentially stressful events—such as financial setback, failed love, career disappointment—as opportunities for change or growth, not as

306

excuses for giving up. Obstacles become stepping stones, not stumbling blocks. And the positive attitude, it seems, can significantly affect how your body *and* soul react to stress.

How Optimists Master Stress

Exactly how do optimists transform positive thoughts into positive results? "By *active* coping," says Dr. Carver.

"Optimists do better in the face of stress, at least in part, because they choose and use specific coping strategies that increase their likelihood of success," says Dr. Scheier. Here's a rundown of some of those strategies.

Problem-focused coping. Optimists are planners, say Dr. Carver and Dr. Scheier. "Examine the situation and, to the degree than you *can* do something, try to resolve it," says Dr. Carver.

"Optimists take action sooner," says Dr. Scheier. Acting quickly often prevents a small stress from snowballing into a big, unstoppable stress.

"Break big problems down into smaller, more manageable problems," says Dr. Scheier. "Optimists tend to formulate subgoals—intermediate steps that will help them to eventually reach their ultimate goal."

You can apply this "paint-by-number" approach to any overwhelming commitment or obligation. "Say you plan to write a book, for example," says Dr. Scheier. "The enormity of the project could be daunting—and paralyze you—unless you say something like, 'I can write two pages a day, so I can write a chapter a month,' and so forth."

Perseverance. Spurred by positive emotions—and past successes—optimists keep going when others might quit.

"Problems often have reverberations that you never expect, beyond the effects on your morale or your finances," says Dr. Carver. So a certain amount of tunnel vision also keeps optimists focused on their objective—and pointed toward active coping.

Positive reinterpretation. People who think positively tend to emerge from their trials thinking, "I developed greater trust in my judgments of situations or people," "I modified personal or career goals to more closely match my true interests, abilities or values," "I gained confidence in my ability to handle other difficulties," or "I discovered I could rely on others for help in getting through difficulties." Such thoughts suggest the person feels that stress enables them to change for the better or grow as a person in a new way, renews their faith or reveals some important truth about life—a kind of modern, personal Aesop's Fables.

"As a coping strategy, positive reinterpretation is important when something happens that you can't do much about—death of a loved one, for example, or an effort that failed," says Dr. Scheier. "There's a lot of confidence and satisfaction to be gained from surviving stress and being able to say, 'I handled that pretty well.'"

"Stress provides 'lessons' that make you more capable of dealing with events in the future," says Dr. Carver. "Optimists tend to see those lessons more readily than pessimists."

Somehow, finding a reason for your suffering makes it more endurable or less devastating. In conversations with Julius Segal, Ph.D., just after their liberation from Iran, American hostages described certain "benefits" of their experience. One said, "Sure, I lost 40 pounds, but I'm now down to my normal weight."

Call it rationalizing perhaps, but reinterpreting trouble in this way preserves your self-esteem, sense of control or mastery over stress, and restores your belief in the world as just, rational and predictable, according to Darlene Goodhart, Ph.D., of the Department of Psychology at the University of Illinois, Champaign.

Social support. Optimists believe others can help. They tend to talk to someone about how they feel under stress, or ask for—and follow—advice.

Acceptance or resignation. Optimists are realists. When reason tells them a situation is out of their hands, they accept it and refuse to dwell on their troubles.

"We don't want to imply that people should put on a happy face and go around being mindlessly cheerful all the time," says Dr. Carver. "Even optimists have occasional doubts or fail sometimes. By resignation, we mean the ability to say, 'I'm not going to pretend this isn't happening, but if I have to put up with it, I will.'"

What's more, optimists seem to instinctively know when to charge forward and when to back off. Dr. Scheier found that optimists leaned toward problem-focused coping in situations they perceived to be under their control. They relied on social support and acceptance or resignation when things were beyond their control. Positive reinterpretation, in turn, seemed to buffer stress in either type of situation.

Negative Thinking: A Self-Fulfilling Prophecy?

You can also identify an optimist by how he or she *doesn't* cope, says Dr. Carver. Optimists don't deny the problem exists, don't blame themselves and don't try to escape through fantasy (such as daydreaming about the perfect revenge or finding a million dollars).

Basically, pessimists tend to think any efforts to change themselves or the situation would be futile, so they don't try, minimizing their chances for success.

"A little bit of denial is good—it prevents us from overreacting," says Dr. Carver. "But I suspect that if a problem is real, the longer you put off dealing with it, the worse it will get."

Instead of focusing on the cause of their stress, pessimists become preoccupied with anger, hurt, frustration or other emotional distress that results. In short, they get upset and give up.

"Acknowledging and expressing your feelings is good–up to a point," says Dr. Carver. "But the more you lie around feeling sorry for yourself, the more you reinforce those negative feelings, until your negative expectations are eventually fulfilled."

Where do negative expectations come from? What makes a Gloomy Gus so glum? "Past experience," says Dr. Scheier. "Pessimists are the way they are because they've experienced trouble in the past and expect more of the same."

"Pessimism, like optimism, is cyclic," says Dr. Carver. "It perpetuates itself."

Can a Gloomy Gus learn to be a Sunny Sam? With a little work, yes. "When faced with a challenge, don't automatically think, 'I can't do it,' " says Dr. Scheier. "You must have had some past successes. Think back to similar situations and ask yourself, 'What worked before that might work now?' "

"Don't overreact to stress or overinterpret events," adds Dr. Carver.

Other negative thoughts to avoid include, "If anything can go wrong, it will," "Nothing ever goes my way," and "Good things never happen to me."

Optimists Suffer Fewer Symptoms of Stress

Winners are healthier than whiners. Studies show that problem-focused coping, of which optimists are masters, is associated with less depression, while simply venting your emotions or refusing to acknowledge the stressful situation is linked with higher levels of depression and other reactions to stress. Optimists also suffer fewer of the physical signs of stress. In one study, Dr. Scheier and Dr. Carver tracked the progress of 141 college students during the final four weeks of a semester. They found that optimistic students reported fewer symptoms of stress–muscle soreness, fatigue, dizziness and coughs–than pessimistic students.

In a related study, the psychologists measured the effect of optimism versus pessisism on how well 54 people dealt with coronary artery bypass surgery–a major stress by anyone's standards. Compared with pessimists, optimists showed fewer signs of complications during the operation, and they recovered faster. The difference seemed to lie in how they expected things to turn out. "Prior to surgery, optimists were more likely to be making plans for themselves and setting goals for their recovery than were pessimists," say the researchers. "In contrast, optimists were much less likely to dwell on the negative aspects of their emotional experience, that is, feeling nervous or sad."

Still another study found that being able to accept physical disability–in this case, from serious injury–is a good indication of how well one will continue to fare psychologically under the stress.

Evidently, optimists tend to be healthier even when injury or illness is the cause of stress. The psychologists suspect they're more apt to follow a prescribed medical program, quit smoking or change other behavior that may cause illness. Optimists also seem less likely than pessimists to rely on alcohol or drugs as an easy escape from stress.

A Tool for Survival

These studies—and others like them—mesh with the widely held theory that "hardy" people have a sense of challenge, commitment and control in the face of stress, while helpless people tend to buckle under more easily.

"Hardiness has overtones of optimism," says Dr. Carver. "Also, there is some speculation that, culturally or societally, people tend to judge situations a bit more optimistically than is realistically accurate. And that's functional, because it keeps us moving forward."

You might say that, in a Darwinian sense, optimism is essential in order for us to survive both as individuals and as a species. Call it "survival of the most optimistic."

PRAYER AND RELIGION

Most chief executives are actively religious, according to a survey of leaders of the nation's top 100 corporations, published in *Forbes*. Sixty-five percent regularly attend church or synagogue. Many start their business day with prayer or devotional study.

"I think management is beginning to say, 'Look, I need help from somewhere else. I need some faith,' " comments one business analyst.

You don't have to be a highly stressed business executive to benefit from some form of spiritual belief, though. Anyone under stress can participate—with blessings not appreciated until recently.

"Prayer is essentially a form of meditation that induces relaxation, including decreased sympathetic nervous system activity," says Herbert Benson, M.D.,"inventor" of the Relaxation Response, a well-known form of calming meditation (see chapter 76), and author of *Beyond the Relaxation Response: Harnessing the Healing Power of Your Personal Beliefs*. "But prayer has an edge over neutral forms of meditation—such as focusing on the word 'one'—because it changes the ways you think about things," says Dr. Benson, who is associate professor of medicine at Harvard Medical School and director of the Division of Behavioral Medicine and Hypertension at Beth Israel Hospital in Boston.

Why Praying Works and Wishing Doesn't

Regular prayer works better than "foxhole" prayers—pleas made under duress, such as "Please, God, help me ace this job interview and I'll never let you down again."

"As a matter of fact, 'foxhole' prayers don't work at all," says Dr. Benson. "But the Faith Factor—a form of meditation, including prayer, that elicits the Relaxation Response, combined with a profound set of personal convictions—

311

works to reduce stress in a number of ways. Prayer elicits relaxation and breaks up the chain of worrisome thought, the anxiety cycle that is so often associated with insomnia, digestive problems and other symptoms of stress. When rooted in religious belief, prayer also helps to put problems in perspective, further reducing overall anxiety. And by acknowledging that there's a bigger force at work in your life, it eliminates the stressful feeling that one is 'all alone out there.' "

Many people feel that their religious beliefs provide them with strength during times of loss or hardship—including the death of a loved one, illness or injury, financial problems (all major sources of stress, according to a widely used scale of stressful life events). Religious feelings and practices, especially those that teach forgiveness, patience and understanding, can also help people cope with internal stress such as blame, bitterness, discouragement, cynicism and hostility.

By establishing guidelines for what's right and wrong, religious convictions also help people make stressful decisions in their lives. "Religious teachings tie an individual into a larger system in which some of these decisions are made for them," says Dr. Benson. If, for example, your religion says "Thou shalt not steal," you may find it easier to resist peer pressure to use the company phone for personal long distance calls.

In addition to serving as a source of spiritual strength, comfort and guidance, a belief system taps into the communal support and values common to people who share that belief—a proven factor in stress resistance.

Religion Is Powerful Medicine

Talking to one's God, then, may not change stressful circumstances, but it can change the way you *perceive* and *react* to stress, both determining factors in how well you weather stress. And anything that buffers stress can help decrease your chances of suffering from the many physical ailments associated with stress.

"People who pray regularly—and attend worship services regularly—have lower blood pressure," says Dr. Benson. They also suffer less irritability, fatigue, tension headaches and various other physical problems often triggered by stress and anxiety.

For years, doctors have observed that the vegetarian diet of Seventh-day Adventists lowers their risk of heart disease and cancer (both of which have stress as a component). Now doctors in Israel have found that religiousness itself, not just diet, may protect against heart attacks. They think that psychological and social factors could play a protective role.

"Orthodox religious Jews are generally characterized by the social cohesiveness and strong social supports of their traditional culture," write the researchers in the *International Journal of Cardiology.* "It is also possible that strong belief in a supreme being and the role of prayer may in themselves be protective."

Breaking the Anxiety Cycle with Meditative Prayer

Dr. Benson says that people of any faith can tap into the Faith Factor and "reduce overall stress and achieve greater inner peace and emotional balance." To combine meditation with your personal beliefs, he suggests the following technique.

Choose a word or brief phrase that reflects your basic belief system. It may be a familiar verse from the Bible or book of your faith, such as a brief phrase from the Twenty-third Psalm or the Lord's Prayer, the word *shalom* (Hebrew for "peace") or another appropriate line or phrase.

"It's important to pick a word that has special meaning to you," says Dr. Benson. "That serves a dual function: It can activate your belief systems and the accompanying benefits by providing a greater calming effect on your mind than you might achieve with a neutral focus word; and it increases the likelihood of your use of the technique."

Choose a comfortable position. Try a cross-legged position or another comfortable sitting position, but not so comfortable that you fall asleep.

Close your eyes easily and naturally. Don't squint or squeeze your eyelids shut.

Relax your muscles. Start with your feet and relax each muscle group of your body. (Tighten your right foot. Hold for ten seconds, then release. Continue, tensing and releasing muscles in your left foot, your legs, your fists, your forearms, your shoulders, your back, your neck and your brow.)

Breathe slowly and naturally. Now, begin to repeat your focus phrase, silently.

Mentally "shrug off" worrisome thoughts or distractions. When a distressingg thought or image enters your mind, simply say to yourself, "Oh, well" and return to your focus phrase.

Meditate for 10 to 20 minutes. You may peek at your watch or a clock from time to time, but don't use a timer.

Practice the technique twice a day, preferably before breakfast and before dinner. "It's interesting to note how many meditative prayers over the centuries have been taught to be utilized with some form of fasting," says Dr. Benson.

Chapter 76

RELAXATION RESPONSE

Whether we tip over the canoe, debut as Otello at the Metropolitan Opera House or merely get trapped in a freeway backup, our body reacts roughly the same way—with the fight-or-flight response to stress that we inherited from our primitive ancestors.

Our heart rate, blood pressure and breath rate leap. Our muscles tense. Our adrenal glands work overtime. This reaction is appropriate for the occasional tiger hunt, but we don't need it for most of life's everyday stressful challenges.

The stress reaction becomes part of our standard routine. As a result, it may usher in a host of stress-induced physical ailments, such as high blood pressure. There are emotional side effects, too. Our inability to cope with the stress may cause us anxiety. And then, of course, there is fatigue.

Wouldn't it be great to be able to invoke the completely opposite response, or to cut the fight-or-flight response off at the pass, unless we really need it?

The great news is that we can. In his famous book, *The Relaxation Response*, Herbert Benson, M.D., introduced Americans to the flip side of the stress response. He dubbed the counterpart to fight-or-flight "the Relaxation Response." And it doesn't occur naturally. You have to summon it in regular sessions of serene solitude.

The Benson Method

The relaxation response is not new. It's been an integral benefit of centuries-old religious rituals. What Dr. Benson did was to study those rituals and devise a simplified way to achieve the same end: flicking the switch that turns off tension and turns on physical and mental peace. Here is Dr. Benson's method, which is a form of meditation.

1. Once or twice a day, sit comfortably in a quiet place and close your eyes.
2. Deeply relax all your muscles, beginning at your feet and working up to your face. Keep them relaxed.

3. Breathe naturally through your nose and become aware of your breathing. As you exhale, silently say to yourself the word 'one' (or another word of your choosing).
4. Maintain a passive attitude. Don't worry about whether you're achieving a state of deep relaxation. Let relaxation come to you. When distracting thoughts enter your mind, try not to dwell on them. Instead, return to your word. Dr. Benson emphasizes that this passive attitude is perhaps the most important element in bringing on the Relaxation Response.
5. Continue for 10 to 20 minutes. You may open your eyes to check the time, but don't use an alarm clock. After you finish, sit quietly with your eyes closed for a few moments. Then open your eyes and sit still for a few more minutes before you stand up.

How It Helps

The many healthful benefits of the Relaxation Response continue for as long as you keep practicing the method. Dr. Benson and others have shown that it counteracts the stress response. It decreases blood pressure, lowers heart and respiration rate, decreases blood flow to the muscles and reduces body metabolism. It also increases alpha brain waves, the waves that are present when you're relaxed. And it decreases blood lactate levels (high levels of lactate are known to produce feelings of anxiety).

If you practice the Relaxation Response regularly, you'll probably sleep better and feel more energetic. If you have high blood pressure, it might drop to normal—without drugs. You may find that you don't fly off the handle or get anxious quite as easily. You'll probably calm down. "I've seen it make people more satisfied, content and peaceful," says Ronald Dushkin, M.D., a holistic physician with the Kripalu Center for Yoga and Health in Lenox, Massachusetts.

That doesn't mean regularly practicing the Relaxation Response will turn you into a wimp who is incabable of experiencing the fight-or-flight response when you really need it. But you'll probably be more calm in the face of those everyday stressors, the hassles that unnecessarily bring on the fight-or-flight response: the overcrowded subway, the shattered jar of jelly on the kitchen floor, the impending work deadline.

Is the Benson method better than other relaxation techniques? It depends on your preference, says Herbert Bloomfield, M.D., a psychiatrist at the North County Holistic Health Center in Del Mar, California.

"There are many techniques that allow us to unwind, and different methods work differently for different people," he says. "So the average person has to be an aware consumer and see what works for him. Some people need something with more of a mystical flavor, like Transcendental Meditation. Some people don't."

Keeping at It

Regardless of what technique you use, the key is to stick with it. "You'll experience more profound results over time," says Dr. Bloomfield. Some folks find it helps to incorporate the Relaxation Response into their daily lives if they use a calendar to keep track of the times they practice it. Make up your own calendar. Write the days of the week across the top of a sheet of paper, then write Week 1, Week 2, Week 3, etc., down the left side. Make a mark at the appropriate spot each time you practice the Relaxation Response.

If you feel you've got too hectic a schedule to fit in the two daily sessions of relaxation that Dr. Benson recommends, consider how some other busy people manage.

Dr. Benson writes about a homemaker who uses the Relaxation Response in the morning after her husband and kids have left the house and again in the late afternoon before her husband returns (she manages to keep her kids from disturbing her for 20 minutes). A businessman takes a Relaxation Response break for 10 or 15 minutes every morning behind his closed office door, while his secretary tells phone callers and visitors that he's "in conference." Others wake up 10 minutes early to practice the technique, do it on the subway, or find a quiet room at work and relax while others drink coffee.

Finally, while this ritual may help you cope with stress, you should take caution not to overdo it. People who meditate several hours a day for weeks at a time have been known to hallucinate. You shouldn't need more than two daily sessions of 10 to 20 minutes each.

And Dr. Benson cautions against using the Relaxation Response to "shield oneself or to withdraw from the pressures of the outside world, which are necessary for everyday functioning." It's a tool to be used wisely.

Chapter 77

RELAXATION TAPES

You've had a miserable day in the city.

You make your way through a crowd of boisterous passengers. You settle into the only available seat on the commuter train, next to a tough-looking individual decked out in leather, studs, chains and—as far as you can tell—hooks.

You adjust a set of headphones over your skull, insert a cassette into your tape player, press a magic button. Before your train leaves the platform you . . . are . . . beginning . . . to . . . feel . . . calm. One by one you relax each and every region of your body.

Suddenly, memories of your difficult day retreat to the tranquil recesses of your mind. As you gain an inner peace, you realize that the day was not such a miserable struggle. Or at least not enough to stress you out. You are enjoying your sublime train ride, leather-and-chains seatmate and all. And you are filled with optimism and enthusiasm for whatever awaits you at your journey's end.

This isn't a fantasy. Relaxation tapes are a marvelous quick retreat, a mood adjuster, an easy and effective method for learning to calm down and reduce stress. Priced as low as $7.95 apiece, they're a lot cheaper than therapy—and available any time you need a boost.

Some of the tapes employ Progressive Relaxation, guided imagery, hypnosis or other methods to get you to relax. Others incorporate a self-improvement theme: increasing your confidence, overcoming loneliness, learning to live with a negative person. Often the self-improvement message is combined with the relaxation techniques, for it is in the comfort zone of deep relaxation that people are most open to suggestions.

Tapes are not just for home (or train) use. Several hundred hospitals keep copies of "Software for the Mind" audio programs produced by Emmett Miller, M.D., a California practitioner of holistic medicine. In the Pomerado Hospital in Pomerado, California, six floors of nursing stations stock tape recorders and Dr. Miller's tapes to help patients with such stresses as preprocedure worry.

317

A Few Words about Subliminals

The same relaxation and self-improvement communiques often come in the form of subliminal (meaning "below the threshold") messages. Here's how it works: You hit the play button and all you hear is the calming sound of soft ocean waves or the tranquil music of violins. Yet in the background, lurking beneath the range of audibility, are messages that will make their way to your subconscious, messages about quitting smoking or taking control of your life or enjoying better table tennis (no lie!).

Before you blow your kid's college education fund on tapes of the subliminal message variety, keep one thought in mind: The effectiveness of subliminal tapes on behavior change is a major topic of debate among psychologists. The messages may make their way to your subconscious, sure, but behavioral experts say they may not do anything once they get there. They cite a lack of substantial scientific proof.

A few scientific studies have indicated that audio subliminals do work—sometimes. In one recent experiment, psychologist Laurence Doche-Budzynski, Ph.D., tested subliminals on two groups of Type A (competitive, impatient, distrustful) men for four weeks. One group listened to tapes that emitted positive suggestions, such as "I am good." The other group listened to neutral subliminal messages, such as "Sky is blue." At a follow-up three months later, the members of the positive suggestion group were reported to exhibit a significant increase in self-esteem (based on standard tests) and a decrease in Type A behavior.

In another experiment, Rita Sullivan, Ph.D., the director of an alcohol and drug treatment center in Medford, Oregon, used subliminal tapes in conjunction with therapy to get alcoholics to cut back on drinking. After three months of therapy and "stop drinking" tapes played during the earliest stages of sleep, her subjects were consuming less than half the alcohol of a control group that didn't hear the tapes.

The best advice is to buy one and listen to it before going to sleep. (Brain researchers say that's when you're most open to the suggestions, so ignore any hype about receiving magnificent benefits while driving your car or steam-cleaning your carpet.) Then determine for yourself whether subliminal tapes have merit, whether you're less bothered by stress or whether your table tennis game improves.

Subliminal or not, if you find the tapes make you *more* anxious, many psychologists suggest you stop listening at once. Tapes are not for everybody.

Once Is Not Enough

Like anything else that's worthwhile, it takes a degree of effort to get the most out of relaxation or self-help tapes. That doesn't mean you have to toil at relaxing. But you may find that you have to use the tape regularly, say two daily 20-minute sessions. Just as it's easy to skip exercising when you haven't become hooked on the benefits, it's easy to turn off the tape in those first few days of use and turn on the TV instead. So don't be discouraged if your relaxation tape doesn't bear any positive de-stressing results after one quick use. Make a *habit* of using it.

If you tire of your tape, if the voice of the person guiding you to bliss starts to sound like your boss or spouse, if the tape's instructions and pace start to bore you, get a few more tapes with similar messages and vary them.

The Choice Voice

With hundreds of tapes on the market, it's often difficult to choose. Here's where you should rely on your personal taste. Do you prefer a male or female voice? Do you enjoy music in the background? Do you prefer a slow or fast pace? Most stores that sell relaxation tapes will let you listen before you buy. Most tape manufacturers (some names and addresses are listed below) provide catalogs of their wares, with complete descriptions that may help you decide.

A word about sleeping with your tapes. Some tapes are designed to help you overcome insomnia, and subliminal message tapes are most effective at bedtime. Whatever the content, if you share your bed with a partner and use tapes that lull you to sleep, it may be wise to buy a pillow-speaker extension. The extension goes under your pillow and, if used properly, will direct the sound to your ears. Not only will your partner be undisturbed but you won't risk ruining your expensive headphones by rolling over on them in your sleep. Another option: use a standard earplug attachment.

Here's a random sample of what's out there.

Executive Anti-Stress Kit
Mindbody, Inc.
4731 West Atlantic Avenue
Suite 13
Delray Beach, FL 33445
(305) 495–4700
$17.95; 30 minutes each side.

First off, there's a bonus if you buy this tape: a package of adhesive stress dots that you attach to your hand. They change color from black to blue, depending on your skin temperature (a measure of relaxation), but they don't appear to work with total reliability. Regardless, the antistress tape itself more than compensates. Developed by Robert C. Sohn, Ph.D., director of the Wholistic Health Center, Manhasset, New York, the tape includes two distinct relaxation formats. Side A uses the voice of Dr. Sohn to guide you through a full-body, flex-then-relax program. Side B, with a different male voice, offers a more general, nontensing relaxation program. Both are accompanied by the lulling sound of waves breaking on a beach. The tape is widely used by businesses in stress-management programs.

Restful, Revitalizing Sleep
Effective Learning Systems, Inc.
5221 Edina Industrial Boulevard
Edina, MN 55435
(612) 893–1680
$9.98; 28 minutes, 45 seconds (a "Love" tape).
Also available in subliminal format.

A soothing tape for those with insomnia. Bob Griswold, the tape's narrator, begins with an encouraging little lecture about how the tape will help you fall asleep quickly and how you will enjoy restful, relaxing revitalizing sleep—and positive awakening. Soon, he says, you no longer will need the tape to produce those results (think of all the money you'll save on AA batteries).

Between the stretch instructions and the guided Progressive Relaxation, the narrator tells listeners to take a moment to set their internal alarm clock. "Your mind is a perfect timepiece, and you can set your mind to awaken at any time you choose. Just imagine yourself setting a clock for the time you will awaken, and you will awaken at that time," he says. To have positive, productive dreams, he instructs: "Just tell your mind what you want." These are useful tools.

Organ music accompanies breathing and Progressive Relaxation, then: "Allow your body to be supported by your bed. You can feel your body sinking heavily into your bed." Later, listeners are told, "Each time you inhale, you're breathing in pure, loving, soothing, healing energy." The energy is to be directed to parts of the body that need special attention.

As the body presumably gets more relaxed, the messages take on a definite note of positive self-affirmation. First, "You are a child of God, you have a right to be here, no less than the trees and the stars." Then, "You can feel the weight lift from you as you forgive yourself and others." Finally, listeners are directed to blow all the resentment they hold for others into a big yellow balloon, to tie it and to release it into the wind. (This tape has the same message on each side. So if you don't fall asleep from one listening, flip the cassette for a repeat performance.)

Deep Relaxation
Effective Learning Systems, Inc.
5221 Edina Industrial Boulevard
Edina, MN 55435
(612) 893–1680
$9.98; 27 minutes, 20 seconds (a "Love" tape).
Also available in subliminal format.

Two relaxation techniques for the price of one. Side A guides you to a relaxed state by simply relaxing the parts of your body, one by one. Side B offers the tense/relax method of Progressive Relaxation. Each is narrated in a male voice and accompanied by ethereal music. The music's driftiness may spellbind some and annoy others. This tape is for those who desire a snail's pace and relaxation guidance so complete that virtually no part of the body is left unnoticed ("even your tongue is relaxing . . . "). The pace offers listeners the opportunity to be meditative in their relaxation. On the flip side, which guides the listener to relaxation without alternately tensing each muscle group, the instructor is delightfully mesmerizing: "As I count down, your body will feel heavier and heavier." He is slow and powerfully effective.

Peace
Effective Learning Systems, Inc.
5221 Edina Industrial Boulevard
Edina, MN 55435
(612) 893–1680
$9.95; about 30 minutes

What if subway vigilante Bernhard Goetz had listened to this tape during his fateful IRT jaunt? It is music, all music—harmonious piano, calming strings—that inspires as it relaxes. Sneak five minutes with this tape to escape the stress of insistent children. (Tell them you're going to the bathroom.) Or listen just prior to nodding off. Indulge in it during your commuter bus ride through an abandoned factory district. (But its soothing tones are not recommended for use in freeway traffic.)

Healing Visualization/Guided Relaxation
Kripalu Shop
Box 774
Lenox, MA 01240
(413) 637–1894
$7.95; 43 minutes

"You can slowly open your eyes and know that whatever your experience has been, you can take that with you, throughout the course of the rest of your activities. When you begin to open your energy like this, the healing process continues to go on and on. You've just made a beginning."

Those encouraging words end the Healing Visualization side of this tape, a guided journey that urges listeners to direct healing energy to parts of the body that require it. The tape, prepared at the Kripalu Center for Yoga and Health in the Berkshires, the largest holistic health center in the country, is narrated by Dr. Dushkin, a holistic practitioner at the center. There's something blissful about Dr. Dushkin's mellow voice. He sounds so worthy of your trust.

On the flip side, he begins with an "awareness check" on each part of the body. ("Let your mental awareness shift into your thigh and hip." Later: "Let the awareness wash over your forehead. Take one or two slow, deep breaths and feel your whole body washed with awareness.") A particularly enjoyable part of the journey takes place when Dr. Dushkin directs awareness to the listener's mind: "Consciously notice where your mind is, what kind of thoughts are passing through your mind. Don't worry about changing them. Just observe and notice." Your thoughts are on parade. Later, when you are visualizing yourself relaxing in a wonderful place, he invites you to take along a special friend or two. Why be alone in paradise?

The Magic of Believing, by Claude Bristol
Order Dept.
Sound Ideas
Simon & Schuster, Inc.
200 Old Tappan Road
Old Tappan, NJ 06745
(201) 767–5937
$8.95; 50 minutes

If you enjoy inspirational literature, you'll probably discover some value in this audio version of Claude Bristol's highly anecdotal 1948 bestseller of the same name. Actor William Kane reads from the condensed book, presented, as Bristol wrote, "in the language of the businessman." (Bristol was a great success in business, following careers as a soldier and a journalist.) The tape includes natural chapter breaks, so you can stop and start. From chapter 2, "The Power of Thought," comes the following: "Thought is the original source of all wealth, all success, all material gain, all great discoveries, inventions, all achievements. With that in mind, it becomes easy to understand that a man's thoughts make or break him." Hard work, says Bristol, will not bring success. It takes creative thinking and a firm belief in your ability to execute your ideas. A great tape for your commute to work or before a difficult meeting.

Ten-Minute Stress Manager, by Emmett E. Miller, M.D.
Software for the Mind Cassettes
Source Cassettes, Inc.
P.O. Box W
Stanford, CA 94305
(800) 528–2737
$10.95; 20 minutes each side.

Here's a not-too-demanding tape that you can comfortably play two or three times a day. Side A consists of Dr. Miller guiding you to relaxation. ("Breathe out unwanted thoughts.") Classical guitar, wind instruments, waves and bird sounds get you in the mood, before and after the ten-minute instruction. Side B offers a selective awareness pep talk "to prepare you for your next challenge." To get energized, you focus on the "little spark of energy that starts each breath." You remember a challenge that you successfully met; you visualize yourself meeting your next challenge with similar success. Upbeat music follows.

Chapter 78

REST BREAKS

Here is an abbreviated version of an "active rest break" devised by Peter M. Miller, Ph.D., author of *The Hilton Head Executive Stamina Program*. These light physical and mental exercises aim to rest the body while rekindling your energy levels.

Deep breathing. Stand with your arms at your sides. Inhale deeply through your nose. Fill your lungs from the bottom up, raising your shoulders. Hold for two or three seconds. Exhale slowly through your nose and slowly lower your shoulders.

Stamina stretches. To stretch tension from muscles and reduce fatigue, stretch your arms over your head and pretend you are climbing up a rope hanging from the ceiling. Next, raise both arms high above your head, reaching as far as you can, until you feel your whole body stretching out. Then shrug your shoulders, concentrating on tightening shoulder and upper back muscles. Hold for ten seconds, then let your shoulders drop. Repeat four times.

Next, stand or sit erect, looking straight ahead. Slowly turn your head first to one side, then the other, then up and back to look at the ceiling, then down toward your chest.

Arm circles. To reoxygenate your blood, stand straight with your arms extended out to the sides. Rotate both arms simultaneously, beginning with small clockwise circles and making bigger and bigger circles. Make ten circles. Repeat counterclockwise.

Brain-boosting imagery. To stimulate your tired brain, sit down, clear your brain of intrusive thoughts and say to yourself, "I am feeling strong, alert and refreshed. Every part of me is full of positive energy."

Power snack. To replenish your brain and muscles with fluid, drink a glass or two of seltzer water, carbonated fruit juice or other cold, carbonated beverage.

Before resuming your work, take a moment to savor the alertness you feel.

Chapter 79

SECURITY BLANKETS

It's a rough world out there, and we all need some comfort from time to time. Thank goodness "teddy bears" come in all sorts of disguises to suit all ages. If you prefer cuddling an actual teddy bear, that's fine. But your "stuffed bear" can be anything: a security blanket, a sailboat, movies, memories, songs, prayers, heroes, even babies.

Objects of consolation, or solacing objects, can and should play a part in every adult's life, according to psychiatrist Paul Horton, M.D., author of *Solace: The Missing Dimension in Psychiatry.* "They're things that give us comfort and peace, that can soothe us in a world that doesn't always seem to offer much tenderness," he says.

As an infant, you develop an emotionally satisfying relationship with your mother, who feeds you and cares for you and seems to belong solely to you. As you grow, you slowly develop a basic trust in others and the world around you. Between the ages of two and six, you realize mom isn't your private possession, so you help to fill in the void when she's not around with a soothing object—a blanket or stuffed animal, perhaps.

From about ages 7 to 13, collections of things—model airplanes, soldiers or dolls, for instance—offer comfort when you're afraid or confused. Then come the years of adolescence between ages 15 and 25. These are the roughest emotionally because you're too old for "kid stuff" like dolls and stuffed animals, yet you're often too young for comforting mature personal relationships. Music often becomes a major source of solace, as do, unfortunately, drugs and alcohol in some cases.

The key, says Dr. Horton, is to realize that it's all right—and in his view, encouraged—to have a "teddy bear" later in life. "Indeed, vehicles for solace may relieve all sorts of pain—physical as well as emotional and spiritual." Many people are too reality oriented and think they have to act grown up all the time. This attitude usually leads to the mistaken belief that it's a sign of weakness to need an object of consolation once in a while.

It's also important to have a "safe harbor" in your home, which can be a time as well as a place. It can be time at dinner for a family talk, or reading or listening to music. The point is not necessarily to find a peaceful location, although it's good if you can; the point is to find an activity that can be somewhat of an island of solace in your daily routine, and make time for it.

Solacing is a personal matter, so don't be ashamed of what you choose for consolation. For one person, it may be playing with a pet. For another, it may be a stuffed animal, a stamp collection or a lasting friendship.

If you're looking for a good object of consolation, why not try a real teddy bear? There's just something about holding one in your arms, and the ensuing feelings of love and comfort and security, that is hard to explain. Besides, they never talk back or tell your secrets.

Chapter 80

SELF-HELP GROUPS

Let's go back to 1905. That was the year that Boston internist Joseph Hershey Pratt organized a group of tuberculosis outpatients who couldn't afford to leave their homes and jobs and obtain treatment at a sanitorium. He brought patients together for weekly meetings to share their experiences and to hear from those who had recovered and were back at work.

It was the birth of modern-day self-help groups.

By the 1930s, the largest and perhaps most enduring self-help group, Alcoholics Anonymous, was formed. During World War II, a shortage of psychiatric workers made individual treatment rare. Thus, group therapy gained acceptance.

Today an estimated 15 million Americans participate in the nation's 500,000 self-help groups. Alcoholics Anonymous alone has a million members. There are women's groups and men's groups, groups for overeaters, groups for single parents, groups for stutterers, groups for the unemployed, groups for the infertile, groups for mothers of twins and triplets.

For the most part, the groups can be divided into two types: those for members who have a problem, such as an addiction, and those for people who are living with a condition or in a situation that causes them stress. There are groups for those who want to stop smoking, and for those people who are in interracial marriages. A growing number of self-help groups support people with sexual problems. If the situation doesn't cause stress, it may be the result of stress. In some groups, members actively practice stress-reduction techniques at meetings.

A Megatrend

It is so great a movement that self-help was one of the ten "megatrends" of John Naisbitt's megabestseller, *Megatrends: New Directions Transforming Our Lives.* He wrote of self-help participants: "These people have decided to bypass the traditional avenues of institutional assistance—churches, social service organizations, the mental health establishments—in favor of dealing with people like themselves who have conquered or are trying to solve the same problem. It is a telling illustration of the shift from institutional help to self-help."

Actually, self-help groups go way, way back. Ancient religious healers relied strongly on group forces. And for centuries folks have found solace and support in tribe members, friends and family. (Part of the reason self-help groups proliferate today is the lack of community that permeates much of our culture.)

But even for folks who have the world's most supportive families and the most dedicated friends, self-help groups provide an important missing element. If you're suffering from a disease, a friend or family member at their most supportive could only say, "I can understand your pain." A group member could say, in all honesty, "I know your pain." There's a special bond that forms between people who share a common problem or goal.

Such assistance is often crucial. In a famous 1976 study, social epidemiologist John Cassel reviewed 100 research papers and came to the conclusion that the biggest single factor in people becoming ill was not a particular cause—such as being overweight—but was the lack of social support.

How They Help

That creates a huge need: the need for support from nonprofessionals, everyday people who are facing the same crises and suffering from the same fears. It can be a group of neighborhood women who meet twice a month and discuss the vicissitudes of menopause and the off-screen lifestyles of prime-time soap opera stars. It can be a group lobbying for benefits for the elderly that also teaches its members self-reliance. It can be a group of new widows, formed by an organizer who scans obituaries and invites the newly grieving. It can be a group of first-time fathers learning to cope with diapers and feeding times, who occasionally end an intense discussion with a stress-busting game of basketball.

One of the marvelous things about self-help groups is that you experience the joys of both giving and receiving. Say your self-help group of hypertensives is focusing on ways to manage stress. Your personal story of the steps you've taken since the most recent meeting may inspire another group member. People learn from seeing how others cope. Likewise, you gain helpful perspective when you listen to other people discuss the dimensions of their problems. "People often find themselves saying, 'My problems aren't so great when I hear John's problems,' " says Alan Gartner, Ph.D., co-founder of the National Self-Help Clearinghouse.

On top of that, your group will reinforce your determination to do whatever it is you've joined to accomplish—cope with a stressful situation, change undesirable behavior. And it provides role models. You can look at others who have successfully tackled a problem or coped with a major stressor, and you can emulate them.

There's still another benefit. "When a comment from a person is addressed to the group, you can listen to it and reflect on it, instead of being the object and feeling pressured to respond," says Dr. Gartner. "You can chew it over in your mind."

How They Operate

Each self-help group is structured differently and tailored to the personal needs of its members. Most groups meet in low-rent or no-rent facilities such as church halls or public buildings. Some groups meet in members' homes. Since the groups are run by members, there are seldom any professional salaries or overhead costs. Since costs are low, dues are minimal, averaging $10 to $15 yearly.

When a group is part of a national parent organization, there may be a newsletter to update members on new research and success stories. There may be a hotline—so you have access to a sympathetic ear between regular meetings. Groups that deal with addictive behavior often use a "buddy system" so members can count on familiar, one-on-one encouragement between meetings.

Your first visit to a self-help group is bound to be a bit awkward for you. It may be frightening to let your guard down and reveal your pains, frustrations, fears and dreams. But veteran members will be there to help make you feel relaxed and welcome.

"A veteran member may begin a conversation and offer literature that outlines the group's purposes," says a National Institute of Mental Health publication. "In an atmosphere that is friendly, compassionate and accepting, new members soon realize that their participation is voluntary with no strings attached—no commitments, no enforced disclosures, no group constraints." You proceed at your own pace.

Something to keep in mind: There's an unofficial code of confidentiality within self-help groups. So if your employer's brother-in-law is in your group of child abusers, word is unlikely to get back to your boss. Your privacy and dignity will be respected.

What to Look For

There is a host of clearinghouses that can refer you to self-help groups in your area. Several of them are listed at the end of this chapter. Among the national organizations with computer listings of groups are the National Self-Help Clearinghouse in New York and the Self-Help Clearinghouse in New Jersey.

Before attending a meeting of a particular self-help group, call to determine if it's right for you. Edward Madara, director of the New Jersey-based

Self-Help Clearinghouse points out that several widely divergent groups offer mutual support for parents of troubled adolescents. If you were to discover your teen was taking drugs, you could join the group that best suited your needs. Toughlove believes in parents taking control and setting limits. Families Anonymous is less directive and more focused on the parents. Parents for Drug-Free Youth looks at the use of drugs as a community problem.

Frank Riessman, Ph.D., the National Self-Help Clearinghouse's co-director, offers some questions to ask when you're considering the value of a particular self-help group.

- Do you feel they'll give you support?
- Is there a new understanding you encounter with group members that you're not experiencing elsewhere?
- Do you feel you can contribute something to the group?
- Are some of your problems being reduced?

Another question to ask is, How accessible are members? Some groups assign each new member to a more experienced member. The point is not only to ease transition into the group but also to provide a person to call upon in times of crisis.

How to Start Your Own

If no suitable self-help group exists in your area, you may consider starting your own. The task can be massive, but it is bound to be worthwhile. Before you start, ask yourself if you are committed to the project and to helping others. If so, find others who are, too. Write to the National Self-Help Clearinghouse, 33 West 42nd Street, New York, NY 10036, for a brochure describing its work. The clearinghouse also sells a manual on starting groups. Contact the organization for information on price and availability.

A first step would be to track down potential members. If you suffer from a particular ailment and want to hook up with others in your predicament, your doctor may be able to assist. Your church, synagogue or local school system can be a source of members. If you plan to start an "anonymous" type of group, contact an existing similar group in another town for some advice. To attract members, take out a small ad in a community newspaper. Or, like a group of widows and widowers does, scan newspaper articles (survivors listed in obituaries, in their case) for potential new members. If it's senior citizens you're after, go to a local seniors' center and post a notice on a bulletin board. It's often that simple.

Once you've attracted a network of members, start establishing some basics: where you'll meet, when and how often, what format the meetings will take, who will take care of administrative chores, who will be the phone contact for new members, etc. One idea: Sit in a circle, so that everyone can be seen, instead of sitting classroom-style.

At your initial planning meeting, draw up a very simple "Statement of Purpose" that defines who you are and what your goals are. Keep in mind always that the point of it all is to help each other—and to receive help in the process.

With that in mind, the group should be structured so that members can join easily. If it's a group to help individuals overcome short-term problems, members should be permitted to leave the group without guilt at the appropriate time. According to the National Self-Help Clearinghouse's "How to Organize a Self-Help Group" publication: "In some groups, such as the Compassionate Friends (for bereaved parents), members recover sufficiently from their bereavement after a time with the group and drop out. However, they might return for occasional reinforcement at a time of stress, such as on the dead child's birthday when the parent is most reminded of his or her loss."

The Role of Professionals

In the early days of the current self-help boom, professional therapists often were at odds with groups. Many therapists believed the trend fostered an overdependency, among members, on the groups. They charged that group members lacked the necessary training in group dynamics. Above all, they felt the self-help group movement took people away from professional therapists. Much of that early criticism has waned as self-help groups became increasingly popular. Now therapists recommend self-help groups to clients as an adjunct to professional therapy. And professional therapists often have a role in starting groups among clients and others, sometimes acting as "facilitators" (the person who runs the discussions). Some self-help groups use a professional as a consultant. While professionals can add immeasurable help in keeping a group headed toward a goal and in easing the therapeutic flow, there's an obvious danger: A therapist can take over a group. If that happens, "the basic sharing nature of the group can be lost and with it the group's effectiveness," according to "How to Organize a Self-Help Group."

If It Ends, It Ends

"I've been involved in many groups of one type or another that outlasted their usefulness. And that's fine," says Dr. Riessman. There comes a point when you or other individuals may no longer need the help of the group. There may come a time when the group itself is no longer needed for any members. People stop coming, the common need is satisfied. Or it just stops working. Dr. Riessman says you should anticipate that such a day may arrive. There's no sense in trying to revive a dead horse, so be realistic about your self-help group's usefulness and life span.

For more help, contact the self-help clearinghouse in your area, some of which are listed below.

For national U.S. listings and directories:

National Self-Help Clearinghouse, N.Y.: (212) 840–1259
Self-Help Center, Ill.: (312) 328–0470
Self-Help Clearinghouse, N.J.: (201) 625–9565

For state and local information:

California: (800) 222–LINK (California only)
Connecticut: (203) 789–7645
Illinois: (800) 322–6274 (Illinois only)
Kansas: (316) 686–3170
Massachusetts: (413) 545–2313
Michigan: (800) 752–5858 (Michigan only)
Minnesota: (612) 642–4060
Nebraska: (402) 476–9668
New Jersey: (800) 367–6274 (New Jersey only)
New York: (518) 474–6293
South Carolina: (803) 791–9227
Vermont: (800) 442–5356 (Vermont only)
Dallas, Tex.: (214) 871–2420
Greater Washington, D.C.: (703) 536–4100
Kansas City, Mo.: (816) 361–5007
Long Island, N.Y.: (516) 348–3030
New York City: (718) 788–8787
Pittsburgh, Pa.: (412) 247–5400
Portland, Oreg.: (503) 222–5555
Scranton, Pa.: (717) 961–1234
Westchester, N.Y.: (914) 347–3620

To contact self-help clearinghouses in Canada:

Calgary: (403) 262–1117
Montreal: (514) 484–7406
Saskatchewan: (306) 652–7817
Toronto: (416) 978–3270
Winnipeg: (204) 589–5500 or 633–5955

There is also a national newsletter, "Initiative," published by the Canadian Council on Social Development, 55 Parkdale Avenue, Ottawa, ON K1Y 4G1; phone (613) 728–1865.

Chapter 81

SEX

Sex alleviates tension; love causes it.

—Woody Allen

It's called "making love." The act is physical, emotional, spiritual, and probably the closest communion two individuals can experience. And after you make love, you usually feel absolutely wonderful. That close expression of caring, passion, tenderness and respect reinforces a couple's shared bond as well as each partner's sense of uniqueness. In such moments of intense intimacy, the world melts away, and worldly stress melts with it.

And why not? Consider the simple act of touching. Touching, as one of the five senses, is just as important as seeing or hearing. And it is vitally important to our emotional well-being. Infants who are not touched, for example, waste away and can even die. Intimate touching, too, is a positive experience, says Harvey Caplan, M.D., a San Francisco psychiatrist. And if sex is an expression of positive feelings toward someone, there's joy, warmth and marvelous human connection. All the nice feelings that help you forget about your impossible sales goals or your balding tires.

On another level, sex is not only an expression of intimacy and a procreative act, it's also physical exercise. As such, it causes your body to produce its own natural tranquilizers. That's one of the reasons you feel so great after a workout—and after sex. So among the many justifications for making love, there's the simple fact that your body probably could use the relaxation it brings.

In certain specific ways, sex often helps to relieve physical problems—such as women's cramps—which may be brought on by stress, says Paul A. Fleming, M.D., a physician and sex therapist who edits the newsletter "Sex over 40." And, he adds, some women even rely on orgasms to help them get to sleep.

If you don't feel comfortable putting sexual intercourse in the same league as, say, tennis, you may be *creating* stress for yourself instead of reducing it, says Dr. Caplan. "There are an infinite number of meanings that sex has, and it does not have to have the same meaning to both partners." Presumably, one person can view it as a workout, while the other may find it a means of spiritual communion.

How to De-stress Sex

"Sex becomes a wonderful coping technique if you think of it as an option—one of many things you *can* do, but one that is not an obligation," says Dr. Caplan.

That may be easier said than done, because each person has their own level of sexual energy. If everybody's different, what happens when one partner wants to make love more frequently than the other? Dr. Caplan suggests the reluctant partner communicate his or her needs and feelings to the other partner. Then listen to each other.

The major problem, says Dr. Fleming, is that people don't have a language in which to communicate their differences in needs and desires. "People often have a language for compromising in other areas where they disagree— say if they don't agree about what to have for dinner or what furniture to buy," he says. "But when it comes to sex, everybody feels they have a right to push for their viewpoint. Since they don't have a language for it, they wind up cutting the other person off or pressuring the other person," he points out. "They need to learn to negotiate, they need to develop options."

Opening such a dialogue with your partner may lead to the most natural and pleasurable way to relieve the stress in your life.

Chapter 82

SLEEP

Don't think of the third of your life you spend sacked out as wasted time. Consider it nature's own stress-management technique. Sleep takes you as far away as you possibly can get from the fight-or-flight response to stress, where your muscles tense, your heart rate speeds up and your blood pressure rises.

When you slumber, several stress-relieving things happen. You breathe more deeply and slowly. Your body temperature drops slightly, and your heart rate and blood pressure go down. Your metabolic rate (the overall pace of your body processes) slows down, too—which may be nature's way of making you conserve energy. (Sleep experts—somnologists—theorize that this nightly energy economy may be one of the major functions of sleep.)

There's even a specific brain pattern to your sleep that makes some of your muscles relax. While you're nodded out, two different sleep states alternate in cycles. As soon as you fall asleep you experience non-rapid-eye-movement (NREM) sleep for about 90 minutes. During this time you move from semiwakefulness to deep sleep. You are not likely to do much dreaming during this phase. It's followed by about five minutes of rapid-eye-movement (REM) sleep where your eyes move beneath closed eyelids as though you were following the action on a movie screen. During REM, you're likely to be dreaming, and your brain waves operate like they do when you're awake. But, you're almost completely paralyzed—so relaxed that certain muscle groups completely close up shop. The NREM/REM cycle repeats itself about five times in eight hours of sleep. NREM periods get gradually shorter; REM periods increase.

The Perfect Antidote to Stress

If you think sleep sounds like the perfect antidote to stress, you're right. "Sleeping enough and well at night certainly helps your mood and capacity to function and cope," says Arthur J. Spielman, Ph.D., a psychology professor at New York's City College and a sleep expert.

Here are tips from the experts to get the best possible sleep.

Stick to a regular sleep schedule. Try to retire and wake up at about the same time each day.

Relax in the hour or so before you go to bed. Take a warm bath, listen to music, practice a relaxation technique—anything that will get you relaxed.

Avoid drugs. Skip the coffee or the nightcap. (Alcohol can make you sleepy, but it may wake you up in the middle of the night.) Nicotine, too, is a stimulant to avoid.

Don't eat a big meal before going to bed. Digesting a lot of food makes your body work overtime—and it may keep you awake.

Sleep in a comfortable environment. Set the thermostat to the temperature that's most comfortable for you. Wear comfortable sleeping clothes that are suitable to the weather. If you're the type who rises with the slightest sound or beam of light, do all you can to avoid those interruptions. (Turn your radio to the very end of the FM band. You'll hear a hum that you can use as "white noise" to help you sleep. Also, try a night mask, to keep light out of your eyes.)

Don't Take Your Problems to Dreamland

"Problems often seem more difficult to deal with when you're tired," says Richard Bootzin, Ph.D., a professor of psychology at the University of Arizona, Tucson. "So I tell people to put their problems aside and look at them again in the morning, when they'll be easier to deal with." After sleep, he points out, you have more resources available—both psychologically and physically. "You're more alert, it's easier for you to think of alternatives, and you don't get frustrated or irritated so quickly," he says.

Sleep research also indicates that people under stress may need more sleep than they normally do. Ernest Hartmann, M.D., a professor of psychiatry at Tufts University School of Medicine, Jamaica Plain, Massachusetts, and author of *The Functions of Sleep*, studied the sleep habits of over 501 people. He determined that among those with changing sleep needs, "sleep requirements increased at times associated with stress, depression, change in occupation and at times characterized by increased mental, physical or emotional work."

Nobody really knows why you may need more sleep during periods of stress. One theory is that sleep helps replenish certain neurochemicals depleted during stress, bringing them back up to a prestress level. For example, after very heavy physical exertion like marathon running, you'll sleep more soundly. "The body seems to be restoring itself," says Dr. Bootzin. There may even be a similar response after emotional exertion.

Take a Nap

And then there are naps. Winston Churchill, an advocate of the catnap, wrote, "Nature had not intended man to work from eight in the morning until midnight without the refreshment of blessed oblivion, which even if it lasts only 20 minutes, is sufficient to renew all vital forces." Theodore Roosevelt, Thomas Edison and Napoleon all swore by naps to resore their famous vigor, as did John D. Rockefeller and the late President John Kennedy. Napping, however, will only refresh you if it doesn't rob you of your nighttime sleep.

To understand how napping can work for you it's important to understand your personal sleep requirements.

"Each person has a genetically determined sleep requirement," says Merrill M. Mitler, Ph.D., sleep expert and secretary-treasurer of the Association of Sleep Disorders Centers. It's a myth that every adult needs eight hours of sleep. (While 90 percent of the population needs between six and nine hours, a minority requires as few as five or as many as ten hours.)

If you're already getting as much sleep as you need at night, a nap may simply make you drowsy. If you're the type who has trouble drifting off at night, you may find it easy to nap during the day. But it's likely to make it even harder for you to make peace with the sandman at night, says Daniel R. Wagner, M.D., assistant professor of neurology at New York Hospital–Cornell's Sleep-Wake Disorder Center.

The first step in effective napping, then, is to learn if you can afford to take a nap. The second step is to determine the time of the day when your body's best tuned for sleep.

Your body's natural sleep-wake cycle has two distinct phases. One consists of the 12 hours that include your 8-or-so hours of sleep. The other is the 12-hour period that incorporates the "awake" part of your day. To determine when you're best suited for a nap—the time at which a nap will be least likely to have an effect on your nighttime sleep—first find the midpoint of your regular sleep schedule. If you typically go to bed at 11:00 P.M. and arise at 7:00 A.M., that midpoint would be 3:00 A.M. According to Dr. Wagner, you're best suited for a nap, and most able to fall asleep, approximately 12 hours later, between the hours of 2:00 and 4:00 in the afternoon.

If you can incorporate such a nap (20 minutes is fine) into your schedule, the benefits may increase when it's done on a regular basis. "If it's regular, then your physical functions can adjust to it," says Dr. Spielman. But if you're a napper and life's stressors are making you lose sleep at night, drop the naps. Eliminating the naps may help you fall asleep more quickly and sleep longer through the night.

Chapter 83

STRETCHING

Yawn.

Go ahead, do it.

Now pay attention to how you feel. Did you get a boost of energy from the oxygen you pulled into your lungs? Did your limbs become a little less tense than they were a moment ago? Did you loosen up your face—often the tensest part of your body?

Yawns are nature's way of forcing us to enjoy the de-stressing benefits of stretching. We can learn a lot from those yawns. Like the fact that beneficial exercise doesn't have to be painful. If it hurts to stretch any more than it hurts to yawn, you must be doing something wrong, says Bob Anderson, author of the best-selling book *Stretching*.

Stretching allows us to bring the same great feeling of a yawn to any part of our body. It gives us something to do with the excess tension we store in our muscle tissues. That particular tension—the result of stress, the result of sitting still at the wheel or at sedentary jobs—can become chronic if we don't release it. The way Craig Daniels, Ph.D., former director of the Stress Research Center at the University of Hartford, West Hartford, Connecticut, explains it, our muscles get tired of being tensed and untensed. So they stay tensed. "It becomes a chronic state so the system doesn't have to keep responding," he says.

Some residual tension is released during sleep and some goes away on its own, but we still may have a lot of tension to get rid of. That's where stretching comes in.

"When you stretch, you get a limbering effect that minimizes any sort of injury," says Dr. Daniels. "As you get older, muscles lose their elasticity. When tensed, the muscles harden. By stretching, you make them looser, make them more elastic." It also forces you to use muscles that you ignore all day if you have a sedentary job.

Layne Longfellow, Ph.D., a psychologist who leads seminars in stress management, explains how stretching also tones up your mind. He says the

337

mind and body are in a "continuous feedback loop." Stressors have a definite impact on the way you hold your body. Exposure to enough fear, for example, will cause your posture to contract. And your body in its contracted position is sending a "fear" message to your mind, says Dr. Longfellow.

You can use stretching to break the loop, to alter chronic tightened postures. "With stretching, your chronically contracted muscles will release, and you will release the psychological contractions that go with it," says Dr. Longfellow.

Learning from Kitty

A daily stretching ritual—or simply stretching whenever you feel tense—is simple, painless and effective. If you don't believe us, just ask the nearest four-legged creature. The delights of stretching have long been known by animals. You've seen your pet dog or cat stretch several times a day. You should do the same.

One of Anderson's favorite stretches is one you can do while sitting in gridlock, instead of fuming. It's called the Shoulder Shrug/Neck Stretch.

The Shoulder Shrug/Neck Stretch. This is great for tension in your neck, shoulders and upper body. Bring your shoulders up to your earlobes for three to four seconds. Then drop your shoulders down and think to yourself: "Shoulders hang, shoulders down." Let your shoulders relax for a few seconds. Do two or three repetitions.

That should help relieve the tension in your shoulders. Now you want to stretch your neck. To do that, tilt your head sideways to the right and visualize your left shoulder going down. Stretch it easily for five or six seconds. Now alternate sides (lean your head to the left and drop your right shoulder). Repeat for each side. This stretches both the neck and the top of the shoulder. "When you're stretching, you should feel that you're in control of the stretch," says Anderson.

Another Anderson favorite is an even simpler stretch, good for long airplane flights or weak moments at work.

Reach for the Sky. Interlace your fingers and raise your hands above your head, palms up. Push your arms upward and slightly back. Feel the stretch in your arms, shoulders and upper back. Hold the stretch for 10 to 15 seconds. Do not hold your breath—breathe normally.

Dr. Daniels offers an all-purpose stretch for the back that you can do while watching the evening news.

Getting a Leg Up. Lie on your back and bend your left knee. Take both hands and put them on your left leg, between the knee and ankle. Pull your left leg up so you are trying to touch your knee to your chest. Hold a few seconds (to start). Bring it back down. Repeat several times.

Do the same with your right leg. Then do the same with both legs together (for this version, make a loop around both legs with your hands).

Another stretch from Dr. Daniels works on the hamstring and calf muscles. It's a stretch that shouldn't be done in the home of people you don't know very well.

Push Down the Wall. Stand about 36 inches away from a wall. Lean forward, placing your hands flat on the wall at shoulder level. Lean into the wall. Slowly walk backward—and keep your feet flat on the floor. You should feel your calf muscles stretch.

Chapter 84

T'AI CHI

At 8:30 on Saturday mornings the football field of Swarthmore College (a small school near Philadelphia) is a study in contrasts. On the running track that encircles the playing field about two dozen beefy, shirtless athletes—and a few companion dogs—pound the cinders.

But on the field itself two trim and relaxed people appear to be dancing a pantomime as they silently—and very, very slowly—lift legs, bend arms, turn. They are teacher Ken Getz and student Lelia Calder, practitioners of the ancient Chinese art of T'ai Chi. And the calmness of their T'ai Chi movement is about as far removed from the grit of football practice as ancient China is from the Superbowl.

But this beautiful exercise can get you in shape—in fact, its adherents believe it can get you in better shape than a traditional gym class regimen of sit-ups and push-ups.

That's because, T'ai Chi experts say, the movements shape up more than your muscles. They help you become aware of and control your *chi*, the subtle energies that flow throughout your body. Does *chi* really exist? When Robert C. Sohn, Ph.D., author of *Tao and T'ai Chi Kung*, directed his *chi* to make himself heavy, two members of the Miami Dolphins couldn't lift him. He even controlled his *chi* to the point where the burly football players fell down when they tried. That's not absolute proof, but it's certainly very intriguing evidence.

An Active Meditation

"T'ai Chi is an exercise involving the maintenance of a particular posture which is held through a series of slow, dancelike motions," says Dr. Sohn. "The motions are designed to allow the free flow of energies through the body. It leads to a high degree of relaxation, strength and alertness."

At its higher levels, T'ai Chi is an active form of meditation, *and* a martial art. Like those two disciplines, when you practice T'ai Chi you are working on breath control and body awareness. "You are continually becoming aware of the parts of the body, everything from the arch of the feet to the curve of the fingers," says Dr. Sohn, who is founder of the Wholistic Health Center in Manhasset, New York.

A so-called "short" form of T'ai Chi includes about 64 different postures bearing names such as "Grasp Sparrow's Tail" and "Snake Creeps Down" and takes about 10 minutes to perform. The "long" form involves 108 postures and typically lasts 20 minutes, according to Lawrence Galante, author of *T'ai Chi—The Supreme Ultimate*. The experts say it may take years to experience the complete richness of T'ai Chi, to master the invisible energy flows of the body. But you can derive stress-reducing benefits from your first workout.

An Ancient Way to De-stress

Don't forget, T'ai Chi is *exercise*. When Galante—who teaches T'ai Chi at corporate stress-management workshops—hooked up a heart monitoring machine to 25 T'ai Chi students, he discovered that they achieved 80 percent of their maximum heart rate within a minute of beginning the bent-knee form of the exercise. Yet even though it can condition the heart, there's little of the strain and difficulty found in other heart-protecting exercises like running. And T'ai Chi has another unique benefit: You achieve a sense of balance.

"T'ai Chi constantly checks alignment and brings you back to your natural alignment—the posture nature gave us," says Dr. Sohn. Your spine straightens out. Your leg muscles strengthen. Your neck muscles strengthen and align properly. With enough practice, T'ai Chi actually changes your regular stance, lifting your head back and up, and lessens the tension you hold in your neck.

"The movement is an external manifestation of what's happening inside. You don't try to use your muscles, you try to utilize the energy—it's a workout from within," says Getz. And the series of movements is intended to be done slowly. "Some people, when they start out, get very uptight because they're so used to rushing," says Dr. Sohn. "It's a movement that's much slower than what we're used to."

Back at the Swarthmore College football field, teacher Getz is giving instructions on the solo short form. "You turn your hips all the way to the front." He pauses to watch. "That's it." He does a movement and then explains what he is doing. "Your left arm does not move much but your right arm does . . . "

After about ten more minutes, he and his students take a quick break. Getz, a college professor, practices T'ai Chi 40 minutes each morning and 20 minutes in the early evening. Does it help him deal with stress? "I don't feel nearly as good if I don't practice," he says. "The quality of my life is not the same." Then he adds: "If I'm in a mood that's stressful, anxious or keyed up, it has the effect of slowing things down."

Most major cities have T'ai Chi instructors. Local YMCA's are beginning to offer classes. Or you can inquire at any of the Kung Fu or Karate schools that are opening in virtually every shopping center in the United States—the instructors there may know of someone in your community who teaches T'ai Chi. It's best if your teacher has at least ten years' experience, says Getz.

Chapter 85

TIME MANAGEMENT

Worrying about having too little time to do what you have to do or would like to do is stressful. But no one can create more time—each day has 24 hours, no more, no less. So the only solution is to better manage the time we do have.

"Pencil and paper are important tools to time management, and therefore to stress management as well," says Cliff Mangan, Ph.D., senior staff coordinator of counseling services, Temple University Counseling Center, Philadelphia. "By writing down how you spend your time and comparing it to what you'd like to do, you can better control time. Having a written agenda, you don't have to worry so much."

Here are some suggestions to use in order to manage this valuable resource.

Take a personal inventory of how you spend your time. "Keep a diary in the form of a compact, portable calendar for a week or two," says Dr. Mangan. Write down, in 15- or 30-minute increments, how much time you spend on various activities—eating, sleeping and getting dressed; cooking, grocery shopping and household chores; childcare, worship and other family activities; and reading, exercise, socializing and other leisure activities, plus various on-the-job tasks. (Don't wait until the end of the day to record your activities. You won't remember accurately.)

"A time-management calendar can be very revealing," says Dr. Mangan. "You may not realize how much time you spend chatting over coffee with co-workers, for example, until you log it on your calendar."

Spend some time thinking about your goals. "What do you want to do over the long run? Where do you want to be five or ten years from now?" asks Dr. Managan. "Fantasize about all your goals, major and minor. Then set intermediate goals. Then set specific, immediate goals—that will help you achieve your long-term goals. Decide how to spend your daily time accordingly." Suppose you want to redecorate your house—that's the long-term goal. This month you plan to install hardwood flooring in the living room—that's your intermediate goal. Tomorrow you plan to buy the wood—that's your daily goal.

Write down what you expect to accomplish. And visualize the finished

343

project. Picture the shiny oak boards. Imagine the smell of new lumber. Feel the wood's warm smoothness. "The more senses you employ in making your plans, the more attainable they seem and the more likely you are to execute them," says Dr. Mangan. "Committing plans to paper makes them less overwhelming and keeps you from worrying about when you'll get to them. Also, more 'urgent' demands are less likely to sidetrack you."

Make an agenda. "Take 15 or 20 minutes before you start the workday day to decide what you're going to do, when you're going to do it—then do it," says Dr. Mangan.

"Planning time saves time," says R. Alec Mackenzie, author of *The Time Trap: How to Get More Done in Less Time.* He cites one study comparing two groups of projects in a company. One allowed a minimum amount of time for planning and the balance for execution. The second group of projects allowed considerably more time for planning, yet were executed more quickly and with better results, saving time and aggravation.

Set specific, realistic deadlines. Rather than making general, indefinite plans, such as telling yourself you would like to paint the bedroom someday, instead, say something like, "I'm going to pick out paint on Saturday and paint the bedroom by September 1" or some specific date.

"One of the problems with setting deadlines is unrealistic time estimates," says Mackenzie. "Poor projections lead to frustration and often to panic and crisis." The secret to getting things done on time is to make allowances for interruptions, distractions, errors and emergencies.

Review your calendar at the end of each month. "As you look over your daily records, think about what you've done to advance your goals," says Dr. Mangan. "Are you progressing? If not, you have all the data right in front of you to show what's stopping you."

Are You Wasting Time?

If your hourglass seems to empty far too quickly, look for stray fragments of wasted time.

Make a " hit list" of your ten biggest time gobblers. "Review your time-management calendar at the end of each day and ask yourself which activities moved you forward toward your goal and which didn't," says Dr. Mangan. A few common time-wasters include meetings, interruptions (such as visitors and phone calls), paperwork, household chores, driving, errands, waiting, watching television. Then look for ways to eliminate or reduce those time-wasters.

Block out interruptions. "Finishing a task in one session saves time because you need not reorient yourself to your work again and again," says Mackenzie. If you need large blocks of uninterrupted time, screen your phone calls (via secretary or answering machine), close your door and schedule meetings for late afternoon—or don't tell anyone where you're going to be.

Sometimes body language alone can discourage interruptions. "Sit facing away from your office door," says Dr. Mangan. "Otherwise, you'll be tempted to say 'hello' to everyone who walks by. If you work in an open office, don't glance up when people pass by. If you make it obvious that you're totally involved, totally committed to what you're working on, people will be less likely to interrupt."

"If others do interrupt, arrange to get back to them later," says Dr. Mangan. "Then write down on your calendar *when* you plan to talk to them. Put your words into action. Again, your calendar can help control how you spend your time."

Give yourself permission to say no. If your calendar is filled with work on school pageants, community bake sales and other commitments, you run the risk of breaking under the weight of time-consuming obligations. The trick is to jettison surplus obligations without feeling guilty.

Delegate. No book on stress management would be complete without mentioning the option of getting someone else to do what you don't have time for.

"Write down what you delegated, to whom, and when you expect it to be done," says Dr. Mangan. "Then you no longer have to do the job *or* worry about it."

The trade-off with delegating is that your delegate may not do the job *exactly* as you would. (For more on this vital time-managment tool, see chapter 59.)

Finding Lost Time

Here are still more rules and tools for chiseling hours off time spent on obligations and channeling it toward what matters the most.

Start the day prepared. Get your clothes (and your kids' clothes) ready the night before, for example. If clothes are color-coordinated, pressed and

---

Take Time to Do Nothing

It's hard to go from trying to do two things at once to doing nothing at all. But everyone needs some "white space" on their calendar, to rest and reflect.

"I hesitate to tell people to *schedule* some 'down time,' " says Cliff Mangan, Ph.D., of Temple University's Counseling Center in Philadelphia. "But down time can be very uplifting. If you don't have time for yourself and yourself alone, to simply relax, you'll be tense, irritable and anxious, which is bound to affect others. So in that respect, I don't think it's selfish to be selfish."

ready to report for duty when needed, you'll be less apt to waste precious time rummaging for a clean shirt or the right belt.

"Your brain is most receptive at two periods of the day—before you go to sleep and as soon as you wake up," says Dr. Mangan. "So make the most of the first and last 20 minutes you're awake. If you take those times to get organized, and perhaps read a brief inspirational message to set the mood, you'll be more efficient and effective throughout the day—and even sleep and dream more productively."

Schedule work that requires energy and initiative for your "peak" times. Energy levels tend to fluctuate in small peaks and valleys throughout the day. To harness natural bursts of energy, do difficult tasks at peak times and easier tasks during dips. After a heavy dinner, for example, you may feel too logy to paint the spare room or fix the leaky faucet in the bathroom. But you could do a routine chore like pairing socks. Conversely, if you're at your best at midmorning or an hour or two after dinner, those may be good times to exercise, organize a new project or tackle some other demanding task.

Set a five-minute limit to rehashing work hassles at the end of the day. "Continuing to think and talk about work problems—whether you're raising children or working in an office—only extends your workday into your scheduled personal time," says Dr. Mangan.

Stand up to sort your mail. Standing to sort your mail discourages you from lingering over bills, bank statements, junk mail, catalogs, flyers, magazines and memos when you could be working on more important tasks. Divide incoming paperwork into three piles: one stack for work you should do as soon as possible, one for semiurgent matters, and one to do whenever you get around to it. Discard the rest. Later, with urgent tasks complete, you can peruse magazines, catalogs or corporate reports at your leisure. (One time-management expert calls this the "art of wastebasketry.")

Shop by mail. With the profusion of mail-order catalogs, there's little you can't buy through the mail. What you don't like, you can send back—without wasting a lot of time circling the block for a parking space or hunting for a salesclerk.

Stock up. To further minimize time spent shopping, stock up on basics or items you use in quantity, like panty hose, all-occasion greeting cards, stamps, laundry detergent, canned goods, vacuum cleaner bags.

Buy Christmas or other presents *anytime*. Whenever you see something that would make a good gift for someone, buy it, even if the occasion is months away. By adding to your gift stash throughout the year, you can avoid crowded stores during the hectic holiday buying season, saving time and aggravation. (By shopping ahead of time, you also avoid selecting gifts by default, under a short deadline.)

Put things where they belong. For sheer exasperation, nothing beats wasting half an hour searching for misplaced car keys—or anything else you can't do without. Always put your keys in the same spot—on the dresser, by the door or in the side pocket of your purse, for example—to avoid wasting a lot of time hunting for them. The same goes for your watch, checkbook, wallet, car registration and other easily mislaid but essential items.

"All this is not as structured as it sounds, and the effort really pays off," says Dr. Mangan. "Paradoxically, the more you write down how long you spend on daily activities and seemingly structure your time, the more time you have for spontaneity and fun, and the less time you spend worrying or feeling guilty. Making conscious choices to restructure your time gives you more control and therefore reduces stress. You'll be more effective at what you do and have more time for fun."

Chapter 86

VACATIONS

*And on the seventh day God ended his work which he had made; and he rested
on the seventh day from all his work which he had made.*

—Genesis 2:2

All creatures great and small experience stress. As such, vacations from
stress have been a God-given right—and necessity—from Day One.

"It is a person's birthright to have some moments alone, to play, to relax,
to rest," say Stephen A. Shapiro, Ph.D. and Alan J. Tuckman, M.D., in their
book, *Time Off: A Psychological Guide to Vacations.*

Given the number of ailments linked to stress, regularly spaced vacations
are downright therapeutic.

"Many physicians believe that vacations often play an important role in
relieving work-related tension," says Geoffrey Godbey, Ph.D., professor of
recreation and parks at the Pennsylvania State University, in his book, *Leisure
in Your Life.* Apparently, the more "R and R" you get on vacation, the bigger
the spillover into daily life. A study of 128 full-time workers before and after
their regularly scheduled vacation showed that overall, people who enjoyed
their vacations generally felt more satisfied with their jobs and life in general
afterward.

Why You Can't Afford
Not to Take a Vacation

Most people need little coaxing to trade in their time card for a get-away
ticket. Yet one out of six people who are entitled to paid vacation doesn't take
one, according to one source. Some think they can't afford a vacation, because
they assume that a vacation by definition has to cost a lot and take you
somewhere exotic. (It doesn't.) Couples with small children often assume

that going off by themselves is simply out of the question. (It isn't.) And many, many people feel guilty about "wasting" their time or money on a vacation. (They shouldn't.) So instead, many well-deserving souls spend their time off washing the car, painting the house, cutting the grass or cleaning out the attic, basement or garage.

Few reasons for not taking a vacation are good enough, though. "Much stress is rooted in feelings of lack of control of the elements of your life," explains Dr. Tuckman. "On the job, your boss has all the control. Or maybe things are *out* of control. Or your home life is controlled by certain demands— the kids, the bills, household repairs. By taking a vacation, you are arranging and controlling your time for one segment of your life. And hopefully, when you return from vacation, you can carry some of that control and the feelings of mastery produced back to your daily life."

Five Signs That Say, "You Need a Vacation"

Do you feel irritable lately? Are you tired even when you first get up in the morning? Are you making more mistakes than usual? Do you think about work and nothing else? Or do you find yourself daydreaming about being somewhere else?

If so, you may not only need a vacation—you may be long overdue for some time off.

"If you're feeling anxious, irritable and overwhelmed, by all means take a vacation, even if you can get away for a long weekend only," says Dr. Tuckman. "But don't habitually wait until you're overloaded with stress before taking vacations. Because if you start your vacation with a high level of tension, that will contaminate your vacation experience and you won't get the full benefit. Similarly, if you want to get full relaxation value out of your vacation, try to resolve marital difficulties or other conflicts *before* you leave. Otherwise, you'll take the baggage of unresolved conflicts along with you on vacation."

Recipe for Relaxation according to Taste

If your idea of the ideal vacation is jetting off to an isolated beach and spending hours lying in a hammock with a cold drink in your hand, you're not alone. In reality, though, few people live out that fantasy—mainly because doing nothing isn't what it's cracked up to be.

"Not many people can remain in a state of continuous relaxation for long without some kind of planned activity to reduce the 'weight' of just doing nothing," say Dr. Shapiro and Dr. Tuckman.

Sun, Surf and Stress Management

The problem with most vacations is that even if you leave your worries behind when you go, they're waiting for you when you return.

Suppose, however, you came back from vacation not only rested and relaxed but with the tools to help you *stay* that way? William R. Newman, Ph.D., psychologist and director of Stress Management Vacations International, organizes planned vacations that provide ample time for fun and sightseeing but also manage to work in time to learn muscle relaxation, deep breathing and other methods of tension control that you can take back home with you.

The trips vary from season to season and include fitness vacations where you can hike, canoe, play tennis, snorkel or enjoy other activities. You can sail in the Caribbean or ski in New England or the West.

For more information on vacations that teach you how to ease tension, at home and away, contact Stress Management Vacations International, Inc., 189 Washington Street, Gloucester, MA 01930; phone: (617) 283–6969.

"Although the *idea* of a holiday 'just to relax' is perhaps the easiest of all to come up with and is, in many ways, the most appealing, it is at the same time a most difficult idea to sustain."

So for many people, the best way to "rest" is to do something different and interesting, especially if their daily routine is, well, too routine. Learning a foreign language. Rambling through the Amish countryside in search of handmade quilts. Carving wooden decoys. Hiking in Vermont. Prowling through flea markets shopping for art deco bric-a-brac.

One important caveat, though: If your vacation begins to resemble your work week, watch out! Should you overschedule your activities, your vacation will demand the same kind of energy and determination as did the responsibilities you left behind.

Case in point: One couple took up scuba diving and, in their initial zeal for the sport, signed up for a full complement of diving on their first couple of trips to the Caribbean. They found, however, that reporting to the dive boat promptly every morning, noon and sometimes night began to feel like a job. On their next vacation, they planned to dive less and schedule some afternoons and at least one whole day for nondiving fun.

Soon, though, the couple loaded up their "free time" scrambling over Mayan ruins, photographing elusive flamingos or exploring rain forests and volcanoes. Once again, they returned from their vacation feeling like they needed a vacation. Clearly, something had to change if these two were ever going to get any stress-reducing benefits from their vacations. So they stretched their next vacation from one week to ten days. That gave them time to "do it all" and still "do nothing."

"A time of recuperation should be an important part of a well-planned [vacation]," say Dr. Shapiro and Dr. Tuckman. "In between the sightseeing, the scuba diving, the dining out, there should be some moments set aside for unwinding and absorbing."

It's a matter of balance: The key to true relaxation is rest and recreation in proportions suited to your temperament and needs. Balancing R and R is especially important for people who feel guilty "wasting" time on vacation or who feel out of sorts away from a highly structured routine.

"A vacation is supposed to reduce stress. Don't defeat the purpose by letting guilt or lack of structure generate stress," says Dr. Tuckman. He suggests that people who have trouble downshifting into the vacation mode do some task—read a book, run, write letters—part of the time so they then feel free to "play"— or do nothing—the rest of the time.

Four Steps to Really Getting Away from It All

Unwinding requires more effort than meets the eye, if you're not used to loafing. Dr. Shapiro and Dr. Tuckman have analyzed the vacation process and conclude that you can't expect to feel instantly relaxed the minute you go off-duty. Rather, "vacating" our normal routine and the tension and worry that often come with it is a step-by-step process. To shed tension—and return refreshed—you have to do the following things.

Stop running—physically, mentally and emotionally. "Learn to let go," says Dr. Tuckman. "The first day on vacation, you're only partly disengaged—you're partly on vacation and partly back home. It takes a day or two to decompress. To put it another way, you can't expect to go from 80 miles per hour to a dead stop."

Resolve feelings of guilt about "wasting time." "This is the barrier between most people and real relaxation," say Dr. Shapiro and Dr. Tuckman in their book.

"Tell yourself, 'It's okay not to work,' " Dr. Tuckman says. "Convince yourself that not only do you deserve it, you *need* it. Otherwise, you can't go on to the next phase."

Learn to tolerate fantasy and play. "Many people find that vacations are an excellent opportunity to play with their kids, get to know them away from the routine of your job, their schoolwork," points out Dr. Tuckman.

Savor the serenity. "Just as sports and games are recreation for the body, so relaxation and the aimless play of the senses are recreation for the mind."

An occasional long weekend may turn your tension meter down a notch or two, but in order to truly relax, you may have to take off for a week or longer. "For a vacation to be of most benefit, it must be extended for at least a week," say the authors. "The first two or three days are devoted to the unwinding process, the gradual letting go of the routines of daily living. Not until the third or fourth day is there a real separation and an unhindered participation in the new environment."

The Right and the Wrong Reasons for Taking a Vacation

"But I love my job!" some will say. "Why should I tear myself away?"

"Nobody can be continually creative—no matter how much you love your job—without breaks," says Dr. Shapiro. "When people say that they feel stable

---

One If by Land, Two If by Sea

Suppose your spouse's idea of an idyllic vacation is piling the kids into the station wagon and driving down to the shore for a jam-packed week of sightseeing, shopping, golf and waiting in line for hours to see Shamu, the killer whale. But you fantasize about back-to-nature treks in the wilderness, sitting around a campfire listening to crickets chirp or shooting the rapids on the Zambezi River. How do you negotiate how and where you spend your hard-earned vacations?

Alan J. Tuckman, M.D., who is well-versed in vacation psychology, offers these tips:

• Discuss your needs. Don't give in without expressing an interest in where to go, what to do. Otherwise, your companions will assume you have no objection.

• Explore new options. Don't get into a rut of spending your vacation at the same place year after year.

• Consider spending time by yourselves, either alone or together. Kids don't need vacations as much as adults do. If you have children, there's nothing wrong with farming them out to a trusted babysitter so you can get away. Or take a babysitter along on vacation so you can enjoy each other undistracted.

• Split the time. Do something you like for part of the trip and something the others like for the rest.

• Be willing to compromise. "It may be impossible to fulfill everyone's vacation needs every year," says Dr. Tuckman. "But don't be rigid in your plans. Improvise."

and healthy without vacations, I want to interview their spouses and co-workers, too. Do *they* agree? Are these nonvacationers as sharp, appreciative and interesting? We're often very poor witnesses about ourselves," adds Dr. Shapiro.

(If you and your family disagree over how to spend your vacations, see the accompanying box.)

One last bit of advice before we bid you bon voyage: A vacation is not a substitute for dealing with the underlying causes of stress in your life. "Refusing to face the problem and going off on a vacation merely ensures its continuation," say Dr. Tuckman and Dr. Shapiro in their book.

"And by all means, don't wait until stress reaches a critical level to take a vacation, even if it means taking 'minivacations' on the weekends—or taking a long walk one Saturday," says Dr. Tuckman. As medicine against stress, a vacation works better as a preventive than as an antidote.

"Vacationing in this taut world is not a luxury; it is a necessity," conclude Dr. Shapiro and Dr. Tuckman.

Chapter 87

WALKING

We're reporting live from the ground floor of the Willow Grove Park Mall in suburban Philadelphia. It's just after 8:00 in the morning, and already just about a dozen enthusiastic souls—mostly retirees—are braving the stares of floor washers on upper levels.

Meet the morning walkers, a crew of exercise enthusiasts who have learned the joys of the latest fitness craze: walking. There's nothing to slow down these folks as they enjoy the climate-controlled, traffic-free, dog-free environment of a largely vacant shopping mall in the two hours before the stores open.

Take Bernard Frank. A heart attack he suffered five years ago convinced the 55-year-old rabbi of the need for regular exercise. And here he is, midway through his daily 40-minute routine of brisk walking. Keeping pace at his side for the 3.5-mile hike (past Sears, Thom McAn Shoes, Everything Yogurt . . .) is his wife, Tobi, 52.

Take Bea Weissman. Perfectly coiffed, wearing earrings and lipstick, this trim 77-year-old woman does a daily eight laps at Willow Grove. She suffered a stroke over a year ago, and as her husband, Seymour, 73, explains, "She's under a lot of stress. This really helps." He lasts for only five laps.

But not everybody here this morning is recovering from a health problem. A trio of women in their sixties say they are walking partly for the regular exercise, partly as an excuse to socialize with each other and partly as a means of quickly checking out the merchandise on display. "Last week I bought a beautiful framed print," explains a woman whose physician suggested this form of exercise. "I couldn't pass it up."

More and more people are saying the same thing about walking itself: They can't pass it up. And it's easy to understand the attraction. This form of exercise is a lifetime activity. It's free—and virtually injury free. It allows you to either enjoy the outdoors or, in bad weather, the controlled climate of a shopping mall. It's fun. And take a look at the healthful benefits.

Using Up the Stress Hormones

"If carried out with enough intensity and for a long enough period of time, walking results in the 'training effect'—your heart becomes more efficient at doing its job," explains Warren B. Howe, M.D., an Oak Harbor, Washington, physician and Fellow of the American College of Sports Medicine.

"Your heart rate decreases. There's usually a decrease in blood pressure. You have a more efficient utilization of oxygen throughout your body. You have an increase in stroke volume—the amount of blood ejected by the heart with each contraction—which means your heart is stronger," he says. "You also can lower your cholesterol by walking. And if you do it regularly without increasing your food consumption, you will lose weight."

Beyond all these physical effects, there are benefits for your emotions. When your stress hormones start pumping through your veins, walking is a way of doing what your body is geared up to do—move. "The body is ready for fight-or-flight, and walking is one of the closest approximations of fleeing that you can get involved in on a regular basis," says William Rosenblatt, Ed.D., clinical director of the Biofeedback and Stress Management Center in Morristown, New Jersey. Walking, like other exercises, uses up the stress hormones in your blood.

"People tolerate stress better when they exercise regularly than when they are sedentary," says Edward Colt, M.D., a Manhattan endocrinologist. "In general, the more intense the exercise, the greater the effect on stress reduction."

And there is the natural "high," a feeling of satisfaction that is probably the result of the rise in the level of specific neurotransmitters that are your brain's own tranquilizers. "These neurotransmitters are released during running, and there is reason to believe that the effect is true of all exercise," says Dr. Colt.

People who walked on a daily basis for 1½ miles at a brisk pace reported fewer symptoms of anxiety and depression than people who did not have a regular aerobic exercise program, says Shae Graham Kosch, Ph.D., a clinical psychologist and associate professor in the Department of Community Health and Family Medicine at the University of Florida, Gainesville.

Got a Problem? Walk It Off

When his clients say they are in the throes of a problem, Dr. Rosenblatt tells them to take a walk. "It doesn't help to sit and worry about the problem. Instead, go out for a walk," he says. But there's one crucial instruction: "As you're walking, don't think about the problem. Spend the time letting go of it." Clearing your mind and enjoying the activity will make you better able to cope when you return home.

"Walking allows you to manage the physical tension generated by the problem," he says. "While you're walking, you're giving yourself the message 'I can control myself.' You'll be more clear about the problem."

He says studies have discovered that people who are walking or exercising don't get the same tranquilizing effect if they are occupied with a problem. He adds that people who insist on approaching walking with great concern for their distance, speed or length of time walked will not achieve the full emotional benefits of the exercise.

How Far, How Fast, How Long

Many experts agree that when you first take up this exercise, you shouldn't be overly concerned about how far, how fast and how long you walk. Instead, here's some advice from Dr. Howe.

Start out easily by strolling at a slow, even pace. Don't worry about how far you go, but try to keep walking for 20 minutes.

Over a week or two, build up to the point where you reach from 1 to 1.3 miles. (At that distance and length of time, you'll be walking at 3 to 4 miles per hour.) Then start to increase the length of time you walk at that pace.

For the best aerobic effect, you should exercise a minimum of three times a week and at a rate sufficient to keep your heart pumping at 70 to 80 percent of the maximum rate you can achieve during exercise. Before you begin walking, have your physician give you a stress test, so you can discover what that maximum heart rate is.

The benefits of walking are achieved if you maintain that 70 to 80 percent of maximum heart rate for 30 minutes. But it's important to work up to it, so Dr. Howe advises you spend the first 5 minutes walking slowly. After the 30 minutes at a more rapid clip, cool down by walking slowly again, this time for 5 to 10 minutes. Again, this routine is a goal you should shoot for. If you can't maintain it, don't. You don't want to overdo it.

Standing and Breathing

In his book, *Walking*, John Pleas, Ph.D., offers some step-by-step advice (and lots of encouragement) for the beginning walker. Dr. Pleas is known in the Nashville area for his well-publicized walks. In an average week he walks 97 miles. He celebrates his birthdays with 24-hour walks.

To get the most out of your walk, Dr. Pleas recommends you practice proper breathing, exhaling twice as long as you inhale. "The process should be effortless and should occur naturally and rhythmically," he says.

As a way to develop proper posture while walking, he suggests you focus on a tree or some other straight object several blocks away and align your body with that object. "Walk toward that object as if you were going to walk through it, keeping your body as straight as possible. As you come within 25 or 30 feet of the object, select another object in the distance and repeat the same procedure," he says. "Although you might not be able to align your body entirely, this procedure will make you more aware of your posture as you are walking."

Do's and Don'ts

If a dog should bother you, *do:*

- Ignore the dog.
- Continue walking briskly and with confidence.
- Stop and tell the dog to go home in a firm voice if the dog pursues you.
- Walk with a friend or in a group on your next outing.
- Check the leash law and call the owner and/or appropriate officials.

At the same time, *don't:*

- Show that you are afraid.
- Run from the dog.
- Intimidate the dog, except to tell it to go home.
- Throw objects at the dog.
- Pet the dog.
- Give up walking.

In addition, *do:*

- Check the weather report.
- Let your family or a friend know your walking route and when you expect to return.
- Go to the bathroom before leaving the house.
- Wear light-colored clothing to reflect the light at night.
- Wear comfortable shoes.
- Carry identification.
- Carry small change for an emergency telephone call.
- Walk facing the traffic on roads that are narrow.
- Call the police if you feel you are being followed and/or if you notice strange cars parked in or cruising the area.

In addition, *don't:*

- Drink coffee or other liquids before walking if you have a weak bladder.
- Continue walking if you become ill.
- Take refuge under a tree when there is lightning.

- Walk briskly at night on a rocky surface or where there are potholes.
- Walk against a red light just to keep up your pace.
- Give up walking.

You'll Never Walk Alone

And if you want to find others to walk with, why not join a Walker's Club? The largest in North America is the *Prevention* Walking Club. For an annual membership fee of $9.97, club members are entitled to an annual magazine called *Walker's World*, which features a 365-day walking log, discounts on walking-related products and an opportunity to sign up for group walking tours of a variety of beautiful locales. In addition, members can participate in an awards program, qualifying for awards as their mileage mounts. (If you walk 5,000 miles in one year, you get awards such as a membership patch, a T-shirt, a minilibrary of *Prevention* Magazine Health Books, and membership in the Walking Hall of Fame.) To join up, write to the *Prevention* Walking Club, Rodale Press, Inc., 33 East Minor Street, Emmaus, PA 18098.

Walking is something you can start anytime, so why not now? Remember that old physics principle: A body at rest tends to stay at rest unless some force acts upon it.

SEEKING PROFESSIONAL TREATMENT

Chapter 88

A CONSUMERS' GUIDE TO PHARMACEUTICAL STRESS REDUCTION

Anxiety. Worry. Insomnia. Depression. They come and go like rain clouds over the emotional landscape. After a day or so, the sun will shine again. Every so often, though, extremely trying circumstances—a disabling illness, financial peril, an accident, the death of a loved one, a messy divorce—stir up an extended forecast of dark, stormy emotional weather. You're depressed, exhausted, tense and preoccupied. And you need help *fast*.

At one time, phenobarbital and secobarbital, which are barbiturates, and meprobamate were standard issue for a bad case of "nerves." But barbiturates depress the central nervous system and proved to be deadly for many—it's far too easy to overdose, especially when barbiturates are combined with alcohol (another central nervous system depressant). So prescribing barbiturates was like calling out the Seventh Fleet to settle a bar fight. Both barbiturates and meprobamate are also addictive: Your body grows accustomed to their effects very quickly, until you can't manage without them.

Today, barbiturates and meprobamate are all but obsolete, having been replaced by so-called minor tranquilizers like diazepam (Valium) or flurazepam (Dalmane). You can even buy over-the-counter sleep aids like diphenhydramine hydrochloride (Sleep-eze 3) to help treat insomnia.

Sometimes anxiety is a symptom of depression, in which case antidepressant drugs like imipramine (Tofranil) or amitriptyline (Elavil) can help in as little as two weeks' time. A third class of drugs, mood stabilizers like lithium (Lithane and others), are prescribed principally for the dramatic mood swings typical of manic-depression. In contrast, "major" tranquilizers like chlorpromazine (Thorazine) are used primarily for psychoses and other serious disorders, which are beyond the scope of this book.

360

At times, these drugs are used in the treatment of anxiety and depression. However, they do not completely replace "talk therapy," a long-standing method of working out problems. Communication between doctor and patient is essential. And while there is no need to fear these drugs themselves, there is need to fear their potential for abuse.

While newer tranquilizers and other stress-management drugs are somewhat safer and less addictive than barbiturates, they are not a panacea for stress and, like all drugs, should be used with caution. Here's why.

Antianxiety Drugs and Sleep Aids

The close-knit family of drugs known as benzodiazepines accounts for 85 percent of all minor tranquilizers prescribed in the United States. Besides diazepam (Valium) and flurazepam (Dalmane), these include:

- Alprazolam (example: Xanax)
- Chlordiazepoxide (example: Librium)
- Clonazepam (example: Klonopin)
- Clorazepate dipotassium (example: Tranxene)
- Halazepam (example: Paxipam)
- Lorazepam (example: Ativan)
- Oxazepam (example: Serax)
- Prazepam (example: Centrax)
- Temazepam (example: Restoril)
- Triazolam (example: Halcion)

"These so-called minor tranquilizers are for pure anxiety without significant depression (with the exception of alprazolam)," says Jacob J. Katzow, M.D., associate clinical professor of psychiatry and behavioral science at George Washington University and director of the Washington, D.C., Clinic for Mood Disorders. If you get jittery before flying or speaking in public—or find yourself so worried and upset that you can barely get through the day—these drugs can help reduce stress. They can control anxiety's most unpleasant symptoms—insomnia, sweating, muscle tension, tension headaches, rapid heartbeat, vomiting and shaking.

In fact, the other benzodiazepines, like flurazepam (Dalmane), temazepam (Restoril) and triazolam (Halcion), leave you so relaxed that they're used specifically to treat insomnia. (Insomnia comes in three types—difficulty falling asleep, frequent awakening during the night and early-morning awakening—and can appear in any combination.) Other antianxiety drugs are a better choice if you want to relax but don't want to fall asleep.

Antianxiety drugs can also help pave the way for effective "talk therapy," if you need it. They can calm you down enough to enable you to talk over your troubles with a professional counselor.

"As for when to prescribe these drugs, how much to prescribe and how long they should be used, that's a matter of the physician's judgment," says Dr. Katzow. Much of that decision is based on how they work in your body.

How Tranquilizers and Sleeping Pills Work

Benzodiazepines like diazepam work by depressing the central nervous system, but to a far lesser degree than barbiturates. That difference makes benzodiazepines a safer pharmaceutical tool to help relieve anxiety. In fact, when these drugs first came out, doctors and patients alike were a bit overconfident. Now doctors are more aware that benzodiazepines can be somewhat risky: They can build up in your system, causing toxicity, and you can become physically or psychologically dependent on them. If they are taken with alcohol, you can go to sleep and never wake up. If you've ever been dependent on alcohol or other chemical means of stress relief, be forewarned: Benzodiazepines are potentially habit-forming.

What's more, dependency can sneak up on you. Anxiety and insomnia tend to be on-again, off-again problems, prompting frequent and sometimes long-term use of these drugs.

Such problems are avoidable, of course. The trick is to select the right drug for the right problem in the right amount for the shortest period of time—and to look for nondrug ways to handle stress or insomnia. You should ask your doctor if the drug prescribed is the safest, most effective drug for your problem.

The type of drug your doctor prescribes may be determined by how long it stays in your system. Some go to work quickly and wear off within hours. Others take more time to kick in, and the effects can linger for several hours. Triazolam and oxazepam, for example, have a short half-life—on the average, your body will use up half the dosage of triazolam in two to four hours and half the dosage of oxazepam in four to eight hours. When used for insomnia, they usually don't leave you with a "drug hangover" in the morning, making them reasonably good sleeping aids for elderly people who experience more than just an occasional sleep problem.

Sometimes, trial and error is the only way to find out which type of tranquilizer is best for you. "If two people take the same drug, one person may get drowsy and another might not," says psychiatrist Lynn Cunningham, M.D.

If short-acting drugs like triazolam don't work, your doctor may try intermediate agents like temazepam or lorazepam. Temazepam's half-life is approximately 10 to 15 hours and lorazepam's is about 12 hours. Unfortunately, they can leave you groggy the next day and are associated with memory loss—decided drawbacks.

Flurazepam is a long-acting drug: It's a powerful sleep inducer, but it has a half-life of 47 to 100 hours. If you need help falling asleep only once in a blue moon, that's of little concern, but with repeated use, the drug can build up in your system. That lingering effect is a special concern for older people, who metabolize drugs more slowly and may take longer to eliminate a drug than young adults do.

For that reason, short-acting benzodiazepines are preferred for older people with more than occasional sleep problems, according to R. Michael Allen, M.D., medical coordinator of adult services at Community Psychiatric Centers, Millwood Hospital, Arlington, Texas.

Diazepam, for example, has a half-life of 20 hours in a 20-year-old but a half-life of 90 hours in an 80-year-old. The difference results from the amount of time the liver takes to process the chemical, says Andrew M. Barclay, M.D., chairman of the Department of Family Practices at the University of Illinois College of Medicine, Peoria. Drugs and their dosages, however, should be dealt with on a case-by-case basis, experts warn.

These short-acting benzodiazepines like alprazolam (Xanax) and oxazepam (Serax) may also be appropriate for older people who experience occasional bouts of anxiety. But for persistent anxiety, intermediate-acting drugs like lorazepam (Ativan) may be the better choice simply because they last longer than short-acting triazolam (Halcion). Be aware, though, that your memory may suffer.

Long-acting agents such as diazepam (Valium) are reserved for people with chronic, general anxiety for whom other nondrug methods haven't brought serenity.

Occasionally, someone taking benzodiazepines like alprazolam (Xanax) will experience what doctors call a paradoxical effect—they become anxious and agitated instead of calm. Should that happen, your doctor may switch you to another benzodiazepine like oxazepam (Serax).

Safety Strategies

"The antianxiety drugs are readily prescribed because they work—and they work fast," says Dr. Cunningham. To minimize any potential problems, doctors suggest these strategies.

Try the drug on a weekend at first, or whenever you don't have to drive. That way, if you become drowsy during the day or develop a "drug hangover," you'll face less risk. If side effects bother you, ask your doctor to change the dosage or switch to another prescription.

Watch for signs of dependency. If you find yourself needing more medicine (that is, more pills or higher doses) than your doctor prescribed, you may have grown physically dependent on the drug. If so, don't stop taking the pills cold turkey—you could become very sick. Completely deprived of your customary dose of sedation, you may feel tense and unable to sleep, or you may go into a full-blown withdrawal reaction, suffering shakiness, headache, nausea and vomiting. You could even experience more dangerous and frightening problems like seizures. To avoid withdrawal, the dose must be tapered off gradually.

Ask yourself if you can manage to cope without the drugs. If you can't, you may be psychologically addicted. "People who are psychologically dependent remember how they felt without the drug, so they're afraid to stop taking it," says Dr. Cunningham. "Also, many refills are called in to the pharmacist over the phone. So it's easy to ask for—and get—unlimited refills without stopping to consider if the drugs are giving relief or if there are other ways to control anxiety."

Be alert for signs of toxic buildup. Warning signs of a sudden overload of these drugs include poor muscular coordination, agitation and slurred speech. Chronic intoxication can lead to disorientation and confusion may easily be misdiagnosed as senile dementia in older people—or just blamed on old age. Falls and fractures, too, are more common in older people who take benzodiazepines, says Dr. Barclay. Once again, tapering the dose gradually reduces toxicity.

How long you can use benzodiazepines varies. According to the *Physician's Desk Reference*, some should not be taken for more than four months. Some doctors feel that's unnecessarily restrictive; in some cases, anxiety may be severe enough to disrupt life for longer than four months, so doctors should decide on a case-by-case basis whether you need to continue or taper off.

Over-the-Counter Sleep Aids

Stroll through any drugstore or the health and beauty aids aisle of a supermarket and you'll undoubtedly run across do-it-yourself sleep aids like Nytol, Sleep-eze 3 and Sominex (which all contain the active ingredient diphenhydramine hydrochloride) or Unisom (active ingredient, doxylamine succinate).

"Why go to a doctor for sleeping pills when you can buy them at the corner drugstore?" you might ask.

Well, it's a matter of using the right tool for the right job instead of improvising with what's easily available.

"Most drugs sold as over-the-counter sleep aids are antihistamines that just happen to make some people drowsy as a side effect," says Magdi Soliman, Ph.D., professor of neuropharmacology in the College of Pharmacy, Florida A & M University in Tallahassee.

Because these antihistamine-type sleep aids are less effective than benzodiazepines, you might have to take a higher dose in order to fall asleep, adds Dr. Soliman. And the more you take, the more likely you are to experience other, undesirable side effects—reduced alertness, foggy memory and confusion. (As with prescription sleep aids, the older you are, the more susceptible you are to drug-induced side effects.) And oddly enough, antihistamines actually make some people edgy or nervous. As a result, Dr. Soliman cautions that they—and prescription drugs, too—should be the last resort when treating insomnia.

Most important, though, artificially induced sleep is not of the same caliber as natural sleep. Antihistamines interfere with rapid-eye-movement (REM) sleep, which is associated with dreaming and considered to be the most restful stage of sleep, explains Dr. Soliman. You may "sleep" all night and still wake up feeling tired. Compounding matters, if you continue to rely on antihistamines, you may experience what doctors call "REM rebound." In other words, you'll eventually spend too much time in REM sleep and have nightmares.

According to studies, prescription sleep aids like flurazepam (Dalmane), temazepam (Restoril) and triazolam (Halcion) have the least effect on REM sleep and therefore the least potential for producing REM rebound. "So while prescription sleep aids are more potent, when prescribed correctly, they are better than over-the-counter preparations," says Dr. Soliman.

If you do try an over-the-counter sleep aid, proceed with care. The label is the closest you'll come to medical advice, so be sure to heed every word. Pay special attention to warnings against taking sleep aids with alcohol or other medicines that also depress the central nervous system.

Tryptophan, a Natural Alternative

"If I were to recommend any over-the-counter sleep aid, it would be tryptophan, an amino acid present in many protein foods and sold as a food supplement in health food stores," says Dr. Soliman. Tryptophan enhances production of 5-hydroxytryptamine, a neurotransmitter in the brain that helps you fall asleep. "A person can take 500 milligrams of tryptophan at bedtime," says Dr. Soliman. "It goes to the brain more readily than other amino acids."

Dr. Soliman says that since tryptophan is a component of food, doctors don't anticipate any adverse effects. The only people for whom tryptophan might pose a problem are those with trytophanuria, an extremely rare defect in metabolism that's invariably diagnosed early in life because of its more overt symptoms.

Beta-Blockers for Anxiety Attacks

In addition to the standard antianxiety drugs, doctors can recommend drugs called beta-blockers, particularly propranolol (Inderal). These may be used to treat anxiety attacks like stage fright.

Beta-blockers block certain nerve impulses to the heart, in effect anesthetizing the heart. They are customarily used to reduce blood pressure, but they can also block a pounding heart, a trembling voice and other physical symptoms of anxiety associated with stage fright and other anxiety attacks. One advantage is that half-life is very short—only four hours—and the drug is completely eliminated from your system by the time the anxiety-causing situation passes.

Because beta-blockers lower your heart rate and blood pressure, they can change the way your body responds to exercise. If your doctor prescribes these drugs, ask if you need to change your activity level in any way.

Drugs for Deep Depression

Most people think of depression as sort of a blue funk—you lie around in your bathrobe all day, on the verge of tears, or just sit and rock for hours. But paralyzing sadness is just one face of depression. Anxiety and agitation may be symptoms of depression, too.

"The person who walks the floor nights wringing their hands may be depressed," says Dr. Cunningham. "We can treat that with benzodiazepines for the short term, to control the agitation, and antidepressants, which work more slowly, to lift the depression. It's a lot like treating pneumonia with cough medicine for the immediate symptoms and antibiotics for the underlying infection."

The arsenal of mood-lifting drugs at a doctor's disposal include:

- Tricyclic antidepressants like imipramime (example: Tofranil)
- Antidepressants with sedative effects like amitriptyline (example: Elavil)
- Combination antianxiety/antidepressant/sedatives like chlordiazepoxide and amitriptyline (example: Limbitrol)
- Monoamine oxidase (MAO) inhibitors like phenelzine sulfate (example: Nardil) for mixed anxiety and depression with phobic or hypochondriacal tendencies
- Mood stabilizers like lithium (example: Eskilith) for the manic phase of manic-depression

Deciding which drug, if any, is best isn't always easy.

"The most obvious, hard-to-dispute uses for antidepressants are for serious depression that lasts for months, where someone stays in the house, crying, and can hardly eat or sleep," says Dr. Katzow. "In those circumstances, it may be obvious to everyone, including the patient, that drugs are an appropriate way out."

According to Dr. Katzow, MAO inhibitors like phenelzine sulfate (Nardil) are often the best antidepressants when individuals aren't responding to other therapy. But they're complicated to use because you have to avoid a long list of foods, beverages and medications (including liver, pickled herring, all cheeses except cottage cheese and cream cheese, yogurt, beer, wine, certain cold and allergy medicines, among many others). Eating any of these while taking a MAO inhibitor could produce a dangerous—and possibly fatal—rise in blood pressure.

So your doctor will most likely try a tricyclic antidepressant like imipramine (Tofranil) first, simply because this type is easier to use.

Mood-stabilizing drugs like lithium (Eskilith and others) are typically used for the extreme ups and downs—the manic highs and depressive lows—experienced with manic-depression. But when used in conjunction with antidepressants, they can help other forms of depression dramatically, adds Dr. Katzow.

When Are Medicines the Answer?

Someone who's suffering a major, short-term stressful event may benefit from a tranquilizer but not from an antidepressant. Also, for milder to moderate depression, extending for months or years, drugs may not be an appropriate treatment.

"Some psychiatrists say that relying on a drug is no better than relying on alcohol, that it sets a pattern, that it's an easy way out, that the correct approach is to work things out in therapy," says Dr. Katzow. "And because many of these drugs are addictive and have possible adverse reactions, it is better to learn to handle problems without recourse to drugs. But psychiatric medications are better than many people think they are."

Still, antidepressants, like antianxiety drugs, carry a long list of possible adverse reactions and cautions. So you have to weigh all the usual disadvantages of treating a problem with a chemical against the benefits. Complicating matters further, you may be depressed and not know it. Sometimes it takes a professional to pick up on the symptoms and determine if drugs, therapy—or both—are warranted.

"Emotional problems can drive people to overeat, or abuse alcohol or illegal drugs," says Dr. Katzow. "Scratch the surface of any behavioral excess and you may discover an underlying difficulty that needs to be resolved."

The question then is whether the underlying problem is a so-called external source of stress (like screaming kids, carpools, deadlines or financial worry) or an internal problem (like guilt, worry or frustration) that can be traced back to an incident in the past. Sometimes only professional counseling can help you to sort it out. Before resorting to drugs, it behooves doctor and patient alike to find out *why* you're down in the dumps.

"Most people fall somewhere in that middle range of the spectrum between easy-to-diagnose depression and more subtle problems," says Dr. Katzow. "And most psychiatrists prefer to try 'talk therapy' first and resort to drugs only if depression doesn't lift."

So, as much of a blessing as these drugs may be in providing relief, they should not be used without some effort to find out the true cause of your anxiety or depression. "Whether these drugs are prescribed by the family doctor, an internist or a psychiatrist, there is the danger of continuing to treat the symptoms but not the underlying disease or, in the case of stress, the cause of the problem," says Dr. Cunningham. "Nor should you assume that just because stressful things are going on in your life, stress is the cause of your depression."

A Lifetime Prescription?

Once you've been prescribed a mood-elevating drug, how long do you have to keep taking it?

"That depends," says Dr. Katzow. "For a short-term crisis you may need it for a short time only. If you have a predisposition toward tension or anxiety, you may need to use the drug off and on for the rest of your life."

"You have to weigh the benefits of a drug against the hazards," says David J. Greenblatt, M.D., chief of the Division of Pharmacology at Tufts-New England Medical Center, Boston. "But as a general rule, use medication in the smallest dose for the shortest possible time."

A Few More Words to the Wise

Here are some suggestions to further help your doctor decide what's best for you.

Discuss any medical conditions you have. Kidney or liver problems, for example, can affect drug metabolism. Also, if you have kidney or liver disease, it could be made worse.

Tell your doctor about any other medication you may be taking. Cimetidine (Tagamet) for example, slows metabolism of diazepam and other benzodiazepines and some antidepressants. Antihistamines (a common ingredient in some cold and allergy medicines) depress the central nervous system, adding to the effect of benzodiazepines.

Tell your doctor if you are pregnant (or planning a pregnancy) or nursing a baby. Some drugs can be passed on to a growing fetus or nursing infant, harming the baby.

Ask what side effects you can expect. Each of these drugs carries a long list of possible side effects, ranging from the mildly annoying (like fatigue) to the rare (like liver problems that turn your eyes and skin a bit yellow). Sometimes they go away, sometimes they don't, so contact your doctor.

Chapter 89

A CONSUMERS' GUIDE TO THERAPY AND THERAPISTS

Today, instead of lying on a couch or interpreting ink blots, someone in counseling is just as likely to be yanking the end of a towel held by a therapist and shouting "I want it!" That's the approach when the therapist is a proponent of bioenergetic therapy. The point of the yanking and shouting? It's a way of developing the capacity for emotional expression and increasing self-assertiveness and affirmative feelings, while releasing negative feelings.

Or if the therapist comes from the school of cognitive therapy, the client may find himself learning how to counter his automatic thoughts in order to build self-esteem. An example culled from *Feeling Good* by David Burns, M.D.: Instead of overgeneralizing and jumping to the wrong conclusion by thinking "Everyone knows how disorganized and selfish I am," a person would learn to think "I'm disorganized at times and I'm organized at times. Everybody doesn't think the same about me."

But why see a therapist? Isn't the best help self-help? Aren't *you* the best expert when it comes to controlling stress?

All that's true. But the therapist can improve and aid your own efforts to rid yourself of stress or emotional tension. He's someone to talk to—someone who won't judge, condemn, belittle or bury you under an avalanche of advice, someone who will *really* listen. He's a professional; it's his *job* to understand troubling emotions and circumstances—where they come from, how they can warp your life and how to deal with them. In short, he's a life assistant, a guide for your personal growth, a friend.

Selecting the therapy or therapies that are right for you is a matter of learning the basic philosophy of each, determining if you feel comfortable

369

with that philosophy, and then deciding whether your goals are compatible with what the therapy has to offer. Transactional analysis, for instance, may be helpful in improving your interpersonal relationships, but may "bypass the inner person and deeper levels of feeling," according to Otto and Miriam Ehrenberg, Ph.D., authors of *The Psychotherapy Maze*.

What follows is a description of different types of professional psychologists and a list that provides the basics of some of the therapies that are used in stress management, adapted in part from the Ehrenbergs' book and Marsha Linehan and Andre Ivanoff's "Guidelines for Getting Help with Problems in Living." Some involve a traditional therapist and client using a verbal approach. Others use the hands-on variety. Some, such as cognitive therapy, lend themselves to specific timetables. If that's the case, during the initial session the therapist may tell you how long the therapy is likely to last. In others, the therapy revolves around the relationship between client and therapist and it's not always possible to predict how many sessions will be needed.

A Who's Who of Therapists

Your physician, clergyman or a trusted friend can be a source of referrals for a therapist. A word of caution before running to your friend's therapist: It's not always a good idea to see someone simply because he helped your friend. "Your friend's problems may have been remarkably different from yours," says Theodore Wasserman, Ph.D., a New York clinical psychologist, "and the therapist's skills may not be appropriate to deal with your kind of problem." Since there are so many types of therapies available, first determine if your friend's therapist's approach is even suitable; maybe another method would be more appropriate to your problem and your personality.

You can hook up with a therapist by contacting a specific therapeutic organization or by getting in touch with the American Psychological Association, 1200 17th Street NW, Washington, DC 20036, (202) 955-7600 for the names of state psychological associations. Call or write the American Psychiatric Association, 1400 K Street NW, Washington, DC 20005, (202) 682-6000 for the names of psychiatric associations in your state or town. Your local community mental health association can also help you find therapists. Another source of referrals: a counseling center at a nearby college or university.

A first session with a therapist is considered a consultation. It's the time to find out whether his or her brand of therapy is likely to be useful to you. And it's the time to determine whether you feel comfortable and confident with the therapist. You will want to discuss your reasons for seeking therapy.

"The most important thing to ask them is the nature of their experience in dealing with your specific problem," says Eric Margenau, Ph.D., a New Jersey psychologist and author of *The Encyclopedic Handbook of Private Practice*. So if you're going to a therapist to stop smoking, for example, and he's a licensed hypnotist, that's fine. A psychoanalyst is probably not what you'd want.

It may matter to you how good a match you are with your therapist. While the job of a therapist is to be objective, be on the lookout for therapists who may have strong values that differ from yours. For instance, if your therapist is an ardent feminist and you aren't, you may have a poor philosophical match. Or if you're seeking therapy because you want to become more successful in business and your therapist is passionately antibusiness, you're not likely to get much sympathy.

Don't be shy when it comes to asking about any side effects of the particular brand of therapy. Relationships may change, comfortable habits may change, you may experience intense pain. Discuss these and other possibilities with your therapist.

Inquire about the therapist's training and qualifications. Therapists can come from all walks of life and several of the therapies listed below can be done by mental health professionals of varying training. Don't by shy when it comes to inquiring about qualifications and background. First question: Does the therapist have a professional license from the state? Here are therapists listed by educational training.

Psychiatric social workers. These therapists have a college degree and at least two years of graduate training in a program accredited by the Council on Social Work Education. For certification by the Academy of Certified Social Workers, a candidate must have a master's or doctoral degree from a program approved by the Council on Social Work Education, two years of postdegree social work experience, and membership in the National Association of Social Workers. They must pass a written exam. Licensing procedures vary from state to state.

Psychologists. These professionals usually have doctoral degrees (Ph.D., Ed.D., Psy.D.), although the requirement varies from state to state. The training programs may or may not be accredited by the American Psychological Association. Most state licensing boards require two years of supervised experience. It's possible after five years to earn a degree in a specialty certified by the American Board of Professional Psychology. Additionally, a psychologist may be listed with the National Register for Health Service Providers. Certified marriage and family therapists belong to the American Association of Marriage and Family Therapists (AAMFT).

Psychiatrists. Psychiatrists must have a medical license. They are medical doctors who have completed four years of medical school and a one-year internship. Most psychiatrists also go through a three-year residency training program in psychiatry.

Nonprofessional therapists. These therapists practice without training or accreditation. They may be individuals who believe their alternative therapies do not require formal education in psychotherapy and recognized credentials or they may be opportunists. Says Dr. Margenau, "You wouldn't want to put yourself in the hands of a nonprofessional therapist if you have a significant problem. You'd only want to go to one if you want to work through something that's not too intense but that's bothering you."

Practical Questions to Ask

There are some practical considerations.

Fees. Don't hesitate to ask what your therapist charges. (You should determine when you make your appointment whether he or she charges for the initial consultation session.) Many therapists charge on a sliding scale according to your income. Don't hesitate to ask a therapist if this is their practice. Some therapists make you pay for sessions you miss or cancel. Some therapists insist on being paid at the end of each session; others prefer to send out monthly bills.

Insurance. Check your policy to see if you have coverage. There is a broad range in what your policy (or your spouse's policy) may pay. Some policies pay for a good portion of your therapy costs, while others offer limited benefits. Some will reimburse only for visits to psychiatrists, or pay for therapy with a psychologist only if he was referred by a physician. Such restrictions are changing, however, as states pass "freedom of choice" legislation. And an increasing number of policies cover therapy by social workers.

Frequency. How many times a week will the therapist want to see you? How long will each session last? How long does the therapist expect treatment to last?

Some Newer Approaches

In the last decade or so a variety of new therapies have blossomed. As a general rule, they offer practical and relatively quick assistance in handling stress.

Behavior therapy. This philosophy asserts that *all* behavior is a learned response to the environment. The goal is to change a person's behavior by replacing old responses with new ones. Most behavior therapists believe that the current environment is the most important in affecting the person's present behavior. Early life experiences, long-time mental conflicts, or the individual's personality structure are considered to be of less importance than what is happening in the person's life in the present. The point of the therapy is to work on problems by working on a person's behavioral skills— not by assuming that there is one underlying psychological problem. A variety of procedures are used to improve the individual's self-control by expanding the person's skills, abilities and independence.

Among the behavioral therapy procedures, one called "stress inoculation" is the most comprehensive for treating the symptoms of stress. It teaches people how to change the thinking that is causing the stress, and it incorporates relaxation techniques and behavior planning.

Behavioral therapist Theodore Wasserman, Ph.D., explains how this works. "Suppose Mary is getting a divorce. A behavior therapist might teach Mary how to behave in the situations that produced stress—how to relax in a meeting with her lawyer, for instance. The therapist would teach her to improve all the techniques that get broken down during stress.

"The therapist might have her engage in 'imaging.' If she had trouble concentrating in her lawyer's office, she would be instructed to imagine herself in the lawyer's office and behaving in a positive way, see herself listening carefully. She would ask herself, 'What is stressing me? What am I saying to myself that's causing the stress? How can I think about it differently to reduce the stress? What can I do differently to reduce the stress?' She might be taught negotiating strategies: how to listen, how to respond.

"Also, the therapist would identify to Mary what she's saying to herself that's causing the stress. In cognitive restructuring she would be given other ways of viewing the events. Suppose the opposing lawyer is nasty. The therapist might say to Mary: 'He's only doing his job,' 'He really doesn't mean what he's saying, he's just doing what's necessary to do his best job for his client.' The therapist would focus on the positive effects of the divorce, and what to do next."

Cognitive therapy. This technique grew out of the work of Aaron Beck, M.D., a professor of psychiatry at the University of Pennsylvania. Its main principle is simple: What you think (your cognitions) may influence how you feel. If you want to change your feelings about something—yourself, for instance—you can change your thoughts first. Your feelings will follow. In one important study, cognitive therapy was suggested to be just as effective as a prescription antidepressant in treating severe depression. Cognitive therapists have discovered that when you feel depressed, most thoughts that create your perceptions of yourself and the whole world are grossly distorted. Cognitive therapy teaches that you can learn to recognize your distorted perceptions and change the way you think. (For further explanation, see chapter 57.)

Gestalt therapy. The German word *gestalt* means "meaningful whole." The goals of this therapy are to help the individual achieve a wholeness in which thinking, feeling and acting are integrated. Exercises in awareness help you focus on the "here and now." You concentrate on releasing or getting rid of old experiences that may be causing you emotional hangups. And body awareness exercises help you assess your feelings. You will learn what your facial expressions or posture might be saying about how you really feel. The awareness experiments and confrontational approach may enable you to experience feelings that were formerly blocked.

Hypnotherapy. "Hypnosis without understanding is a scalpel in the hand of a 12-year-old," says Murray Needleman, Ph.D., a Philadelphia psychotherapist with a popular radio program. Like many other psychotherapists, Dr. Needleman points out that hypnosis itself, which is merely heightened concentration, will do little to help a person manage stress in the long run if not accompanied by high levels of faith, cooperation and trust. While the state of hypnosis can be therapeutic because it is associated with deep relaxation, many psychotherapy professionals caution that it should be part of a broader therapy strategy. "The importance is not the state but what the hypnotist should do with it," says William Fezler, Ph.D., coauthor of *Hypnosis and Behavior Modification: Imagery Conditioning*. He emphasizes the importance of finding a hypnotist who is also a psychotherapy professional. Many hypnotists have no training or expertise in psychotherapy and are unlikely to help you by knowing what to do with the state of hypnosis once they've got it. Dr. Fezler warns that they can even produce the opposite of the desired effect. "A therapist using hypnosis has to know what's going on with the patients. Otherwise he could create anxiety instead of relaxation."

Primal therapy. Primal therapy gets a person to experience and express feelings that have been blocked. Techniques vary, but the more famous versions involve screaming out pain—the primal scream. What therapists try to achieve is an in-depth, unimpeded expression of your pain. In primal therapy you could find yourself beating a mattress to express anger. But it's not all screaming and beating. You talk with your therapist, too, although that's not the emphasis. One of the goals is to relive your painful memories. Once you do that, proponents of primal therapy say you will become a feeling person and "clear."

In its original format, primal therapy consisted of three weeks of intense therapy followed by months of group sessions. Now primal practitioners vary the schedule and format of the therapy. To learn more about primal therapy and to track down a list of primal therapists, write to the Los Angeles Information and Referral Center, 8380 Melrose Avenue, Los Angeles, CA 90069, or phone (213) 272-1478.

Rational-emotive therapy. Developed by Albert Ellis, Ph.D., it teaches people to think rationally. By focusing on a client's belief system, a rational-emotive therapist teaches the client that it is the beliefs about events—and not the events themselves—that cause an emotional upset, even though both may be disturbing. It's a short-term, problem-oriented therapy that does not dwell on one's past. If a person were to visit a rational-emotive therapist for stress-induced problems, the first thing the therapist would do is to identify the stressors—a bad marriage, say, or job burnout. Then the therapist would point out the effects these stressors have on the individual and his beliefs about them. Suppose the client believes it's wrong or cowardly to escape either the bad marriage or the impossible job. Then the object of therapy is to change those beliefs so that they are more in the person's best interest.

Transactional analysis. This therapy was developed by Eric Berne, M.D., and popularized in his book *Games People Play*. It is based on the concept that people are motivated by social hungers in addition to biological drives, and that the social hungers are satisfied by stroking—which is any act that recognizes another person. According to the theories of transactional analysis, each of us has three aspects of personality that determine our behavior: the parent, the child and the adult. Each of the roles fills a function for us, but if one role is either excluded or used *too* much, it can throw us out of balance and affect our relationships. Also, we can communicate satisfactorily only when our roles are complementary. But conflicts arise when, for instance, one person's "adult" is talking to another person's "child." Transactional analysis encourages you to get into adult-adult relationships.

What If You're Dissatisfied?

The Association for Advancement of Behavior Therapy's "Guidelines for Choosing a Behavior Therapist," by Marsha Linehan, R. Stuart, T. Risley, P. London, M. Parloff, J. Cautela and R. Bootzin, includes some sensible advice for those who may be dissatisfied with a therapist.

Talk with your therapist. That's what he's there for. If you're angry or frustrated, if you're not getting anywhere, discuss your dissatisfaction with the therapist. "A good therapist will be open to hearing any complaints and discussing your dissatisfaction with you," say the guidelines.

Get a second opinion. If your problems don't appear to be getting resolved, consider a consultation with another professional. Your current therapist can suggest someone for a consultation. If he objects to this, find a new therapist.

Consider changing therapists. "Good therapists realize that they might not be appropriate for every person," say the guidelines. So don't buy the line that it's unacceptable to change therapists once therapy has begun.

According to the guidelines, "The most important thing you need to ask yourself when deciding to continue with a particular therapist is, 'Am I changing in the direction I want to change?' If you do not feel that you are improving, and if, after discussing this with your therapist, it does not appear likely to you that you will improve with this therapist, you should consult another therapist."

KEEPING A STRESS DIARY

A diary can often reveal clues to the causes of stress-related illness, such as headaches, backaches, stomach troubles, colds and flu. To help determine if a persistent but unexplained health complaint is related to stress, keep a brief diary of how you're feeling and what stresses you are coping with on a week-to-week basis.

In column one, fill in the dates, starting with week 1. In column two, jot down your symptoms, and in column three, briefly list any problems you may be having with work, deadlines, children, spouse, finances or other stressful demands. In time, you should be able to see any connection between health complaints and stressful events.

WEEK	SYMPTOMS	STRESSFUL EVENTS
1.		
2.		
3.		
4.		
5.		
6.		
7.		

WEEK	SYMPTOMS	STRESSFUL EVENTS
8.		
9.		
10.		
11.		
12.		
13.		
14.		

WEEK	SYMPTOMS	STRESSFUL EVENTS
15.		
16.		
17.		
18.		
19.		
20.		
21.		

WEEK	SYMPTOMS	STRESSFUL EVENTS
22.		
23.		
24.		
25.		
26.		
27.		
28.		

WEEK	SYMPTOMS	STRESSFUL EVENTS
29.		
30.		
31.		
32.		
33.		
34.		
35.		

WEEK	SYMPTOMS	STRESSFUL EVENTS
36.		
37.		
38.		
39.		
40.		
41.		
42.		

WEEK	SYMPTOMS	STRESSFUL EVENTS
43.		
44.		
45.		
46.		
47.		
48.		
49.		

	WEEK	SYMPTOMS	STRESSFUL EVENTS
50.			
51.			
52.			

INDEX

A

Abdominal breathing, 254
Abdominal pain, 176
Abrahms, David B., 227, 228–29, 230
Abrahmson, David I., 242, 243
Absenteeism, 7
ACTH, 270, 271
Acupressure, 295
Adrenaline, 68, 69. *See also* Epinephrine
Affairs, love, 291–92, 293
Aggressive behavior, versus assertive behavior, 232–33
Aging. *See also* Retirement
    benzodiazepines and, 362–63, 364
    hot baths and, 243
    loneliness and, 57–58
    of parents, 31–33
    sleep and, 197
Agoraphobia, 97, 99
Ahrons, Constance, 123–24, 125, 128–29, 130

Alcohol, 101
    barbiturates and, 360, 362
    insomnia and, 194
    performance jitters and, 69
    sexual performance and, 201
    sleep and, 335
Alcohol abuse, 6, 210–13, 318
Alcoholics Anonymous, 213, 326
Allen, R. Michael, 363
Allen, Steve, Jr., 285, 286, 287
Alpha brain waves, 271, 315
Alprazolam (Xanax), 361, 363
Altfest, Lewis J., 156, 157
Amitriptyline, 360, 366
Amphetamines, 211
Anger, 84–86
    discharging, 47
    after divorce, 129
    job-related, 61
Antianxiety drugs, 361–62, 367
Antidepressants, 360, 366, 367, 368
Antihistamines, 364–65, 368

B